Rebel Girl and the Godfather

SUNY series in Italian/American Culture

Fred L. Gardaphé, editor

Rebel Girl and the Godfather

New York City's Italians and the Fight for Civil Rights

JEFFREY LOUIS DECKER

excelsior editions
State University of New York Press
Albany, New York

Cover Credit: Elena Civoli Brittain, *Paesaggio* (2020–2021). Acrylic on wood. Courtesy of the artist and Museo Italo Americano, San Francisco.

Published by State University of New York Press, Albany

© 2025 State University of New York

All rights reserved

Printed in the United States of America

No part of this book may be used or reproduced in any manner whatsoever without written permission. No part of this book may be stored in a retrieval system or transmitted in any form or by any means including electronic, electrostatic, magnetic tape, mechanical, photocopying, recording, or otherwise without the prior permission in writing of the publisher.

Links to third-party websites are provided as a convenience and for informational purposes only. They do not constitute an endorsement or an approval of any of the products, services, or opinions of the organization, companies, or individuals. SUNY Press bears no responsibility for the accuracy, legality, or content of a URL, the external website, or for that of subsequent websites.

EU GPSR Authorised Representative:
Logos Europe, 9 rue Nicolas Poussin, 17000, La Rochelle, France
contact@logoseurope.eu

Excelsior Editions is an imprint of State University of New York Press

For information, contact State University of New York Press, Albany, NY
www.sunypress.edu

Library of Congress Cataloging-in-Publication Data

Name: Decker, Jeffrey Louis, author.
Title: Rebel girl and the godfather : New York City's Italians and the fight for civil rights / Jeffrey Louis Decker.
Description: Albany : State University of New York Press, [2025] | Series: SUNY series in Italian/American Culture | Includes bibliographical references and index.
Identifiers: LCCN 2024057650 | ISBN 9798855803433 (hardcover : alk. paper) | ISBN 9798855803440 (ebook) | ISBN 9798855803426 (pbk. : alk. paper)
Subjects: LCSH: Italian Americans—Civil rights—New York (State)—New York—History—20th century. | Italian Americans—New York (State)—New York—Biography. | Sansone, Mary (née Crisalli), 1916–2018. | Colombo, Joseph, Sr., 1923–1978. | Congress of Italian American Organizations. | Italian American Civil Rights League. | Community activists—New York (State)—New York—Biography. | Mafia—New York (State)—New York—Biography. | New York (N.Y.)—Politics and government—1945–1980. I. Title.
Classification: LCC F128.9.I8 D44 2025 | DDC 974.7/1043092
[B]—dc23/eng/20250310
LC record available at https://lccn.loc.gov/2024057650

For my mother,
Cesira "Cile" Cloranda Maria Marinaro Decker,
and in memory of my grandmother,
Domenica "Mary" Costello Marinaro

Contents

List of Abbreviations   xi

List of Illustrations   xiii

Preface   xvii

Prologue   xxi

Part One. South Brooklyn

1. Mary and Joe   3
2. Family Room Crime   11
3. Mrs. Sansone and *Capo* Colombo   16

Part Two. Civil Rights Confidential

4. A Rage in Harlem (1960)   25
5. Boycott (1961)   30
6. Knotty Pine Politics (1962)   32
7. Racial Equality on the Waterfront (1963)   34
8. Most Wanted (1964)   40
9. Mafia Literati (1965)   46
10. Black Power Provocation (1966)   47

11.	Exclusively Italian (1967)	53
12.	Ethnic Harmony Amidst Civil Disorder (1968)	59
13.	"The Mark of an Emergent Self-Consciousness" (1969)	72

Part Three. Rise Up!

14.	Day 1 (April 30, 1970)	87
15.	Picket (May)	91
16.	The League (June)	97
17.	Unity Day (June 29)	105
18.	Alliance Averted (July)	115
19.	The M-Word (August)	124
20.	San Gennaro Handshake (September)	127
21.	Some Kind of Wonderful (October)	132
22.	The Offer (November)	139
23.	Sister Joe (December)	144
24.	Man of the Year (January 1971)	153
25.	Hollywood Deal (February)	156
26.	No Show (March)	161
27.	Park-Sheraton Slap (April)	167
28.	CIAO Coalition (May)	175
29.	Scorpio (June)	187
30.	Columbus Circle (June 28)	199

Part Four. Stayin' Alive

31.	Nowhere Man (1971)	205
32.	Cellar to Suite (1971)	208

33.	Button Men (1971–72)	211
34.	Wobbly and Quaker (1971–72)	218
35.	New League Retreat: Canarsie's Busing Crisis (1972–73)	222
36.	"A Model for All New Yorkers" (1973–75)	232
37.	A League of Their Own: Williamsburg's Neighborhood Women (1974–77)	241
38.	Requiem and Redemption (1977–79)	252
39.	The Machine Strikes Back (1977–79)	255

Coda	266
Notes	267
Selected Bibliography	303
Acknowledgments	307
Index	311

Abbreviations

ADL	B'nai B'rith Anti-Defamation League; B'nai B'rith
AFSCME	American Federation of State, County and Municipal Employees
AIADL	American Italian Anti-Defamation League (renamed Americans of Italian Descent)
AID	Americans of Italian Descent
ARI	American Relief for Italy
BPP	Black Panther Party for Self-Defense
CCC	Concerned Citizens of Canarsie
CETA	Comprehensive Employment and Training Act
CIAO	Congress of Italian American Organizations
CORE	Congress of Racial Equality
FIADO	Federation of Italian American Democratic Organization
HRA	Human Resources Administration (New York City)
IAC	Italian American Coalition
IACRL	Italian American Civil Rights League; the League
IACUA	Italian American Center for Urban Affairs
IAMSC	Italian American Multi-Service Center
IASO	Italian American Service Organization
ILA	International Longshoremen's Association

ILGWU	International Ladies' Garment Workers' Union
IWW	Industrial Workers of the World
JDL	Jewish Defense League
MARC	Metropolitan Applied Research Center
NAACP	National Association for the Advancement of Colored People
NCNW	National Congress of Neighborhood Women
NCUEA	National Center for Urban Ethnic Affairs
NFIAO	National Federation of Italian American Organizations
NOW	National Organization of Women
NUL	National Urban League
OAAU	Organization for Afro-American Unity
OEO	Office of Economic Opportunity (replaced by Community Services Administration)
RICO	Racketeer Influence and Corrupt Organizations Act
SCLC	Souther Christian Leadership Conference

Illustrations

P.1.1	Junior Wobblies, 1920s.	1
2.1	Television image of Frank Costello's chest, arms, and hands, 1951.	12
P.2.1	Confidential FBI memo identifying Top Echelon Criminal Informant Greg Scarpa, 1962.	23
4.1	Apalachin summit headline, *New York Daily News*, 1957.	28
7.1	International Longshoremen's Association Vice President Anthony Scotto speaks to Local 1814 members on the Brooklyn docks, 1965.	36
8.1	Andy Warhol's *Thirteen Most Wanted Men* at the New York World's Fair in Queens, 1964.	42
10.1	Little Apalachin defendants hide their faces while exiting a Manhattan jail, 1966.	48
11.1	Sammy Davis Jr. and Frank Sinatra sing during an American Italian Anti-Defamation League fundraiser in Madison Square Garden, 1967.	56
12.1	Congress of Italian American Organizations founder Mary Sansone and others celebrate the opening of CIAO's first storefront in South Brooklyn, 1968.	63
12.2	US Vice President Hubert Humphrey joins Mary Sansone and other National Federation of Italian American Organizations leaders in Washington, DC, 1968.	64

P.3.1	Italian American pickets in front of FBI headquarters in Manhattan, 1970.	85
16.1	Italian Civil Rights League advertisement in the *Long Island Post*, 1970.	102
17.1	US Congressman Mario Biaggi campaigning for NYC mayor, 1973.	107
17.2	US congressional candidate Bella Abzug attends Italian American Unity Day in Columbus Circle, 1970.	110
17.3	IACRL founder Joe Colombo carrying AFL-CIO placard while marching alongside Anthony Colombo and other supporters on Italian American Unity Day, 1970.	112
18.1	Joe Colombo interviewed by the *New York Daily News*, 1970.	116
20.1	NY Governor Nelson Rockefeller accepts IACRL membership while shaking hands with Anthony Colombo at the San Gennaro Festival in Manhattan's Little Italy, 1970.	128
21.1	Sammy Davis Jr. joins hands with New York politicians while attending the grand opening of IACRL Chapter 4 in the Bensonhurst section of Brooklyn, 1970.	134
23.1	A woman speaks into an open mic at an IACRL meeting in Manhattan's Park-Sheraton Hotel, 1971.	150
25.1	Joseph Colombo Jr., along with his mother and father, exits the federal courthouse in Brooklyn after his acquittal, 1971.	157
26.1	*The Godfather* producer Al Ruddy, alongside IACRL leaders Nat Maricone and Anthony Colombo, announce an agreement between Paramount Picture Studios and the League, 1971.	162
27.1	Joe Colombo, Anthony Colombo, and Steve Aiello on *The Dick Cavett Show*, 1971.	169
27.2	Balcony view of Joe Colombo addressing an IACRL meeting from the dais in the Park-Sheraton ballroom, 1971.	170
28.1	Program cover for an annual CIAO dinner dance held at the Cotillion Terrace in Bensonhurst, 1971.	178

28.2	Rev. Silvano Tomasi accepts an award from NYC Mayor John Lindsay at the annual CIAO dinner dance, 1971.	180
29.1	*New York* magazine cover featuring Nicholas Pileggi's report on Italian Power, 1971.	187
30.1	Jerome Johnson filming Joe Colombo at the Second Annual Italian American Unity Day in Columbus Circle, 1971.	201
P.4.1	Teens pose in front of a graffiti-tagged wall in South Brooklyn, 1977.	203
33.1	Greg Scarpa testifies in front of US Senate organized crime commission, 1971.	212
33.2	Sammy Davis Jr. guest stars on *All in the Family*, 1972.	217
33.3	The IACRL pin worn by Sammy Davis Jr. on *All in the Family*, 1972.	217
34.1	Bayard Rustin gives the featured address at CIAO's Ethnic Communities and the Challenge of Urban Life symposium in Manhattan's Statler-Hilton Hotel, 1972.	219
35.1	New League President Carl Cecora poses in front of IACRL's relocated national headquarters in the Canarsie section Brooklyn, 1974.	224
35.2	A Black parent leader converses with an IACRL representative during the school busing crisis in Canarsie, 1972.	226
36.1	Mary Sansone is joined by Bayard Rustin and other supporters at a CIAO press conference, 1975.	237
37.1	IACRL Chapter 23 storefront in the Williamsburg section of Brooklyn.	242
37.2	IACRL Multi-Service Center Director Sally Martino-Fisher is joined by Kellie Everts and other Center staff at a Chapter 23 event, 1975.	248
39.1	Campaign poster for NYC mayoral candidate Mario Cuomo, 1977.	258

Preface

Rebel Girl and the Godfather tells the true story of a pair of improbable social justice crusaders from Brooklyn—Mary Sansone, a homemaker, and Joe Colombo, a gangster—and their rivalry over the powerful community organizations they founded. This book challenges stereotypes of the docile Italian wife and the parochial Mafia boss by recasting these actors as a rebel girl and a renegade wiseguy. More broadly, it provides an alternative history of the 1960s and 1970s, when it was presumed that working-class white ethnics living in urban America were predisposed to responding to the civil rights movement with backlash and the women's movement with scorn.

Sansone and Colombo built their political networks in the traditional fashion: by relying on the Italian family. Beyond family, however, they both looked to the Black freedom struggle for inspiration, guidance, and assistance. Around 1970, when their grassroots organizations were ascending, they were championed by some of the most important Black political activists of the day. Bayard Rustin—the genius organizer behind the 1963 March on Washington, whom Rev. Martin Luther King Jr. praised for his unassailable commitment to nonviolent resistance—was Mary Sansone's lifelong friend. He was also an unflagging ally of her progressive community action coalition, the Congress of Italian American Organizations. Sammy Davis Jr.—who, after King, was arguably the foremost fundraiser of the civil rights movement—was introduced to Joe Colombo by their mutual friend Frank Sinatra. Davis surpassed even Sinatra as the most resolute, high-profile supporter of Colombo's social justice organization, the Italian American Civil Rights League.[1]

The main characters in this book are at once exceptional and recognizable, idealistic and fallible; they make bold decisions and they miscalculate, which can lead to their downfall and, in the case of Joe Colombo, death.

Colombo was shot in Columbus Circle at a Unity Day rally sponsored by a civil rights organization he led, over the objections of other Mafia dons, who were growing weary of his activism when they became ensnared in an FBI dragnet targeting his operation. Mary Sansone became an urban folk hero when she stood up to Mafia boss Joe Colombo . . . and prevailed.

Sansone spent years plotting to open multiracial community centers in New York City that assisted the poor. By 1970, she finally succeeded in doing so. Colombo, in an attempt to confer legitimacy on his civil rights outfit through her crime-free organization, made Sansone an "offer" to form an alliance. She refused. Soon after, Colombo was gunned down but Sansone's trouble with racketeers didn't end. During the 1970s, she was forced to fend off hostile take-over bids from machine politicians who were once allied with Colombo and who now sought to abscond with her multimillion-dollar municipal contracts. In Italian Williamsburg, on Brooklyn's Northside, white ethnic women who once served as foot soldiers in Colombo's civil rights outfit or the Catholic Church began organizing women in their community. Melding Sansone's coalition-building efforts with an emergent second-wave feminism, they launched the National Congress of Neighborhood Women, an interracial organization that addressed the needs of working-class women.

Rebel Girl and the Godfather is based on as-yet-unmined archival documents as well as author-conducted interviews. Considerable effort went into establishing chronology, because without a reliable timeline for the sequence of events, it is often difficult to understand a person's motivation or the full scope and trajectory of an organization. Newspapers—the proverbial first draft of history—were essential to establishing chronology, but they were also a double-edged source. For the post–World War II period, they provided the most immediate and extensive account of New York City's people and events. Nonetheless, newspaper stories are mediated by an array of factors, from a reporter's personal bias to institutional constraints based on industry standards. Those factors are incorporated into the reconstruction of events wherever possible and highlighted when journalists or the newspapers for which they work acknowledge these constrictions inside their coverage.

The Federal Bureau of Investigation's documents on racketeering are a singular source of information. They too are double-edged. On the one hand, they offer a peek into the criminal underworld; on the other, their reliability is indelibly compromised. Redactions conceal information the government deems too sensitive to make public. Moreover, much of the information revealed in these confidential FBI documents is gathered in the context of a precarious relationship between undercover informants and their Bureau handlers, who are often motivated by dubious considerations, monetary and professional. A part of the story this book tells turns on a civil rights protest against the FBI's clandestine and sometimes nefarious information-gathering practices.

Details and dialogue in my narrative are not only informed by what was recorded in writing and on film but inspired by what was told to me by more than a dozen people—including Mary Sansone and Anthony Colombo Sr. (Joe Colombo's son)—who were directly involved in or else witnessed the events recounted. The feelings conveyed to me by my interviewees about past events were placed into the service of composing a narrative from the perspective of the community activists whose stories remain untold.

Prologue

On or about June 28, 1971, Mary received a phone call from Nick, her close friend and confidant.

"Colombo was shot in Columbus Circle."

"Who did it?"

"A Black guy. He was shot too."

"Shot dead?"

"I don't know. They took them to Roosevelt but I think the Black guy is." Mary was silent. Nick added, "My guess is they'll go after Joey Gallo."

Mary knew the rumors. Since his release from prison a few months earlier, word around South Brooklyn was that Gallo was aligning with Black hoodlums while angling to take out Mafia boss Joe Colombo for refusing to pay off debts he believed were owed to him.

Mary too had been feuding with Colombo but she was no Mafioso. In fact, her contempt for the Mafia ran deep. Her beloved father, Rocky Crisalli, was a Wobbly labor organizer who despised the mob. At age nineteen, Mary, happily unmarried and following in Rocky's footsteps, agitated on behalf of the International Ladies' Garments Workers' Union. It was the middle of the Great Depression, when organizers regularly fought mobsters hired by garment industry owners to keep unions out their shops. Soon after the war, Rocky's brother, Jimmy Crisalli, a high-ranking racketeer, tried to persuade his niece to terminate her activism, which was damaging his reputation among business associates. Mary refused her uncle's request.

Nicholas Pileggi, born and raised in Bensonhurst before becoming a journalist, knew a lot of people. But he never met anyone like Mary. They were introduced in the 1960s. Mary, the wife of a longshoreman, ran a coalition—the Congress of Italian American Organizations, which went by the snappy acronym CIAO—out of the wood-paneled basement of her two-story attached brick home in Boro Park while looking after a house full of children. Nick found CIAO extraordinary not just because it was commandeered by a Brooklyn homemaker. Among New York City's nonprofit organizations, CIAO held the proud distinction of operating multiracial community centers that served the poor. Moreover, it did so in predominantly Italian American neighborhoods where—according to conventional wisdom—it couldn't be done.

Pileggi was a leading New York City crime reporter when, in the spring of 1970, Joe Colombo suddenly stepped out from behind the veil of syndicate secrecy in order to lead the fledgling Italian American Civil Rights League—known to locals as the League—to hell with objections from rival mob bosses about unwanted publicity. Soon after, Colombo sought out Sansone and invited her to a private meeting to discuss her community-based service delivery operation. Any hesitation she might have had to meet with Colombo vanished when Pileggi encouraged her to go. During their sit-down, Colombo pitched an alliance—Sansone's organizational drive and CIAO's pristine reputation paired with his deep pockets and the League's massive membership rolls. She turned him down on the spot. And she did it again a few months later, her second refusal performed peremptorily, in front of hundreds of outraged League supporters.

Today, hearing Nick utter Gallo's name over the phone in connection with Colombo's shooting, Mary's mind raced. She recalled an unsolicited message she recently received from Gallo. It was dispatched by her Uncle Joe, a third-rate Brooklyn mobster, who phoned her to say that when Gallo got wind of Mary's brazen dismissal of Colombo's offer, he told him to deliver a message to his niece: "Tell Mary not to worry because Colombo is gone."

That disquieting recollection was followed by the thought that Colombo's guys might think that she was somehow connected to Gallo and that she had a hand in the shooting. That amused her—she couldn't kill a fly—before she sobered.

"Jesus, is this where I get it next?"

Part One
South Brooklyn

Members of an unidentified local chapter of the Junior Wobblies, girls and boys, Black and white, 1920s. *Source:* Walter P. Reuther Library, Archives of Labor and Urban Affairs, Wayne State University. Public domain.

Chapter 1

Mary and Joe

Mary Crisalli and Joe Colombo were born poor, Mary in 1916 and Joe in 1923, and both were raised in a tough neighborhood known to locals as South Brooklyn. Mary and Joe's families had Italian roots in Calabria, an impoverished region located deep in the boot of southern Italy, where the ruthless 'Ndrangheta crime syndicate operated with impunity around the time Mary's and Joe's parents left for America. For many Italian immigrants, the promise of a better life in the New World was met with the disappointing reality of New York City. Maria Forte, who came through Ellis Island in 1920, recalled, "I hear, 'America! America! It's beautiful!' And when I see Bank Street, I don't know if you ever see South Brooklyn, but I no see no beautiful thing."[1]

Growing up in one of Brooklyn's Italian ghettos between the two world wars, Mary witnessed gangsters gunned down in the street in front of her family's Henry Street pastry shop. It was an establishment her racketeering Uncle Jimmy had bought as a front for her father to run. Jimmy might have been surprised that Rocky wasn't grateful for the opportunity to run his own business but Rocky wanted no part of his brother's life.

Rocco Crisalli had studied in Italy to be a priest but escaped from the seminary to come to America, where he spent his days organizing workers on the waterfront and in restaurants for the revolutionary Industrial Workers of the World (IWW). He also wrote for *Il Proletario*, a popular Italian-language Brooklyn newspaper that was a part of the radical immigrant subculture. What little money Rocky made was spent on books. "Feed the mind," he'd say with a wink at his daughter. Running the pastry shop from morning to night was left to Mary's mother, Martha. During the Great Depression, the family business was sometimes all that separated Mary's family from starvation.[2]

Joe Colombo's father, Anthony Colombo, went missing on January 28, 1938. Nine days later, a boy named Nathan Hawkes, who was the same age as Joe, was airing his terrier, Spot, on Shore Drive in Brooklyn when he noticed a woman's bare leg sticking out from the rear door of a parked car. The boy peered through the sedan's window. On the back seat he eyed a pale green drape dappled with tiny identical dancing couples. He notified the authorities. By the time the police arrived, several hundred people crowded the crime scene. Investigators found two corpses, a man and a woman. "Crowded in with the bodies was a full set of golf clubs," noted *The New York Times*. The man had been left gasping in a noose—a bloodied sash cord coiled three times around his neck. The woman, also strangled, wore a white metal wedding ring on her left hand. She was left naked from the waist down.[3]

Nathan Hawkes's grisly discovery inspired next-day, coast-to-coast tabloid headlines—frequently front-page and occasionally supplemented by photos.

"Frozen Bodies Found in a Car" (*Detroit Free Press*)

"Nude Woman and Man Slain" (*Los Angeles Times*)

"Woman, Man Garroted in Mystery Tryst" (*Washington Post*)

"Woman Strangled with Golf Romeo in Automobile Tryst" (*New York Daily News*)

"Dead 3 Days, Semi-Nude Woman and Man Found Garroted in Auto" (*Atlanta Constitution*)

"Stranglers Kill Missing Woman and Golf Player; Semi-Nude Body of Mother Shows Terrific Fight" (*Chicago Tribune*)

"Woman, Escort Found Slain by Strangler; Gangster Don Juan and Young Mother Murdered; Jealousy Is Blamed for Double Killing" (*San Francisco Examiner*)

One victim was identified as Christine Oliveri, a twenty-four-year-old mother of two. The other was Joe's forty-one-year-old father. Anthony Colombo was known locally, according to the *Times*, "as a dealer in cheeses and oils and as a frequenter of the municipally operated Dyker Heights Golf Club, where his partners often were women." He was known to law enforcement as Tony Durante, an ex-convict and racketeer. On the streets, he was Two-Gun Tony.[4]

As a girl, Mary had a vague idea about what her Uncle Jimmy was mixed up in—the mob, the rackets, the syndicate, whatever they called it—but no one talked openly about it or the Henry Street shootings she witnessed. From the time she started elementary school at Brooklyn's PS 29, Mary loved nothing more than sitting on a soapbox in Manhattan's Union Square while her father, Rocky, make a fiery speech before a gathering crowd about the Italian immigrant anarchists Sacco and Vanzetti and how they had been railroaded in a US court of law. Mary listened, the excitement building, for the moment when Rocky invoked the IWW motto: "An injury to one is an injury to all!" That was her cue to sing "The Rebel Girl," which she memorized from her copy of *Little Red Songbook*, a gift from father to daughter she'd treasure for years to come.[5]

> Yes, her hands may be hardened from labor
> And her dress may not be very fine
> But a heart in her bosom is beating
> That is true to her class and her kind

Mary followed Rocky around like a puppy. At the ripe age of twelve, with her father's blessing, she delivered her first speech as president of the Brooklyn chapter of the Junior Wobblies. Mary urged the other kids to join her in looking forward to the day when they too would become organizers like her father. Rocky beamed from the back of the room.

At age fourteen, Mary wanted to go to high school but her mother thought it more practical for her daughter to become a dress designer. As a compromise, Mary matriculated at Textile High School in Chelsea. Her first school assignment was to sew sleeves on a woman's suit. She sewed them upside down, thereby putting to rest any lofty aspirations her mother might have had for Mary's career in fashion.

At the time of her high school graduation, Mary's father took ill with a heart condition. It was 1934, the height of the Great Depression, and Mary was eager for a paycheck to help support her family. She still hated sewing but found a job in a nonunion factory in Midtown's garment district. It was menial work but it was also an opportunity for Mary to see for herself the inside of a sweatshop. She wanted to know if what her father said about the horrible conditions was true.

Garment manufacturing was New York's largest industry at the time, and it employed large numbers of Jews and Italians. Mary found life inside the sweatshop worse than she had allowed herself to imagine. The factory floor was not just hot but stifling. No fans, no nothing. Lunchbreaks, the only time talking was allowed, were as short as ten minutes. Sexual abuse in the factory was rampant. Women, some barely high school age, suffered unwanted groping from male supervisors. The only guaranteed way for a girl on the floor to get a pay raise was to sleep with the boss. Mary hated the work, and she despised the factory owners and the gangsters who they hired to keep unions out of their sweatshops.

After working for a year on the factory floor, Mary's father procured a full-tuition union scholarship for his daughter at the Rand School of Social Science. She attended classes at night so that she could continue in the sweatshop by day. The next summer, an official with International Ladies' Garments Workers' Union Italian Dressmakers Local 89—a foreign-language local with membership approaching 40,000, of which more than 80 percent were women—suggested to Mary that she organize the seamstresses where she worked. That was all the encouragement Mary needed. She went straight to her father for advice. Rocky gave her lessons on how to talk up a strike with her coworkers, on when would be the best time of day to pull the shop out, and on ways to negotiate with the factory's owner. Martha, knowing any expression of concern for her daughter's safety would be ignored, sat silently while Mary and Rocky conspired together like partners in crime.[6]

A week later, Mary huddled with her garment industry coworkers and told them that if they didn't want to be treated like slaves, they had to join the union and demand higher wages and better working conditions. Her coworkers didn't need much prodding. Most were eager to follow Mary's lead and join the tens of thousands of Italian American women entering the labor movement in the 1930s. The next morning, Mary walked into the factory, instructed the women to shut down their machines, and pulled the shop out on strike. The factory owner was livid. Two weeks into the strike, he settled. Mary, battle-hardened, was ecstatic.

The double murder of Anthony Colombo and Christine Oliveri was never solved. In 1939, one year after his father's death, Joe Colombo dropped out of New Utrecht High School in Bensonhurst. He began hustling—stealing cargo off the back of delivery trucks, running crap games in the neighborhood, hanging out with his crew on the Coney Island boardwalk. At five foot, six inches, Joe wasn't tall, but his solid 165-pound frame and a strong left jab made him a formidable street fighter. After crossing paths with the men who ran local labor unions, he found a well-paying job as a shop steward in a nearby factory.[7]

That's where he met an attractive brunette named Lucille "Jo-Jo" Faiello, a scrap dealer's daughter from Staten Island. She worked on the floor. They dated. She took him home to meet her father. Mr. Faiello offered Joe a glass of wine. Joe declined, saying he didn't drink. He offered Joe a cigar. Joe declined, saying he didn't smoke. After Joe left, Mr. Faiello said to his daughter, "What kind of man doesn't drink or smoke."[8]

Twenty-six-year-old Mary Crisalli received her certificate in social work from the Rand School just as the US entered World War II. During the war, Mary applied for an intake caseworker position in the social work department of the Brooklyn Red Cross and began helping draftees and their families. She assisted soldiers seeking emergency furloughs and hardship deferments. She investigated soldiers who exhibited mental illness or behavioral disorders but were unable to avoid the draft. She made sure late allotment checks weren't lost in the mail. She counseled Italian women who had married US servicemen but spoke no English.

Mary's most challenging cases involved Italian nationals who, having wed African American soldiers stationed in Europe, were unaware of US attitudes toward mixed-race marriages. For guidance on counseling interracial couples, Mary consulted thirty-year-old Bayard Rustin, who was field secretary for the Congress of Racial Equality. She was introduced to Rustin by her father, Rocky. The two men previously worked together on campaigns to support Norman Thomas, a leader of the democratic socialist movement in America. They shared each other's ideals. Bayard shared with Rocky the IWW's commitment to organizing Black and white workers on the basis of complete equality; Rocky shared with Bayard, a Quaker, the Religious Society of Friends' belief that racial prejudice is a violation of God's law of love.[9]

Mary and Bayard became loyal friends and lifelong collaborators.

A year after the United States entered World War II, Joe Colombo enlisted in the Coast Guard. Joe held the rank of seaman first class on a destroyer that provided protection against submarine and air attacks on US Navy vessels in the Atlantic Ocean. Joe's ship was under constant threat of assault from German submarines as it escorted allied war ships to and from Africa. To make a little extra money while helping to pass time, Joe held impromptu crap games with his mates. When they docked in New York Harbor in December 1943, the crew was given a three-day furlough. Joe went to see Jo-Jo and didn't return for a week. For the infraction, Joe was punished with a short confinement and a small fine. Six months later, his boat docked again in New York but this time the crew was not given furloughs. Desperate to see his girlfriend, Joe disembarked without permission. While AWOL, he and Jo-Jo quickly arranged to be married in South Brooklyn at Our Lady of Peace Church. Returning to his ship, Joe pleaded for leniency after showing his marriage certificate to his commanding officer. Joe was disciplined without being court martialed. Back at sea, Joe received word from Jo-Jo that she was pregnant. Joe's past infractions made him ineligible for furlough. Nevertheless, when his ship docked in New York the following August, he snuck off the boat to be with his wife. When he returned to his ship, Joe was thrown in the brig, court martialed, and sentenced to a year's confinement on Hart Island.[10]

Hart Island had been occupied by the military as far back as the Civil War, when it served as a Union Army prison for Confederate soldiers. Later, it was the site of a workhouse for the poor, and after that, a women's asylum. In the twentieth century, Hart Island was mainly operated as a public burial ground, the nation's largest, for the city's unknown dead. There, Joe underwent psychiatric evaluation, which concluded that he was "unable to adapt to the restrictions of military life because of tension and instability." On February 25, 1945, Joe was still imprisoned on Hart Island when Jo-Jo gave birth to their first child Anthony, named after Joe's murdered father.[11]

On February 26, the day after Joe Colombo's son Anthony was born, Mary Crisalli's father died suddenly of a heart attack. At the funeral, while mourners prayed goodbye to the rebel, Rocky, his widow Martha whispered seven words to her daughter: "I bet you wish it were me." Mary pretended not to hear her mother's reproach. Not one to dwell on loss—even of her dear father—Mary, now twenty-eight years old, threw herself back into her work with the Brooklyn Red Cross. Her M.O.: Move on.[12]

At the time, there weren't too many women or Italians employed as social workers in New York. Mary, however, never shied away from a challenge and gained a reputation among her colleagues for her restless energy. After the war's end, Mary was hired by the United Nations Appeal for Children to raised money for Italian war orphans. In her first month on the job, she received a $25,000 check from the Ford Foundation. Before long she was receiving accolades for the amount of money she had raised, which eventually reached $200,000. Mary's successful efforts on behalf of the UN caught the attention of American Relief for Italy (ARI), a charity organization that hired her as executive secretary and where she continued to raise money for war orphans.[13]

Mary's fundraising prowess also caught the attention of her racketeering uncle Jimmy Crisalli. ARI donations were solicited on the organization's letterhead with the name Mary Crisalli printed at the top, and the publicity was inadvertently causing trouble for Jimmy. He was determined to put a stop to it. One afternoon in January 1948, Jimmy hurried up Henry Street gripping an ARI flyer in his hand. When he reached Cammareri Brothers Bakery, a block and half from Mary's home, he crossed Henry Street and entered the pastry shop, where he found his widowed sister-in-law standing behind the counter. He asked her where he could find Mary.[14]

"Out doing her father's business," Martha replied.

"*Crazy* like her father," Jimmy said, biting his lip.

"You might catch her at the house tomorrow before she leaves for work," Martha offered.

The next morning, Jimmy climbed the stoop at 489 Henry Street and made his way through the door, past the stairs and into the kitchen, where he found Mary leaning her four-foot-eleven frame over the *Brooklyn Eagle*. She didn't look up from the paper when he entered the room.[15]

Jimmy, removing his hat, cleared his throat.

Mary raised her eyes. "Uncle Jimmy, what brings you around?"

"Can we sit?" he asked, placing one hand on a kitchen chair.

"I can't, Uncle Jimmy. I've got to run to the UN. We're in the middle of fundraising—"

Jimmy interrupted, "That's what I want to talk—"

But Mary was so excited she didn't pause.

"—and I'm meeting this morning with these adorable kids, war orphans named Rosie and Vic. Relief for Italy is sending us to Washington next week to raise more money. Rooney, the congressman, he's arranged tours for the kids—the Capitol, the White House, the FBI Building . . ."[16]

Mary and Joe | 9

Jimmy blurted, "I need you to quit what you're doing."

Mary recoiled but said nothing. Jimmy checked himself.

"Let's sit," Jimmy said with quiet restraint as he slid into the chair. Mary remained standing.

"Your name is in all the papers," he began in a soft tone. "Stories about you raising money for Italian orphans."[17]

Mary listened with polite impatience.

"Your flyers are blowing around the docks. They ask for money. Italian relief. Your name on top. A guy sees 'Mary Crisalli' and he thinks, Jimmy Crisalli must be in on this. Then he thinks, where's mine?"

Jimmy gave his niece a knowing look before saying in a soothing voice, "If I can tell them you've quit . . ."

"My father wouldn't tell me to quit."

Jimmy was stung. He looked up into her eyes, searching for his brother but found only his own reflection.

"I'm trying to protect you," he pleaded.

"Drop dead," she snapped, cold with offended dignity.

The front door slammed shut before Jimmy could rise from his seat. For more than a year, she refused to speak to him.

Chapter 2

Family Room Crime

Neither Mary nor Joe would soon forget the ignominious spectacle of March 13, 1951. On that day, fifty-year-old mob boss Frank Costello testified on live television before the US Senate Special Committee to Investigate Organized Crime in Interstate Commerce. The hearings took place in a room on the twenty-sixth floor of the Foley Square United States Courthouse, a neoclassical structure fronted by imposing Corinthian columns and rising thirty-seven stories into the sky. The committee was chaired by Democrat Estes Kafauver from Tennessee. The courtroom was crammed with TV cameramen along with newspaper and radio reporters. Five stations in New York City alone broadcast all or part of the hearings, which reached an estimated two and a quarter million homes and taverns in the metropolitan area.[1]

The day before, in a first-floor room inside the same courthouse, key prosecution witness David Greenglass began his testimony in a week-old espionage trial. Greenglass wove a fascinating verbal web of wartime criminal conspiracy that ensnared his wife Ruth, his sister Ethel Greenglass Rosenberg, and Ethel's husband Julius Rosenberg. The courtroom's high chandeliers, as described by a *New York Times* reporter on the first day of the trial, contributed to a "somber and dimly lit" aura of "deceptive quiet."[2]

In the midst of Greenglass's testimony, just as the witness began disclosing the composition and function of the "super secret" atomic bomb, Federal Judge Irving R. Kauffman interrupted him to announce that "in the interests of national security," visitors—including the press—would have to leave. For ten minutes, under the watchful eye of the Federal Bureau of Investigation, only the jury and court officials were permitted inside the cavernous room. Later, the judge recalled the newspaper reporters; spectators, however, remained barred.[3]

The following day, up on the twenty-sixth floor, the air was electric. Even before cameras began rolling, Frank Costello caused a stir when, after expressing reluctance to accommodate the media circus, he made special demands about the conditions of his television appearance. Not wanting to lose their star witness, the senators, led by Kefauver, agreed to Costello's conditions. The cameras were not to reveal Costello's face and could exhibit only his chest, arms, and hands.

When TV audiences tuned in, cameras were trained on Costello's fingertips. His nails were buffed to mirror-like brightness. They danced impatiently back and forth from a half-empty glass of water to the rims of his spectacles, lenses reflecting klieg lights (Fig. 2.1).

When Costello addressed the Senate committee, he betrayed an awareness of aural etiquette—and perhaps his own inadequacies—by opening with

Figure 2.1. Television image of Frank Costello's chest, arms, and hands, US Senate Special Committee to Investigate Organized Crime in Interstate Commerce hearings, Foley Square federal courthouse, Manhattan, March 1951. *Source:* Burton B. Turkus Papers, Lloyd Sealy Library Special Collections, John Jay College of Criminal Justice, City University of New York. Used with permission.

an apology for his slow and guttural delivery. "Mr. Chairman, please excuse my voice for I am suffering with a touch of laryngitis." After broadcasting his testimony, Kefauver anointed Costello "The No. 1 racketeer in this country."[4]

If in middle of the twentieth century the word Mafia was still foreign to the American tongue, it was now being broadcast on family room TVs coast to coast.

Good Friday. In the midst of the hearings that made Costello into the new medium's first real-life villain, Senator Charles W. Tobey appeared on *Meet the Press*. The ranking Republican member on the committee, Tobey fielded questions from a panel of national correspondents working for big city newspapers.

Paul Leach from the *Chicago Daily News* began the questioning. Perhaps unexpectedly, he asked Senator Tobey not about organized crime but about the impact television was having on the hearings.

"You've had very broad newspaper coverage of this, newsreels, from the very beginning," Leach began.

Tobey, nodding in agreement, confirmed: "Nothing like it ever known before."

Leach: "Then along comes television with millions of people watching it. Has that merely been entertainment for the people who've been reading it or watching it?"

Tobey pointed his finger at Leach, shook his head, and replied with a dismissive "Oh, no!" before turning away to take the next question from another panelist.

When Leach's turn came around again, he didn't pursue his earlier line of inquiry about how the new medium might be turning news into entertainment. Instead, he asked about the hearings themselves. Would federal agencies, such as the Department of Justice and the Bureau of Internal Revenue, be "following up some of the revelations that this committee has made?" Leach tried to clarify his question with another. "I mean in respect to the Mafēa or Mafia or whatever you call it?"

Leach's mispronunciation of the word "Mafia" drew a vexed response from Tobey. "I don't know about the Mafēa or Mafia," retorted the Senator, "but I do know that out in California we found . . ."[5]

Mafēa. Mafia.

The reporter's verbal stumble might have been dismissed as an isolated anomaly. However, TV audiences witnessed a repeat performance with different players a week later when Senator Kafauver, committee chair, was the guest on *Meet the Press*.

April 1. During the broadcast, Scripps-Howard Newspaper reporter Marshall McNeil questioned the senator about the hearings. Twice McNeil offered a third shade of the word "Mafia."

"Your committee report," the journalist began, "said that the Māfēa might be the adhesive between gangs around the country."

The senator, slack-jawed, stared at the reporter with a bewildered look.

"You said you were going to look further into that," McNeil pressed on. "Now have you shown any additional evidence that shows the Māfēa is the glue that holds this thing together?"[6]

Mafēa. Mafia. Māfēa.

If the federal government was going to get people to take seriously the pervasiveness of organized crime, it needed not only to standardize the pronunciation of the word "Mafia" but also to normalize its existence in the hearts and minds of the American public. In the same year, 1951, Kefauver published his jeremiad, *Crime in America*, based on testimony taken from the hearings. A better title might have been *Mafia Literacy 101*.

"A nationwide crime syndicate does exist in the United States of America," Kefauver exhorted. "Behind the local mobs which make up the national crime syndicate is a shadowy, international crime organization known as the Mafia, so fantastic that most Americans find it hard to believe it really exists."[7]

In certain respects, Kafauver's anti-Mafia campaign was cut from the same cloth as Joseph McCarthy's anti-communist crusade. Both were launched by US senators at the outset of the 1950s, when Cold War paranoia about foreign-influenced domestic conspiracies was heating up. By 1953, both were challenged by articulate liberal commentators. Anti-anti-communism found its voice in an unexpected place: television. Reporter Edward R. Murrow, along with his producer Fred Friendly, exploited the new media in five episodes of *See It Now*, starting in the fall of 1953. While a perhaps less reckless iteration of anti-communism survived the broadcast, Senator McCarthy's reputation never recovered.

Liberal dissent toward the Mafia conspiracy found an outlet in a highbrow venue: the literary quarterly. Sociologist Daniel Bell, writing in the summer 1953 issue of the *Antioch Review*, dismantled Kefauver's proclamation that Italian criminals were coordinating a stealth attack on America, particularly its big city municipalities, police departments, and labor unions, by means of a "nationwide crime syndicate." "Unfortunately for a good story—and the existence of the Mafia would be a whale of a story—neither the Senate Crime Committee in its testimony, nor Kefauver in his book, presented any real evidence that the Mafia exists as a functioning organization."[8]

Kefauver's Mafia was a myth. Just as Murrow was not denying the existence of communists in America, Bell was not so naive as to claim that criminals, Italian or otherwise, didn't operate inside the United States. Both Murrow and Bell were insisting, however, that the level of threat to internal national security did not match the hysteria launched by overzealous elected officials and disseminated through an acquiescent news media.

According to Bell, the Kefauver hearings produced no proof of an omnipresent criminal conspiracy inside America. While criminals with mutual interests sometimes coordinated operations—and while coordination might occasionally cross state lines—the government had found no concrete evidence of a ubiquitous syndicate. The committee was "taken in by its own myth of an omnipotent Mafia and a despotic Costello," argued Bell, due to "its failure to assimilate and understand . . . institutionalized crime in relation to the political life of large urban communities in America."[9]

Soon after the hearings ended, Frank Costello sought to speak out in his own defense. He agreed to sit down for a newspaper interview with leading gossip columnist Walter Winchell, who had recently dubbed Costello "Public Enigma No. 1." From his flagship at the *New York Daily Mirror*, Winchell dispatched Costello's contention "that his only interest in politics (at any time) stemmed from a 'religious desire' to see Italian-Americans get a 'better break' in the distribution of good political jobs in New York where the heaviest Italian population is."

Sitting across from Costello, Winchell asked, "What was your first mistake?"

Costello's reply: "If you can call it a mistake, I guess it was being born of poor parents and raised in a tough neighborhood."[10]

Chapter 3

Mrs. Sansone and *Capo* Colombo

A few months after her bitter run-in with her racketeering Uncle Jimmy, Mary Crisalli was approached by a political neophyte named Joseph R. Corso to run his New York State Assembly campaign. She declined. Mary was as distrustful of politicians as she was of gangsters. Most Brooklyn campaigns were run out of local clubhouses, the base of political power in the city. Clubhouses were ruled by men who operated the political machines, and Mary wanted no part of that. She cherished her independence as a democratic socialist and the freedom to speak her mind that came with it.

Corso, however, had two things going for him. First, he was an insurgent candidate running against a Republican Party incumbent. Second, he knew Mary from her work on behalf of American Relief for Italy and told her more than once how much he admired her spunk. Corso pressed Mary. She reconsidered his proposition. A few days later, she told him she would run his campaign on the condition she could do it without interference. She was surprised when Corso agreed to her terms. Mary recruited an army of volunteers, mainly drawn from her network of female colleagues in social work, and commandeered a relentless door-to-door campaign.[1]

To the surprise of political insiders, Corso won the election. Mary was pleased until the victorious candidate gave his acceptance speech. While Corso thanked his pals profusely, he failed to even mention Mary's name. It then dawned on her that among those standing alongside Corso in the front of the room, she was the only woman.[2]

Nevertheless, Mary loved her work and had little interest in marriage. Once Mary turned thirty, however, the pressure to get married mounted. She expected it from her family, and wasn't surprised when, upon returning home at night, she'd find her mother making a novena, imploring the Virgin Mary to intercede on her daughter's behalf for *someone* to marry her. She didn't expect it, however, from just about every woman's magazine she picked up. Now that the war was over, magazines were full of stories promoting "housewife" as the most fulfilling occupation imaginable for the modern woman. Mary, a freethinker like her father, wasn't buying it.

489 Henry Street, where Mary continued to live with her mother after the war's end, was originally purchased by her *nonna*. Before the turn of the century, Mary's grandmother came to the United States with three-year-old Martha from coastal Reggio Calabria, an Italian city separated from the island of Sicily by the Strait of Messina. To pay for the row house, she took in boarders by converting a single-family residence into a four-family house. She occupied the basement. Mary lived with her parents and siblings—now just her mother—on the first floor. The upper floors were rented to a steady stream of recent arrivals.

Not long after getting off the boat in Manhattan, Zachary Sansone made his way across the bridge to South Brooklyn in search of Mary. Zach was born in the United States but was raised in Italy from the age of eight. His older brother, Gerry, had met Mary a few months earlier when she was hired as his translator at a medical conference he was attending at the United Nations. Gerry found Mary fascinating, and upon his return to Italy, he encouraged Zach, who was planning a three-month vacation in the US, to call on Mary when he visited New York.

For Zach, the trip was more of an escape than a vacation, although he expressed this sentiment to no one. By all appearances, Zach was a successful lawyer who had served as mayor of Sant'Antonio Abate, a small municipality south of Naples. But he suffered chronic stress as a result of his military service during World War II. At the outset of the war, Zach tried to avoid conscription by claiming US citizenship, but the Italian government refused to acknowledge his birthright and the American Consulate declined to intervene. When the fighting was over, he returned home to a ravaged village. It was a daily reminder of the war. He battled postwar stress by throwing himself into his mayoral duties, generating detailed proposals for the reconstruction of his village, which included everything from soccer fields to senior citizen centers. It didn't help. The only thing he looked forward to was leaving Italy.

Zach was immediately smitten with Mary Crisalli. On their first date, which took place in January 1949, she found him to be a good listener with great ideas for how to design community development projects. After that, Zach and Mary saw each other almost every day for the next couple months. When Zach expressed his love for Mary and desire to remain in the States, Mary surprised herself by suggesting they go to city hall to get married. For two weeks, Mary and Zach lived separately while she kept the elopement a secret. When she finally told her mother, Martha was relieved that her spinster daughter had found a husband but distressed that she hadn't married in the church. She pressed Mary: "What would Zach's family back in Italy think of marrying without a priest?" Mary, like her father, despised the clergy, but she wanted to please her mother. Mary had zero interest in planning her own wedding and was happy to relinquish control of the event to her mother. That meant Mary couldn't protest when Martha arranged for Uncle Jimmy, who had taken a shine to Zach, to walk her daughter down the aisle on June 30, 1949.

During his seven-month wartime incarceration on Hart Island, Joe Colombo was diagnosed as suffering from "psychoneurosis," a condition likely the result of trauma caused by the unsolved murder of his father as well as by the carnage he witnessed in the war. After his discharged from the Coast Guard, he returned to his wife Jo-Jo and their newborn Anthony, who were residing in a two-bedroom apartment inside the home of Jo-Jo's sister on President Street in Red Hook. Joe sought an outlet to manage the stress in the form of a refuge from the city. He found one upstate in Kingston, New York, where he rented a secluded bungalow atop a tree-covered mountain at the end of a dirt road. In the first half of the 1950s, it was the spot where he and his family vacationed.[3]

Back in Brooklyn, Joe signed on with Local 1814 of the International Longshoremen's Association, a union run by labor racketeer Anthony Anastasio and controlled by the Gambino crime family. On the waterfront, Joe began his rise up the ranks of organized crime. He earned enough to move his family out of his sister-in-law's President Street home and, with the addition of two more sons Joe Jr. and Vincent, into a three-story house on Seventy-Seventh Street in Bensonhurst.[4]

In the mid-1950s, just after the Waterfront Commission to combat labor racketeering in the Port of New York Harbor was established, Joe Colombo left his union job with Local 1814 to be a salesman with Pride Wholesale Meat Company, another Brooklyn operation controlled by the Gambino crime family.[5]

Joe could now afford to drive a new Cadillac every year. In Bensonhurst, he opened a social club named Café Royale and was a silent partner in the Como Lounge. When the cops closed down Café Royale, Joe moved a few blocks west and reopened under a new name. On weekends, Joe motored upstate to the little town of Blooming Grove, where in 1955 he bought a knotty-pine cottage on three acres of land, where his family spent the entire summer.[6]

Mary worried that her marriage would change her life. She believed marriage should be a partnership and she was determined to make it so. In 1950, less than a year after they wed, Mary and Zach secured a storefront on Brooklyn's Court Street and opened the Italian American Service Organization. IASO offered new immigrants and the working poor in need of neighborhood-sponsored social services an alternative to turning to the local Mafia for help. In IASO's office, the newlyweds worked together: She performed social work; he provided legal advice. Mary's wide-ranging network of contacts among elected officials and government bureaucrats, priests and rabbis, business owners and union leaders, made IASO a one-stop shop for assistance, everything from a green card to rent relief. Mary privately hoped that once Zach mastered English he would take the New York State bar exam and practice law. Zach couldn't live up to those expectations. He associated practicing law, like being mayor, with Italy. Mary sensed that her husband's anxiety was fueled by the neighborhood men who stopped by the IASO office and, in her presence, would say to Zach, "If I had a wife like yours, I'd be president."[7]

In the spring of 1950, Mary gave birth to their first child, Carmela. Her doctor insisted on performing a cesarean because of her "advanced age." Mary intended to go back to work on Court Street after recovering from surgery, but soon after giving birth she contracted a pulmonary embolism that settled in her left leg. Her illness kept her housebound for months and she was forced to rely on her mother's help with the care of Carmela. Then, just as Mary was finally getting back on her feet, her mother took ill with a heart condition. Now the daughter cared for the mother and the newborn. In an odd twist of fate, the domestic responsibilities that sidelined Mary from community organizing also helped shield her from becoming ensnared in Senator Joseph McCarthy's Red Scare. Even so, Mary feared accusations of being a communist. The Rand School, which she attended prior to the war, was a self-described "workingmen's college" and "auxiliary for socialist movements." Now, with the onset of the Cold War, she guarded her affiliation with Rand as a secret to protect herself and her family from persecution.

The Sansone's IASO struggled financially due to Mary's absence from the office. She didn't protest when Zach closed the storefront for good. At the start of 1951, Zach took a better paying job on the Brooklyn waterfront, where within a few years he was promoted to the rank of shop steward with the International Longshoremen's Association. Mary, pleased that her husband had found steady work that could support a family, was consumed with caring for her daughter even as her mother's health improved. It seemed like only yesterday that Carmela was getting out of diapers when Mary discovered she was pregnant for a second time. She didn't have a moment to stop and think about whether Uncle Jimmy had a hand in Zach's hiring or in securing her husband's promotion inside the union.

Marriage ended Mary's life as she once knew it. She now struggled to find fulfillment in her prescribed role as wife and mother of two, Carmela and newborn Ralph. For the first time, she battled depression. She spent evenings—children asleep, Zach working the night shift on the docks—alone, sometimes crying. Distressed by her daughter's uncharacteristic unhappiness, Martha blurted, "I can't understand how you gave up your life for a man!" Mary, caught off guard, said nothing. But her mother's rebuke set off something inside Mary. She was determined to make a change.[8]

Magazines were full of stories promoting home ownership as the ideal setting for housewives seeking fulfillment. By 1956, Zach's job on the waterfront allowed them to save $2,000, enough to put a down payment on a two-story attached brick home on Fifty-Ninth Street near New Utrecht Avenue in Boro Park, a neighborhood adjacent to Bensonhurst and considered "mixed" because it was evenly divided between Italians and Jews. The home in Boro Park had three levels. Upstairs, there were three bedrooms. On the middle floor was a rear kitchen with dining and living rooms out front. Stairs from the kitchen led down and into a finished basement.

Mary was left with two problems. The first was financial: Although they had money for a down payment, how could they afford the $100 monthly mortgage? The second was emotional: She struggled to play the role of domestic angel. She hit upon a scheme, one that drew on the twin inspiration of her work with orphans through Relief for Italy and the enterprising example set by her nonna, who paid off her Henry Street mortgage by renting out the upper floors.[9]

Mary's plan: foster care. In collaboration with Catholic Charities, Mary took in children who had been abused, neglected, or abandoned by their parents or guardians. Some of the kids she welcomed into her home were Italian but others were Irish, German, Polish, and Puerto Rican. All were from poor families. For a dozen years, Mary housed as many as five foster kids at a time. Guests remarked that spending time at Mary's was like visiting "Little UN."

In the winter of 1959, while his family was back in the city for the school year, Joe's Blooming Grove summer house burned to the ground. More bad news followed in the spring when Joe learned that his eldest son Anthony was kicked out of St. Francis Prep—a prestigious Catholic high school in the Williamsburg section of Brooklyn—after failing Latin.

Anthony's expulsion was a big blow to his father. Joe, who dropped out of high school after the death of his father and for whom his children's education was paramount, had gone to great lengths to secure a seat for his son at St. Francis. He asked his brother-in-law Joe LaRosa to pull strings with his cousin Father Brendan, who taught at the school. However, after Anthony matriculated at St. Francis, the school found out that law enforcement listed his father as a Brooklyn mobster. Joe later discovered that the informant was, allegedly, a police officer named Walter F. Henning. Henning had recently been promoted to deputy chief inspector with the NYPD's Central Investigation Bureau in what *The New York Times* called an all-out effort "to spur a drive against racketeers." Chief Inspector Henning's son Dan, a future NFL quarterback and coach, was an all-city quarterback on the powerful St. Francis football team. Anthony, who loved football, had earned a position as an undersized but hard-nosed linebacker on the school's team. During the season, Anthony had become acutely aware—without knowing why—that Dan Henning disliked him.[10]

Once St. Francis administrators got wind of Colombo's criminal profile, Anthony's F in Latin was the excuse they needed to rid the school of any connection to Joe's family. Joe was powerless in the face of law enforcement officials determined to weaken him by harassing his family, including his own children. Without thinking, Joe unleashed his fury on Anthony. In the basement of their Brooklyn home, he pummeled his son with his fists before giving him the belt. For good measure, he took a dull pair of scissors to Anthony's prized pompadour. It was a beating Anthony would never forget, partly because his father, while a strict disciplinarian, only rarely raised a hand toward his children. It also confirmed, in Anthony's mind, the importance his father placed on his children's education.

By the fall, Joe had collected $37,000 on his homeowner's insurance and began rebuilding on the site where the small Blooming Grove summer cottage once stood. After the run-in with Anthony's school the prior spring, Joe decided to move his family from Bensonhurst to Blooming Grove year-round, where they could live in comfort, safety, and relative anonymity. On weekends, Joe commuted to Blooming Grove, where he joined the nearby Otterkill Country Club, listing his occupation on the membership application as "chicken farmer." He was known to regulars at the private club as an avid golfer, a passion he shared with his deceased father.[11]

Back in the city, Joe purchased a split-level at 1161 Eighty-Third Street, just off Dyker Beach Park, for $47,000. In Blooming Grove, he purchased an additional forty-four acres and, over the next decade, turned the property into an estate, replete with swimming pool, tennis and handball courts, a horse racing track, a tack room, and six stables for four horses and two Sicilian donkeys. The donkeys were a gift from Joe's close friend Carmine Persico. Together, they had climbed the crooked ladder to become *caporegimes* or "captains" of their own crews inside the Profaci crime family by end of the 1950s.[12]

Part Two

Civil Rights Confidential

Confidential FBI memorandum addressed to Director J. Edgar Hoover and from New York Special Agent in Charge with information regarding Gregory Scarpa's designation as a Top Echelon Criminal Informant on November 21, 1961. *Source: The Vault/the FBI: Federal Bureau of Investigation. Public domain.*

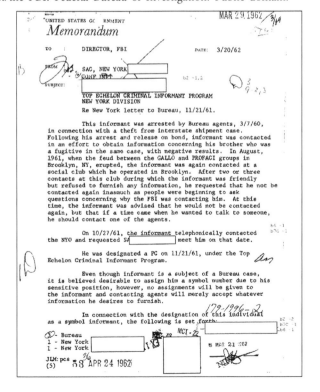

Chapter 4

A Rage in Harlem (1960)

Just days before the dawn of the new decade, US Congressman Adam Clayton Powell Jr., a flamboyant reverend-politician, announced before one thousand parishioners at Harlem's Abyssinian Baptist Church that "Italian bankers have run the Negro banker out of business in Harlem." From the pulpit he made a promise—a vow that echoed across the East River to South Brooklyn, where Mary Sansone and Joe Colombo lived. Powell pledged that, upon his return to Washington in January, he would use his congressional immunity to place into the congressional record the name and address of a numbers bank that the police had not yet raided. "I am against numbers in any form," Powell preached. "But until the day when numbers is wiped out in Harlem, I am going to fight for the Negro having the same chance as an Italian."[1]

During his most recent congressional campaign, Powell had defeated a candidate handpicked by Carmine DeSapio, the first Italian American boss of the once-powerful Tammany Hall political machine. Powell won the election handily. At the time, sociologist Daniel Patrick Moynihan examined the results to assess how Powell pulled off the resounding victory. Moynihan concluded that Harlem's numbers runners were the difference-makers in the election. Powell's "popular support came from the Negro numbers runners," wrote Moynihan, "who were tired of working for white men who ran policy from outside Harlem." With Harlem's local economy awash in the numbers game, opportunities for enterprising Black bankers should have been plentiful. Yet, Moynihan noted, even after Black racketeers helped the reverend repel Carmine DeSapio's candidate, "Negroes still did not control policy."[2]

Powell believed permissive crime, such as numbers running, was a civil rights issue. Fellow Harlemite and civil rights champion Kenneth B. Clark conceded that Powell's approach to permissive crime as a social justice cause had a pragmatic appeal. "He understood this society and its corruption," Clark said by way of commenting on Powell's political acuity, "and he just refused to be taken in by it. He took as his responsibility one of the most difficult civil-rights responsibilities, the integration of corruption."[3]

Powell kept his word. At the start of 1960, the congressman began making public on the House floor "a list of alleged gamblers and gambling places in New York City," reported Chicago's Black newspaper the *Daily Defender*, and "also gave law enforcement agencies some advice on 'how to track down the Mafia' which he said controls gambling rackets."[4]

From the House floor, Powell was heard.

> I am not afraid of the Mafia, the syndicate, the gangsters and hoodlums. I have specifically asked the police department to not provide me any bodyguards.
>
> I am stating one unchallengeable fact, that the Mafia and the syndicate are in complete control of Harlem.
>
> I refuse to allow myself to be pauperized and criminalized by the sickness of gambling and the sinister forces of the Mafia.[5]

The following Sunday evening, in a television interview, the routinely unrepentant Powell surprised his audience by walking back his statements associating "Italians" with organized crime. He offered viewers an oblique apology for his defamatory remarks—"Maybe I should have said that the [policy] bankers in Harlem are white."[6]

Powell aired his reluctant mea culpa on television at a time when Italian Americans were raising objections to prime-time depictions of themselves as mobsters on a new cops-and-robbers TV drama called *The Untouchables*. Produced by Desilu studio and sponsored by Liggett & Meyers Tobacco Company's Chesterfield King cigarettes, *The Untouchables*, starring Robert Stack as real-life federal agent Eliot Ness, was an overnight ratings hit for the American Broadcasting Company when it premiered in October of 1959. The show, premised on the unimpeachable moral standing of special units within federal law enforcement, was shot in a documentary style that gave its largely fictionalized stories a realistic look.

"It has got so bad that people have started referring to 'The Untouchables' as 'The Italian Hour,'" complained Dominic H. Frinzi, president elect of the Italian American service organization UNICO. A. A.

Marcello, national chairman of the Sons of Italy, made an appeal to Walter Winchell, the leading tabloid columnist of the day. Winchell had been hired on *The Untouchables* to provide the show's signature narration—terse, high-pitched, breathless—over the melancholy strings of Nelson Riddle's orchestra. "On behalf of the Sons of Italy in America," Marcello pleaded to Winchell, "we ask you to champion our cause and have ABC delete the telecast which slanders millions of Americans through the use of the word Mafia."[7]

Although *The Untouchables* treated crime, including the drug trade and prostitution, with frankness, its relentless depiction of Italians as criminals made it a veritable slander sheet to many Americans of Italian descent. In its inaugural episodes, for instance, members of the Capone outfit voiced cartoonish Italian accents. Another first season episode, titled "The Noise of Death," was singled out by anti-defamation groups as particularly noxious. In the fall of 1959, the *Los Angeles Times* ran an ad for the episode containing the copy: "*Untouchables* from the silence of the cold, cold room . . . comes the awful noise of death . . . Joe Bucco he's through as a Mafia boss."[8]

Without warning, however, "The Noise of Death" episode, scheduled for an evening in October, was pulled by the network. The day before its air date, Walter Winchell's gossip column explained the delay in a dispatch. "Memos of a Girl Friday. Dear W. W.: The ABC-TV press staff called. Said the best of 'The Untouchables' episode so far is 'The Noise of Death' (about the Mafia)—originally scheduled for last Oct. 29th. It was held up at the request of the Dept. of Justice, which feared it might cause a mistrial of the Apalachian [*sic*] mob if shown before the trial ended. It will be shown on the 14th [of January 1960], the date they are to be sentenced."[9]

Two years earlier, in November 1957, police accidentally stumbled on a mob summit inside Joseph "Joe the Barber" Barbara's stone mansion near the small upstate New York town of Apalachin. According to law enforcement, the parley was held to decide how to divide the holdings of Murder Inc.'s Albert Anastasia, who once controlled the syndicate's enforcement arm but who, a month earlier, became the victim of a gangland assassination. The resulting "Apalachin trial" gave the government the biggest boost to its case for a ubiquitous Mafia since Frank Costello appeared on broadcast television at the start of the decade. Beginning in the 1950s, politicians framed organized crime as a threat to national security perpetrated by unassimilable foreigners, namely Italian Americans. It didn't take long for mass media to

Figure 4.1. Half-page headline announcing the arrest of "Apalachin summit" attendees, *New York Daily News*, November 1957. *Source:* New York Daily News. Used with permission.

make the Italian word "Mafia" a synonym for organized crime inside the United States. In the process, Italians in America were criminalized in the popular imagination. By 1957, news outlets no longer relied on officials to sound out the hidden underworld threat. It had a name—Mafia—that was shouted in bold headlines for everyone to see (Fig. 4.1).

Among those on trial for their participation in the Apalachin summit were the heads of two New York crime families, Carlo Gambino and Joseph Profaci. Gambino, a friend of Joe Colombo's father, was Joe's longtime mentor. Profaci, who had once been Joe's father's boss, was now his. Men like Gambino and Profaci worried that the media's spotlight on the Mafia, in entertainment programming as well as on the news, would result in heightened scrutiny by law enforcement of their underground operations. But what could they do about it?[10]

According to three discrete insider accounts, a Profaci crime family associate named Joseph Colombo masterminded what would become a successful anti-defamation picket against ABC-TV for broadcasting *The*

Untouchables. One account of Joe's leading role in organizing the demonstration was offered by Joseph Luparelli, who, like Colombo, was an associate in the Profaci outfit. Luparelli recalled a "day in 1960" when Profaci complained about how crooks on *The Untouchables* were always Italian. "Colombo suggested forming a legitimate association of Italian-Americans to boycott *The Untouchables* and the program's sponsors."[11]

Chapter 5

Boycott (1961)

Joe Colombo was a businessman. He recognized that simply picketing the network would not get the job done. Pressure had to be put on the show's corporate backer—specifically Liggett & Meyers, the sponsor who paid for *The Untouchables* by purchasing ad time. According to Luparelli's account, "Profaci took this novel plan to the Commission, presenting it as his own brainchild." Joe's putative idea of launching an anti-defamation organization was set aside. However, "after lengthy debate," the mob bosses approved his scheme to boycott Liggett & Meyers.[1]

On Amerigo Vespucci Day, March 9, one hundred members of the International Longshoremen's Association (ILA) gathered outside the American Broadcasting Company headquarters at 7 West Sixty-Sixth Street in Manhattan. They were there to protest *The Untouchables*. More pointedly, they were making public their threat to boycott of the show's sponsor, Liggett & Meyers, by refusing to move its products unless *The Untouchables* stopped stereotyping Italians as criminals. The unannounced picket was led by Anthony "Tough Tony" Anastasio, president of AFL-CIO ILA Local 1814. With a membership of 10,000, it was the largest and most powerful local in the union. Tough Tony, brother of Murder Inc.'s Albert Anastasia, was a member of the Gambino crime family, which controlled Local 1814.[2]

Eyebrows were raised when, in a matter of days, Liggett & Meyers announced it would drop its sponsorship of *The Untouchables*. Television industry magazine *Broadcasting* noted that it was "probably the first time in TV history that a sponsor's decision to get out of a show had coincided so closely with announced boycott plans intended to achieve that same result." The boycott worked. Desilu stopped giving its gangsters Italian names and cartoonish accents. A year and a half later, in the face of the show's declining ratings, Lucille Ball, head of the studio, was asked if she was aware of the ILA boycott (she was) and if she would reverse course in an effort to regain audience share. The famous redhead replied: "I'm not that brave."[3]

US Congressman Alfred E. Santangelo, whose Upper East Side Manhattan district included Italian East Harlem and who was also president of the New York State Democratic Party's five-hundred-member Federation of Italian American Democratic Organizations (FIADO), tried to claim credit for the victory. It was apparent to anyone paying attention that the tobacco company caved only when Local 1814 threatened to boycott. In an interview with *Broadcasting*, Tony Anastasio was pleased to take credit for contacting "men from Liggett and Meyers" with a proposition. "It's going to be tit for tat. You play ball with us and we'll play ball with you. I also tell them . . . that my men would not handle their stuff. I say to them, I'll cause them as much trouble as I cause Mr. Castro."

Anastasio was referring to his Local's refusal to move Cuban goods through Brooklyn's industrial waterfront in protest of the country's turn toward communism. After Liggett & Meyers dropped its sponsorship of *The Untouchables*, Anastasio wired the company's president, W. A. Blount, to express his "sincere appreciation on behalf of his membership and their families" for the decision. He assured the reporter from *Broadcasting* that he had "no reason to cause Liggett & Meyers any more trouble." A FIADO spokesman told the same reporter that the Democratic Party organization was not connected to Mr. Anastasio. "We didn't sanction anything he did," the spokesman said, while conceding that the labor boss's efforts had been "helpful to the Italian-American cause." Anastasio, before dying from natural causes, built a $2 million medical clinic to serve Brooklyn dockworkers and their families, thereby cementing his commitment to helping Italian Americans.[4]

Chapter 6

Knotty Pine Politics (1962)

Mary Sansone sidelined her passion for community organizing in order to mother a house full of foster kids along with her own two children. A dozen years later, however, she was itching to find a way to reactivate her political career. Mary began reestablishing her social network, yet she struggled to regain her public speaking voice. Mary found a remedy in the most unlikely place—on her kitchen wall. Armed by Ma Bell, she jump-started her service delivery operation. Her knotty-pined basement became the bunker from which—phone tucked between chin and shoulder—Mary commandeered political campaigns while dressed in her housecoat and performing domestic chores. Even when notable politicians and community leaders became a regular presence in her finished basement, Mary couldn't be bothered changing out of household garb. "I'm just at home," she reasoned. Strategy sessions at the Sansones' were a mix of children's rumpus and the aroma of frying peppers to be followed by Mary's family-style meatball dinners, the recipe for which was often requested and happily shared.

1. Preheat oven to 375 degrees.
2. Mix 12 slices of crumbled stale white bread, 2 medium chopped onions, chopped parsley, 2 tablespoons grated Parmesan cheese, 4 eggs, 2 pounds ground beef, salt and pepper to taste, and form into 34 golf-ball-size meatballs.
3. Put 8 tablespoons olive oil into baking pan and heat in oven until hot.
4. Add meatballs to oil and bake until brown, about 15 minutes, turning once.

5. Heat homemade tomato sauce on stove.

6. Finish cooking meatballs in tomato sauce, simmering about 20 minutes.

7. Check seasonings, and serve with cooked pasta.

Serves 12 guests.[1]

Soon, there was scuttlebutt around the borough and beyond about an Italian housewife who was a political power broker and a great cook. This was confirmed for all to see when, one Sunday afternoon in the spring of 1962, Vice President Lyndon B. Johnson and his entourage showed up on Mary's doorstep for a homecooked Italian meal. LBJ was there to thank Mary and her army of volunteers for their work on behalf of his friend, four-term Congressman Victor Anfuso. A civil rights movement champion, Anfuso was in the political fight of his life after a redistricting decision pitted him against the machine-backed candidate, John Rooney, whose district included South Brooklyn's waterfront, where the mob ruled.[2]

Chapter 7

Racial Equality on the Waterfront (1963)

International Longshoremen's Association Local 1814, which remained under the control of the Gambino crime family, brought the Southern civil rights movement to the Brooklyn docks. In May 1963, newly installed Local 1814 leader Anthony M. Scotto told Harlem's *Amsterdam News*, "We openly admire the Rev. Dr. Martin Luther King Jr.; we agree wholeheartedly with his philosophy of militant but non-violent protest; we are with him and the CORE freedom fighters all the way."[1]

Scotto, who had worked on the waterfront since the age of sixteen, was a new breed of union leadership. He was groomed to take the reins by his father-in-law, Local 1814 boss Anthony Anastasio. "A 28-year-old former longshoreman who majored in political science while swinging a bailing hook on the Brooklyn waterfront is at the helm of the largest local in the 70,000-member International Longshoremen Association," an April 1963 *New York Times* profile began. "Dressed to the nines with the accent on the conservative side, Mr. Scotto almost looks out of place amid the rough-and-tumble atmosphere of the piers and warehouses." On the political front, "Mr. Scotto is in almost daily communication with politicians in Washington, Albany and City Hall," to which the reporter added, "Mr. Scotto is a founding member of the New York Trade Union Committee for the Congress of Racial Equality (CORE)."[2]

In October, Scotto led thirty picketers from the New York chapter of CORE and the American Committee on Africa in a blockade of a Brooklyn dock. The aim of the protest was to halt operations on the South African *Pioneer*, a ship doing business with the apartheid government in South Africa. The nonviolent direct-action campaign was consistent with the tactics of CORE, whose Black and white Freedom Riders had attracted national headlines two years earlier when they challenged the segregation of interstate transportation in the Jim Crow South. It was also reminiscent of the gambit used by Scotto's father-in-law to protest a communist dictatorship in Cuba. In this case, three twenty-one-man dockworker crews, all members of Local 1814, honored the pickets and refused to unload the *Pioneer*. Scotto, in a press conference, said that the ILA's refusal to cross the picket line was a "gesture of cooperation in protest against racism and white supremacy practiced by the South African Government." In the *Chicago Daily Defender*, Scotto was quoted as stating, "We are happy to take part in any action against racism . . . our men decided that this was one way of contributing to the cause."[3]

Scotto's commitment to the cause was not limited to politics abroad. Early that year, in May 1963, the newly installed ILA boss pledged his union's support for the civil rights movement. In a press conference covered by the *Amsterdam News*, the charismatic leader announced that the executive board of Local 1814 had authorized a $1,300 donation to fund a CORE task force leader who would travel to "the deep south educating Negro citizens in their constitutional rights and responsibilities, persuading them to register and vote, urging their participation in techniques of peaceful protest such as sit-ins and freedom marches." As a part of his reform effort at home, Scotto also arranged for the Brooklyn local's participation in the Southern campaign. "By exchanging letters, photographs and progress reports" with the CORE worker down South, Scotto explained that "Brooklyn Longshoremen will be in close touch with their 'adopted' task force leader—thus creating a sense of personal involvement in the fight for civil rights." He urged Brooklyn longshoremen "not dodge controversial social issues."[4]

Scotto's challenge in bringing the spirit of remote social justice activism into his own backyard was chronicled the following winter. Journalist Tom Brooks, in a day-in-the-life feature story on the union boss published in the *New York Herald Tribune*'s new "New York" magazine Sunday supplement, shadowed Scotto, starting at dawn when the union boss arrived at Bush Terminal, Pier 4, on Brooklyn's waterfront. The reporter watched and listened as Scotto was pulled aside by a dockworker, "a short barrel of a man who wanted to know if there would be an election," to which Scotto said, "Yes . . . in 30 days."

"What about *them?*" challenged the longshoreman, jerking his thumb at a group of African Americans who belonged to one of the labor gangs on the pier.

"They vote," Scotto replied. "The election . . . will be held according to the constitution . . . C'mon, you know if they don't vote here they won't vote anywhere else."

Figure 7.1. ILA Vice President Anthony Scotto (second from left) talks to Local 1814 members, Brooklyn, 1965. *Source:* Meyer Liebowitz/New York Times/Redux. Used with permission.

Another dockworker, observing Scotto's presence among the old-timers, reassured Brooks that "real longshoremen . . . they go for this kid, the real longshoremen." Overhearing the dockworker's comment, Scotto admonished the reporter, "Don't . . . disassociate me from the membership. I'm not unique as far as they are concerned. They've changed, too."[5]

Nineteen sixty-three was a year of sweeping change inside the world of organized crime. The prior year, after Giuseppe Profaci died of natural causes, Giuseppe Magliocco took over as boss. Then in 1963, Joe Colombo learned from boss Magliocco that he and boss Joseph Bonanno were conspiring to assassinate boss Carlo Gambino. Joe, rather than take part in the murder plot, sided with his mentor and double-crossed Magliocco and Bonanno by reporting their scheme to the Mafia Commission. Colombo's tip thwarted the coup. After Magliocco died, apparently of natural causes, at the end of that year, Joe Colombo was rumored to be next in line to head the Profaci crime family.

The Federal Bureau of Investigation picked up talk of Joe's rise from Gregory Scarpa Sr., a soldier in the Profaci outfit. Scarpa was one of the earliest criminal recruits to FBI Director J. Edgar Hoover's nationwide Top Echelon Criminal Informant Program, which was inaugurated in 1961 and to which Scarpa was "converted" on November 21, 1961. Informants were underworld double agents employed as gangland spies for the FBI. The darkest side of the top-secret Top Echelon program was the license it gave informants to commit crimes—theft, extortion, assault, even murder—with impunity. Cover was provided by handlers, who were unsupervised special agents responsible for informant oversight.[6]

Scarpa—who is classified in FBI files as informant NY 3451-C-TE and as racketeer NY 92-2657—was providing the FBI with the most detailed information available on the inner workings of the secret society.

```
During night of 6/5/62, a lengthy interview
was had with informant during which he fur-
nished information on the history and back-
ground of the Italian criminal organization,
the organizational set-up; procedure and ritual
for inducting new members, certain rules of
organization and penalty for violation; and
the identity of the officers of the PROFACI
family.⁷
```

In a September 1962 FBI memo, Scarpa had named Joe Colombo a "Captain in the PROFACI family." By November, Scarpa was identifying Joe as a captain in "the leadership of the family formerly controlled by the late JOSEPH PROFACI," which was now headed by "JOSEPH MAGLIOCCO." In mid-December 1963, with Joseph Magliocco on his deathbed, Scarpa informed his FBI handlers that Joe Colombo was the heir apparent to the Profaci crime family throne.[8]

```
The informant stated that from all appear-
ances JOE COLOMBO is presently running the
MAGLIOCCO "family" and it is the informant's
guess that COLOMBO will emerge as the new
"boss" in the "family." Informant stated
that COLOMBO is receiving a large number
of visitors from members of the "family" at
```

>   Cantalupo Realty Company at the present time.
>   He stated that COLOMBO uses the last office
>   in the rear of Cantalupo for meeting with
>   member of the "family."[9]

Joe had left his job at Pride Meat Company the year prior and taken a position as a salesman for Cantalupo Realty, located at 1434 Eighty-Sixth Street in Bensonhurst. Even within high-ranking organized crime circles, Joe's purported elevation to boss of his own family was unexpected.[10]

At that time, the fall of 1963, the American public was served a TV diet of "insider" information on the Mafia that Greg Scarpa had been covertly feeding the FBI for more than a year. In October, Joseph Valachi, a sixty-year-old, low-ranking thug in the Genovese crime family, became the first Italian American gangster known publicly to have turned state's evidence and broken *omertà*, the Mafia code of silence, when he testified before the United States Senate Select Committee on Improper Activities in Labor and Management, also known as the McClellan Committee.

The *Boston Globe*, hometown newspaper to President John F. Kennedy and his brother US Attorney General Robert F. Kennedy, scooped Valachi's immanent testimony. The initial *Globe* coverage, published August 4, 1963, and appearing on page 1, spotlighted the attorney general rather than his star witness. Valachi's name was withheld until paragraph 10 on page 7. The story opened instead with misinformation about the unnamed witness—describing him as "a figure once fairly high in the mob hierarchy"—before stating, "Justice Department officials . . . consider this a major victory in Attorney General Robert F. Kennedy's coordinated attack on organized crime." When Valachi finally appeared on TV before the McClellan Committee a month later, he testified to the lurid workings of New York's underworld, which he identified as "Cosa Nostra" and which he translated as "our thing, our family."[11]

Valachi's televised testimony, while less dramatic than Costello's, was nonetheless a major setback to the anti-defamation victory supplied by *The Untouchables* boycott. Italian American service organizations across the country immediately attacked the hearings as slanderous toward twenty-one million Americans of Italian descent. They argued that making a spectacle of Valachi was part of a Kennedy administration smear campaign orchestrated by the attorney general. A high-ranking Democrat told *The New York Times* that there was a "strong feeling" within the Italian community that Valachi was being deployed by the administration as "a diversionary tactic" to draw public attention away from the civil rights movement down South, where less than a month earlier four Black girls had been murdered by Ku Klux Klansmen in a Birmingham, Alabama, church bombing that had sent shock waves across the nation.[12]

Chapter 8

Most Wanted (1964)

In the spring of 1964, Top Echelon FBI informant Greg Scarpa provided the following information about Joe Colombo to his handler.

> Informant advised that on Sunday night, 4/5/64, JOE COLOMBO was confirmed as "boss" of the MAGLIOCCO "family." Informant related that the ceremony was attend by representatives from seven "families" and all the "Captains" in the MAGLIOCCO "family."[1]

At only forty-one years of age, Joe was the youngest crime boss in the country and the youngest to head one of the Five Families since the Prohibition era, when twenty-nine-year-old Joseph Bonanno ascended to the top.

> On 6/3/64 . . . Colombo advised [informant] that he would be assigned directly under COLOMBO for the present and that COLOMBO desired to keep his eyes and ears open and learn everything for him. COLOMBO further advised that he had a plan whereby he would gradually retire all the old "Captains" in the "family and replace them with younger men."[2]

A federal agent characterized the fledgling Colombo family as a new generation of Mafia. "Most of its members are American-born, free-wheeling men not so bound to tradition and eager to find new ways to exploit the system."[3]

***

At the start of the year, just months after Valachi publicly testified in front of the McClellan Committee, FBI Director J. Edgar Hoover used an appropriation subcommittee hearing in the US House of Representatives as an occasion to dismiss Attorney General Robert Kennedy's claim that Valachi's reveal was "the biggest intelligence breakthrough we have ever had." The House Appropriation Committee hearing was run by Congressmen John Rooney, whose district included the South Brooklyn waterfront. As chair of the powerful subcommittee, Rooney had a well-deserved reputation inside the Capitol for axing bureaucratic budgets he believed too extravagant. However, Rooney was one of the few politicians in Washington who had a close working relationship to the Bureau director. As chronicled by *The Washington Post*, never once during Hoover's long tenure did Rooney give the FBI a penny less than what Hoover asked for. Sometimes he added money to the Bureau's request. Beltway reporters noticed that when the director appeared before Rooney's subcommittee, the hearing frequently turned into a love fest between the two men.[4]

During the subcommittee hearing, Rooney questioned Hoover about the quality of intel the Department of Justice had procured from informant Valachi: "There is very little of that you have not known for years?"

Hoover replied, "That's correct."

"Has Valachi ever been of any assistance to the Bureau?"

"There has been no person convicted as a direct result of any information furnished by Valachi."[5]

Perhaps the most startling disclosure solicited from Valachi was obtained during an interrogation by an FBI agent, where the informant claimed the word "Mafia" was never uttered by his criminal associates. "It's not Mafia," Valachi insisted. "That's the expression the outside uses."[6]

The Italian American outcry over Valachi's televised testimony coincided with the moment when pop artist Andy Warhol began work on a mural called *Thirteen Most Wanted Men*. Still largely unknown outside the art world, Warhol was commissioned to create the mural for the 1964 New York World's Fair. Prominent architect Philip Johnson asked Warhol and nine other artists to produce large-scale pieces that would hang on the exterior of Johnson's panoramic theater for the New York State Pavilion.

In mid-April 1964, on the eve the fair's opening, workers hung *Thirteen Most Wanted Men* (Fig. 8.1). It displayed blown up mug shots of

Figure 8.1. Andy Warhol, *Thirteen Most Wanted Men*, New York State Pavilion, New York World's Fair, Queens, April 1964. *Source:* © 2024 The Andy Warhol Foundation for the Visual Arts, Inc./Licensed by Artists Rights Society (ARS), New York. Used with permission.

the New York City Police Department's "Most Wanted" fugitives on large Masonite panels. The *New York Journal-American*, a paper with a sizable Catholic readership among the city's dailies and that advertised itself as "New York's World's Fair Newspaper!" previewed Warhol's installation with a photograph of the twenty-by-twenty-foot mural beneath a cheeky headline "Some Not-So-Fair-Faces."

The article accompanying the *Journal-American* photo asked the artist, "Andrew Warhol," to defend his contribution to the fair in anticipation of "howls of protest." Warhol initially brushed off disapproval with a camp-ish retort: "I had thought about doing great big Heinz pickle." Next he tried to deflect criticism of the mural's content by appealing to its modest price tag. "The whole thing cost about $4,000. That's all they gave me to do it. It took one day. I got the pictures from a book the police put out. It's called, 'The 13 Most Wanted Men.' It just had something to do with New York, and I was paid just enough to have it silk screened. I didn't make any money on it."[7]

According to a memoir penned by Italian American poet John Giorno, a friend of Warhol's, the idea to silkscreen criminal mug shots was conceived at a dinner party hosted by painter Wynn Chamberlain, who had an intimate connection inside the NYPD. "My boyfriend is a cop," Giorno, who was in attendance, recalled Chamberlain saying. "He can get you all the mug shots you want." Chamberlain's lover, identified as Jimmy O'Neill, was a third-generation New York City cop—half Italian, half Irish—and, according Giorno, "gorgeous" and "hip." He recalled that Jimmy "gave Andy a big manila envelope filled with crime photos, mug shots, archival photographs." Among these treasures, Warhol discovered a 1962 NYPD bulletin titled "The Thirteen Most Wanted," which contained the raw material for his World's Fair mural. Warhol's *Thirteen Most Wanted Men*, within the context of pre-Stonewall gay life, offered a set of insider codes connecting outlaw masculinity to homosexual desire and homoeroticism to illicit rough trade, which was punishable by jail in New York at that time.[8]

In the early 1960s, however, public expressions of homosexuality remained verboten, so it was unlikely that most fair-goers recognized the mural's queer allusions. Fair officials, led by the event's president, the powerful Robert Moses, weren't going to take any chances. They were determined to scrub all traces of outlaw culture from the surrounding area. In anticipation of opening day, "authorities launched a clean-up campaign of such ferocity," according to a *New York Times Sunday Magazine* investigation, that "New York's famous homosexual bars"—"the best known of them . . . run by syndicates"—were "rapidly disappearing."[9]

At the opening of the 1964 World's Fair, authorities in New York, having shuttered gay bars and driven their patrons deeper into the closet, worried about how the public would view *Thirteen Most Wanted Men*. In light of the recent outcry over the Valachi hearings, would Warhol's mural be seen as the Worlds Fair's tacit endorsement of the Mafia stereotype? If so, protests were sure to follow. During the week, between when the mural was hung and when the World's Fair opened, a decision was made to silver over *Thirteen Most Wanted Men* in aluminum paint. According to one source, "Word had come from Governor Nelson Rockefeller," who in 1964 was in the midst of an uphill primary campaign for the Republican Party's presidential nomination, "that the painting might be insulting to some of his

Italian constituents, since most of the thirteen criminals were Italian." Philip Johnson, who was responsible for acquiring the art that hung outside the pavilion he designed, confirmed that Rockefeller had been given the names of the mugs pictured in *Thirteen Most Wanted Men*. "You see," he explained, "we have a terrible problem in this country. The Mafia is reputedly Italian, you see, and most of these 'Thirteen Wanted' were Mafiosi."[10]

On June 21, three activists with the Congress of Racial Equality—Michael Schwerner, Andrew Goodman, and James Chaney—went missing under suspicious circumstances at the start of a massive three-month voter registration drive in Mississippi. The disappearance of the CORE workers was followed by a national media frenzy over the federal government's inability to maintain law and order in the face of violent Ku Klux Klan resistance to desegregation. In Southern civil rights movement lore, Top Echelon informant Greg Scarpa was utilized by the FBI in J. Edgar Hoover's desperate attempt to break the "Mississippi Burning" case.

Scarpa's FBI deployment to Mississippi was confirmed by former federal agents, including his handler Anthony Villano. Scarpa was purportedly tasked with interrogating, by whatever means necessary, Lawrence Byrd, a local salesman and Klan member. Byrd was thought to have participated in the disappearance of the young men. To elicit a confession, Scarpa put a gun in the Klansman's mouth and threatened to pull the trigger. On August 4, Byrd sang. The young men's bodies were found beneath an earthen dam out on Highway 21.[11]

In the same week that the three Mississippi CORE activists went missing, *The New York Times* warned that in New York City "a murderous war is in the making between a group known locally as 'the Black Mafia' and a white syndicate." A couple days later, on June 28, during a speech in Harlem at the founding of the Organization for Afro-American Unity, Black nationalist leader Malcolm X called for "an all-out war on organized crime in our community." In mid-July, residents in Harlem rioted when a white police officer shot and killed a Black youth in front of a dozen witnesses.[12]

Black and white CORE demonstrators protested the alleged police brutality by picketing NYPD headquarters on Centre Street, located next door to Lower Manhattan's Little Italy. The nonviolent pickets were immediately met by a counterdemonstration consisting of local Italian youth. The teenagers, calling themselves "the Mulberry Boys," assaulted the "the pickets with firecrackers, bottles, and racial insults." For three uninterrupted nights, white kids attacked and injured some CORE demonstrators, along with some police assigned to protect them. Attempts to disperse the counterdemonstrators were futile. Each time the cops disbanded the teenagers, they would reassemble a half hour later on the cobbled streets and chalk-scrawled sidewalks to do battle again. By the third night, the confrontation was threatening to turn into another riot. Robert Perrella, a priest from Church of the Most Precious Blood on Mulberry Street, was summoned to keep the peace, or as he put it, "to make sure none of the neighborhood young men get into trouble." The teens, ignoring the reverend's plea, refused to stand down.[13]

That night, a bystander to the CORE–Mulberry Boys melee came to a conclusion shared by others in the neighborhood. "They should turn this thing over to the Mafia," a local resident told one reporter, adding "they would clean this up." Although not made public at the time, that's exactly what city hall did. As an official in Mayor Wagner's administration explained to crime reporter Nicholas Pileggi, "We went right to those guys around the corner sitting in their clubs . . . and told them if they didn't call those jerky kids off, we were going to have to lean on them harder than they would want." The official added, "Mind you, nobody actually said they would take care of anything, it was more like we just talked about how unfortunate all of these demonstrations are and how wonderful it would be for the community if some people with influence and respect could exert their prestige in the direction of subduing the wild kids."[14]

The next day, on the fourth night of CORE picketing, the violence subsided. Not one Mulberry Boy showed his face. Peace on the mean streets, for the moment, was restored. "The local priest might advise," Pileggi deftly observed, "but the local Don could *order*."[15]

Chapter 9

Mafia Literati (1965)

One night, three wise men—Mario Puzo, Gay Talese, and Nicholas Pileggi—met for a meal in Bensonhurst. The trinity gathered at the kitchen table in Nick's boyhood home along with Nick's parents, Susan and Nicola. Susan happened to be Gay's aunt. Nicola was an avid reader, and he told Mario that he'd just finished his recently published autobiographical novel, *The Fortunate Pilgrim*. Nicola admired the book. It reminded him of New York City before World War II. Mario's portrait of his mother, an indomitable matriarch who struggles to build a new life in Hell's Kitchen for her immigrant family, left a deep impression on Nicola.[1]

But Nicola said he was disappointed that Mario hadn't given more attention to a minor character in the novel. "You should have done more with the mob boss," he said, referring to a gangster named Signore Le Cinglata, who is characterized in the book as "almost a godfather" to Mario's older brother. He added, "Now that's someone no one has *really* written about."[2]

Nicola, the proprietor of a nearby garment shop on Eighteenth Avenue and New Utrecht Street, wasn't a wiseguy, but he knew plenty of them, including the late Albert Anastasia. Most of the Italians in the neighborhood, like him, were Calabrese.

"I never met a real honest-to-god gangster," Mario told the table. "But I've started a book about the mob. I'll call it 'Mafia.'"[3]

Chapter 10

Black Power Provocation (1966)

When, in the spring of 1966, Joe Colombo made his first appearance as a Mafia godfather in the press, little was known about him. In an April story that was buried on page 58 of *The New York Times*, crime expert Charles Grutzner explained to readers that according to law enforcement, Joe was "a 'sleeper'—a Mafioso with no record of convictions"—which, authorities believed, was why Joe was chosen to head the former Profaci crime family. Indeed, Grutzner reported, around Bensonhurst Joe had built a reputation not as a ruthless mob boss but as a salesman—specifically, according to Grutzner, "as a highly successful salesman" with Cantalupo Realty.[1]

In September, Joe was arrested in an NYPD raid on a gangland meeting at La Stella restaurant in Forest Hills. In attendance at the sit-down were thirteen racketeers, including Joe and his mentor, boss Carlo Gambino, along with mobsters from cities as far away as Tampa and New Orleans. The meeting was dubbed "a little Apalachin" by Chief Inspector Sanford D. Garelik. *The New York Times* gave the arrest page 1 coverage, which included an above-the-fold photograph of the arrestees leaving jail, "trying to hide their faces behind coats and handkerchiefs as they ran to five waiting autos" (Fig. 10.1). Joe, like the other mobsters ensnared at Little Apalachin, wanted no publicity at all.[2]

Shortly after the "Little Apalachin" raid, Colombo was approached by FBI special agents outside Cantalupo Realty. To the surprise of the G-men, Colombo didn't dodge their questions but invited them into his office because "he desired to converse." He told them that he had never met the men from outside New York City who were arrested along with him at La Stella restaurant. He expressed concern over Carlo Gambino's ill health. He

Figure 10.1. "Little Apalachin" defendants hide their faces outside Civic Jail, Manhattan, September 1966. *Source:* New York Times/Redux. Used with permission.

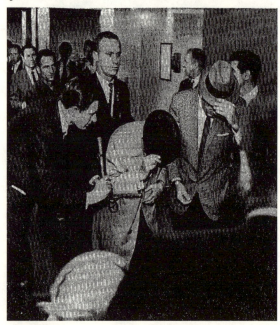

talked about his oldest sons, both of whom were currently dating young women who happened not to be Italian. "COLOMBO further noted that he does not speak Italian noting that he was born in the United States."[3]

Before the year's end, New York crime families were subjected to more unwanted publicity in the press. "Black Nationalist literature accusing the Cosa Nostra of activity in Harlem" was how *The New York Times* characterized the leaflets posted on lampposts and sidewalk billboards in upper Manhattan. "The Cosa Nostra is flooding our communities with narcotics, destroying our families and getting rich at the same time," the leaflets read. "They have chased decent black number bankers from Harlem."[4]

Joe Colombo—aware of the fledgling Black Power movement's growing threats to the mob's control over Black ghettos—decided to act. He organized an Italian American anti-defamation league. It was modeled on the proposal he made five years earlier, when as a captain in the Profaci family

48 | Rebel Girl and the Godfather

he drew up plans for *The Untouchables* TV boycott. The stated purpose of the anti-defamation organization was to protect Italian Americans, including his own wife and kids, from the slander caused by the Mafia stereotype, which criminalized Americans of Italian descent. Its stealth purpose was to reduce law enforcement pressure on organized crime triggered by the media's focus on the Mafia.

In November, *The New York Times* used the headline "New Body Decries Slurs on Italians" to announce the formation of a Brooklyn-based civil rights organization calling itself the American Italian Anti-Defamation League. AIADL's founding made news across the country. Like the *Times*, Chicago's leading Black and white papers, the *Defender* and the *Tribune*, covered AIADL's launch as an Italian American retort to an emerging Black Power threat.[5]

Joe kept his name out of the press. Confidential FBI documents, however, identified him as the mastermind behind AIADL and the individual responsible for bankrolling the group.

```
The informant advised that Colombo was the
originator of the Italian Anti-Defamation
League and the financier of the league.⁶
```

Despite his leading role in organizing AIADL, FBI files indicate the degree to which Joe was determined to maintain his anonymity.

```
Informant stated there are numerous people of
Italian descent who are legitimate and front
for the organization. Informant stated that
COLOMBO and other members of LCN are actively
backing this organization and are going to
great lengths to keep their connection with
the organization unknown to the public.⁷
```

In November, a month after Joe Colombo's AIADL was launched, the Congress of Italian American Organizations (CIAO) was chartered in New York State as a nonprofit organization. Mary Sansone and her husband Zach had spent more than a year making their dream of starting a social-action coalition a reality. He had endless ideas; she had inexhaustible drive. Together, they believed that the Italian poor were being ill-served by power brokers at all levels, from the federal government and city hall to the Catholic Church and the local mob, and that they could do a much better job. The key was to keep the coalition free of politicians and racketeers—no small task in Brooklyn. CIAO, instead, would be populated by progressive-minded citizen activists even if it meant Mary and Zach would have to go into debt to keep the organization afloat.[8]

At the time CIAO was awarded nonprofit status, it consisted of a handful of professional and business associations as well as civic groups that collectively operated out of the Sansones' Boro Park basement. The alliance included the Italian Welfare League, a women's group led by Angela Carlozzi, which assisted new immigrants with naturalization, employment, and housing. Another founding member was the newly formed Carroll Gardens Association, a South Brooklyn neighborhood association run by an energetic thirty-five-year-old undertaker named Salvatore "Buddy" Scotto Jr. (no relation to Anthony Scotto).

In November, the same month that CIAO was chartered, Mary became aware of a legal dispute over adoption that was making headlines across the nation. The case pitted Italian American foster parents, like herself, against the upstate Ulster County welfare agency. It involved second-generation Italians Michael and Mary Liuni, an IBM employee and housewife. The Liunis owned a three-bedroom brick home in the town of Tillson. They lived with their three biological children, ages nine, ten, and fourteen, and a foster child, age four, who had been with the family since birth.

The child the Liunis were fostering, born Elizabeth St. John in a nearby hospital on July 4, 1962, was surrendered by her biological mother to the county's child welfare services at birth for adoption. The mother's decision was driven by the fact that the baby was illegitimate, fathered by someone other than the mother's husband. The Ulster County welfare agency, however, deferred adoption and instead chose foster care for the infant for two reasons. First, neither mother nor putative father bothered to sign welfare agency consent forms allowing for the infant's legal adoption. Second, baby Elizabeth, blond-haired and blue-eyed, was born with birthmark on her left temple. According to county records, authorities felt the blemish so disfiguring that "welfare did not wish to place the child until this matter cleared up."[9]

On her fifth day, in lieu of adoption, the baby was placed into the care of foster parents Michael and Mary Liuni. Before the end of the child's first year, her foster family inquired about legally adopting the baby they called Beth. The welfare agency caseworker explained to the Liunis that their prospects for adoption were dim due to the legal entanglement caused by the natural parents' failure to sign consent forms. By the child's second birthday, however, the agency had located Beth's birth mother. She willingly signed the adoption papers, and failing to find the biological father, the agency settled for the signature of the mother's husband.

Meanwhile the Liunis pressed their case for adopting Beth. Welfare never seriously considered it. The child was into her fourth year when authorities discovered, during a routine medical exam, that the birthmark had "receded naturally." Adoption, the agency determined, could move forward. Beth's foster parents were instructed to turn the girl over to county authorities immediately. Once again, the Liunis requested they be allowed to adopt Beth, who had lived with her foster family without interruption during her four years. Authorities again refused, citing four reasons.

First, foster parents in Ulster County had no legal claim on children in their care. Mary Sansone fostered children in her Brooklyn home under the same condition, which initially made her skeptical that the Liunis' case was legitimate. Mary felt outrage, however, when she learned the other reasons cited by welfare to deny the Liunis' request. The second rationale given by Ulster County authorities was that the Liunis, both age forty-eight, were too old by child welfare standards to care for a preschooler. Mary Sansone, two years older than the Liunis, cared for a full house of foster kids, including preschoolers. The third reason was that Mrs. Liuni's medical records showed that a year earlier she had been hospitalized and given electroshock therapy for what her physician diagnosed as "menopausal depression." Her doctor reported that she no longer showed any signs of emotional distress, but the welfare agency used this information to call into question the mental health of the only mother Beth had ever known. Mary, from personal experience, was familiar with the mental stress that motherhood and menopause might cause. Finally, Ulster Country welfare determined that the Liunis, a swarthy couple of Italian stock, were an ill-fitting match for a fair-skinned girl sans disfiguring birthmark. For Mary, it was this last reason, rooted in ethnic prejudice, that convinced her to support the Liunis.

In June of 1966, Ulster County Family Court, after hearing testimony, ruled in favor of the county's welfare agency. The Liunis were denied custody of the child. Widespread condemnation followed the court's decision, which included censure from the B'nai B'rith Anti-Defamation League (ADL). In mid-November, the ADL—an organization dedicated to fighting prejudice wherever it was found—committed its ample resources, including legal counsel, to file an appeal on behalf of the Liunis with the state supreme court to vacate the family court ruling. The national media took notice. On November 27, *The Washington Post* published an editorial opposing the ruling titled "Ethics and Ethnics." The following day, New York Governor Nelson Rockefeller held a press conference to make his first public pronouncement, calling it "a tragic case" and ordering the state's department of welfare to make "a full investigation" into Ulster County's adoption policies.[10]

The Liuni adoption court case dragged into the new year, by which time Governor Rockefeller was receiving daily reports from the state welfare commission. Mary was relieved to learn that the legal battle had finally been put to rest when the county's welfare commissioner reluctantly dropped his support for the initial ruling and surrendered the child to the Liunis for adoption. In the end, *Ulster County Welfare Commission v. Michael and Mary Liuni* became a landmark case in United States adoption law.[11]

Chapter 11

Exclusively Italian (1967)

The Liuni adoption case presented Joe Colombo's American Italian Anti-Defamation League with a perfect opportunity to demonstrate its commitment to defending Italians from slander. Anti-defamation was, after all, in the organization's name! But as the case wound its way through the courts, AIADL was missing in action. A few years later, Joe would publicly distance himself from the organization's failure to intervene on behalf of the Liunis, but at the time he was obliged to remain behind the scenes and keep quiet. *The New York Times*, however, raised a stink. "It's hard to find where 'anti-defamation' enters the picture," a May editorial criticized. "The organization that helped the Liuni family in their dramatic fight to keep their blonde adopted daughter," the *Times* pointed out, "was the local branch of B'nai B'rith."[1]

At the time, B'nai B'rith was not only working on behalf of the Liunis but fighting against AIADL for using the phrase "anti-defamation league" in its name. The B'nai B'rith Anti-Defamation League, a reputable Jewish organization, had issued a cease-and-desist order to AIADL. When AIADL ignored the order, B'nai B'rith sued, accusing the defendant of "unfair usurpation" with "no other design but unlawfully to pirate and exploit the plaintiff's name."[2]

The same *Times* editorial that criticized AIADL for failing the Liunis also took aim at the organization's recent announcement that Frank Sinatra had been appointed the group's national chairman. FBI files reveal that Joe Colombo had secretly orchestrated the appointment of Sinatra, a close friend. In the following memo, a Bureau handler provides an account of his informant's observations.

> He stated that prior to the letters sent out
> to important people regarding the league,
> Colombo personally contacted Frank Sinatra
> to head the league. Informant believed that
> the get-togethers were in connection with the
> forthcoming American-Italian Anti-Defamation
> League [for which] Colombo was a big time
> fund raiser.[3]

With great fanfare, the AIADL had publicly proclaimed that "La Voz" would "add luster to the group's cause." *Times* editors countered that Sinatra's chairmanship made AIADL more suspect than ever. To New York City media elites, few of whom were Italian, Sinatra was a dubious choice as chairman of an organization appealing to the moral conscience of America. Hadn't Sinatra, the *Times* asked, refused to renounce his "associations with underworld figures"? The editors were referring to, among other recent statements made by Sinatra, his January 1967 testimony before a grand jury investigating Mafia control of Las Vegas casinos.

The *Times* editorial pointed out that beyond Sinatra, "among the names of the board of directors of this new organization . . . are several who by no means will add 'luster' to the Italian-American image." Most of them, according to the editors, "are connected with Brooklyn politics." The phrase "Brooklyn politics" was code for graft in New York City's largest borough. One member of AIADL's board was Amadeo "Meade" H. Esposito, a powerful Brooklyn Democratic district leader whose political machine ran on patronage. "Getting citizens municipal or government jobs hardly comes under the heading of 'anti-defamation,'" rebuked the *Times*. Other AIADL board members, such as convicted racketeer Daniel J. Motto and Tammany Hall kingmaker Carmine DeSapio, would be convicted the following year on charges of kickbacks and bribery on city contracts.[4]

"Italian-Americans have always been a puzzle to outsiders," journalist Nicholas Pileggi has noted. Despite naysayers such as *The New York Times*, keen observers understood why Frank Sinatra might have been the best choice to head an Italian American anti-defamation organization. Gay Talese, in his celebrated 1966 *Esquire* magazine article "Frank Sinatra Has a Cold," assessed Sinatra's standing with the Italian American community. "Sinatra is, in this country, the most powerful American of Italian descent." By appointing

Sinatra as its national chairman, Mario Puzo observed, "the American Italian Anti-Defamation League . . . knows very well what it is about."[5]

Frank Sinatra's willingness to lead AIADL, an organization modeled on B'nai B'rith, was consistent with the singer's reputation for being one of the most politically outspoken entertainers of his generation. He was an early champion of the civil rights movement. In 1945, as servicemen were coming home from World War II, he crisscrossed the country, appearing before teenagers at schools, condemning "racial and religious intolerance" particularly as it related to anti-Semitism. During the 1950s, Sinatra lobbied against racial segregation in Nevada casinos and hotels before it was popular to do so. In January 1961, Sinatra not only organized (along with Peter Lawford) president-elect John F. Kennedy's inaugural gala in Washington, DC, but he also played Carnegie Hall (along with Dean Martin and Sammy Davis Jr.) in a wildly successful pro-integration benefit honoring Martin Luther King Jr., with all proceeds going to King's Southern Christian Leadership Conference.[6]

Six years later, Sinatra took his most public stance against the defamation of Italians when he agreed to chair the AIADL. In this role, he organized a membership drive and hosted a fundraiser at Madison Square Garden. At the time Sinatra joined AIADL as its national chairman, the organization claimed 7,200 members paying $10-a-year dues. Less than six months later, on the eve of the fundraiser, AIADL boasted a membership of 20,000. The event jammed upward of 18,000 Italian Americans into Madison Square Garden to honor Sinatra as their standard-bearer.[7]

Showman Sammy Davis Jr. and ILA Vice President Anthony Scotto shared master of ceremonies duties. Scotto read a telegram saluting AIADL from the president of the United States. "I'm sure that every American applauds your purpose," Lyndon B. Johnson proclaimed, "in focusing national attention on this long and cherished legacy." Scotto was a vocal supporter of LBJ during his 1964 presidential campaign, during which the ILA union boss was photographed sitting next to the president on multiple occasions.[8]

Once Sammy Davis Jr. took the mic, the entertainment portion of the program was in full swing. The lineup included Dean Martin, Connie Francis, Diahann Carroll, and the Four Seasons. Near midnight, more than three hours into the show, Davis introduced "the noblest Roman of them all," and AIADL's chairman appeared on stage wearing a red handkerchief in his tuxedo (Fig. 11.1). Before he sang a note and without ever saying a word, Sinatra drew a four-minute standing ovation. He then performed several of his hits from the *Great American Songbook*, finishing with "I've

Figure 11.1. Sammy Davis Jr. and Frank Sinatra, AIADL fundraiser, Madison Square Garden, Manhattan, October 1967. *Source:* William Sauro/New York Times/Redux. Used with permission.

Got You Under My Skin." Sammy Davis joined Sinatra during his final number. Hundreds of people rushed the stage.

Davis, who only a month earlier had given up his conk for untampered hair, exhorted, "You cats better dig this organization, or you cats gonna be riding in the back of a bus." After his encore, Sinatra bowed, blew a kiss, adjusted his collar, and walked off the stage. According to an AIADL spokesman, the fundraiser drove membership to 27,500 people.[9]

At the 1967 Madison Square Garden fundraiser, the keynote was given by Civil Court Judge Ross J. DiLorenzo, who in 1948 had sponsored Mary Crisalli's Relief for Italy fundraising campaign. DiLorenzo now presided over AIADL. In his speech, he sounded the organization's mantra: "We must uncover and combat the fallacy that organized crime is in control of Americans of Italian ancestry."[10]

Earlier in the year, *The New York Times* ran a headline announcing "City Police Expert on Mafia Retiring from Force." The expert's name was

Sergeant Ralph Salerno, an Italian American who had worked for the NYPD for twenty years as a specialist on racketeering and, according to the *Times*, had "gained a reputation of knowing more about the Mafia than any other non-member." Olive-skinned and broad shouldered, the forty-two-year-old Salerno, who had grown up the Bronx, was a hardened anti-Mafia crusader determined "to fight any criminal association that could rule a community." The article highlighted Salerno's expressed concern over "reports from Washington that the National Crime Commission, under President Johnson, had backed away from a recommendation to permit wiretapping and electronic eavesdropping by police."[11]

When, a few months later, the president's National Crime Commission held hearings in Washington on its findings and recommendations, Salerno participated as a special consultant. It was there, during hearing's public testimony, that Salerno encountered Mary Sansone for the first time. He listened as she spoke passionately and authoritatively about the need inside close-knit Italian communities for leaders who were brave enough to stand up to the Mafia but also smart enough to reject the Mafia myth. In fact, she had traveled to DC on her own dime to take issue with a claim made in the organized crime section of the commission's report, which read: "Today the core of organized crime . . . membership is exclusively Italian."[12]

Exclusively Italian?

She was determined to set the record straight by correcting the crime commission's overreaching statement. According to an account of Mary's testimony in the press, "She took her small self to Washington and gave the members of the Crime Commission a substantial piece of her well-organized mind." Salerno, listening to Mary testify, was thoroughly impressed. She was articulate and gutsy. Mary explained her concern about the defamation of Italian Americans in the commission's report—a complaint, she said, voiced even louder by members of her organization, CIAO. After her testimony, Salerno introduced himself to Mary. He offered to speak to members of her group on the topic of organized crime when they returned to New York. Mary heartily accepted his offer.[13]

Soon after, Salerno attended a CIAO gathering held in Mary's basement, where he faced nothing short of an inquisition. The meeting was called to order at nine o'clock at night, according to an account in a local tabloid, amid a "charged atmosphere." It didn't adjourn until four o'clock in the morning. CIAO officials were described as intelligent and knowledgeable, "but they were angry!" Salerno, according to the reporter, "was hard put to expound" on the defamation of Italian Americans in the crime commission's report, but "the good cop stood his ground . . . answering questions, giving explanations, posing hypotheses." Salerno did his best "to shed light upon the very few whose activities are casting darkness upon the many." It was trial by fire for the former detective, but Mary came out of the overnight confab with nothing but admiration for him.[14]

Chapter 12

Ethnic Harmony Amidst Civil Disorder (1968)

Race riots had become commonplace in US cities across the country by 1968. In an attempt to dampen racial unrest, politicians and government bureaucrats funneled antipoverty resources to communities of color. This approach to race relations was buttressed by LBJ's National Advisory Commission on Civil Disorders, established after three consecutive summers of urban riots. Released in February 1968, the commission's grim findings, known as the Kerner Report, put most of the blame for deteriorating conditions in the ghettos—which caused the riots—where it belonged: on white America. "White society is deeply implicated in the ghetto," the report stated before bluntly summarizing, "White institutions created it, white institutions maintained it, and white society condones it." However, for readers sympathetic to the plight of ethnic whites, one of the report's conclusions was a dubious illustration of the have-a-lots criticizing the have-littles for the problems of the have-nots. In Chapter 9 of the report asserted that an African American "escape from poverty has been blocked in part by the resistance of European ethnic groups; they have been unable to enter some unions and to move into some neighborhoods outside the ghetto because descendants of the European immigrants who control these unions and neighborhoods have not yet abandoned them for middle-class occupations and areas."[1]

New York's John Lindsay—who at the time had a well-earned reputation for being tone deaf to the needs of outer borough ethnic whites—was the loudest voice on the president's commission. Having also earned a riot-proof reputation as mayor, Lindsay was the prime mover behind the Kerner Report. In many respects, the report mirrored the mayor's bracing insight into US race relations. To Lindsay's credit, New York City never suffered a race riot on the scale of Watts, Detroit, or Newark. For instance, in the immediate aftermath of Martin Luther King Jr.'s assassination, when Chicago's Mayor

Daley told the press he had ordered his police "to shoot to kill arsonists and shoot to maim or cripple looters," Lindsay, an advocate for police reform, walked 125th Street and listened to the people living there. He showed he cared by giving Harlemites an opportunity to be heard. This, Lindsay's finest hour as mayor, was the culmination of his administration's systematic effort to hold the city together in deeply troubled times. After entering city hall in 1965, Lindsay had the foresight to deploy a temporary task force designed to ease slum tensions. Just after the Kerner Report appeared, he signed an executive order making the Urban Action Task Force, headed by mayoral assistant Barry H. Gottehrer, a permanent part of the city's budget.[2]

The *New York Times Sunday Magazine* profiled Barry Gottehrer in a piece on the mayor's task force. The article, authored by Nicholas Pileggi, found that Gottehrer and his staff used an innovative, hands-on approach to providing city support to underserved Black and Puerto Rican areas. The task force, he concluded, performed near miracles in keeping New York's ghettos cool while other cities burned.[3]

The reach of Lindsay's task force stretched only as far as Black and Puerto Rican ghetto neighborhoods. It ignored the unraveling of ethnic white enclaves, such Greenpoint in Brooklyn (Poles), Corona in Queens (Italians), and the Grand Concourse in the Bronx (Jews). If the task force wanted to expand its reach beyond Black and brown communities, it would be wise to solicit input from progressive-minded white community activists who lived in the outer boroughs. Lindsay was told about an Italian housewife living in Brooklyn leading the fight for social justice in underserved poor communities. Soon after, Nicholas Pileggi escorted Lindsay to 1451 Fifty-Ninth Street in Boro Park.

At the time of Mayor Lindsay's first visit to the Sansones', Nick Pileggi had known Mary for less than a year. They met through a mutual acquaintance, Ralph Salerno, who had known crime reporter Pileggi since his days on the force. Ralph told Nick about his new friend Mary. Nick's first thought: She sounds like a good source, maybe a great story. Nick asked to be introduced. Ralph told Mary about Nick, who he described as a tough guy from Bensonhurst who knew all about the mob. Mary told Ralph, "I can always use a tough guy. Send Nick over."

On a summer's day in 1968, Nick made his first visit to Mary's. She was expecting him. She heard an engine idling outside her home and pulled back her living room drapes. She was surprised to see a VW bus on the curb sporting yellow curtains in its windows. Her first thought: "How tough can a guy be who drives around with yellow curtains?"

Mary and Nick hit it off immediately.

Nick was no tough guy, but he was taller than Mary expected and in possession of a disarming, impish grin. He was smart and alert, having grown up in Bensonhurst before attending a local college, where—prior to landing a job with the Associated Press as a reporter on the city desk—he aspired to make his Italian family proud by becoming a professor of English. Nick, for his part, was drawn to confident, independent-minded women who were determined to not only survive but also thrive in a world dominated by men.[4]

The two shared a love for their Calabrian fathers, anti-fascist Italians who rejected the pieties of the Catholic Church. It was not long before Mary and Nick began helping one another. Mary, who was friendly with civil rights movement leaders, provided Nick inroads to the world of progressive social-action politics. For his part, having earned a press pass to the underworld, Nick was Mary's guide to how the city was run behind closed doors.

Pileggi was one of the few New Yorkers at the time—Ralph Salerno being another—who could truly claim to know much about the intricacies of organized crime. He began working for the AP in 1956 and, in the decade that followed, had earned the trust of cops and gangsters alike. This gave him exclusive sources, which, coupled with a knack for writing compelling stories, made him among the best crime reporters in the city.

Early on, Mary told Nick about her Uncle Jimmy (who, like his brother Rocco before him, had recently died of a sudden heart attack) including what little she knew about his underworld activities.

Jimmy Crisalli had a reputation for being very sharp, Nick told Mary. He identified Jimmy as a "sleeper" who ran the waterfront with a knack for avoiding violence.

"How high up?" Mary asked.

"Back in the day," Nick said, "Albert Anastasia was *his* driver!"

That summer, Pileggi brought the mayor to Boro Park to meet Mary Sansone. When Lindsay, who stood six feet, five inches, arrived at the Sansones', he was surprised to see a woman standing in the doorway—a full foot and a half shorter than he—wearing a housecoat. Mary invited him in and led him down the back stairs into the finished basement. The mayor, sitting

Ethnic Harmony Amidst Civil Disorder (1968) | 61

across from Mary, expressed his frustration with white youth and with the city's struggle to keep them from fighting with Black youth.

"With all due respect," Mary responded, "you're doing everything wrong. You're organizing Black youth with programs aimed at them but you're neglecting the needs of poor white kids."

"How would you handle the problem?" asked the mayor.

Mary had been sitting on an answer to that question for years. "Let CIAO open a storefront in an Italian neighborhood for whites but which also actively welcomes Blacks and Puerto Ricans," she said, invoking the spirit of the Industrial Workers of the World, the revolutionary union that encouraged racial minorities to join by appealing to working-class solidarity. "We'll run after school tutoring and offer the dropouts counseling in everything from drug treatment to job placement."

Mary persuaded Lindsay to commit $25,000 in "seed money" to CIAO for what the *New York Daily News* characterized as "an experiment to create greater understanding and harmony among troubled South Brooklyn's ethnic groups." Funding would come from the Youth Services Agency, which was originally designed by the Lindsay administration to thwart gang activity by providing educational opportunities to the city's Black and Puerto Rican youth. The "new venture," according to the *Daily News*, "will be sponsored by the Congress of Italian-American Organizations, known as CIAO, and is believed to be the first time an Italian-American group has received government funding for a community project in the United States."[5]

At long last, Mary had achieved a breakthrough. As reported in the *Daily News*, CIAO "aims to draw South Brooklyn's large Italian-American population, traditionally family-oriented, out into community activities to help them work with Black and Puerto Rican groups in the changing neighborhoods." For Mary—having spent years in dialogue with civil rights crusader Bayard Rustin—interracial cooperation was a key component in any attempt to keep urban youth in school, off drugs, and out of trouble. Mary had made her home—CIAO's headquarters—one of the few places where the city's white, Black, and Puerto Rican movements came together.

The first CIAO youth center opened in November (Fig. 12.1). The *Daily News* announced: "The storefront facility, at 260 4th Ave., near Carroll St., will serve the youth of all ethnic groups, according to Mrs. Zachary Sansone, president of CIAO." The center was located in a predominantly Italian community and served the neighborhoods of Park Slope, Carroll Gardens, and Red Hook. Operationally, it functioned as a service delivery program for after-school recreation. The program, coordinated with the board

Figure 12.1. CIAO center opening, South Brooklyn, 1968; Black, Puerto Rican, and Italian youth join (right to left) Mary Sansone, CIAO president; Theresa Melchionne, NYC deputy police commissioner; Lucas Longo, of the NYC Youth Services Agency. *Source:* The Tablet. Used with permission.

of education, prepared dropouts for high school equivalency diplomas and facilitated job placement.

On May 1, 1968, the first annual conference of the National Federation of Italian American Organizations wrapped up three days of meetings at the historic Beaux Arts–style Willard Hotel, located a couple blocks from the White House. On that day, the national organization, with one hundred Italian leaders in attendance, was founded. Plans for NFIAO, which would operate as a national "clearing house" for Italian American organizations fighting discrimination, had been in the works for a year. In October 1967, CIAO sponsored a symposium at New York City's Waldorf-Astoria Hotel to lay the groundwork for launching the National Federation. Mary's organization invited eighty civic leaders representing fifty groups in the metropolitan area to take part in the day's discussions. The Jewish service

Ethnic Harmony Amidst Civil Disorder (1968) | 63

group B'nai B'rith, "desirous to see the federation come into being," was one of its earliest organizations to sign on. Conspicuously missing from the symposium were representatives of the American Italian Anti-Defamation League. When a *New York Times* reporter questioned Mary about AIADL's absence, she replied that "the league had been invited but failed to respond."[6]

The next year, at the inaugural May 1968 NFIAO conference in Washington, the conferees were charged with the task of approving the organization's mission statement and electing the new group's president. While the mission statement ("True Americans first, last and always is the primary concerns among Federation founding fathers") was passed by unanimous voice vote, electing the organization's first president proved arduous. When, after much haggling, a candidate could not be agreed upon, those in attendance turned to Mary Sansone. She was offered the post with the caveat that her appointment would carry the provisional title of "interim" president. That wasn't the first—or last—time Mary confronted male chauvinism while organizing on behalf of Italian Americans. Her instinct was to turn the interim post down—to tell the men to go to hell. But a major political development had taken place that weekend that convinced Mary to put aside the slight and accept NFIAO's provisional presidency.[7]

Vice President Hubert Humphrey had declared himself a candidate for president of the United States, and NFIAO attendees were abuzz because

Figure 12.2. First annual conference of the NFIAO, Willard Hotel, Washington, DC, May 1968; left to right, Congressman Frank Annunzio, Victor J. Failla, Vice President Hubert H. Humphrey, Interim President Mary Sansone, Interim Director Michael A. Rivisto, Congressman Peter Rodino, Mario O. Rubinelli, and Congressman Joseph Minish. *Source:* Fra Noi. Used with permission.

64 | Rebel Girl and the Godfather

Humphrey had chosen to kick off his national campaign at their meeting. NFIAO would be the first stop for candidate Humphrey on his cross-country tour of rank-and-file Democratic Party ethnic groups. When it was time for a photo op, Interim President Sansone, appearing in a brunette bouffant and wearing a smile, posed in front of six founding NFIAO members—all men—which included three members of Congress, plus the candidate, who stood directly behind Mary, his hands resting on her shoulders (Fig. 12.2).[8]

Mary knew the value of the political networks. Humphrey—a longtime supporter of labor organizers and civil rights workers—was the kind of presidential candidate she could enthusiastically endorse. A few weeks later when New York Citizens for Humphrey ran a full-page ad in *The New York Times*, among the diverse group of supporters listed were New York politicians Victor Anfuso and Abraham Beame; Hollywood actress Tallulah Bankhead; jazz singer Sarah Vaughan; celebrated authors Ralph Ellison, James T. Farrell, and John Steinbeck; and NIAO President Mary Sansone.[9]

In mid-June, a missive on White House letterhead arrived at 1451 Fifty-Ninth Street addressed to "Mrs. Mary C. Sansone, President, Congress of Italian American Organizations, Inc." It read,

Dear Mrs. Sansone,

It was a pleasure to see you a few weeks ago. As I promised, I am sending bracelets for you and your daughter, Carmella [sic], under separate cover.
    Hope to see you again soon.
    Best wishes.

Sincerely,

Hubert H. Humphrey

No member of the Colombo-backed AIADL was listed among Humphrey's supporters. AIADL had, near the start of the year, lost its long-running legal battle with B'nai B'rith and was forced to drop "anti-defamation league" from its name, thus becoming Americans of Italian Descent, or AID. When asked to assess the political efficacy of the Sinatra-led organization now called AID, seasoned Brooklyn community activist Mary Sansone was quoted in *The New York Times* saying, "It's going to take them a while to clean up the mess of the group's first two years of existence."[10]

AIADL's national chairman, Frank Sinatra, was a friend of Vice President Humphrey and was eager to contribute to his campaign. For Sinatra, stumping for Humphrey had the added benefit of helping thwart Bobby Kennedy's bid to win the Democratic Party nomination. "His distaste for Bobby Kennedy," reported the *Chicago Tribune* at the time, "goes back to the early J.F.K. White House years." Sinatra told *Los Angeles Times* gossip columnist Joyce Haber, "I'm not angry at Bobby." The denial was in reference to a question about whether he was still sore at RFK who as US attorney general in 1961 advised President Kennedy to distance himself from Sinatra due to information he had received from J. Edgar Hoover regarding the singer's underworld connections.[11]

A week before the 1968 Democratic National Convention, *The Wall Street Journal* published a front-page story exposing, for the first time in public, FBI intelligence used by Bobby Kennedy in the early 1960s to convince his brother to cut ties with Sinatra. The article, dated August 19, reported that Sinatra was scheduled to emcee "a musical tribute to Mrs. Humphrey staged by the United Democrats for Humphrey" on the opening night of the DNC. The *Journal* exposé begged the question: Is Sinatra angling to reprise with Humphrey the role he played for JFK eight years earlier? On the eve of the benefit, Sinatra canceled his appearance due "pressing recording commitments in California." The apology only fueled speculation about the entertainer's alleged friendship with "Mafia elite," which, true or not, could compromise the Humphrey campaign.[12]

After Sinatra, the most high-profile Italian American supporting the vice president's candidacy was San Francisco Mayor Joseph Alioto. Like Sinatra, Alioto was both a liberal Democrat and, as described in the press, "an active advocate of Humphrey's nomination from the start." Alioto had recently become the first mayor of San Francisco to hail from North Beach, an Italian American neighborhood. A rising star in the Democratic Party, Alioto was also the first mayor to endorse the vice president's presidential bid, and he was rewarded with the national chairmanship of Mayors-for-Humphrey.[13]

While candidate Humphrey was shedding his ties to Sinatra, he was strengthening them with Alioto. A few weeks before the DNC, *Chicago Sun-Times* syndicated columnist Carl Rowan, who had reported widely on the civil rights movement before joining the Kennedy administration, described the San Francisco mayor, son of a Sicilian-born fisherman, as "suddenly . . . the brightest light among West Coast Democrats." When Democrats met for their national convention in Chicago, Humphrey and Alioto had "developed an increasingly close relationship." Unnamed Humphrey insiders, characterized by Rowen as "absolutely authoritative," told the columnist that Alioto "is now the number one contender for the vice presidential nomination if Hubert Humphrey wins the presidential nomination."[14]

Humphrey knew who his challengers in the general election would be: Alabama Governor George Wallace and former Vice President Richard Nixon. Both Wallace and Nixon were courting the backlash vote by running as "law and order" candidates. Humphrey's handlers believed that the best way for the campaign to neutralize their opponents' appeal to white voters was to choose a running mate, as characterized by *The New York Times*, "who is both Roman Catholic and a member of an ethnic minority." Those qualifications whittled the field of candidates down to two. "Senator Muskie, who is of Polish extraction, and Mayor Alioto, an Italian-American, meet these tests and would presumably cut Democratic losses in the so-called 'backlash' areas where racial fears are strongest."[15]

On the next to last night of the raucous Democratic National Convention, the mayor of San Francisco, described in the press as a "debonair, alert-eyed, man of 52," delivered the nominating speech for candidate Humphrey.[16]

On the convention's last night, Humphrey chose his running mate: Edmund Sixtus Muskie. Why didn't Humphrey tap Alioto? The reason was not made public for almost a year. In a September 1969 *Washington Post* column, Jack Anderson revealed that immediately after the convention, one of Humphrey's campaign managers told him that "Alioto has acted as attorney for Mafia leaders." Anderson's source added that "while every man has the right a lawyer, politics being what it is, Alioto had to be crossed off." Anderson made the disclosure only after learning from the press in Sacramento that *Look* magazine was about to release a sensational exposé identifying Alioto as "enmeshed in a web of alliances with at least six leaders of La Cosa Nostra."[17]

A leak inside California Governor Ronald Reagan's office had revealed the *Look* piece. What might motivate the governor's men to divulge this information? A year earlier, prior to the convention, Alioto told the national media that despite being seriously considered as a vice presidential candidate, he was "not excluding the option" of running for California governor in 1970. Republicans judged Alioto a formidable obstacle to Reagan's reelection. The governor's handlers, determined to tarnish Alioto's rising star, did so by exploiting a political weakness: prejudice against Italians in the Golden State. When, on September 4, 1969, the governor's office received an advanced copy of a *Look* magazine article, it immediately leaked it to the Sacramento press.[18]

"Mayor Joseph L. Alioto of San Francisco, the rising politician who came close to the Democratic nomination for the Vice Presidency in 1968," the *Look* exposé began, "is now preparing to challenge Republican Ronald Reagan for the governorship next year. But the public Joseph Alioto," *Look* ominously reported, "bears little resemblance to the private Joseph Alioto, whose name appears on dozens of pages of law-enforcement intelligence reports in California and Washington." The following day, Alioto issued a strongly worded public denial. The *San Francisco Chronicle* immediately investigated the allegations of skullduggery and concluded that *Look* "did not have sufficient facts to justify" the nefarious "stories" about Alioto's business associations. But the *Look* piece crippled the mayor's ambition for higher office.[19]

Alioto sued *Look* for $12.5 million in libel damages. It was the beginning of what *Time* magazine later described as "a long odyssey through litigation and apparent scandal." During the May 1970 trial, two FBI agents were identified as the sources for the *Look* article. One was Special Agent Charles Bates, who was previously in charge of the San Francisco FBI office but had been suddenly transferred to the Bureau's Chicago office. Another, Herbert K. Mudd, a crime force agent and a twenty-six-year Bureau veteran, had recently retired with a full pension. During the court proceedings, Mudd testified that his FBI "superior had called him into his office and asked him to talk to the *Look* writers."[20]

The revelation that the US Justice Department was selectively disclosing sensitive intelligence information to the press brought Assistant Attorney General William Rehnquist before the Senate Judiciary Subcommittee on Constitutional Rights. Forty-five-year-old Rehnquist, who was six months removed from taking a seat as on the US Supreme Court, characterized abuses in the Alioto case as an isolated instance of "excessive zeal" on the part of rogue FBI agents. The government's overzealousness in the case of Alioto stretched from Sacramento to Washington, from Reagan's State House to Nixon's White House. Although Alioto ultimately won his suit against *Look* when the Supreme Court upheld the award in 1981, he never recovered politically, withdrawing from the governor's race in 1970 and again in 1974.[21]

When Congress passed the 1968 Omnibus Control and Safe Street Act, it included a provision (Title III) permitting the FBI to request warrants for legal wiretapping in criminal investigations. Included in the guidelines was a controversial emergency provision giving designated officials permission to wiretap without obtaining a warrant from a judge in organized crime cases. President Johnson's liberal attorney general, Ramsey Clark, refused to allow the Department of Justice to deploy unwarranted wiretaps. Richard Nixon's election to the White House in the fall, however, brought with it a new sheriff: strongman John Mitchell. As attorney general, Michell authorized wiretapping within weeks after the president's inauguration. In conjunction with stepped-up electronic eavesdropping, Mitchell bolstered the Department of Justice's new Organized Crime Strike Forces, which deployed DOJ prosecutors to conduct long-term racketeering investigations in targeted cities.[22]

It was in this less fettered law enforcement environment, according to *Washington Post* columnist Jack Anderson, that Hoover, for the first time, consented to partnering the Bureau with Justice task forces. "Inside the Justice Department's Organized Crime Section, top officials are talking excitedly of breaking the back of the Mafia," Anderson revealed. "The weapons will horrify civil libertarians: widespread use of bugs and wiretaps, singling out top hoods for prosecution and harassment, release of raw, unverified information on crime lords. But Attorney General John Mitchell has subtly let his crime fighters know that he won't object if they need to use a little fire to fight fire."[23]

No one, including Mary Sansone, needed Ralph Salerno to tell them that organized crime's raison d'être is to exploit the public's demand for goods and services prohibited by law. Prior to the 1969 riot at the Stonewall Inn, the truism applied as much to "homosexuals" who socialized in unlicensed bars as it did to gamblers who patronized local numbers runners. Syndicate control of gay night life helps explain the ambivalence with which some gay men at the time perceived organized crime.

The uneasy relationship between the gay community and the syndicate was illustrated just months before the Stonewall rebellion when Steve Ostrow, an opera singer and proprietor of the recently opened Continental Baths, located in the basement of the Ansonia Hotel on Manhattan's Upper West Side, was visited by a pair of gangsters. Ostrow's business was booming. When the uninvited wiseguys appeared at the Baths, they tried to shake down its proprietor. Ostrow hesitated. They dialed back the pressure but promised to return in a week.[24]

That very next day, Saturday, Ostrow told Joe, his barber and also close confidant, about the shakedown. As the barber leaned in with a blade to trim Ostrow's mustache, he whispered, "Look, you come back here Monday morning, 10AM sharp. I got a regular customer comes in for a shave who might be able to help you out."

On Monday morning, before Ostrow arrived, Joe told the young man sitting in his chair about Ostrow's problems. When Ostrow arrived, Joe had just finished the man's shave. Joe introduced the man to Ostrow as a lawyer. The man held out his hand and said, "My name is Barry Slotnick. I'm a criminal defense attorney. Joe tells me you own the Continental Baths on 76th Street. I hear it's quite a spot. I also hear you're in trouble. Maybe I can help."

"How?" asked Ostrow.

"I'll explain."

The two men left the barbershop and shared a taxi uptown. On the ride, Slotnick told Ostrow that he lived only a couple blocks from the Baths with his new wife, who was pregnant with their first child. The more Slotnick talked, the more Ostrow sensed that Slotnick wasn't gay. He was just a stargazer who loved rubbing elbows with performers. The Baths was gaining buzz in the city's underground night club scene for booking not only up-and-comers like Bette Midler and Barry Manilow but veterans like Linda Hopkins and Sarah Vaughan. The Baths was far afield from Slotnick's haunt, the Copacabana, where one of his most favored clients arranged for Slotnick to hobnob with Vegas acts like Frank Sinatra and Sammy Davis Jr. while sitting front and center.[25]

"If you agree to my conditions, then I'm your lawyer now," Slotnick said.

Ostrow didn't object, but the expression on his face conveyed his uncertainty.

"If and when those guys come back, just show them my card, and I don't think you'll have any more problems," Slotnick assured him. "Trust me. I represent a lot of important people." Slotnick was a persuasive man, a trait that served him well in front of juries, and Ostrow finally agreed to take him up on the offer.

A week later, the wiseguys returned to the Continental Baths intending to shake down the owner. Without saying a word, Ostrow handed them Slotnick's business card. They stared at it. They looked at each other. One of the two men glanced at Ostrow, who finally spoke. "You should talk to my lawyer." The other man signaled toward the door, and the two promptly exited the Baths.

The next day, Saturday, Ostrow was back in barber Joe's chair. He could hardly contain himself. "Who the fuck is this guy Barry?"

The barber smiled in the mirror and said, "Oh, he's Joe Colombo's lawyer, that's all."

On Saturday night, Linda Hopkins was booked at the Baths. Slotnick was in attendance. After the performance, Slotnick took Ostrow aside and asked him if everything was all right.

"You know very well how it went, Barry," Ostrow said.

He replied, "Oh well, they just know who's boss, I guess."

Slotnick knew the timing was right to pitch Joe's proposition: If Ostrow allowed the "boss" to take over "the garbage removal, the cigarette machines, the jukebox, and any other vending machines in the place," Joe would pay the proprietor 5 percent more than whatever deal he had now, "plus . . . better service and new machines . . . and . . . you'll also have a friend as a bonus." This time Ostrow didn't hesitate.

"You won't be sorry," Slotnick assured him.

Looking back years later, Ostrow reflected, "And you know what? I never was."

In the late 1960s, most gay men were less sanguine than Ostrow about syndicate protection. Mob-run gay bars, operating under the "protection" of corrupt police, were known to traffic in boys and to blackmail the rich and famous. Distrust toward organized crime within the gay community would be militantly expressed during the June 1969 Stonewall uprising. Agitating for the decriminalization of homosexuality, for gay pride, and for community self-determination, ballsy agitators chalked a notice on the Inn's boarded-up windows, proclaiming, "GAY PROHIBITION CORRUPT$ COPS FEED$ MAFIA."[26]

Chapter 13

"The Mark of an Emergent Self-Consciousness" (1969)

NYPD Chief Detective Albert A. Seedman put word out on the street that he wanted to interview Joe Colombo at Brooklyn headquarters. This was Seedman's first encounter with Joe. Aware that mob bosses never met with law enforcement without legal counsel by their side, Seedman was shocked when Joe showed up at police headquarters unaccompanied by his attorney Barry Slotnick. "Till that day I had never seen a man in Colombo's position enter a station house without lawyers," he remembered, but that day "Joseph Colombo walked into my office alone." Seedman was himself something of an anomaly. He had personally experienced his share of ethnic bias during his remarkable rise up the ranks before becoming chief detective. One of the few high-ranking Jews on a police force dominated by the Irish, Seedman wore his curly gray hair slicked back while donning tailored suits, an onyx pinky ring on his right hand and a diamond-spray on his left. One veteran cop characterized the cigar-chomping chief detective as "what a Jewish gangster is supposed to look like."[1]

After Joe sat down, Seedman explained that he wanted to question him about a recent gangland murder. "Colombo shook his head and looked troubled." He then expressed distress. "Chief, I give you my complete cooperation in this. It was a terrible thing. But I do not understand why you're coming to me about it. So help me, I don't have any connection with this." After making his denial, Joe pleaded his case more broadly.

"If I was a Jewish businessman, you'd never dream of calling me down here on a murder I had no connection with. But because my name is Italian, that's different. I'm a goombah mobster, not good people like you. But I don't expect you to think differently, no matter what I say or do . . . I know that when you're done, I can walk out of here. At least, today I can.

But I also know this: as sure as I sit here, I fully expect to be harassed by the law for the rest of my life. Not by you, necessarily—the detectives who work for you are on the whole good guys—but the Federal men are lousy. They are bigots. I expect they will be after me before long." Finally, Joe appeared to resign himself to fate, surrendering to what poor Italian immigrants called *destino*. "I'd never say this to my family, but I swear to God the FBI is going to frame me somehow. Maybe it will be income-tax evasion, maybe one of those conspiracy deals. Whatever it takes, they will throw me into prison. I expect to die there." The interview ended, Joe exited and Seedman was left wondering: Who *is* Joseph Anthony Colombo Sr.?[2]

That same year, in one of the earliest published accounts of Joe Colombo's rise in the ranks of the underworld, a *Life* magazine profile reminded its readers that Mafia bosses "got where they are—and have managed to stay there—by killing people." However, in the case of Colombo, the reporter conceded that he "doesn't stack up as much of a headbreaker" and instead described the forty-three-year-old don as "more of an angler than a triggerman." According to law enforcement officials, Joe's rackets operated almost exclusively inside Brooklyn and Long Island and were limited to "numbers and sports gambling, hijacking, fencing in stolen goods and loan-sharking." His moneylending operation totaled in excess of $3 million annually. Colombo family members numbered approximately two hundred, a relatively small outfit when compared to the operation of his mentor Carlo Gambino, which was believed to be four times that size.[3]

Evidence indicates that Joe Colombo, like Frank Costello before him, prohibited underlings from engaging in the drug trade. Joe knew that narcotics, while highly profitable, were also very risky. On the inside, dealers might turn into users and undermine the operation. On the outside, the feds were pouring huge sums of money into busting the drug trade. Who wanted all those narcs running around your neighborhood? Beyond business considerations, there was also some evidence that Joe Colombo was personally opposed to dope. According to an FBI memorandum, in the late 1960s, Colombo expressed to a federal agent his "surprised at all the 'heat' being brought on his family stating 'they' should be greatful [sic] at the way his 'family' behaves, noting that he would not tolerate narcotics, prostitution or disrespect in general."[4]

Law enforcement officials identified Joe as a new breed of crime boss. Affable and low-key, Joe dressed "expensively but conservatively." His personal style rubbed off on his business associates. "The Colombo group has a style and character all its own," an assistant district attorney in Brooklyn told

New York Times organized crime specialist Nicholas Gage. A federal agent profiled the Colombo family as follows: "Most of its members are American-born, free-wheeling men not so bound to tradition and eager to find new ways to exploit the system." And like their boss, "the family's capos are well-spoken, polished and innovative." For Joe, innovation meant investing in legal enterprises. A federal agent estimated that Joe had "interests through fronts in about 20 businesses in New York." Encouraging his men to get involved in legitimate operations had become "almost a fetish with him."[5]

By decade's end, Joe Colombo and his associates were keenly aware of stepped up federal law enforcement efforts to pursue organized crime, which had spread like a seismic wave from out West. In August 1969, a month before *Look* magazine published classified information on San Francisco Mayor Alioto leaked by FBI Agents Bates and Mudd, another G-man—this one operating out of Arizona—was enmeshed in a tangled web of intrigue. The bizarre tale was brought to light in a sleepy Tucson courtroom. It centered on Joseph Bonanno. The crime lord had fled New York in the mid-1960s after his plan to become the "boss of all bosses" by assassinating Gambino backfired when Joe Colombo, assigned to carry out the murder, tipped off the commission to Bonanno's planned coup. In exchange for surrendering control of his family business, Gambino spared Bonanno's life. Bonanno retired to Tucson, where he had maintained a homestead since the early 1940s.[6]

Tucson in the late 1960s was home to 300,000 people, which included about a dozen underworld gangsters whose reputations were made elsewhere. The city's organized crime expert was FBI Special Agent David Olin Hale, a ten-year veteran of the Bureau. Sometime during the summer of 1968, Hale arranged a meeting at Iron Mask restaurant with three locals: racecar driver William John Dunbar; electrical engineer Paul Mills Stevens, who was employed by Hughes aircraft; and real estate developer Walter Prideaux.[7]

Over dinner, Hale—who was described as tall and thin with blond hair and who dressed, according to a friend, "like a blue-suited Baptist minister"—divulged that he was in charge of an FBI program to drive the mobsters out of Tucson. He wanted to enlist the three men in the government's effort to end the scourge. Hale leaned in and told the would-be recruits that his plan involved bombings—even murder. The aim was to instigate warfare between gang factions. The three civilians were intrigued by the opportunity to carrying out Old West–style vigilante justice under the cover of FBI covert operations. They signed on.[8]

The special agent sweetened the pot for Dunbar by promising, in exchange for his services, to wipe a 1963 felony conviction off his record. Dunbar, a weapons enthusiast, mail-ordered a custom-made crossbow from Los Angeles for $275. Hale suggested he put poison on the shaft to make sure the job was done right. An AR-15 semi-automatic rifle was also purchased, and practice sessions were arranged in the mountains surrounding the high desert valley. Stevens, a twenty-three-year-old ex-Marine trained in demolitions, assembled the bombs from dynamite procured from a mine he partly owned. Prideaux, in addition to storing the explosives in his office safe and putting up the money to purchase Dunbar's crossbow and a rifle, agreed to drive the getaway car.[9]

Hale told his recruits that if they got caught, the FBI would protect them, but it's unlikely that his assurances carried any weight with the Bureau. For years, the FBI had executed clandestine operations labeled "black bag jobs," which a 1966 FBI memorandum acknowledged as "clearly illegal. . . . Despite this . . . an invaluable technique in combating subversive activities." However, as the second-in-command in the Chicago FBI office told a special agent assigned to a black bag squad, "Hoover would fire and disown us if we ever got caught in the act."[10]

On July 21, 1968, explosives ripped through the Tucson garage of former Detroit crime boss Peter J. "Horseface" Licavoli Sr. A day later, two bombs were detonated at the base of the patio wall outside the house of deposed Mafia kingpin Joseph Bonanno Sr. His son, thirty-seven-year-old Salvatore Vincent "Bill" Bonanno, fired his shotgun at a fleeing man, hitting him the leg before he jumped into a car, which sped away. According to journalist Gay Talese, who at the time of the bombing was embedded with the Bonanno clan while gathering material for the book that would become *Honor Thy Father*, no one inside the home knew what to make of the attack. "And while no one in the Bonanno house had any idea who was behind the destruction," Talese observed that "the police seemed certain that the 'Banana War' had extended to Tucson."[11]

The local press ran with the story dispatched by local law enforcement. The *Tucson Daily Citizen* had recently published editorials urging Bonanno and his kind to get out of town. The bombings appeared to confirm its presumption. "Has gangland warfare come to Tucson?" an editorial in the *Citizen* asked. It was campaign season and even Barry Goldwater, former Republican Party presidential nominee and current US senator from Arizona, got into the act. Talese reported, "In a speech delivered to members of the Pima County Republican Club, Goldwater criticized the Lyndon Johnson

Administration in general, and Attorney General Ramsey Clark in particular, for failing to deal adequately with organized crime in America." Goldwater finished with an exhortation: "The reign of the Princes of the Cosa Nostra must end."[12]

The following day, Hale visited Stevens in the hospital, where he was recovering from a gunshot wound. The FBI special agent was getting cold feet about using the rifle and crossbow for the planned assassinations. But Hale nevertheless wanted the bombings to proceed as planned. He asked Stevens if he could assemble the bombs now—under his hospital bedsheets! Stevens complied.[13]

Between July 1968 and July 1969, a total of fifteen bombs targeting syndicate leaders and people connected to them were detonated in Tucson. The bombs appeared to target property rather than people. During the same period, Stevens and Dunbar were aware that Hale had been traveling back and forth between Washington and Tucson.[14]

On July 21, 1969, exactly one year after Bonanno's home was bombed, the Tucson police finally made an arrest in the case. The suspect was Paul Stevens.[15]

During the first week of August, Wes Mauldin, a captain with the Arizona Department of Safety, received a tip that Stevens, along with an accomplice named William Dunbar, bombed Bonanno's house. Even more shocking: The two men were working for FBI Agent David Hale. A day or two later, State Police Captain Mauldin received the same information—that Stevens and Dunbar bombed the Bonanno home on Hale's orders—from a different source. On August 7, the FBI announced the suspension of Special Agent Hale. On August 12, Stevens and Dunbar appeared in court for a preliminary hearing, where Stevens's girlfriend testified that "an FBI agent named Dave" masterminded the bombings in order to start a gangland war. This was the first time an FBI connection in the case was made public.[16]

The Nixon administration, which had pledged to make the war on organized crime a top priority, was now in the awkward position of possibly having its Department of Justice file charges against an FBI agent for depriving a crime boss of his civil rights. On the same day that the FBI agent's name was spoken in a Tucson courtroom, David Hale resigned from the Bureau. Through his attorney, Hale released a statement explaining that US Attorney General John Mitchell had ordered him to remain silent about anything he had learned in his official capacity as an FBI agent.[17]

On August 18, Paul Dean, the editor of the *Arizona Republic*, the state's largest newspaper, published an open letter to FBI Director J. Edgar Hoover asking for answers. The letter began with a friendly reminder that he and Hoover shared correspondence "reaching back years to when you [Hoover] commended an article I wrote on the work of the FBI in Arizona." Next, Dean got down to business. "That was June 1965. This is August 1969. And today, a segment of the efforts of the FBI in Arizona no longer merits my approval." The rebuke, Dean said, was based on "allegations made in Tucson last week that your bureau, or at least one of its agents, attempted a CIA-type fait accompli," adding, "you have personally confirmed an FBI man was 'allegedly involved' in the bombing of Bonanno's home." Then, the admonishment: "My God. This is like finding out that Eliot Ness was on Al Capone's payroll," a reference that any reader familiar with *The Untouchables* would catch. Dean closed by stating, "This Tucson business is ridiculous. Suddenly, the FBI is tangoing with the truth to save face." Hoover's reply to Dean's appeal was nothing more than "formalized evasiveness." When Dean responded with a second, private missive to the director requesting a substantive reply, he received nothing at all.[18]

One evening, Gay Talese offered Joe Bonanno's son Bill something to read. It was a novel Talese received in the mail from a friend, who also happened to be the book's author. In Talese's account, Bill "stayed up half the night reading the book that he held in his hands, a new novel about the Mafia called *The Godfather*." Talese was eager to know what Bill thought of the book. "He was half-finished, and so far he liked it very much, and he thought the author, Mario Puzo, had insights into the secret society." Talese pressed him. "Bill found the central figure in the novel, Don Vito Corleone, a believable character. . . . The Sicilians described in *The Godfather*—not only Don Vito Corleone and his college-educated son Michael (with whom Bill identified) but other characters as well—were endowed with impressive amounts of courage and honor, traits that Bill was convinced were fast deteriorating in the brotherhood." Reading the book, reported Talese, the Bonanno scion "became nostalgic for a period that he had never personally known."[19]

Mary Sansone, after opening her organization's first South Brooklyn storefront the year prior, set out to lobby Mayor Lindsay to expand CIAO services targeting the city's Italian poor. But by 1969, her plans were stalled—a casualty of election year politics. Lindsay was fighting for his political life. The mayor was unpopular with voters in the polls and facing an uphill reelection campaign. His handlers knew that only by forging a top-bottom coalition of high-income liberals and low-income minorities could he find a path to victory. As a result, city hall's token commitment to a working-class white ethnic antipoverty organization, namely CIAO, was shed like excess baggage. When approached by a reporter wondering why Mary Sansone wasn't campaigning for the incumbent, she replied rhetorically, "If you were Italian who would you work for?"[20]

Mary was working for mayoral candidate Mario Angelo Procaccino, who was born into a working-class family that emigrated from Italy to the Bronx when he was nine years old. Procaccino was elected city comptroller the same year Lindsay entered city hall. By the summer of 1969 and with the help of neighborhood activists like Mary Sansone, who had taken charge of Brooklyn's Citizens for Procaccino campaign committee, he was the front-runner, having opened up a comfortable lead in the polls over Lindsay and other rivals.

Earlier that year, in the spring, thirty-three-year-old Brooklyn-born journalist Pete Hamill identified what came to be understood as the most pressing political problem facing the next mayor. "But for the moment," Hamill pleaded, "it is imperative for New York politicians to begin to deal with the growing alienation and paranoia of the working-class white man." Hamill was sounding an alarm over the simmering discontent of the white lower middle class. "I really don't think they can wait much longer, because the present situation is working its way to the point of no return. The working-class white man feels trapped and, even worse, in a society that purports to be democratic, ignored. The tax burden is crushing him, and the quality of his life does not seem to justify his exertions. He cannot leave New York City because he can't afford it, and he is beginning to look for someone to blame. That someone is almost certainly going to be the black man." Keen observers of the outer boroughs, like Hamill, recognized that the white backlash—stoked by George Wallace and Richard Nixon during the 1968 presidential race—portended an approaching racial apocalypse in America. Just months after Richard Nixon's January 1969 inauguration, the president circulated Hamill's article among his inner circle.[21]

New York City mayoral candidates on the November ballot included the incumbent mayor and the city comptroller along with State Senator John J. Marchi and the writer Norman Mailer. The Brooklyn-born novelist, whose running mate (seeking the office of city council president) was the Queens-born journalist Jimmy Breslin, campaigned on the slogans "no more bullshit" and "throw the rascals in." Lindsay lost his party's primary to Marchi, a soft-spoken conservative Republican whose "law and order" campaign was notable for the vigor with which its candidate, an Italian American, attacked the Mafia as a scourge on the city. The prohibitive favorite to win the race was tough-talking Procaccino. Having coined the term "limousine liberal" to besmirch Lindsay and his wealthy Manhattan backers as elitists, he was popular in outer borough neighborhoods, particularly among the city's largest ethnic voting bloc—Italians.

"Ethnic in the extreme," was how journalist Nicholas Pileggi profiled Procaccino. And his followers: "The candidate of the shirt-sleeve, stoop-sitting voters of the city." On the campaign trail, Procaccino had a glaring weakness. Prone to speaking from the heart, he had a propensity to shout or weep in public. Mary sometimes winced at the antics of her candidate, who was more *un pagliaccio* than Fiorello La Guardia on the stump. On the campaign trail, for instance, when a reporter asked Procaccino the obligatory question about the existence of the Mafia, the candidate's choleric disposition came off as panic. "I don't know any Mafias," Procaccino declared in a *New York Times Sunday Magazine* feature. "I never have and never will. Don't talk about the Mafia to me because I think it's insulting. . . . There's always a connection of trying to put some Italian name with a Mafia. There's a Jewish Mafia, an Irish Mafia, a black Mafia." In Procaccino's campaign playbook, combating the Mafia myth meant refusing to condemn crime organized by Italians. It was a damaging proclivity he shared with the leadership of the American Italian Anti-Defamation League, a group now operating under the acronym AID (Americans of Italian Descent).[22]

Lindsay, after losing in the primary, jumped back in the race by launching a new party—the Independent Party of New York City—formed, according to *The New York Times*, as "the crux of Mr. Lindsay's battle to stay in office after being rejected by his own party." The Independent Party was composed of seventeen sponsors, fourteen Democrats and three Republicans. One of the sponsors was Anthony Scotto, whose close political ties to the mayor went back to the start of the first Lindsay administration. In May 1966, with the immanent closing of the 165-year-old Brooklyn Navy Yard less than a month away, Lindsay tapped Scotto for membership in the city's newly formed Council on Port Development and Promotion, where he served as head of the marine port committee.[23]

The closing of the Navy Yard was a consequence of the loss of thousands of industrial jobs each year in New York City during the prior decade. Lindsay was keen to redevelop the site not merely to attract new businesses that would create blue-collar jobs. He was also looking for ways to avert civic unrest. At a luncheon to announce the mayor's plans, Donald Shaughnessy, Lindsay's economic adviser, warned that "unless we create industrial job opportunities we will have a Watts here." It was a sentiment with which Congressman Hugh Carey concurred. "We don't want a Watts in Brooklyn," Carey said, "but the possibilities are there."[24]

The federal government handover of the Navy Yard to the city was stalled by the Johnson administration's reluctance to assist a Republican politician, even one as liberal as John Lindsay. New York was only handed the keys to the facility after 1968, when Richard Nixon entered the White House. During the presidential campaign, Nixon's handlers promised Lindsay the prize if he agreed to second the nomination of their candidate's vice presidential running mate, Spiro T. Agnew, at the party's national convention in Miami. Lindsay swallowed hard and agreed to the deal. Five days after the Nixon-Agnew inauguration, the vice president flew to New York and ended what one journalist characterized as years of "tortuous negotiations" leading to a city takeover of the Navy Yard. In June of 1969, the federal government sweetened the redevelopment deal by allowing New York to lease Brooklyn's dormant Army Terminal. In a joint news conference with Mayor Lindsay, Vice President Agnew stated that the Navy Yard and Army Terminal projects would generate more than 1,500 new jobs on Brooklyn's waterfront by making new maritime and manufacturing space immediately available.[25]

This was music to the ears of Anthony Scotto, whose ILA membership had suffered the brunt of waterfront deindustrialization during the 1960s. Scotto's willingness to sign on as a founder of the new Independent Party, whose sole purpose was to reelect Mayor Lindsay in 1969, "hinged at least in part," according to one post-election analysis, "on getting the dock project out of mothballs."[26]

The only other labor leader among the seventeen sponsors of Lindsay's Independent Party was Victor H. Gotbaum, head of District Council 37 of the American Federation of State, County and Municipal Employees. Scotto and Gotbaum, although both were Brooklyn-born and held political science degrees from Brooklyn College, gained a reputation among political insiders as the "Madison Avenue boys." Young, handsome, and progressive-minded, they led unions with huge memberships. Local 1814 of the powerful ILA had 9,000 members. District Council 37 represented 80,000 civil service workers. Gotbaum was described by the *Times* as "a maverick . . . constantly at war with its Old Guard leaders over Vietnam, Jim Crow union practices and politics." Of his fellow Brooklynite Anthony Scotto, Gotbaum remarked, "He's probably the most socially motivated guy I know. Whether it's fighting against welfare cuts, splitting with the other union leaders to endorse Lindsay, or pushing voter registration, this guy was always there. As for this talk about the Mafia, I've dealt with him intensely and I've never seen any connection, I've never seen any dealings."[27]

Gotbaum's defense of Scotto was motivated by the publicity surrounding the federal government's release in October 1969 of the ILA leader's name in connection to organized crime. As far back as 1966, an FBI-organized crime chart listed Scotto as a *capo* in the Gambino crime family. At the time, however, the chart "was given in secret to the House Appropriations subcommittee," chaired by Brooklyn Congressman Rooney, an ally of J. Edgar Hoover. Rooney, who was elected to represent South Brooklyn and its waterfront interests for thirty consecutive years, could not have survived as the district's congressman without the political machine's backing and the tacit approval of its underworld associates. Perhaps this explains why, in 1966, Rooney's subcommittee—during a closed-door meeting requesting more money for the FBI to fight organized crime—withheld the Gambino crime family chart.[28]

In 1969, in the heat of Lindsay's reelection campaign, the veil of secrecy was lifted when the 1966 FBI Gambino family chart was made public by newly appointed US Attorney General John N. Mitchell. Scotto denied the federal government's accusation that he held a high-ranking position in an underworld crime conspiracy. When Scotto offered to remove himself from the Independent Party's sponsorship committee, the mayor refused to accept Scotto's resignation.[29]

John Lindsay, the underdog incumbent, won reelection. One of the key factors in his unlikely victory was the hiring of Richard R. Aurelio, a former newspaper man who had also worked for liberal Republicans, to orchestrate the Independent Party campaign. Aurelio ran a sophisticated operation that exploited Lindsay's Kennedy-esque televisual appeal while pillorying Procaccino as an unsound candidate seeking to impose "leadership by hysteria." Marchi, the Republican Party candidate, was easily dispatched as a dangerous "candidate of the far right." Aurelio also lined up a string of liberal celebrity endorsers, including Coretta King, the widow of Martin Luther King Jr., and Frank Sinatra, who performed at a $150-a-ticket gala at Madison Square Garden's Felt Forum.[30]

Lindsay's path to victory came by way of a coalition of Blacks, Puerto Ricans, and affluent Jews. Working- and middle-class Jews went for Procaccino. The large, white Catholic vote split between Italians for Procaccino and Irish for Marchi. The Independent Party line on the ballot drew 140,000 votes, the equivalent of 77 percent of Lindsay's margin of victory. The mayor received a respectable 258,946 out of the 718,310 total ballots cast in Brooklyn. How many ballots Lindsay picked up among members of Scotto's ILA is unknown, but preelection predictions of a massive anti-Lindsay vote in Brooklyn never materialized.[31]

Within a month of his reelection, Lindsay installed Aurelio as his deputy mayor. This prize was bestowed upon Aurelio for his shrewd management of the campaign, but it was also a tacit acknowledgment by the second Lindsay administration that city's Italian electorate could no longer be ignored. During a 1969 Christmas Eve interview, which appeared on the front page of *The New York Times*, Lindsay acknowledged that the "greatest lesson" of his first term of office "was how terribly complicated this city is, and how deeply embedded are the network of power structures." It was, according to the mayor, "a city that's very sensitive about its representative nature"; namely, "it's a highly ethnic city."[32]

For the majority of the city's Italians, Democrat and Republican, the twin defeat of Procaccino and Marchi was a slap in the face. Adding salt to the wound was the indictment, the following month in nearby Newark, of two-term Mayor Hugh J. Addonizio by a federal grand jury on charges of conspiracy and extortion in a bribery case involving illegal gambling. Six months later, Addonizio, still awaiting trial, ran for reelection in New Jersey's largest city. A liberal, Addonizio was challenged by Kenneth A. Gibson, a Black engineer who the mayor had appointed to the Newark Housing Authority, and by Anthony Imperiale, an ultra-conservative who had gained notoriety as a racist vigilante in the wake of the devastating 1967 Newark riots. Imperiale's candidacy functioned as a spoiler by drawing white votes away from Addonizio and helping to propel Gibson to victory as the first African American elected mayor of a major Northeastern city.

To political observers, the Italian American reputation for political ineptitude was confirmed by the electoral failures in Newark and New York. In 1970, native New Yorkers Daniel Patrick Moynihan and Nathan Glazer reissued their classic academic treatise *Beyond the Melting Pot*. It proffered a new, one-hundred-page introduction where they bemoaned the vacuum of political leadership within the Italian American community and the overall "failure of Italians to make a larger impact on the city scene," citing, as an example, "the near to total failure of the Italian-American 'Anti-Defamation League' . . . to combat anti-Italian prejudice." Moynihan and Glazer identified Mario Puzo's 1969 bestseller, *The Godfather*, as "the mark of an emergent self-consciousness but," they bleakly concluded, "not necessarily of emerging competence in the encounters that count."[33]

Part Three

Rise Up!

Italian American pickets, New York City FBI headquarters, Manhattan, May 1, 1970. *Source:* Donal F. Holway/New York Times/Redux. Used with permission.

Chapter 14

Day 1 (April 30, 1970)

For a price, Top Echelon FBI informant Gregory Scarpa, name redacted, rats out Joseph Colombo Jr., the twenty-three-year-old son of Scarpa's boss.

> This is to recommend continuation of authority to pay —— on a C.O.D. basis. —— who has been a top echelon informant since 1962, is one of the most effective sources developed to date in the organized crime field. He is a veteran member of La Cosa Nostra (LCN) and affiliated with the Joe Colombo "family." He consistently supplies extremely valuable and sensitive data regarding top level LCN activity. His information enabled our New York office to arrest Joe Colombo Jr., and two racket associates in April, 1970.[1]

Joe Jr., who is the spitting image of his father, is picked up by FBI agents on a bright but cool Thursday afternoon at the end of April and charged with conspiring to melt down silver coins into more valuable ingots. The United States Treasury prohibits melting coins to recover their silver content. The obscure federal law, only recently passed, is set to expire next month. Joe Jr. and his two older accomplices are temporarily held in the Bureau's New York Office at Sixty-Ninth Street and Third Avenue on the Upper East Side of Manhattan while they await transfer to the Federal House of Detention downtown.[2]

When, within an hour of Joe Jr.'s arrest, Joe Colombo receives word, he snaps. Junior's arrest confirms, in his mind, that the FBI will stop at nothing—not even ruining the lives of his children—to get to Joe Colombo. Why do they go to such great lengths to slander and defame him? Because I'm Italian, Joe thinks. They don't even treat Jews this way. Wasn't Meyer Lansky allowed to send his son to West Point?[3]

FBI informant Scarpa provides an eyewitness account of Joe's initial reaction to the news during a hastily arranged meeting in his private office in the back of Cantalupo Realty. "He met with Colombo who was in worst rage he had ever observed Colombo in. Colombo was shouting that his son had been framed and that we 'turned enough cheeks.' Colombo ranted 'we got to take steps, enough is enough.' "[4]

Joe steams. He's desperate. He'll do whatever it takes to get his son back. Twenty-five-year-old Anthony Colombo, Joe's oldest son, who is married with a newborn, has never seen his father in such a state.

Joe's longtime friend, fifty-six-year-old Natale Marcone, rushes over to Cantalupo's from his Staten Island home. He tries to rein in Joe's rage with an appeal to reason. Born in East Harlem and raised in Bensonhurst, Marcone is a retired labor organizer and Joe's partner in a local furniture factory. Marcone, whose name is redacted in the following information provided to the FBI by informant Scarpa, maps out a plan "on the spur of the moment."[5]

> Also present was —— who insisted that they picket the FBI "around the clock" and that they should seek assistance from AID (Americans of Italian Descent).[6]

Joe backs the idea of picketing the New York FBI headquarters but wants nothing to do with AID, an organization he contends has been co-opted by self-serving *prominente*—Italian American community leaders, mostly small businessmen and local politicians and professionals, who give little more than lip service to helping those in need for fear of losing their precarious hold on middle-class respectability.

Picket signs are hastily made, family and friends are phoned, and the first wave of protesters—about thirty people—is dispatched to 201 East Sixty-Ninth Street. They arrive at 7:15 p.m. Marcone hands out sandwich boards. The signs are scrawled with messages—

ITALIANS WANT EQUAL JUSTICE

TIME HAS COME FOR ITALIANS TO TAKE A STAND

FBI, HOOVER, WHY FRAME ITALIANS?

PRESIDENT NIXON, WHY ONLY ITALIAN AMERICAN CRIMINALS?

Along with a dozen women and children, the men march single-file in a circle on the sidewalk outside the FBI office, shouting "FBI are Gestapo!" and "FBI frames Italians!"[7]

Inside FBI headquarters: confusion among those working late tonight. Agents gather at windows. Looking down, they wonder: Who are these people? What do they want?

Fifteen minutes later, a second wave of picketers arrive. Someone peeking out a window from inside headquarters identifies the man leading a small boy by the hand as crime boss Joe Colombo. Inside the building, confusion turns to disbelief. There's a bleached blonde by Joe's side. It must be his wife, Jo-Jo.

Outside, the ranks swell to sixty and then to nearly a hundred and include what agents will describe in the next day's *Daily News* as "a sprinkling of identifiable Mafia." Are they carrying guns? Someone decides to secure the doors. From behind closed windows agents can hear Jo-Jo shouting "Give me my son back!"[8]

Joe breaks from the line, leaving the boy behind with his wife. He tries to enter the building. Locked. Joe kicks the door and yells, "Here I am! You want me? You want my family? Come on down here and open the door!"[9]

"Extraordinary" is the word used in an initial dispatch by law enforcement to describe the pickets.[10]

Has the boss of the Colombo crime family gone mad?

It's 1970. Street demonstrations in America are commonplace. But two things make this action different. Never before have anti-government protesters picketed the FBI, which was previously assumed to be untouchable. And never before has a crime lord conspicuously exercised the full range of his First Amendment rights—free speech *and* peaceful assembly—to challenge law enforcement. One journalist characterizes Joe's demonstration as "the first recorded example of lese majesty toward the aged director," J. Edgar Hoover.[11]

According to FBI informant Scarpa, even *capos* in Joe's crew, such as Nicholas "Nicky" Bianco, are vexed by the boss's public broadside against the Bureau.

> Informant advised that NICK BIANCO advised he was disgusted but resigned to the fact that he must placate COLOMBO. . . . Source advised that he discontinued picketing at approximately 1 a.m. and then had a discussion with JOE COLOMBO who advised he intended to get more people and continue picketing in the morning.[12]

Day 1 (April 30, 1970) | 89

Five hours after the sidewalk pickets commence outside the FBI building, they shut down. But not before Joe, energized by the night's activity, instructs his minions to prepare for day two.

> Source [Gregory Scarpa] emphasized that this was JOE COLOMBO's "thing" and that he did not have any set plan or regularly scheduled conferences with either his captains or other "families," that COLOMBO consulted with his close associates but depended primarily on ——.[13]

Chapter 15

Picket (May)

The first night's protest, done on the spur of the moment, is covered in an eight-paragraph scoop in the May 1 edition of the *New York Daily News* under the headline "Mafia Chief Organizes a Picket Line at the FBI." Buried in the middle of the article is an acknowledgment that the paper's coverage is sourced by federal "agents who remained in the headquarters" during the demonstration. The cozy relationship between the Bureau and the *News* is highlighted in a confidential FBI memo.

> ——— of the New York Daily News (both he and his paper are very close supporters of Bureau) has advised that his paper is considering running an article concerning Colombo and his associates, which will show just what a "bum" he is and his past criminal activities. The information in the attached memorandum is strictly public source information, and if approved by the Director, would be utilized by the New York Daily News without any attribution whatsoever to the FBI.[1]

"We regularly leaked stories to a reporter on the *New York Daily News* that were calculated to cause bad feeling," revealed Anthony Villano, FBI special agent assigned by the Bureau to be Scarpa's handler.[2]

Only one local newspaper steadfastly refuses to go along with the Mafia frame when covering Joe Colombo's FBI pickets—the *Long Island Post*, a weekly tabloid whose circulation doesn't extend far beyond Queens and parts of Brooklyn. One week into the demonstrations, the first article on the pickets appears in the *Post* under an Alice-through-the-looking-glass headline, "FBI Accused of Harassment." The *Long Island Post* makes no mention of Joe Colombo or the Mafia. Instead, the paper profiles ordinary people, including women and children, who walk the picket lines and appear energized by the boldness of their action. "There were as many women, carrying signs and chanting slogans, as there were men. Some of the women had brought their children, and the young ones marched alongside their mothers seemingly enjoying the whole thing."[3]

The inaugural coverage of the FBI pickets in the *Long Island Post* opens with an exchange between the unnamed reporter and "Mrs. Cam Fiorello of Howard Beach, Queens, the mother of three children, the eldest a student at St. John's University." The story's author uses an intimate, first-person voice. "I asked her why picket the FBI?" Mrs. Fiorello answers, "Because it all starts here." She points to the New York FBI headquarters building. "They gave the stories to the newspapers," Mrs. Fiorello explains without disclosing how she knows this to be true, "and the newspapers have a field day. This is only the beginning." As she turns to rejoin the marchers, she adds, "We will picket until hell freezes over, or until the Italians are treated with the respect they deserve."

The May issue of *The Challenge*, Americans of Italian Descent's new monthly newspaper, reports on the FBI demonstrations by quoting extensively from *Long Island Post* coverage. *The Challenge* adds nothing new to the reportage except to inform its readers that AID launched its own investigation to determine the veracity of the protesters' charges against the Bureau but that the paper's investigation proved inconclusive. According to *The Challenge*, when AID executives "ask the demonstration leaders whether we could act as intermediary between them and FBI authorities in the hope of coming to an understanding and stopping the picketing," Joe declines their offer. Tagged on to the end *The Challenge* coverage is a framed sidebar in bold font stating: "As we go to press, AID has stopped its investigations since the protest leaders seem determined to continue the demonstration and have not accepted our offer to act as intermediary."[4]

On May 18, eleven demonstrators are arrested while waiting for transportation to FBI headquarters at Expresso Café on 123 Avenue S in Brooklyn. As reported by the *Long Island Post*, when the demonstrators appear before a judge, they "answered all questions and when found to be without [criminal] records they were paroled for trial . . . on charges of loitering." That evening, Philip Vitello, outgoing AID president, stands on the trunk of a car speaking through a megaphone to an angry crowd numbering in the thousands. "Tonight," Vitello begins, his voice quivering

92 | Rebel Girl and the Godfather

with emotion, "I witnessed the most flagrant case of harassment I have seen in my 30 years as an attorney."[5]

The same evening, Reverend Louis Gigante, pastor of Saint Athanasius Parish, located on Tiffany Street in the poverty-ridden Hunts Point section of the Bronx, takes his turn on the bullhorn. Handsome and athletic, with wavy black hair and heavy-framed glasses, Gigante accuses the US Justice Department of defaming Italian Americans. "They try cases in the newspapers," he charges, "cases they seldom win in a court of law, and the word Mafia is plastered on all the front pages."[6]

Louis Gigante was a street priest. Born the youngest of five sons to Neapolitan immigrants in Greenwich Village, Gigante was a basketball star at Georgetown University. After graduation, he entered the priesthood and was selected by the church to study in Puerto Rico. Upon his return to the States, he was assigned to a Hunts Point parish.

"Father Gigante was our priest at St. Athanasius," recalled Sonya Maria Sotomayor, who was raised in majority Puerto Rican South Bronx and would later be appointed United States Supreme Court justice. "I would only gradually become aware that the familiar figure at the altar was a larger-than-life presence beyond the sanctuary, an activist for tenants' rights who famously walked the streets with a baseball bat as he negotiated with gangs and landlords. . . . Father Gigante was working to reclaim buildings that were abandoned or gutted by arson and renovate them as low-cost housing. It wouldn't have occurred to me to call him a freedom fighter, but why not?[7]

In May 1970, Father Gigante attended an all-day City Council Housing Committee hearing at city hall, where he joined tenants to protest the Lindsay administration's proposal to relax rent control. "We believe it's about time that the real-estate industry is destroyed," he declaimed. "When the capitalist system begins to destroy the human beings in places where we live such as the South Bronx . . . then we have to throw that system away."[8]

The reverend was also known to law enforcement agencies as the brother of Genovese crime family capo Vincent "The Chin" Gigante.

Reverend Gigante tells the picketers that his family has been persecuted by law enforcement. "The Federal Government framed my brother and put him away for four and a half years."[9]

Law enforcement agents, who sit hour after hour listening to bugs of Joe's conversations, are struck by the sincerity of Colombo's dedication to his cause. Joe confides to Father Gigante, "There's a larger thing here beyond Junior and the safety of my own family."

You might wonder why, for the first time in anyone's memory, large numbers of Italian New Yorkers leave the safety of their neighborhoods in the name of social action. Imagine you're from the neighborhood, the son of Italian immigrants, raised on American ideals of political freedom and economic opportunity, but now you feel used and abused by the mass media, big business, and patronizing government officials. Word has spread about Italian Americans, led by Joe Colombo, actively protesting their mistreatment. You decide to check out the nightly pickets for yourself. You take the train to FBI headquarters in Manhattan, exit the subway station at Lexington Avenue, walk up to East Sixty-Ninth Street, turn the corner, and suddenly see hundreds of picketers occupying the sidewalk. You stand across the street at a safe distance. Someone on the line looks like Joe Colombo from the papers but you can't be sure. The man—short, medium build with smooth skin and thinning hair—is not an overwhelming presence, but when he stops and speaks, he attracts a crowd. You cross the street to get within earshot. "We need more young men like you," you hear the man say, soft but firm, to someone unseen. "If you like what we're doing here, we hope you'll join us." You breathe it all in. Traveling home on the South Brooklyn Line, the man's words are lost in the scrape of rubber on iron, leaving only the messianic pitch of his voice.

The sheer size of the nightly pickets is proof that the demonstrations might be more than a con. *The New York Times*, in its initial coverage of the demonstrations on the second night of protests, reports that the picket lines "had grown to several hundred people." A month later, the *New York Post* observes that the nightly demonstration "has been rallying crowds of up to 4000 for six weeks."[10]

The national press takes notice. A *Newsweek* dispatch: "In car pools and buses, pickets from as far away as Jersey City have been arriving nightly in a blare of honking horns. Chanting slogans ('Hi-dee, hi-dee, hi-dee, ho, the FBI has got to go'), thumping placards ('FBI—Fascists'), they snap off Nazi salutes with roars of '*Sieg Heil!*'" Joe to *Newsweek*: "They're framing our children and harassing our pregnant women. We want them to stop."[11]

The New York Times estimates that transporting a crowd of this size to the FBI building in Manhattan five times a week involves arranging for "10 to 20 chartered buses . . . each night." In order to make transportation free of charge, Joe relies on personal contacts in a Brooklyn-based school bus company (Varsity Bus Inc.) and its drivers' union (Local 1181 of the

Amalgamated Transit Union, AFL-CIO), both of which have Italian American leadership, some of which the FBI identifies as mob-affiliated. Journalist Nicholas Pileggi details the reasons why the syndicate finds the school bus businesses so attractive: "First, of course, the profits are high, especially if some of the employees are paid off the books at reduced rates. Also, school-bus companies can efficiently launder illegal earning and can serve as excellent employment centers for jailed hoods looking for work-release programs and early parole."[12]

Joe instructs his men to transport picketers to the FBI building, as spelled out in FBI informant Scarpa's May 11 report to his handler: "Informant advised . . . he was instructed to have a bus load of pickets report to the NYO, which he did." Another informant report describes "the daily arrival of a food truck," also furnished to picketers free of charge.

With so much invested in the nightly demonstrations, Joe keeps track of his men's participation. "Informant advised that he has attended the picketing on a nightly basis and that COLOMBO has been keeping a 'head count' of all those attending and is angry at those who haven't shown regularly." Joe also counts heads, according to an FBI press leak, because some pickets are "debtors of loan sharks or bookmakers whose tabs are reduced by $35 for each four hour stint on the line." FBI informant Scarpa observes Joe Colombo monitoring the behavior of picketers. His boss is adamant that the FBI protest remains nonviolent, going so far as to discipline one of his own in the presence of law enforcement officials.[13]

> At one point [ANTHONY] AUGELLO falsely claimed an FBI agent had torn his placard off him, and spit on him and an incident almost ensued. After this incident, JOSEPH COLOMBO took him aside and severely censured him. . . . Informant advised previously BLACK SAM had attempted to start trouble and COLOMBO likewise berated him.[14]

Joe is wary that law enforcement will use the stereotype of short-tempered Italian men to discredit the pickets in the press. The month's news is awash in the kind of white working-class violence Joe is trying to avoid in connection with his FBI picketers. On May 8, two hundred construction workers storm the streets of Lower Manhattan and brutally assault peaceful anti–Vietnam War protesters marching against the recent Kent State student massacre and the Nixon administration's secret bombing of Cambodia. The press dubs the event the "hard hat riot." Conflicting news reports appear about whether the hard hat riot is spontaneous or orchestrated by contractors and union leadership. Two weeks later, Peter J. Brennan, president of the Building and Construction Trades Council of Greater New York and New York State, along with Manhattan union boss Thomas "Teddy" Gleason, general president of the International Longshoremen's Association, organize a pro–Vietnam War rally of tens of thousands of construction workers and their cohorts in front of Manhattan's city hall. The primary target of their rage is New York City Mayor Lindsay, an outspoken critic of the war. According to crime reporter Fred Cook, the hard hat rally is assembled in collusion with the employer-contractors, who pay the workers to march. Before the month is out, Brennan and Gleason are invited to the White House, where they present President Nixon with an emblematic hard hat along with an American flag pin and a pledge to continue their support for his Vietnam policy.[15]

While the hard hat riot receives blanket coverage, the large and boisterous but peaceful nightly pickets in front of the FBI building—what, according to informant Scarpa, Joe privately "continues to refer to it as 'my' demonstration"—garner scant media attention. Every now and then, when the press covers the FBI pickets, it treats the League as a Mafia hoax. Out of frustration, Joe considers expanding the demonstrations beyond the Bureau to the headquarters of news outlets throughout the city. According to an FBI memorandum, "COLOMBO desires to picket all the NY papers because of their lack of coverage at the NYO and because they are involved in discrediting Italian-Americans."[16]

Joe wants to form an organization to build on the picketing and push beyond a single-issue campaign. He envisions a new group, a community organization that will agitate on a variety of social justice issues. He's adamant that this group will have the power to ensure that when victories are achieved, promised concessions are delivered. The organizational leadership will be drawn from family, trusted associates, and allies. Nat Marcone will be in charge of day-to-day operations and hold the title of president. Joe's firstborn, Anthony, will serve as vice president and act as the group's chief spokesman. A family friend, Caesar Vitale, will be hired as secretary-treasurer. Joseph DeCicco, on loan from the Gambino crime family, will be lead organizer. Joe will remain behind the scenes. Barry Slotnick, Joe's lawyer, suggests "Italian Civil Rights League" as a name for the organization.[17]

Chapter 16

The League (June)

Since mid-May, Nat Marcone has been thinking out loud about an idea he has for staging "a big thing . . . a demonstration, sometime next month." At the start of June, Joe signs off on Marcone's idea—"Italian Unity Day"—for winding down the pickets without losing the momentum gained over the last month. As described by FBI informant Scarpa to his handler, "COLOMBO intends to keep enlarging the picketing for approximately 3 weeks to give him an opportunity to organize one massive march from city hall to the NYO which will 'cap-off' the demonstrations honorably."[1]

Most members of the media, even those who don't trust J. Edgar Hoover, cover the FBI pickets as a fraud. Park Slope's Pete Hamill, in his op-ed column in the *New York Post*, comes off as a scold when he berates the demonstrators. "Make no mistake: Mob guys are . . . degenerates. . . . So when I see the Italian-Americans picketing the FBI I wish they would also face some realities . . . they are kidding themselves when they try to say there is no Mafia in this country . . . Joe Colombo, head of the Mafia in Brooklyn . . . is now holding press conferences on the sidewalks. . . . If the Italian-American community really wanted to improve its image in the U.S. it would be picketing Joe Colombo's house. . . . They wouldn't come to Third Av. in buses provided by Joe Colombo's button men. . . . Meanwhile, someone should mount a counter-demonstration across the street from the anti-FBI pickets."[2]

Long Island Post op-ed writer Lou Benton responds to Hamill's rebuke with some ethnic sniping of his own. " 'Petey Boy' is a pretty smart kid, make no mistake about that, and when he says the Italian-Americans should clean their houses before they have the right to picket the FBI he is tossing another defaming curve. The Italian-Americans are sick and tired of that kind of tripe, and . . . united in their fight against defamation and discrimination, and Americans will be a little better off because of it."[3]

Even readers of the *New York Post*—which has a liberal reputation among the city's afternoon tabloids—who agree with Hamill's anti-anti-FBI picket indignation might still be left wondering: What outlets for streetwise political activism are available to outer borough ethnic whites seeking social justice? The labor movement is in decline; its national leaders, taking a defensive posture, increasingly align themselves with reactionary forces. The civil rights movement, having lost its integrationist momentum, has given ground to Black Power and identity-based politics. To many observers, the city's working-class Italians have only two choices: riot with the hard hats or join Colombo's League.

The date for Unity Day is set: Monday, June 29. The event will provide a venue where the Italian Civil Rights League can present itself to the world as a multifaceted social-action organization. Manhattan's Columbus Circle—a site marking Italian contributions to the making of America—is chosen as the rally site. The rally will conclude with a peaceful march to FBI headquarters and thereby also serve as a culminating event for the two-month-old demonstration.

Preparations for Unity Day are in full swing by the start of the second week in June. Joe rents a suite on the twenty-second floor of the Park-Sheraton Hotel, at 870 Seventh Avenue in midtown Manhattan, to house League headquarters. *The New York Times* notes the frantic pace inside the organization's offices as "pretty girls in miniskirts and men in pastel-colored turtle neck shirts scramble to answer the calls."[4]

There are only twenty-four days until the rally. Speakers need to be invited and the entertainment needs to be booked. Buses need to be hired to bring rally-goers to Manhattan from as far away as Chicago and Miami. Union support needs to be secured to allow local workers to take the day off. Shop owners need to be encouraged to close during the rally. Mailings, press releases, advertising. City permits need to be obtained for the rally site, vending rights, and the post-rally march to FBI headquarters.

The city permit required to route the Unity Day march from Columbus Circle to FBI headquarters during Monday afternoon rush hour traffic reaches an impasse with the police department. Joe asks for a meeting and is invited to NYPD headquarters. He arrives at the Centre Street location with his lawyer Barry Slotnick, along with League executives Nat Marcone and Anthony Colombo. They enter the building and are seated in a conference room.[5]

Anthony looks up as two dozen officers, many highly decorated, file through the door and into the room. He's a little anxious about the sit-down. *Will they try to arrest my father?* he wonders. His apprehension turns to bemusement when some of the policemen who walk past Joe pause to shake his hand. Anthony smiles to himself, thinking, *I wonder if they expect a bribe.*

A huge map of midtown Manhattan is tacked to the wall. Joe and his entourage listen while officials debate various parade routes from Columbus Circle to FBI headquarters. There's no consensus on how to get people from the starting point to the finish line without causing a traffic nightmare.

Joe interjects, "What if we march through the park—from Central Park driveway to Center Drive to East Drive, which dumps us at 72nd Street?" He gets up from his seat, walks up to the map, and traces it with his finger. He continues, "72nd is wide so we'd only block one side." Heads are nodding. "From there it's just four blocks to 3rd Avenue, where we turn right. Then it's just three short blocks to the corner of 69th Street."

The officer standing alongside Joe at the map says, "That might work. We'd only have short tie-ups at 5th and at Park." Fifteen minutes later, NYPD officials agree to Joe's idea for the parade route and the meeting ends amicably.

To build momentum for Unity Day, the League begins opening storefronts, called chapters, in borough neighborhoods. The first chapter opens on Saturday afternoon, June 13, on the corner of West Fifteenth Street and Neptune Avenue in Coney Island. Marcone boasts to reporters that the League will open twenty chapters before the June 29 rally.[6]

Only three chapters open prior to June 29, all in Brooklyn. The fourth won't be launched until to mid-October. For now, the League's energy is focused on Columbus Circle. Operations inside Park-Sheraton headquarters are documented in an FBI memorandum document.

> During the week of June 15, 1970 COLOMBO's headquarters in mid-town Manhattan hotel mailed out 79,000 pieces of first class mail urging support for the June 29, 1970 demonstration. They also have printed 500 arm-bands for "parade marshalls" [sic] and reportedly have engaged in some training of the selected marshalls.[7]

The five hundred parade marshals are "volunteer captains" recruited from the nightly picket lines and comprise what a League official describes as a "coordinating group" for the rally.[8]

Marcone explains to reporters that members of the coordinating group have been instructed to "go around in pairs visiting Italian-owned businesses to tell them of the rally." Anxious phone calls from a few shop owners trickle into news rooms. They claim that League captains are trying to bully them into hanging signs in their windows announcing they will close on June 29. Midway through the month, the *New York Post* investigates and finds most storekeepers who placed Unity Day signs in their windows are unwilling to talk to the press. One owner, however, is quoted as saying, " 'I'd rather lose a day's business than my entire business' . . . adding that two 'well-dressed men' came into his store last week and handed him the neatly printed poster which now hangs in his window. 'In honor of Italian-American Unity Day this store will be closed,' the sign proclaims."[9]

The League denies the rumored threats ("close on Monday or sweep up on Tuesday"). FBI informant Scarpa confirms that Joe prohibits the use of pressure tactics to force stores to close during the rally.

> He [informant] stated that COLOMBO gave strict orders before-hand to individuals who were supervising the canvassing of neighborhood stores and handing out of Unity Day posters not to use any coercion or threats whatsoever.[10]

Beyond any real or perceived pressure from League captains, store owners who close shop on Unity Day do so out of respect for their Italian customers or, if they are Italian, as a display of ethnic pride.

Joe appeals directly to labor leaders, many whom he knows personally, hoping to persuade them to give members a June 29 holiday in observance of Italian Unity Day. According to FBI informant Scarpa,

> COLOMBO advised he has been approaching various labor leaders in NYC who are sympathetic to Italian-American rights and is attempting to organize them with "shutting down NY" by leaving their jobs for a massive demonstration.[11]

The day before the rally, it's widely reported in the press that the event has "gained considerable union support." Progressive labor leaders, like Anthony Scotto of ILA Local 1814 and Victor Gotbaum of AFSCME District Council 37, publicly endorse Unity Day. Gotbaum confirms that District Council 37 has "arranged for members who wish to attend the gathering to charge the hours to their vacation time." Scotto anticipates his Local will shut down Brooklyn's piers. "I would assume that this port would be virtually wrapped up on Monday," he tells *The New York Times*.[12]

Beyond the Brooklyn waterfront, the piers of Manhattan, Staten Island, Newark, Elizabeth, and Hoboken will also shut down on June 29. Sanctioning a work stoppage on this scale requires the approval of crime boss Carlo Gambino.

```
Informant [Gregory Scarpa] stated that COLOMBO
had the complete blessing of CARLO GAMBINO
during the past 8 weeks, as well as the moral
support from other "families," some of whom
sent some of their people to march.[13]
```

The only news outlet expressing unconditional support for Unity Day is the *Long Island Post*. On its June 25 editorial page, *Post* publisher Lou Bruno prints an open letter to his son Joseph. "Dear Joseph," it begins, and reads in part, "You may have wondered why I have devoted as mush space as I have to the demonstrations by the Italian-American Civil Rights League. The answer, Joe, is very simple. For the past ten years I have stood by, as have all the other Italian-Americans, and allowed a proud people to be defamed and degraded by the American press. . . . Seven weeks ago, a group of courageous people fought back. . . . They went after those who had offended most, the FBI. Whenever an Italian-American is arrested . . . the FBI news release mentions Mafia and Cosa Nostra. The implication being that crime is an Italian evil, bred by Italians and committed by Italians. Nothing could be further from the truth."[14]

On page 8 of the same edition of *Long Island Post*, the "Italian Civil Rights League" runs a full-page ad for "Italian Unity Day"—the first to appear anywhere (Fig. 16.1).

The advertisement's assertion that Italians are not only "degraded" and "defamed" but also "discriminated against" suggests widening scope of the League's political agenda. Three days later, the League buys a near identical quarter-page ad in *The New York Times*. The *Times* ad, however, inserts Bruno's letter to his son and includes the word "American" in the organization's name, which henceforth will be officially known as the Italian American Civil Rights League (IACRL).[15]

Figure 16.1. Italian Civil Rights League advertisement, *Long Island Post*, June 25, 1970. *Source:* Long Island Post.

> **If you are an Italian-American and tired of being DEFAMED, DEGRADED and DISCRIMINATED AGAINST, there is only one place for you to be on the occasion of the . . .**
>
> **1st ANNUAL**
>
> **ITALIAN UNITY DAY**
>
> ON
>
> **Monday, June 29th, 1970**
>
> AT
>
> **Columbus Circle**
>
> AT
>
> **12 NOON**
>
> Sponsored by
> **ITALIAN CIVIL RIGHTS LEAGUE**

The *New York Daily News* also publishes a quarter-page ad for the event the day before the rally, but unlike the others, its Unity Day ad space is bought by Americans of Italian Descent and signed "Alfred E. Santangelo, Pres. AID." Conspicuous in the ad is the absence of any mention of the League.[16]

This is indicative of the rift between AID and IACRL, as well as perhaps the *Daily News*'s interest in fueling the feud between rival Italian groups. In Joe's eyes, AID has become indistinguishable from *prominente*-led organizations like UNICO and Sons of Italy. He's finished with AID. He won't give them another dime. According to an FBI memo, informant Scarpa "learned that AID will be discontinued as an organization and the balance of its treasury transferred to COLOMBO's new organization."[17]

The *Daily News*, the outlet most hostile to the League, allocates "guest editorial" space to John Marchi, state senator from Staten Island and unsuccessful Republican Party candidate for New York City mayor. He relishes his role as the only elected politician unwavering in his attacks on the legitimacy of the FBI pickets. "I can't buy the story that the FBI is in a conspiracy against the Italians," Marchi maintains. His words also appear in a *New York Post* piece, where he characterizes the League's FBI demonstrations as a "futile exercise in ethnic paranoia." In *The New York Times*, the state senator denounces other officials, particularly those planning to show their support for Italian Americans by participating in Unity Day. "You can forgive the people who come in good faith, but any public official who shows up is incredibly naïve or has lost his perspective and sense of values."[18]

In his *Daily News* guest editorial, Marchi chides his colleagues for breaking trust with the people they serve. "Having been put on notice that the circumstances are suspect, I think it's a failure to appreciate the responsibilities that go with public office." He concludes his editorial with a warning, one that associates Joe Colombo with confessed serial rapist and murderer Albert DeSalvo. "You go to a public affair and you might wind up with your arm around the Boston Strangler." An FBI anti-racketeering file titled "Gregory Scarpa" advises:

> The subject was a nighty member of the picketing demonstrations which were organized and run by JOSEPH COLOMBO in front of offices of the FBI in NYC, from 4/30/70 to 6/29/70. . . . During the course of these demonstrations it was observed that SCARPA frequently consulted with JOE COLOMBO, NICK BIANCO, DOMINICK "Mimi" SCIALO, and ANTHONY AUGELLO.[19]

The state senator's tabloid homology notwithstanding, the difficulty, as understood by journalist Nicholas Pileggi, is that while Marchi "has very clearly pointed to the hole in Joe Colombo's boat," he offers "nothing to the men and women on board by way of alternatives."[20]

Nagging questions abound: How long can the IACRL's boat stay afloat? Would Joe consider relinquishing command? If so, can the League sail without its Ahab?

During preparation for the following day's Unity Day rally, there's confusion among city employees regarding the Columbus Circle fountain, which surrounds the central pillar and around which is to be built a temporary stage where dignitaries will speak. Who knows how to shut off the water? And who has the authority to do it? Department of Water Supply? Parks? Cultural Affairs? Somebody suggests the mayor's office. Work on the stage comes to a halt. Joe puts his own men on the case. Nicholas Pileggi reports that "unidentified plumbers, armed with blueprints of their own, turned off all the proper nozzles and valves themselves." A city official, questioned about the League taking matters into its own hands, concedes, "Sure we were impressed. Most of our own guys wouldn't know how to turn that thing off."[21]

Chapter 17

Unity Day (June 29)

Day sixty. A stiff breeze coming off Gravesend Bay winds through empty streets and alleyways, snaps the bunting draped from the top of storefront windows and rustles the small Italian and American pennants strung across the street from the top of telephone poles to the elevated subway tracks. A sun-bleached flag of Brooklyn, inscribed with the Old Dutch phrase *Een Draght Maekt Maght*, is unfurled from the third story window of a stucco apartment building.

It's noon and the normally noisy thoroughfares in Brooklyn's predominantly Italian Bath Beach are abandoned. Shops are shuttered along Eighty-Sixth Street. A sign in the darkened window of the Hy Tulip Delicatessen reads, "This Store Will Be Closed Until 3:30 P.M. on Monday, June 29th in support of our many good friends & customers on their Italian-American Unity Day." Silence is suddenly shattered by the rataplan of a four-barrel carburetor under the hood of a black Pontiac GTO, *Bad Sicilian* etched on its rear fender.[1]

Soaring seventy-five feet above Midtown Manhattan—atop a granite rostral column—stands a sun-kissed marble statue of Cristoforo Colombo looking down through a canopy of red, white, and green streamers and on to a sea of nut-brown faces. The crowd spills out of the circle, flowing into the streets and onto the grass at the southwest corner of Central Park.[2]

Columbus Circle resembles an Italian *festa* as much as a political rally. The sound of Staten Island's Bob Chevy eight-piece orchestra delights the crowd with a spirited rendition of "You've Got to Change Your Evil Ways." The band strikes up "Neapolitan Tarantella," and Mrs. Jennie Ricchio, a tiny eighty-year-young resident of East Harlem (to whom Joe has bestowed the title "Mother of the League") begins to whirl.[3]

Hawkers move through the throng selling buttons—"I'm Proud to Be Italian," "Kiss Me, I'm Italian," and "Italian Power"—fifty cents each. Supporters hold up signs reading "There Are No Italo-Americans on the Board of Education" and "25% of WWII Vets Are Italian Americans." A Jewish teenager, Steven Teitel, leans against a light post. One hand holds an Italian ice, the other a poster proclaiming, "Jews of Flatland Support Americans of Italian Descent." Someone in a gorilla costume wears a placard carrying the words "F.B.I. Is Using Gorilla Tactics."[4]

Police on horseback cluster on the perimeter. Joe, dressed in light gray slacks and a yellow polo shirt with white and blue stripes, works quietly throughout the day to keep things running smoothly. FBI informant Scarpa tells his handler that "COLOMBO gave . . . strict orders to maintain order at all costs at the Unity Day Rally."[5]

Reporters and cameramen dot the crowd, which—depending on your source—is estimated at anywhere from 50,000 to 250,000 people (the actual number is probably closer to 100,000). Longshoremen, construction workers, service industry employees, and their families are well represented. FBI informant Scarpa claims that for the Unity Day rally "he personally supervised the unloading of about 100 chartered buses from his area alone."[6]

The audacity of Joe arranging for his lieutenants to fill Columbus Circle with tens of thousands of working- and middle-class Italians is, as assessed by journalist Nicholas Pileggi, "something that none of the *prominenti* would have dared even during their best years."[7]

Dignitaries invited to make short speeches sit on stage beneath an Italian American Civil Rights League banner adorned with the group's logo: an outline of a United States map cut through the middle with a large number 1 and filled with the stripes of the Italian flag. The orchestra strikes up "The Star-Spangled Banner," after which Father Louis Gigante, who has assumed the mantle of League chaplain, opens Unity Day ceremonies with an invocation. "We come as humble and proud, good and bad, rich and poor, to pray out against the injustices which have long plagued the Italian-Americans."[8]

Anthony Colombo, vice president of the League, kicks off the rally with passionate statement on the origins of the Unity Rally. "Yesterday," he roars, referring to the night of April 30, "thirty courageous Italian American people started a fight against discrimination, harassment, and defamation at the hands of the FBI. The FBI laughed and called it a passing fancy.

The news media ridiculed us in print. Today, we are united. Today, we are one. I thank you all and God bless you all." He pauses before lifting his hoarse voice. "Unity. We are one!" The crowd joins in, "One! One! One!"[9]

Congressman Mario Biaggi, the vigorous fifty-three-year-old Democrat from the Bronx, sets the tone for subsequent speakers. A former police officer, Biaggi, citing FBI statistics, declares that out of 22 million Italian Americans in the United States, only 5,000 are involved in organized crime, or less than 1 percent. Biaggi's gloss: "That's better than the 99 and 44/100ths purity of Ivory Soap."[10]

Biaggi, an urban ethnic populist, was identified by The New York Times *as the League's "political hero." A La Guardia Democrat who received campaign endorsements from New York's Republican and Conservative Parties, Biaggio was the quintessential "service congressman." According to a 1972 profile in* New York *magazine, he offered personalized assistance to his constituents in a manner evoking Don Corleone at his most benevolent in Mario Puzo's* The Godfather.[11]

Biaggi was a neighborhood guy. Born in an East Harlem tenement to poor Italian immigrant parents, he was a shoeshine in his youth. After graduating

Figure 17.1. Mario Biaggi, US congressman (D-Bronx), president of the Grand Council of Columbia Associations, while campaigning for the office of New York City mayor in 1973. *Source:* Ron Galella/Getty Images. Used with permission.

high school at the height of the Great Depression, he worked in a factory before landing a coveted job as a mail carrier for the US Postal Service. He married, had children, and moved to the Bronx before joining the NYPD in 1942, which, along with the fact that he had two brothers already fighting overseas, made him exempt from the draft. By the time he retired from the force twenty-three years later, Biaggi was New York City's most decorated police officer, having been wounded eleven times and receiving dozens of citations for valor. From the start of his NYPD career, Biaggi was active in the Patrolmen's Benevolent Association, and in 1952 he became president of the Grand Council of Columbia Associations—a fraternal order representing 80,000 Italian American civil servants in New York government—which would become his political power base.[12]

But by the mid-1950s, The New York Times reported that Biaggi "was clearly out of favor" with NYPD higher-ups as rumors began to swirl around his leadership of PBA and the Grand Council, which "brought him into frequent contact with politicians, city contractors, hangers-on, and, according to unverified reports, figures in organized crime." A turning point in Biaggi's career came in 1959, when he was caught in a wild gun duel that bolstered his law enforcement legend and buttressed whispers of his involvement in shady dealings. Biaggi's account of the incident is as follows. In the middle of the night, while off duty and in civilian clothes, he was at the wheel of a Cadillac, driving a friend who was letting him try out his new car. While the two men waited at a red light, a hooded stick-up man jumped into the back seat, put a gun to Biaggi's head, and tried to rob them. Biaggi, fearing the robber also planned to kill his mark, discreetly removed his revolver from its holster and, counting on the element of surprise, whirled around and fatally injured the gunman with five shots, four of which hit home. The gunman, a twenty-three-year-old ex-convict, returned volley with five shots, four of which missed their target and one of which inflicted a minor injury to Biaggi's thumb.[13]

"Although not all police authorities were said to have been satisfied with his explanation of the event," the Times reported, "the department awarded him its highest decoration, the Medal of Honor." Word on the street was that the gun battle was the result of Biaggi's involvement in protecting a Mafia bookmaker. Soon after, Biaggi retired from the force and began his political career with an appointment as assistant secretary of state in Republican Governor Nelson Rockefeller's administration. In 1968, Biaggi ran for Congress as a Democrat in what had been a Bronx Republican stronghold, won handily, and easily held on to the seat for the next twenty years.

Speaking to Unity Day rally-goers, Biaggi admonishes the press to "break away from the easy headline words and the continued indiscriminate use of 'Mafia' and 'Cosa Nostra' as synonyms for organized crime—an equation that carries with it the connotation that crime is the exclusive preserve of Italian Americans."

Former Controller Mario Procaccino, last year's Democratic Party nominee for mayor, draws righteous applause when introduced. "Don't let anyone imagine," he says in his hoarse voice, "that we are going to stand by and permit smearing and harassment of innocent people whose sole crime is that they are related, friends or neighbors, or just happened to be Italian-American."[14]

Frank Russo, a Lower East Side district leader and candidate for the New York State Assembly declares, "Eighty thousand Italians can't be wrong. You can't coerce and intimidate that many people." Former Police Lieutenant Rocco Scarfone proclaims: "The Mafia is . . . a myth. . . . It doesn't exist."[15]

Newark Councilman Anthony Imperiale's rousing speech takes note of the Italian American propensity for political apathy and mistrust of authority. He shouts, "Don't take the lies. Boycott the newspapers." He implores, "Picket and boycott, do what your enemies do. How many Italians do you have on the Board of Education in the city of New York? None." He reviles, "What do you do about it? You stay home and watch television." He warns, "If you leave this place and forget what you have to do, you deserve what you get."[16]

ILA union head Anthony Scotto jabs at the League's nemesis. "I urge you not to vote for a man just because he has an Italian name. Like that clown from Staten Island by the name of Marchi. Any time the media wants one Italian to rap another Italian, they call on Marchi." The crowd applauds Scotto's accusation. Marchi, for his part, has told the press that "he had been invited to attend the rally but declined because 'I couldn't buy this conspiracy bit.'" Speakers at the rally label State Senator Marchi and retired NYPD Detective Ralph Salerno "Uncle Tomes."[17]

Democratic nominee for US Congress Bella Abzug—the only woman invited to speak at the rally (Fig. 17.2)—catches some off guard by slipping in an antiwar message. "We do have a problem of organized crime." Her head bobs to the left on the beat and punches the words, "It's war."[18]

Abzug senses the crowd's ambivalence—or is it confusion?—about her pro-Italian/antiwar message. Finished, she steps away from the podium and saunters back to her chair. Seated, Abzug pokes a burly League representative with her elbow. "Do you think they'll murder me for that approach?"

Other notable liberal politicians are given a few minutes to speak, including Allard K. Lowenstein, Richard L. Ottinger, and Paul O'Dwyer. Deputy Mayor Richard Aurelio—the sole Republican Party speaker on the platform—attends the rally as John Lindsay's representative. Aurelio is there to demonstrate city hall's support for Unity Day. For many in attendance, however, the scrapes from last fall's defeat of Italian mayoral candidates Procaccino and Marchi remain raw. When the deputy mayor—who, wearing his trademark lavender shirt, is easy to spot from a distance on the dais—mentions his boss by name, the boos are so loud his voice becomes inaudible.[19]

Congressman Adam Clayton Powell Jr., the only African American on today's program, is also met by a chorus of boos. There are many in attendance who haven't forgiven him for his outspoken condemnation, a decade ago, of the "Italian" gangsters who controlled Harlem's numbers game. Powell is unbowed. He has been Harlem's representative in Congress for twenty-five years but he's currently fighting for his political life, having narrowly lost a primary for the first time in his career.[20]

Dressed in a white turtleneck sweater adorned with a large medallion that hangs from his neck (a gift presented to him many years ago by Emperor Haile Selassie of Ethiopia), Powell begins, "We have come here today for one reason." He pauses before starting again, this time raising his voice above the din. "We have come here today to ask one question. Is this a nation for all people or just for a privileged few?" The crowd settles

Figure 17.2. US Congressional candidate Bella Abzug, Italian American Unity Day, Manhattan, June 1970. *Source:* Ron Galella/Getty Images. Used with permission.

down. "I say it's a nation of all people and I'm with you in anything you want to do to make this the kind of nation it should be. A nation *of* the people, black and white," his right fist punches the air above and the crowd begins to applaud, "*for* the people, Puerto Rican," rolling his R's as the crowd becomes swept up in his speech. He drops his right fist as the left one rises, "and *by* the people, Protestant and Catholic." Both fists are now raised. The roar—a raucous mix of cheers and boos—is pierced by Powell's final words: "I say, "Right on! Right on! *Fight* On!""[21]

Next, a boy named Anthony LaRosa, son of Joe's sister, whose head barely crests the massed microphones, speaks. "I'm a twelve-year-old Italian American boy who does not want to grow up labeled. I want to grow up with my equal constitutional rights, not to be harassed and discriminated against." His accent is earnest Brooklynese. "As a young boy, reading the newspaper, watching TV, I asked my father, 'Dad, do only Italians commit crimes in this country.' And my father answered, 'Son, according to statistics, only one percent of all Italians commit crime, which is an exceptionally small ratio. Italians are hard workers, lovers of their home and family.'" The crowd goes wild with applause. The kid doesn't miss a beat. "And this is the reason I'm depending on you, the people, to unite and protect what is most precious to me, my Italian heritage. And to overcome the stigma that has been placed upon us. And so I won't have to explain to my children what my father had to explain to me. Please, don't let me down. Thank you and God bless you."[22]

Thunderous applause before the rally breaks into a restless chant, "We want Joe!" Father Gigante tucks a Bible under his arm and returns to the microphone to introduce the man of the hour. "Ladies and gentlemen, it is my honor and privilege to introduce a man *who knew* that he would be discriminated against, *who knew* that he would be unjustly accused, *who knew* that his name would be in every paper and completely condemned, *and yet* came out to help his son, his grandchildren, to stand up for their rights. I give you, Joey Colombo." The orchestra strikes up "For He's a Jolly Good Fellow" and Joe steps to the speaker's mic beneath a statue of Columbus to a deafening ovation. "I thank you for this honor and again I say, I thank God I was born of Italian birth [applause]. Today, this day belongs to you, the people. You are organized. You are one." The crowd chants, "*One! One! One!*" "You have the ball. You have to carry it. Let no one, but no one, come between us. God bless you and thank you!"[23]

The New York Times estimates that 12,000 rally-goers remain long after the speeches to participate in a *passeggiata* from Columbus Circle through Central Park to the FBI building on Sixty-Ninth Street and Third Avenue. The line, stretching twelve blocks, weaves its way through the park.[24]

Figure 17.3. IACRL founder Joseph Colombo Sr. holds a District Council 37 American Federation of State, County and Municipal Employees sign while marching from Unity Day in Columbus Circle to a League-sponsored rally outside FBI headquarters, Manhattan, June 1970; Colombo is flanked on the left by his son, IACRL Vice President Anthony Colombo. *Source:* Santi Visalli Inc./Getty Images. Used with permission.

Late Monday afternoon, the marchers reach their destination in front of FBI headquarters. Two police officers have been injured in skirmishes along the parade route. The NYPD, worried about escalating violence, asks Joe to help disperse the demonstrators. He mounts a sound truck with his son, who grabs a bullhorn. "We have achieved greatness here today," Anthony reminds the crowd. "We are one now. We must keep this peaceful and nonviolent." Joe takes charge. "Please be careful," he says through the bullhorn. "You have your mothers here, your daughters, your sisters. Be careful and go home. God bless you and go home."[25]

Less than twenty-four hours after Joe was showered with applause in Columbus Circle, he surrenders to Nassau District Attorney William Cahn on a charge of criminal contempt in a grand jury investigating mob infiltration into legitimate businesses. The indictment had been returned a week earlier but DA Cahn, without explanation, withholds announcing it until the last day of June. Five buses carrying two hundred Italian American Civil Rights

League picketers arrive along with Joe to the Mineola Court House office. Demonstrators beat a staccato rhythm on placards and shout "Cahn is a tool of the FBI" and "Cahn only did this to discredit our rally."[26]

As Joe is led from Judge Paul Kelly's chambers into court, the press asks him to comment on his arrest. Joe, with his attorney Barry Slotnick by his side, pleads his case. "It is unbelievable . . . I can't believe it." Shaking his head, "I answered each and every question every time I was there. I never refused to answer any questions. I promise I will let the press read the minutes of the grand jury. You will see for you see for yourselves. This is their version of Italian justice. This type of arrest is exactly what we have been trying to get across. If this isn't harassment, then I don't know what to call it."

The judge releases Joe on $5,000 bail.

For the League, there is an unexpected silver lining to Joe's arrest. For the first time in years, a US district attorney appears to go out of his way to avoid using the words Mafia or Cosa Nostra while arguing his case before the court. Instead he identifies those indicted, including Joe, as "members of organized crime."

The press takes note. When asked by the reporters about the conspicuous absence of the inflammatory words, the DA becomes visibly annoyed. "I have never used a phrase or a word that would lend credence that crime is controlled by any ethnic group," Cahn responds, while adding: "I am convinced that Joseph Colombo is an important figure in organized crime and does operate a crime family."

The same day, the director of the FBI composes a letter addressed to John Marchi. The missive reads,

```
My dear Senator:

I have learned about your remarks regarding the
completely unfounded charges of discrimination
made against this Bureau by certain elements
in New York City and want you to know I
sincerely appreciate your staunch support in
this matter . . . [and your] incisive com-
ments on the total impropriety of determining
the guilt or innocence of criminal conduct
on the picket lines.

    Sincerely yours,

    J. Edgar Hoover.[27]
```

The director deposits a copy of the letter into the Bureau files. Before now, when the League is captioned within an FBI document, it's classified under LCN "File No. 92-5509: JOSEPH ANTHONY COLOMBO." Beginning today, the FBI assigns the League a discrete criminal identification number that classifies the organization under racketeering: "File No. 92-12264: ITALIAN AMERICAN CIVIL RIGHTS LEAGUE."

Chapter 18

Alliance Averted (July)

The FBI monitors growing underworld support for Joe's crusade against the Bureau. According to Scarpa's FBI handler,

> Informant noted that COLOMBO was very pleased with the outcome and felt that he had scored an impressive success in being able to sustain picketing of the FBI for 8 weeks and climaxing this with a rally. Source advised that many of the COLOMBO "family" members who initially thought that the boss had made a mistake, now agree that COLOMBO has made his point.[1]

Joe is less interested in the approval of his associates than in winning over the court of public opinion. He takes his case into the belly of the beast, agreeing to do his first in-depth interview with *New York Daily News* crime reporter William Federici. "Yesterday," Federici writes in the preface to his interview, "Colombo broke the 'omerta,' or iron code of silence reportedly binding every 'family' member to talk about his troubles in an hour-and-a-half interview with a reporter." Federici notes that the room where the interview takes place is stifling hot. Despite the heat and the fact that the interviewee appears visibly agitated while discussing his harassment at the hands of the FBI, the reporter observes not a single bead of sweat on Joe's brow (Fig. 18.1).

In response to Federici's opening question about how he pulled off the events of the last two months, Joe flatly states that "the whole thing would have collapsed if I didn't work at making it a success," adding: "Picking the FBI was my thing but the rally was for all Italian-Americans." On his reputation as a crime lord: "The FBI and Justice Department made me the

Figure 18.1. Joseph Colombo Sr. speaks, interviewed by *New York Daily News* reporter William Federici. Colombo's lawyer, Barry Slotnick, sits between them. *Source:* New York Daily News/Getty Images. Used with permission.

boss of a Mafia family. . . . If I'm a leader of the Cosa Nostra or Mafia or whatever they are calling it then maybe the rumor that I'll be killed is true. I've broken all the rules I've heard about. I'm talking to the press." On his business associates: "I've known many people like Carlo Gambino since I was this high (holding his hand two feet off the ground) . . . I've always tried to help friends. . . . When there was trouble in the streets, they came to me because I knew everybody. Yes I knew the Gallo brothers. I know a lot of people. I will help them if I can." On what motivates him to speak publicly: "They have to stop defaming Italian-Americans. Guilt by association or ancestry is not the American way."[2]

Less than a week after Joe's *Daily News* interview, Mary Sansone appears on *Newsfront*, an hour-long civic affairs broadcast aired on New York City's public television station, Channel 13 (WNDT-TV). The topic is "the ethnic syndrome." Host Michael Krauss is joined by a group of Italian Americans with diverse political perspectives. As is so often the case, Mary is the only woman on the panel. Aside from the Congress of Italian American Organizations president, guests include Frank Arricale (leader of the Lindsay administration's Youth Board), Rev. Geno Baroni (founder of the DC-based National Center For Urban Ethnic Affairs), John Marchi (Republican state senator from Staten Island), Ralph Salerno (former NYPD detective and an authority on organized crime), Ronald Formisano (history professor at the University of Rochester), Salvatore LaGumina (history professor at Nassau Community College in Garden City, NY), and Aldo Tambellini (a multimedia artist who lives and works in Manhattan's Lower East Side).[3]

After introducing his guests, Krauss's opening remarks reference last week's "first Italian American Unity Day." The specter of the League rally hangs over the entire broadcast. Krauss asks the panelists to respond to the question "American melting pot—fact or fiction?" Baroni, a leading figure in the emerging white ethnic movement as the head of NCUEA, rejects the melting pot, characterizing it as a myth. Arricale, a passionate and outspoken social worker, is blunt: "We're not a melting pot society. We're a pluralistic society in which we have a co-existence of different cultures. The Italian suffers from the residue of a certain kind of racism."

Host Krauss turns to Mary and asks, "In the so-called hard hat phenomenon among construction workers, were there a disproportional number of Italian Americans?" She offers context: "In the last 10 years, when everything has become ethnic—you get the Blacks, the Puerto Ricans, the Jews—they're all are striving for their own ethnic groups. The Italians have become sensitive to this and I think that they, too, feel they need an identity, and the only way they can obtain this is by organizing and uniting." Krauss asks, with reference to Italian Americans who protest the Mafia stereotype, "Isn't this what the Italian American Unity Day was all about?" Mary aligns herself with the League's position on the defamation of Italian Americans in the mass media. "This constant talk of Cosa Nostra and the Mafia," she says, "I think it's unfair."

Ralph Salerno, Mary's close friend and ally, along with John Marchi, scoff at the assertion that the press is unfair to Italian Americans. Marchi states that he has no tolerance for ethnic tribalism and dismisses it as a dangerous fad. Salerno identifies the elephant in the room: "I'm most concerned about organized crime's sponsorship of Unity Day."

Krauss returns to Mary, addressing her as the grassroots activist among the eight panelists. "Mrs. Sansone, getting down to the level of the street where people live, how do they feel about this?" Mary seizes the opportunity to speak: "This is what I was hoping to say something about."

> For the last twenty-five years, I've been working with the very poor Italian, and I'd like to make everyone aware that we do have a tremendous amount of very poor Italians. . . . And, for a couple of years now, I've been bringing to the Lindsay administration—trying to make him [Mayor Lindsay] aware of—the needs of Italian Americans. I've been working with the Italian American kids in the Italian American areas by helping them to live and work with other ethnic groups. Our organization has been doing this on our own . . . I, as the director of the Congress of Italian American Organizations, have been working very closely with Mr. Aurelio, deputy mayor, and Deputy Commissioner Robert Malito, and I've been introducing them to the poor Italian American community, which doesn't relate to outside ethnic groups as easily as some other ethnic groups do.

Unbeknownst to Mary, enthusiasm for the Italian American Civil Rights League has reached CIAO's inner circle. Some executive board members, swept up in the fervor surrounding the League and its appeal to New York's 1.6 million Italian Americans, have joined IACRL. Some members of CIAO's board have had informal conversations with League officials about aligning the two organizations.

At a meeting of the executive committee—attended by twenty-two board members at Mary's Boro Park home—a small but powerful group of men on the executive board voice their enthusiasm for a CIAO-League alliance. Everybody wins, they contend. CIAO gets badly needed funding and the League gets CIAO's programming. The pro-alliance faction is led by CIAO President Dr. Joseph F. Valletutti.

When he joined CIAO, Joe Valletutti impressed Mary with his interest in pursuing big ideas about how to help Italian Americans. Later, when the board was electing the organization's next president (which essentially meant rubber-stamping the executive director's choice) Mary endorsed Valletutti's candidacy. More recently, however, Mary has become suspicious of Valletutti's loyalty to CIAO's social-action principles. He seems more interested in the plight of Italian American professionals—doctors, lawyers, teachers—than in the welfare of the poor. Along these lines, it also bothers her that he insists that others address him as *"doctor."* Everyone knows the title is puffery, the result of an honorary degree conferred in "commercial science," bequeathed only after he raised enough money operating a Thursday night bingo game on Queens Boulevard to endow a chair at St. John's University.

Mary is caught off guard. CIAO's pro-alliance faction explains that they're impressed by the League's audacity. They're committed to showing up at nightly pickets and capable of holding massive rallies. CIAO, they contend, does good work but struggles to pay its bills. The IACRL commands the respect and loyalty of hardworking men and women. Their dues-paying membership grows by the hundreds every week. They have money and power. They get media attention. CIAO flies under the radar.

Mary knows intuitively that IACRL appeals to some men on her board because their leader operates like a king and the League is organized like a fraternal order. Some board members, even those not in the pro-alliance camp, see Mary as an undersized woman with an outsized ego. They stick with her because she's sincere about working on behalf of the poor and—more than any man they know—she gets things done.

A motion is made by Valletutti for CIAO to align with IACRL. Mary is furious. Any pity she might have felt for Valletutti turns to distrust. She reminds everyone in the room about who it is that allegedly runs the League and about how even the appearance of an alliance between their organization and IACRL would besmirch CIAO's spotless reputation. Finally, she issues an ultimatum. "If we vote to join the League, I'm out! . . . And I'll take CIAO with me." A vote is taken. It's tied, 9–9, with three abstentions. Mary, as director, gets to break the tie. Before she does, however, a school administrator on the board named Ralph Calaceta, who had abstained, changes his mind. "I'm voting no," he says. "I'm going with Mary."[4]

Valletutti resigns from CIAO. He joins the rival group Americans of Italian Descent (AID), serving on its board of directors and as editor of *The Challenge*. Mary learns a lesson. From now on, she'll fight fire with fire by packing CIAO's board with people she can trust. Like it or not, it's what she must do.[5]

The League, despite losing the CIAO vote, gets a hearing inside city hall. Eleanor Holmes Norton, head of New York City's Human Rights Commission, agrees to investigate IACRL's charges of government bias against Italian Americans. In a *New York Daily News* article describing the recent Lindsay appointee as "the tall, slender, militant and black city commissioner of human rights," Norton acknowledges that her office "has no jurisdiction over the FBI, but we do have jurisdiction over the way ethnic groups are accepted in the city." Norton announces that a "preliminary [HRC] investigation shows us that there is some basis for the belief that a significant number of New York City residents do indeed stereotype Italian-Americans unfairly."[6]

In a July *New York Times* story, for example, a source inside the Manhattan district attorney's office admits to crime reporter Lesley Oelsner, "When we went after organized crime we only went after Italians."[7]

We only went after Italians.

Norton concludes her press conference with the statement "We will do everything possible to eliminate this injustice where it exists."[8]

US Attorney General John Mitchell, fearing a League-led counter-backlash against the Nixon administration, is forced to respond. On July 21, he issues a memorandum to all Justice Department agencies, including the FBI, to stop using Mafia and Cosa Nostra in internal reports and press releases because they offend "decent Italian-Americans." A special assistant to the attorney general, Richard A. "Red" Moore, announces this month's executive order on behalf of the DOJ. Moore, an Irishman from Brooklyn and friend of Mitchell's, has been hired by the administration to give Mitchell a makeover as "a softer-tonged law enforcer." Moore makes a point of denying the obvious when he states that the new policy is not the result of recent demonstrations by the IACRL.[9]

Hoover is furious. Just having hung up the phone with the president, the Bureau director fires off a memorandum dated July 24 to his longtime aide Clyde Tolson.

> I commented that I was very much surprised this morning when I heard on the air that the Attorney General has issued orders that no reference henceforth should be made to La Cosa Nostra or Mafia but be referred to only as organized crime because it is offensive to Italians. I said I would imagine the Press is going to tear into that; the La Cosa Nostra does exist and all the members are dedicated to murderous activities . . . most of the cases in organized crime are headed up by the Cosa Nostra, but I have not seen the order, just heard about it. The President said he would take a look at it.[10]

Hoover also complains privately to Mitchell that wiretaps have picked up Joe Colombo boasting to his associates that the DOJ's directive is "our first public victory and there will be others."[11]

Mitchell works for Nixon, not Hoover. The order stands. Mitchell appears on NBC's *Today Show* and reiterates the DOJ directive that all federal law enforcement agencies censor the words "Mafia" and "Cosa Nostra." This directive has the full support of the president, he adds. Mitchell ends by repeating Moore's denial that the League's activism influenced the president's decision, which is "in no way connected with a recent mass demonstration in New York City protesting alleged harassment of Italian-Americans by the Federal Bureau of Investigation."[12]

On the other side of the country, in the desert city of Tucson, Arizona, William Dunbar and Paul Stevens appear in Superior Court before Judge William Frey for the first time since their preliminary hearing last August. They are charged with bombing the home of Joseph Bonanno. Both Dunbar and Stevens plead guilty and, in their serpentine testimony, implicate former FBI Agent David Hale. Judge Frey calls Hale to the stand to respond to the criminal allegations leveled against him. (This will be Hale's only court appearance.) After stating his full name, the former FBI agent answers each question by claiming executive privilege and his Fifth Amendment right against self-incrimination.[13]

In frustration, Judge Frey shakes his finger at Hale and scolds, "You have led two young men down the primrose path." Rather than impose harsh penalties on Dunbar and Stevens, he disposes their testimony, fining them $286 each. The judge's last words are saved for Hale and his attorney. "I think it is a disgrace that the nation's top law enforcement body should neglect the prosecution of this case."[14]

The day after Hoover sends his memo to Tolson complaining that the press is certain to "tear into" the DOJ prohibition on using the word "Mafia," his fears are realized. On July 25, a front-page *Washington Post* article embarrassing to the Bureau appears under the headline "Judge Says Ex-FBI Man Caused Tucson Bombings." The piece, authored by *Arizona Republic* investigative reporter Logan McKechnie, who is also a correspondent for the *Post*, is a cogent recap of what Judge Frey characterized as the "fantastic" events in Tucson over the past two years, culminating this month with FBI Agent Hale's tight-lipped performance in Superior Court. The article is reprinted in news outlets nationwide, including the *New York Post* and *The Challenge*.[15]

McKechnie's story is a colorful tale about bungled FBI bombings and their aftermath. It opens with reference to Joseph Bonanno as "a so-called 'Mafia' chieftain." Mafia, which appears five more times in the story, is always bound by scare quotes (i.e., "Mafia"). The scare quotes distance the reader from the taken-for-granted meaning of the word and, in this instance, increase the likelihood that the reader might think twice about the stereotypical connection between criminality (Mafia) and ethnic identity (Italian American).[16]

The League, despite the administration's denials, takes credit for Nixon's executive order squashing the federal government's use of the words "Mafia" and "Cosa Nostra." Now IACRL demands the same from others. It aggressively goes after Hollywood studios, advertisers, and news outlets that circulate defaming stereotypes of Italian Americans. The League even targets the Paper of Record. During the first six months of 1970, the word "Mafia" appears in *The New York Times* an average of 149 times a month. In the month of June alone, the word is used a whopping 504 times. On the third Sunday in July, the *Times* publishes an article particularly offensive to IACRL supporters. Titled "Mafia Believed Behind the Italian-American Protests Over 'Harassment,'" the seven-column story asserts that the League is a hoax. It includes Joe Colombo's photo beneath an organizational chart labeled "New York City Mafia Families." It details his personal history.[17]

In late July, Joe contacts leadership in the newspaper truck drivers' union and alerts them to an upcoming League action against *The New York Times*. He solicits their sympathy for his picket in order to mitigate the potential for violence. At seven o'clock in the morning on the last Thursday in July, League demonstrators are dispatched to the newspaper's printing plant near Lincoln Center to protest "the *Times*' use of the term 'Mafia' in their copy." Joe joins the picket, two hundred strong, which forms an unbroken chain across the plant's trucking bays on West Avenue at Sixty-Fifth Street.[18]

During its venerable 118-year history, the *Times*, at its corporate offices, has been picketed on occasion by its unionized workforce and, more recently, by organizations connected to the civil rights movement. But before today, no one has dared shut down production or delivery of the newspaper. Three hours into the blockade, at the paper's nearby Times Square headquarters, a meeting is hastily convened between officers from the League and *Times* editors, who are led by forty-eight-year-old A. M. "Abe" Rosenthal, a man as much feared as revered among colleagues. His abrasive managerial style coupled with a volcanic temper is legendary. The League is represented by Barry Slotnick and Anthony Colombo, the latter with a short fuse to match Rosenthal's.

The next day's *Times* coverage of the parley is thoroughly sanitized. A story without a byline reassures readership that the paper is "sensitive to all aspects of the problem of discrimination in America and would review its performance with reference to Italian-Americans to see if there are deficiencies." The piece, buried on page 20, states that issues raised will be "discussed among editors and reporters." However, the article concludes with Rosenthal's reassurance "that under no circumstances would the *Times* respond to pressure tactics."[19]

Scrubbed from the *Times* coverage is an account of the heated exchange, which lasts two hours and ends with the Anthony Colombo giving the *Times* editor an ultimatum: "You want the trucks to leave the plant, then stop all the bullshit. Stop using the words." League representatives exit *Times* headquarters and head toward the printing plant, where fifty police officers prepare to clear street access to the truck bays. Upon arrival, Slotnick consults privately with Joe before debriefing the demonstrators, after which they disperse.[20]

Chapter 19

The M-Word (August)

The word Mafia makes sixteen appearances in *The New York Times* this month.

The League mails letters to media outlets in New York City and across the country demanding they "follow in accordance with the directive of President Nixon that the words 'Mafia' and 'Cosa Nostra' should be stricken."[1]

Joe knows that the League's anti-defamation campaign is an uphill battle. He also knows that the only way to control the message is to own the messenger. Joe purchases the *Long Island Post*. The paper's publisher, fifty-one-year-old Lou Bruno, is a Brooklyn resident. The *Long Island Post* differentiates itself from all other news outlets by keeping the organized crime angle out of its coverage of League activities. The *Post* even avoids publishing Joe Colombo's name.

According to Bureau documents, Joe encourages his "close associates" to buy shares in the paper. FBI informant Scarpa "advised that he learned that the Italian Civil Rights League was buying the 'Long Island Post' newspaper and that COLOMBO was exerting his close associates to purchase a share of this newspaper venture for $1500."[2]

The paper is renamed the *Tri-Boro Post*, and its circulation is expanded beyond Queens and parts of Brooklyn to all of Brooklyn and Staten Island. In a letter from the governor's desk dated August 26, Nelson Rockefeller congratulates the *Tri-Boro Post* on its "leadership in your ever expanding community," its recent "growth from a neighborhood publication . . . to a borough-wide newspaper," and its future "coverage into Brooklyn and Staten Island."[3]

The following day, Rockefeller directs New York State law enforcement agencies to halt the use of Mafia and Cosa Nostra when discussing organized crime. He one-ups his intraparty rival Richard Nixon by urging public servants outside the executive branch—judges, prosecutors, law enforcement—"to forsake the easy, vivid catchwords that unjustly slander Americans of Italian or any other descent." The *New York Daily News*, which one week earlier had received a friendly visit from Nixon in its Manhattan offices, and which has never been particularly fond of moderate Republicans, mocks Rockefeller's prohibition in a headline for treating the press like a disobedient child.

" 'Mafia' Now a No, No."[4]

Before the month is over, Slotnick's office on the fifteenth floor of 15 Park Row in Lower Manhattan is bombed. The explosive, a pipe bomb, is placed in an unoccupied waiting room. When it goes off, Slotnick is inside an adjoining room meeting with League officers, including Caesar Vitale. The explosion makes a thunderous noise, blowing out ceiling tiles and wall plaster and shattering the glass doors of other law offices along the 100–ll corridor. Slotnick's ears ring. He smells smoke. He tastes dust. Within minutes, ten fire trucks surround the twenty-seven-floor building located across from city hall. An FDNY investigator describes the fact that nobody was hurt in the explosion as "practically a miracle." Police detectives discover a shredded note in the rubble outside Slotnick's office, which they characterize as "a warning of some sort."[5]

They show the note to Slotnick. It reads "You help the Mafia. We don't like them." An FBI agent informs Slotnick that the Bureau believes the bomb was planted by one of Joe Colombo's underworld rivals. Slotnick doesn't trust the FBI any more than Joe does.

Unlike news reporting elsewhere, *The New York Times* piece on the Park Row bombing is remarkable for its constraint. It describes the fifteenth floor law offices as handling "mainly corporate law, with only a few criminal cases." Most news coverage is eager to make the connection between the bombing and the underworld. *The Washington Post*, for example, picks up a UPI story with the title "Bomb Rocks Office of Gangsters' Lawyer" and opens with a reference to "gangland boss Joseph Colombo."[6]

Closer to home, the *New York Daily News* coverage, headlined "Bomb Criminal Lawyer's Office," opens with a reference to Slotnick's "clients," which "include a number of mob big shots." However, both the *Post* and the *Daily News*, like the *Times*, refrain from using the words "Mafia" or "Cosa Nostra" in their stories.[7]

Chapter 20

San Gennaro Handshake (September)

The League places a full-page advertisement in the newly christened *Tri-Boro Post* announcing its first membership drive. IACRL membership currently stands above four thousand. Joe wants to expand it tenfold. He's willing to commit the necessary resources. "A mass membership drive has already been initiated," FBI informant Greg Scapra tells his handler, "with each COLOMBO associate required to enlist a quota of new dues paying members."[1]

League membership gets a boost from the annual Feast of San Gennaro Festival, which runs for nine days in the middle of the month on Little Italy's Mulberry Street. On the first night of the *festa*, September 11, Governor Rockefeller arrives along with New York Secretary of State John P. Lomenzo, his chief aide on Italian American affairs. The governor, campaigning for reelection while visiting the festival, issues a proclamation declaring September 19 San Gennaro Day, the same date Zsa Zsa Gabor will make an appearance at the League's festival booth. During his stroll down Mulberry Street, Rockefeller makes a scheduled stop at the League's booth, where he's given a hero's welcome. On the spot, IACRL officials make the governor, along with Secretary of State Lomenzo, honorary League members. IACRL lead organizer and Gambino crime family associate Joe DeCicco fastens a League pin to the governor's left lapel above a big "Italian Power" button. Cameras capture the moment. The governor shakes Anthony Colombo's hand while Lomenzo drapes his arm around the shoulder of Nicky Bianco, a made man in the Colombo crime family (Fig. 20.1).[2]

For Rockefeller, accepting an honorary membership in the IACRL is part of a campaign strategy sweeping much of the nation. Up and down the Atlantic seaboard and across the Midwest, 1970 is shaping up to be the year of the white ethnic voter. According to *New York Times* political reporter Richard Reeves, politicos identify white ethnics as "Roman Catholics of Irish, Italian and Polish ancestry who are usually registered Democrats." The League appeals to candidates like Rockefeller, a moderate Republican with a reputation as a political pragmatist. The payoff: After receiving only 34 percent of the Italian vote in 1966 and narrowly winning the election, Rockefeller takes 65 percent of the Italian vote statewide in November and wins reelection in a landslide.[3]

Perhaps the most blatant instance of Rockefeller's election-year opportunism occurs when, during September, he dispatches his secretary of state to advocate on behalf of a group of working-class Italian American residents from Queens—known as the Fighting Corona 69—in their four-year-old battle against the Lindsay administration's decision to demolish their homes under the city's eminent domain law in order to make way for a school. The state has no jurisdiction in the dispute, which makes little difference to the governor.

Figure 20.1. New York Governor Rockefeller accepts honorary membership in the IACRL, San Gennaro Festival, Little Italy, Manhattan, September 1970; left to right, Anthony Colombo; Joseph DeCicco, IACRL lead organizer and Gambino crime family member; Nelson Rockefeller; John Lomenzo, New York secretary of state; Nicholas "Nicky" Bianco, Colombo crime family member. *Source:* Anthony and Carol Colombo Family Archive. Used with permission.

128 | Rebel Girl and the Godfather

***

The Fighting Corona 69 is New York's first urban neighborhood preservation "cause." It pits powerful interests in city hall against an urban ethnic community that is unwilling—or cannot afford—to take part in the middle-class exodus to the suburbs. Overall, 40 percent of the city's Italian American population live in the same neighborhood where their family originally settled, making them three times less likely than Jews or Irish to participate in white flight.[4]

The first Lindsay administration, knowing the Italian American community's reputation for political apathy, ignored them. The Corona residents, however, defy tradition by standing their ground. They rummage for ways to make the mayor listen to their demands. They are led by two homeowners, Lillian Manasseri, a small woman with a big voice, and Ralph Dellacona, who explains to Jack Newfield of the *Village Voice*, "There was a city dump here when the Italians first came here in 1900. We took the worst land, and we build homes with our bare hands. Because I want to live with my friends and keep my home, they call me Mafia."[5]

In *The Great Gatsby*, F. Scott Fitzgerald calls this place "the valley of ashes." From those ashes grew an urban village, an enclave of Italian immigrants and their extended families, most of whom work blue-collar jobs and retreat into homes made of brick, shingle, and frame. A *New York Times* reporter describes the neighborhood as "perhaps one of the few crime-free oases left in the city" where residents still "do not even bother to lock doors."[6]

The Corona homeowners hire an unknown thirty-eight-year-old lawyer from Queens named Mario Cuomo to help stave off eviction. But by September 1970, they are forced to pay rent to the city, which has taken title to their homes while preparing to enforce eviction notices. Frustrated by the slow pace of negotiations, they turn away from the counsel of their soft-spoken, scholarly lawyer. They gravitate toward Vito P. Battista, a brazen Brooklyn state assemblyman who's itching to lead them into battle even if it plays out as Corona's Last Stand.[7]

During the prior decade, Battista, a picaresque figure and perennial conservative Republican candidate, gained a well-deserved reputation for political theater, which he skillfully used to stage his opposition to the liberal policies of the mayor. For example, after losing the 1965 Republican Party mayoral primary to Lindsay, Battista exhibited his consternation by parading an elephant and a monkey down Wall Street. He explained to onlookers that the elephant, which he dressed in a pink banner, showed the "pink-tinged" turn toward communism the Republican Party made when it nominated Lindsay for mayor. The monkey signified how the Liberal Party, which also endorsed Lindsay, "is making a monkey out of the elephant."

Battista—short, stout, and rumpled—used his Wall Street circus to rattle off a litany of conservative complaints, including nuisance taxes, rent control, forced busing, public housing, a proposed civilian review board for the police department, and the fluoridation of water. According to a report in The Wall Street Journal, *a law enforcement officer gave the elephant's owner a summons for allowing a wild animal to roam the city's streets. Coverage of the spectacle in the* Journal *concluded with the droll observation that "the policeman didn't challenge the monkey."*[8]

Despite Battista's reputation for being a difficult politician to work with, Joe is determined to help the Fighting Corona 69. On September 15, four hundred IACRL demonstrators assemble on the steps of the Queens Supreme Court building to join Battista and the embattled residents in persuading a judge to postpone the decision on eviction.

At the courthouse rally, Battista stands atop a ladder holding a battery-operated microphone. He reminds the Corona 69 demonstrators that the homes threatened by the bulldozer contain 138 families that have sent 71 young men to fight in Vietnam. Battista asks the crowd, "How do you tell those boys that when they were fighting to protect the homes of others, they lost theirs?" Before the day's end, the judge decides to postpone the decision pending further investigation of alternative sites for the school.[9]

Before the month's end, Battista, backed again by hundreds of League members, holds another Corona 69 rally. It takes place at City Hall Plaza, where the protesters demand an audience with the mayor. Mario Procaccino, who like Battista is a friend of the League's and no friend of Lindsay's, participates. When it's Procaccino's turn to speak, he shouts: "It's about time they stopped treating us like second class citizens. We demand equal treatment!" The protesters grow increasingly agitated. Mounted police crowd their horses at the base of the steps to keep the gathering storm of demonstrators from blocking city hall's main entrance.[10]

In the meantime, another contingent—unaffiliated with the Corona 69 cause—arrive in the plaza. This group is much smaller than the Corona brigade and consists mainly of Black and Puerto Rican mothers and children who are there to protest overcrowding in Public School 11 in the Bronx. Someone inside city hall decides to turn the Bronx protest into an educational opportunity. The children, along with their parents and teachers, are invited inside for a tour.

The PS 11 assembly begins to file into the building. Confusion and then mayhem overtake the Corona 69 demonstrators. Battista, gesturing wildly toward city hall, shouts to his followers: "Go in there! Go in there!" Corona protesters surge. They break through the police line and scramble up the steps. Police pursue. Fists fly. Punches are thrown. Battista, charged with inciting a riot and endangering the safety of children, is handcuffed. Restraining Battista only serves to intensify the siege. The assemblyman is preemptively un-cuffed.[11]

Deputy Mayor Aurelio appears on the steps of city hall and tries to restore order. He announces that the Lindsay administration will negotiate on one condition. Vito Battista, who has shown himself to be a headline-seeking obstructionist, must be excluded from discussions inside the mayor's office.

The Corona delegation is led by the IACRL's Anthony Colombo. The deputy mayor has been sympathetic to IACRL activities ever since he attended the League's Unity Day as city hall's representative. He is also genuinely concerned about the plight of the Corona homeowners. At the meeting's end, Aurelio grants Anthony access to Room 9, the city hall press room, where IACRL's vice president announces that the deputy mayor has given his word that he will "look into the equities of the situation" and keep the lines of communication open. On behalf of the League, organizer Joe DeCicco pledges, "We will be on hand whenever and wherever we are needed." Anthony asks the demonstrators to leave the area peacefully and return to their homes. Before departing, the crowd, led by bandleader Bob Chevy, erupts into a chorus of "God Bless America" and finishes with IACRL's unity chant, *"One! One! One!"*[12]

Chapter 21

Some Kind of Wonderful (October)

Columbus Day parade organizer Fortune Pope, scion of ur-*prominente* Generoso Pope, refuses IACRL's request to participate in the annual event by joining the march up Fifth Avenue. Fortune publishes the nation's largest Italian-language daily newspaper, *Il Progresso Italo-Americano*, inherited from his father, who founded the city's Columbus Day parade and who used his newspaper to raise money for the statue of Columbus erected at the center of Columbus Circle.[1]

League officials are not deterred by deliberate snubs. They celebrate the holiday by holding a wreath-laying ceremony in Columbus Circle. Upon arrival on the morning of October 12, they discover vandals have smeared red paint on the statue's base and written the words "Indians Discovered Columbus." League members in attendance, including Congressman Mario Biaggi, scrub the graffiti before raising a six-by-ten-foot floral tribute with the words "Italian American Civil Rights League Honors Cristoforo Colombo." Although *The New York Times* and the *Daily News* publish stories on the Columbus Day vandalism, only the *Tri-Boro Post* covers the League's tribute and cleanup operation.[2]

News outlets, with the exception of the *Tri-Boro Post*, fail to cover IACRL community-building activities and events. A case in point is the grand opening of Chapter 4 on the corner of Eighty-Fourth Street and Seventeenth Avenue in Bensonhurst on October 18, the Sunday after Columbus Day. The League refers to it as the "mother chapter" because it's Joe's home club, located less than six blocks from his split-level home on Eighty-Third Street in Dyker Heights. Only *Tri-Boro Post* reporters are on the scene. According to the paper's estimates, over thirty thousand people attend the noon to midnight block party, which includes political speeches by some of the biggest names in New York City politics alongside entertainment from big-time acts (Fig. 21.1).[3]

Headlining the event is "Mr. Wonderful" himself, Sammy Davis Jr. He's currently appearing at the Copa in Manhattan. During the League event, Davis is asked to sing the new "Italian American Civil Rights" anthem. It was recently recorded by the League's official vocalist, Tony Darrow, as a 45-rpm single released on the Sanfris label. Unfamiliar with the song, Davis is handed a copy of the lyrics and stumbles through it.[4]

> The Italian American Civil Rights League has a heritage we boast about to-day . . .
> We're going all out to do the things we believe in, and that is the reason why we say . . .
> We'll help the kids along . . .
> We'll make drug addiction a thing of the past, and give legal aid to all who ask . . .
> Join our ranks, Come along . . .

Before departing the stage, Sammy Davis reminds the audience to "stay united and continue to grow." Joe walks up to Sammy Davis and pins a League button on his close friend, making him an honorary League member. No non-Italian is a more enthusiastic supporter of Joe's crusade. "Whenever you need me," Sammy Davis tells the crowd before his exit, "I am at your disposal."[5]

League leadership express their gratitude to Sammy with a large banner, made of green, white, and red felt fabric, with the organization's logo at its center and "To Sammy Davis Jr." written in cursive at the upper left-hand corner. It will be presented to Sammy, along with a gold-covered album with forty-nine pictures commemorating the October 18 event. In one happy photograph, Joe stands between Sammy and his third wife, entertainer and Brooklynite Altovise Davis, his arms wrapped around the guests of honor.

While attendees at the block party feast on free sausage and peppers, franks, hamburgers, chicken, Italian eggrolls, and pastries, a litany of candidates, dignitaries, and public officials line up to speak. The list includes former US Senate Democratic Party nominee Paul O'Dwyer, New York Secretary of State John Lomenzo, Congressional candidate Bella Abzug, State Senator Basil Paterson, State Senatorial candidate Ted Pulaski, and Kings County Leader Meade Esposito, who had recently hand-picked Sebastian

"Sam" Leone, little known outside Bensonhurst Democratic circles, as Brooklyn borough president.[6]

Stephen Aiello, a twenty-seven-year-old public school educator who joined the nightly pickets in June and was named chairman of the League's newly formed Italian American Political Unity Association, is tapped to introduce the guest speakers at Chapter 4's opening ceremonies.

The son of Italian immigrants and a 1960 graduate from Lafayette High School, Steve Aiello grew up on West Thirteenth Street in Bensonhurst. Aiello was a New York City hundred-yard-dash champion in high school, he graduated from New York University, and he earned a master's in history from Columbia University. He taught in New York City's public schools. He played sax in a jazz band on weekends for the love of it. When Brooklyn's John Dewey High School, which adhered to a progressive curriculum, opened its doors in 1969, Aiello accepted a job as coordinator of student activities while also teaching

Figure 21.1. Grand opening of Chapter 4 in Bensonhurst, Brooklyn, October 1970; left to right, civil rights lawyer and politician Paul O'Dwyer, Kings County Democratic Party Leader Meade Esposito, Sammy Davis Jr., Brooklyn Borough President Sebastian Leone, State Senator Basil Paterson. *Source:* Anthony and Carol Colombo Family Archive. Used with permission.

134 | Rebel Girl and the Godfather

social studies. But outside the classroom, he still searched for a way to make a difference in the neighborhood where he was raised.

From behind a podium, Steve Aiello speaks to the crowd, urging them to support an eclectic mix of candidates—conservative, moderate, and progressive, Italian and non-Italian, Black and white, men and women. Among today's guests, Basil Paterson and Bella Abzug, stand out as the only Black and the only woman invited to speak. Perhaps the League's boldest endorsement goes to Bella Abzug, a leftwing Democrat, running for US Congress in Manhattan's Nineteenth Congressional District. Steve Aiello knows that Abzug's association with the women's movement doesn't play well with this audience. However, her outspoken opposition to the Nixon administration's omnibus crime bill is her ace. She's promising to introduce legislation to overturn the crime bill.

In Lower Manhattan, IACRL members work on behalf of Abzug's campaign from the League's newly opened Chapter 7, located in a nondescript storefront off Houston Street. The storefront is used as a base from which to organize campaign volunteers. Abzug, who embraces her identity as a "tough broad," is determined to win the working-class vote. "I was the first to talk with the hard hats," she reminds the *Daily News*. Abzug embraces the League's support. Her campaign manager, Doug Ireland, generates a special leaflet for distribution in Little Italy that targets the candidate's opposition to Nixon's crime bill. The flyer's headline reads "It's Not a Crime to Have an Italian Name." When Abzug wins in November, she will be the first radical leftist elected to the US House of Representatives since East Harlem's Vito Marcantonio left Congress in 1951.[7]

You might wonder how the League goes about opening a storefront, such as Chapter 7. Imagine you're a neighborhood guy—not a wiseguy but a small-time bookmaker—and you're looking for a secure location from which to take bets. By chance, League officials are interested in starting a chapter in the same neighborhood. The local crime boss, a trusted friend of Joe's and a League supporter, controls gambling in the area. He approves the location on the condition that the bookmaker, who is already a League member, opens an IACRL chapter in the same storefront. Mob money, not the bookmaker's, initially pays the rent, but before long hundreds of citizens from the community join the League and are paying dues, which now cover the cost of the storefront.

Membership is $10-a-year, of which $5 is returned to the local chapter and the balance is spent by the national organization, which, during the month, moves IACRL headquarters from the Park-Sheraton Hotel to a spacious, five-room suite on the seventeenth floor at 635 Madison Avenue and Fifty-Ninth Street.[8]

Prior to the beginning of the month, only three local chapters are launched and all of those are opened in the weeks leading up to the first Unity Day. Over the next eight months—just prior to the end of June, when the second Unity Day is scheduled—the League will open thirty more chapters. Located as far south as Miami and as far west as Las Vegas but mostly in the greater New York area, chapters are organized by 2,000 neighborhood captains and serve 50,000 members.[9]

Each chapter has its own president, vice president, and treasurer. Members who demonstrate an extraordinary commitment to League actions, occasionally women but mostly men, are recognized as captains after signing a League form titled Oath of the Captains.

> I, _____, before God, do hereby solemnly and sincerely promise and swear that I will abide by and uphold the rules and regulations of the Italian American Civil Rights League . . .

The task of inserting a captain's pin in the lapel of a newly recognized captain is typically performed by chapter presidents or one of the four League executives. There's even a junior captain's badge awarded to youth who pledge allegiance to the League.

> Must obey Mother and Father. Homework must be done every day. No Hookie playing. No smoking without parent's consent. Be warned that drugs are our enemies—Pot, Heroin, Pills etc.

No one seems to find it ironic that Joe Colombo insists on presiding over the junior captain awards ceremony, where badges are awarded for following the rules of good behavior. It's a League activity that he appears to relish more than all others and, up to this point, it's one of the few occasions where onlookers, including cameramen, observe Joe out in front of an IACRL function.

Since the start of the fall, the League has been holding semi-monthly meetings on Thursday nights in the Park-Sheraton Hotel's grand ballroom, where hundreds of members and nonmembers gather to discuss the organization and its activities. Over the summer, the hotel was used for League meetings but without regularity and, perhaps most importantly, without Joe in the spotlight.

The arrangement didn't go unnoticed by the press. "Sitting in the back of the hotel auditorium, Joseph Colombo," reports *The New York Times*, "greeted friends warmly with an easygoing confidence." After granting the post–Unity Day interview to the *Daily News*, Joe decides it's best not to draw attention to himself. "I don't want to hurt what this organization is doing," he explains. "My sons are up there and I don't want to hurt what they're doing."[10]

However, starting this month, Joe no longer sits, self-exiled, in the back of the ballroom. He's on stage alongside his son Anthony and Barry Slotnick, Steve Aiello, and Father Gigante, who blesses each gathering with an invocation. Invited speakers also sit on the dais. Nat Marcone, League president, chairs the meeting.

There's an open mic on the floor, allowing anyone to speak on any topic. Meetings are noisy, argumentative, and evangelical. However, as journalist Nicholas Pileggi observes, "debates between the various officials and their supporters end only when Joe rises from his seat, walks toward the microphone shaking his head, and begins to address the various sides like a stern father." Pileggi adds that Joe "has never yet been contradicted or challenged from the floor."[11]

When, on occasion, a wiseguy grabs the mic to testify, he's doing it to win Joe's favor. This is how the IACRL functions to enhance Joe's power within the Colombo crime family. Imagine you're a made man. Normally, you can't get close to Joe. He's like the pope—isolated from underlings within his own organization. If you want to speak to Joe, you follow protocol. If you encounter Joe by accident, you don't speak to him unless he speaks first. Wiseguys in the Colombo family embrace the League because it gives them an opportunity to get closer to Joe than ever imaginable. Talking into the floor mic, they are free to speak directly to Joe. Since the League is Joe's passion, it's their passion too.

At the meetings, most decisions, particularly relating to raising money, are made by Joe. Here's one instance. A penniless single mother living in East Harlem with three kids loses her home in a fire. The hardship is brought to the attention of the local IACRL chapter. She is invited to the next League meeting, where the chapter president testifies from the floor to the plight of the woman and her children. Joe sits and listens. When the chapter president is finished, Joe moves to the mic at the podium and says,

"OK, we're gonna need money to help this poor woman and her kids." He walks in front of the dais and stands before the seated audience. He points to his wife. "Jo-Jo donates $300." He points to his mother. "My mother gives $100." He points one of his sons. "Joey Jr. gives $400." And so on.

Before he's finished, guys "with long pockets," as Pileggi describes them, are lining up in the center aisle. One by one, they walk up to Joe and—*bada-bing-bada-boom*—they're dropping hundred-dollar bills at his feet. Joe's shoes disappear beneath a pile of green reaching his ankles. It's a win-win-win. The woman cries tears of joy. Joe beams. Wiseguys bask in his sun.

Chapter 22

The Offer (November)

Even with the accolades, Joe recognizes that the League is hamstrung by law enforcement, which thwarts the organization's plans build community service centers. The only Italian American organization doing this work is Mary Sansone's, and hers has a spotless reputation. He knows that Mary has seized a firmer grip on power within the Congress of Italian American Organizations since the summer, when she nearly lost the vote to keep her organization from allying with the League. CIAO has grown into a parent organization comprising over fifty Italian American groups representing almost fifty thousand members throughout the city.[1]

Under Mary's leadership, the organization in its first few years of existence has borrowed thousands of dollars with First National City Bank to keep it afloat. Now that the city is starting to fund its programs, CIAO is beginning to pay down its debt. Over the past six months, Mary has overseen the opening of a drug rehabilitation center in Greenwood to go along with CIAO's community center storefront in Park Slope. Demand for CIAO services has outgrown accommodations inside its modest storefronts. Mary lobbies the Lindsay administration's Human Resources Administration (HRA) for funds to expand CIAO's current locations and open daycare centers. Mary is working with HRA's head, Jule M. Sugarman. In a push for "maximum feasible participation" under the auspices of the federal government's War on Poverty, Sugarman pledges to finance, for the first time, daycare centers managed not by city bureaucrats but by organizations such as CIAO, which "operate under the principle of community control" and serve "low-income people." The phrase "low-income people" has been code in city hall for Blacks and Puerto Ricans—until now.[2]

CIAO has been gathering statistics using the government's own data to demonstrate that drug abuse and high school dropout rates among Italians in the city is closer to that of Blacks and Puerto Ricans than WASPs or Jews. Mary demands that the city approve daycare centers in predominantly low-income Italian neighborhoods. She pledges that CIAO will continue to serve racial minorities alongside ethnic whites. This has made her a darling inside city hall among the most progressive-minded Lindsay appointees, including an African American woman named Gladys Harrington—a high-ranking HRA official and one of the only women, Black or otherwise, holding a leadership position in the administration.

In 1960, Harrington was elected New York CORE's first chairperson. She led the interracial civil rights organization through 1963, when the group formed an alliance with Anthony Scotto's ILA Local 1814 in support of Black freedom struggles in South Africa and in the southern United States. She was also one of the few invited Black leaders who agreed to stand alongside Malcolm X at an August 1963 "unity" rally in Harlem organized by Black Muslims who were skeptical of the Kennedy administration's eleventh-hour endorsement of the March on Washington for Jobs and Freedom organized by Bayard Rustin. From the podium, Malcolm X urged Black militancy by calling on "so-called Negro leaders to submerge our trivial differences by forming a united black front." When it was Harrington's turn to speak, she warned, "Watch out for the black moderate, the white liberal and those who would sell us out."[3]

Harrington trusts Mary Sansone. She works behind the scenes to shepherd Mary's programs through the city's bureaucratic maze. Word around South Brooklyn is that CIAO is on the verge of securing funds for a daycare center in Carroll Gardens. Lindsay, since his reelection a year ago, is eager to make inroads into the outer boroughs' white enclaves without making his administration beholden to patronage organizations, such as Brooklyn boss Meade Esposito's powerful political machine. Mary disdains the Democratic chairman of the County of Kings as much as she does the local crime kingpins. Maybe more. Guys like Esposito pull the strings, making politics just another racket.[4]

Mary encourages Lindsay, "If you keep up what you're doing, I'll work for you."[5]

Joe looks for another angle to get Mary to agree to ally CIAO with IACRL. He's heard about CIAO's debt to First National City. He could pay it off. In order to make the offer to Mary, Joe goes through a mutual friend named Rosemary, who worked with Mary on last year's Brooklyn Citizens for Procaccino campaign and who has been a devoted League member from start.[6]

Rose phones Mary. "Guess who wants to meet with you?"

"Who?"

"Joe Colombo."

Mary takes a breadth. "What does he want with me?"

All Rose knows is that Joe asked her to ask Mary if she would meet him at the League's Chapter 4 storefront on Eighty-Fourth Street and Seventeenth Avenue. "He knows you don't drive so he'll arrange to have someone pick you up." The League storefront is a ten-minute walk from Joe's Dyker Heights home but a ten-minute drive from Mary's.

Mary tells Rose she'll think about it.

Mary hangs up and tells her husband. Zach, worried about his wife's safety, cautions her against going.

Mary calls Nicholas Pileggi and Ralph Salerno.

"Go," Pileggi tells her.

Ralph says, "Don't worry. Colombo knows your closest friends are me and Nick."

Mary phones Rose to arrange the meeting.

On a gray November morning, a limousine pulls up in front of Mary's home. The doorbell rings. Mary opens it and greets Rose, who stands before her in a mink and high heels. Mary wears her housecoat.

"Aren't you getting dressed?" Rose asks with a nervous smile.

Mary thinks, *This is exactly what I think of him* but pretends not to hear. She pushes past Rose and hops into the warmth of the waiting limo.

When they arrive in front of Chapter 4, Mary exits the car but Rose stays behind. Mary enters the storefront and is led by a young man through a large front room, down a hallway, and into the rear office, where she finds Joe behind a large desk. He invites her to take a seat across from him.

Joe begins, "I admire you, Mary, and I think the world of the work you're doing with CIAO."[7]

"We do the best we can with what we have," Mary says.

"That's what I want to talk to you about. I'd . . . the League would like to help CIAO do more."

"I'm not sure I understand," says Mary.

"We're both doing the same work, right?" Joe pauses to make sure Mary understands his meaning. She remains civil but Joe senses her impatience.

He continues, "So why not do it together? We'd get a lot more done."

Mary figures it's best not to mince words. "The day I start working with you," she says matter-of-factly, "is the day I lose my good name."

"Do I seem like a bad guy to you?" Joe says.

Joe's question reminds Mary of her Uncle Jimmy. Growing up, she never knew her uncle as a bad guy but she knew he must have done bad things. Her run-in with Uncle Jimmy twenty years ago taught her that even if Joe is sincere in his desire to keep the League free from corruption, his business associates would eventually demand their share of any money raised by the League. And if CIAO were aligned with IACRL, they'd come after her next.

"Well, I guess there's a little good in everybody," she says.

"What is it you want?" Joe asks. "What does CIAO need?"

"Well, maybe one day we can have a building like everybody else has. You know, the Blacks have one for the Urban League and the NAACP, the Jews have one for B'nai B'rith and the American Jewish Congress. So maybe we could have a place for CIAO, where Italians can go when they need help."

"What's it cost? Half a million? A million?"

"I don't know much about real estate but it could."

Joe jumps in, smiling. "Good, you got it."

"All I know is that if CIAO goes with the League, we'll lose our credibility. That's not something you can buy."

"There's good and bad in every group," Joe counters.

Mary isn't interested in debating. "I think I should leave now."

Joe doesn't want the meeting to end badly. "Before you go, I'd like to invite you to a benefit concert for the League on Friday."

Mary has heard all about it. "I can't afford the $200 ticket."

Joe says, "I want you and your husband to come as my guests. It won't cost you a dime." He senses Mary's continued reluctance. "Paul O'Dwyer will be there and so will Deputy Mayor Aurelio."

"I don't think so," Mary says.

"What are you afraid of?"

Mary, unsure what to make of Joe's question, decides to leave. She says her goodbyes and is out on sidewalk before he can get out of his seat.

At the curb, the limo—along with Rose—is gone. Mary reaches for cab fare but her housecoat pocket is empty. Shoulder against the wind, she walks down Seventeenth Avenue before turning up on New Utrecht Avenue and heading home under the El.

IACRL high-profile activities are organized by its leading men. Joe arranges for his son Anthony to meet with his friend Frank Sinatra to work on plans for the League's November 20 fundraiser in Madison Square Garden's Felt

Forum. From Sinatra's Manhattan office, Anthony and the singer discuss arrangements for the benefit concert, which Sinatra will headline and which will raise money to build an Italian American hospital, a drug rehabilitation center, and a home for the aged.[8]

The League has recently taken an option on a 10.5-acre parcel of land overlooking a Gravesend Bay site. The purchase price is $3.5 million.[9]

Sinatra insists on personally arranging invitations for other entertainers. In anticipation of the gala event, FBI informant Scarpa tells his handler "that all entertainers appearing at the 11/20/70 rally have donated their services to the event."

> Informant stated that FRANK SINATRA was actually "ramrodding" the obtaining of talent, and that the entertainers had agreed to appear as a favor to SINATRA. Informant stated as he has previously reported SINATRA and JOSEPH COLOMBO, LCN boss, enjoy a close personal relationship going back a few years. Informant stated that he did not know basis for this relationship, but it is a result of this association that SINATRA has taken it upon himself to recruit talent for the event.[10]

"Sold Out" reads the full-page ad in *The New York Times*, which accompanies an announcement of the eight o'clock start time for the IACRL event.[11]

Times coverage describes IACRL's charity show as having "an opera-night air of anticipation and elegance." The 5,600 guests, who make donations ranging from $100 to $200 to secure a seat in the Felt Forum, arrive "in furs and tuxedos." Among the guests are prominent New York politicians such as Democrat Paul O'Dwyer and Deputy Mayor Aurelio. Conducting the orchestra is Don Costa, arranger on last year's Sinatra hit "My Way." Ed McMahon is flown in from California to emcee the black-tie event. He opens the gala affair with "Good evening, fellow Italians."[12]

The show, which runs past midnight, features a host of singers and comedians, including Frankie Valli and the Four Seasons, Connie Francis, Vic Damone, Ross Martin, and Godfrey Cambridge. In a reprise of the 1967 AIADL benefit, Sammy Davis Jr. and Frank Sinatra take the spotlight for the grand finale.[13]

The event raises $487,000 for the planned League hospital.[14]

The Offer (November) | 143

Chapter 23

Sister Joe (December)

New Yorkers join IACRL in droves. They do so for lots of reasons. A handful of League members are affiliated with organized crime and, among them, those who don't share Joe's passion for the League are nevertheless pressured into paying dues.

Most of the thousands who join IACRL are law-abiding citizens. They support League causes or seek its services, and an increasing number of them are not Italian but working-class Jews who feel abandoned by the Jewish elite, including those who run their powerful anti-defamation organizations.

There are outliers among those signing up with the League. Radical feminist Ti-Grace Atkinson is one of them. She and Joe happen to share the same lawyer, Barry Slotnick, who has been working on her personal injury lawsuit against the NYPD. Atkinson alleges that after being arrested at a women's liberation demonstration earlier in the year, she was brutally strip-searched in Manhattan's Fourteenth Precinct.

Atkinson is in Slotnick's law office to discuss her case but he keeps bringing up Joe and the League, talking about Unity Day and how she should check it out. She's too busy on the lecture circuit, and besides, for the past year Atkinson has refused to appear in public with a man.

Back in February, thirty-one-year-old Atkinson issued "The Political Woman," a mimeo denouncing men as the "enemy," and, in doing so, making the political personal. "The price of clinging to the enemy is your life . . . I, personally, have taken the position that I will not appear with any man publicly, where it could possibly be interpreted that we were friends."[1]

Atkinson, daughter of a prominent Baton Rouge Standard Oil executive, had gained a reputation as an original thinker among women liberationists. She was responsible for helping the women's movement conceive the radical possibilities for second-wave feminism. She did not argue that individual men were the problem but that—*based on sex roles*—men as a class *were the enemy of women. She called for nothing short of a revolution that would destroy sex roles by abolishing the institutions of marriage and the family.*

Until October 1968, Atkinson was the first president of the National Organization of Women's New York chapter. She was appointed to that post in December 1967 by national president Betty Friedan, author of The Feminine Mystique, *who viewed Atkinson as her protégé. Friedan also recognized the benefits of having, as the face of the movement, someone tall, blond, slender, and in possession of a flawless complexion.* The New York Times *branded Atkinson "the militant's haute thinker" and gushed, "Whereas Mrs. Friedan is low-pitched and brusque, Ti-Grace Atkinson emotes in a dreamy, softly sexy style."*[2]

Slotnick, who is very persuasive, convinces Atkinson to join him and attend the next League meeting. Upon arrival, she feels like a fish out of water but finds the fervor inside the Park-Sheraton ballroom extraordinary. Atkinson has been involved with movement politics for years but has rarely witnessed this kind of energy.

After the meeting, she pulls Slotnick aside and asks him to arrange a meeting between her and League executives.

Atkinson sits beside Slotnick and across from Joe at a large mahogany table in a conference room at the League's Madison Avenue headquarters. She explains that she is working on a case for the DC-based organization Human Rights for Women, for which she is president. The case involves an Italian American woman named Darlene "Corky" Willis, a janitor at a downtown bank who has been fired by her employer, Allied Maintenance, for complaining about the unequal treatment of male and female employees. Willis, after consulting coworkers, discovered that male maintenance employees make fifty cents more an hour than females for doing the same job, are guaranteed forty-hour workweeks, and get ten-minutes longer for lunch breaks. Supervisors are men. Women are only hired to mop, dust, and lug garbage.

Despite these dismal work conditions, Willis wants her job back. She needs the money. Her husband is seriously ill.[3]

"I've tried everyone else," Atkinson explains. "The bank won't help her. Her union, Service International Employees, won't help her. The State Human Rights Commission won't help her. And the women's movement has tried and," she looks directly at Joe, "Barry says helping people in trouble is what the League is all about."

"What about filing a grievance with the union?" Joe asks.

Atkinson explains that the union is segregated by sex. One local, 32B, represents men; the other, 32J, represents women. Segregated unions encourage sex discrimination—separate and unequal—and Willis's union wants to maintain the status quo.

Joe agrees to help. He puts the League's lead organizer, Joe DeCicco, on the case. DeCicco schedules a meeting with representatives from Willis's union and lawyers from Human Rights for Women.

By the week's end, Willis has her job back.

Atkinson is not just grateful. She's elated. Her enthusiasm for the League is in inverse proportion to her growing disillusionment with the women's movement. From her perspective, the women's movement spawns radical theorizing while avoiding revolutionary practice. She begins to think that people who call themselves militant, particularly white folks like herself, should study the Mafia.[4]

She types a press release. The "organizational structure" of the Mafia, she writes, offers "the framework within which activists can live outside the law (can actively attack the class in power) and survive." Atkinson is "convinced that any significant change depends upon an alliance between the Left and the Mafia."[5]

A series of events toward the end of 1969—the dangerous folly of the Weathermen's Days of Rage demonstration in Chicago, for instance, which was followed by the police killing of local Black Panther leader Fred Hampton—drove some members of the radical Left underground. To kick-start the revolution in the immediate aftermath of the 1960s, a few prominent militants looked toward the Mafia as either a political ally or a model for organizing militarily. In New York, Ti-Grace Atkinson was contemplating a Left-Mafia alliance, and in the San Francisco Bay area, members of the Black Panther Party noticed that Huey P. Newton—having read and been inspired by Puzo's The Godfather while in prison—was reorganizing the Panthers along the lines of the mob. David Hilliard, Newton's boyhood friend and BPP chief of staff who ran the Party during Newton's nearly two-year absence while in jail, identified The Godfather as "a new influence guiding Huey." He elaborated as follows: "Now Mario Puzo's novel provides the organizational map, a patriarchal family, divided into military and political wings." Even Dr. Tolbert Jones Small, national chairman of the BPP Sickle Cell Anemia Project, "noticed a new spirit" among Party cadre *who were once instructed by Mao's* Little Red Book *but were now "reading* The Godfather."[6]

Atkinson dismisses *The Godfather* as little more than an airport novel. Her only interest is in those she identifies as "political Mafiosi"—revolutionary gangsters whose primary objective is to "rip off people in power" by targeting corporations and challenging the "criminal conspiracy" that aligns government and big business.[7]

In the midst of partnering with the IACRL on Willis's sex discrimination case, Atkinson is approached by documentary filmmaker Inez Gottlieb, a producer at WCAU-TV, the CBS affiliate in Philadelphia. Gottlieb is doing a segment on the radical wing of the women's movement. She wants to profile Atkinson.

Atkinson wants to give back to the IACRL for its work on behalf of Willis. She tells Gottlieb she'll participate in the documentary if it includes a tribute to the League. "I want to show that Italian-Americans are discriminated against—like blacks and women," Atkinson explains to friend and journalist Joan Kron, who, on assignment for *Philadelphia* magazine, tags along with Gottlieb's film crew. "I want to tell how the League helped an Italian-American cleaning woman get her job back after she lost it unfairly."[8]

Kron's *Philadelphia* magazine coverage appears under the title "Radical Chick," a nod to renowned New Journalist Tom Wolfe who, a few months back, published a sensational *New York* magazine cover story on Leonard Bernstein's party for the Black Panthers. It is, Wolfe proclaims, "the season of Radical Chic." He observes how, at the present moment, style has trumped substance in radical politics. Kron sees Atkinson's radicalism through a different lens, writing, "She uses her life-style as a political statement."[9]

Kron and Gottlieb, along with camera and sound operators, jam into Atkinson's tiny two-room, rent-controlled apartment in an East Side Manhattan townhouse. Its residents include New York's hip glitterati, such as Dick Cavett, who lives on the second floor in a flat that used to be Woody Allen's. Kron observes the surroundings and makes note of status details in her steno pad. Atkinson's dress, for instance: braless underneath white Banlon sweater; suede pants over Saks boots. Atkinson's locution: "Her lingo is part Harvard, part Black Panther. Her diction is part Oxford, part Southern Belle." Willis is there too, wearing a lavender pants suit topped by a brown chiffon babushka.

Atkinson has prepared a press release. Once everyone is settled, she hands it to Gottlieb. It reads, in part, "For the first time in a year, Ti-Grace

Sister Joe (December) | 147

Atkinson will appear publicly together with, and in support of, certain men. The men are of Sicilian descent [*sic*] and are alleged Mafia chiefs and/or relatives. . . . She will appear with them because they have made some significant contributions to the Women's Movement."[10]

After the interview with Atkinson and Willis, everyone piles in the WCAU-TV news van, which heads to League headquarters at Fifty-Ninth and Madison. Upon arrival, they take the elevator to the seventeenth floor and step out into a waiting room, which is covered in what Kron describes as wall-to-wall burnt sienna.

Seated on a couch across from three mini-skirted receptionists is a stylish young woman who looks out of place, wearing pants and a sheepskin-lined coat and holding a small Bonwit Teller holiday shopping bag. Kron instantly recognizes her as *New York* magazine writer and celebrity feminist Gloria Steinem, a friend of Atkinson's. Over the summer, Steinem opened her *Los Angeles Times* review of Joan Didion's *Play It as It Lays* with a deft assessment of Atkinson's status in "Women's Lib" as the "most intelligent and least practical of the movement's theorists."[11]

Atkinson has been urging Steinem to publish a piece in *New York* on the League's fight against discrimination. Steinem is skeptical but agrees to check it out. She's sitting in IACRL headquarters today at Atkinson's invitation. When Atkinson arrives, Steinem rises from the couch and joins her at the front desk. A secretary escorts the entire group to a conference room down a hall.

Once inside, Atkinson and Willis take a seat on either side of League Vice President Anthony Colombo, who wears a navy blue suit with an IACRL pin stuck in the lapel. Steinem positions herself behind the camera.

Anthony speaks. He rattles off the origins of the League, its purpose, its achievements—running the words together having said them so many times before.

When he's finished, Willis thanks the League for helping her get her job back. She then describes her employer's unequal treatment of male and female maintenance workers, which led to her complaint and caused her to be fired.

When Willis is finished, Steinem jumps in with a question for Anthony. "Has the Italian American Civil Rights League taken a public stand against sexism?"

The question blindsides Anthony. He's never felt comfortable around Atkinson, and Steinem's presence today only adds to his unease. Dismayed, he says, "I'm not sure I understand what that's got to do with the League."

Steinem redirects. "What's *your* position," she asks, looking at Anthony, "on male chauvinism?"

Atkinson is furious with Steinem for baiting Anthony. She speaks before Anthony can respond. "These Italian men are depicted in the media as male chauvinists," Atkinson says. "However, their willingness to support a working woman like Corky Willis in her fight with her corporate employer and her union over pay equity demonstrates that the sexist stereotype is a lie." Pointing at Anthony, she states, "They're taking the risks when no one else can or would. *They* are doing the work of feminism."

In Anthony's ears, the word feminism is a red herring. He opposes feminism, and he believes that by raising the specter of women's lib, Atkinson is working at cross-purposes with the League. "I don't know about feminism," he says while shaking his head, "but I'm glad to help with this case."

The meeting fails to win over Steinem, who dismisses Atkinson's advocacy of the League. On their way out of the office suite, Steinem walks past the receptionists at the front desk. She speaks to the room. "I understand there are no women in *executive* positions here." Steinem turns to the secretaries, who are minding typewriters and phones. "Are *you* paid well? Do they make you sew on buttons? We may come back and organize you."

Men run the League. Although women hold the title of captain in various chapters, no woman holds a position of power within the national organization. It seems obvious to an outside observer like Steinem that women in the League are treated like second-class citizens. Only once does Kron hear Atkinson, in a moment of frustration while dealing with League officials, vent about how these guys treat women. It happens when IACRL executives, without warning, back out of press conference arranged by Atkinson, which was supposed to take place on the steps of a Brooklyn courthouse. The snub, Kron observes, puts Atkinson in a fury. "I feel like an Italian wife," she chides before offering an excuse for their behavior. "They're distrustful of the press." It's a cursory rationale and rings hollow even for Atkinson. Finally, she explains her frustration: "I'm breaking my ass for them and they treat me like the other woman."

Atkinson feels differently about Joe. She finds no trace of phoniness in him. He isn't paying lip service to organizing working-class Italians. He just does it every night.

Ti-Grace walks the League picket line outside the FBI building alongside Joe. She calls him Papa. She's impressed by his curiosity. He asks lots of questions about the women's movement. She gives him a "Freedom for Women" button and he wears it while picketing. Nobody laughs. Next spring, when Joey Gallo visits the picket line, he'll introduce her to Gallo as "Women's Liberation." That fall, she will publicly bestow upon him the radical feminist honorific "Sister Joseph Colombo."[12]

Women in the League are keenly aware of women like Atkinson when the latter show up at IACRL functions. Imagine you're a dues-paying woman in the League. You can't help but notice how these outside women draw a different kind of attention to themselves—not as wives or daughters or sisters or even mistresses but as outspoken and independent women who are not shy of the camera lens. When these outside women make an appearance at a League event, they mainly interact with leadership. Given that the organization is run by men, it's rare that they speak to women who are regulars in the League.

It goes almost unnoticed that Italian American women comprise the vast majority of the League's foot soldiers, responsible for the grunt work that sustains community organizing. Just as with the church—without these women, there is no League.

Figure 23.1. A woman speaks into an open floor mic, IACRL biweekly meeting, Park-Sheraton Hotel Ballroom, Manhattan, 1971. *Source:* Anthony and Carol Colombo Family Archive. Used with permission.

For instance, Joe's wife, Jo-Jo, relies on her network of female friends, including her nine sisters, to support the organization's activities. In the League's early months, she coordinates the transportation of hundreds of picketers to and from the nightly demonstrations in front of FBI headquarters in downtown Manhattan. After Thanksgiving, Jo-Jo is responsible for contacting local businesses for contributions to the League's toy drive. As the winter holidays approach, garages of friends and family are stuffed with more than a thousand donations. League women haul hundreds of toys to locations throughout the city, such as the Foundling Hospital in Manhattan and the Angel Guardian Orphanage in Brooklyn, where they are distributed to children between the ages of two and five by a League-sponsored Santa Claus.[13]

Joe and his driver, Rocco "Rocky" Miraglia, sit in Miraglia's Buick wagon, which is parked behind the federal courthouse building in Foley Square. Joe's trial for perjury is scheduled at the courthouse today. Two FBI agents approach the car. One raps on the window and asks the men to step out. It's a bitter cold mid-December morning. More harassment, Joe thinks.

Miraglia is being arrested for allegedly giving false statements to a federal grand jury earlier in the year. Miraglia is holding a black briefcase. The agents ask to see its contents. Miraglia hesitates but the agents seize it.[14]

A report in "File No. 92-12264: Italian American Civil Rights League" describes the contents of the briefcase.

> At the time of his arrest, Miraglia was carrying a briefcase belonging to Colombo containing records of the IACRL. The records dealt specifically with ticket sales for a rally sponsored by the League at the Felt Forum. . . . Among the individuals listed as having purchased tickets for this affair were: Carlo Gambino, Thomas Eboli, Russell Bufalino, Raymond Patriarca Jr., ———, and Joseph Straci, all of whom have been publicly identified as members of LCN.[15]

Dollar amounts also appear next to the names, including "Carlo Gambino . . . $30,000."

"Oh," Joe says matter-of-factly to the FBI agents, "that's how much Carl raised selling tickets to the League's benefit concert at Felt Forum." Before returning the list to Joe, the Bureau makes copies and circulates them among law enforcement officials.[16]

Denis E. Dillon, director of the Federal Strike Force Against Organized Crime for the Eastern District of New York, studies the list before writing a memo to J. Edgar Hoover's second-in-command, William Sullivan, for "File No. 92-5509: Joseph Anthony Colombo."

> This list would form an excellent basis for a Federal Grand Jury Investigation under Title 18, Section 1962, United States Code, which makes illegal the investment of funds derived from racketeering activities in any enterprise affecting interstate commerce.[17]

Dillon, who in the early 1960s worked in the US attorney general's office under anti-Mafia crusader Robert F. Kennedy, is referring to the Racketeer Influence and Corrupt Organizations Act, or RICO, signed into law in October by President Nixon. RICO gives the US Department of Justice—and by extension its Organized Crime Strike Force—jurisdiction over large-scale gambling operations even in cases that do not cross state lines.

Since Al Capone, the government has found success prosecuting organized crime kingpins on income tax evasion charges when insufficient evidence exists to try them for non-tax-related crimes. The government attempts to cripple Joe's multimillion-dollar gambling operation by using the IRS to adduce that Joe can't possibly maintain his upstate Blooming Grove estate solely on his income as a real estate salesman. In addition, he is charged with lying on his state broker's license application.[18]

The IRS refuses to grant the League tax-exempt status because the FBI alleges that the organization is a front for Joe's illicit operations. Without tax-exempt status, there are limits on how much a donor can give to the League and every dollar donated must be reported along with a list of donor names. The donor list confiscated from Joe's briefcase is used by the FBI to stymie the IACRL fundraising activities and build the government's case for indicting League officers on tax evasion. This likely explains why the League is classified in FBI files under criminal "racketeering" rather than designated—a la COINTELPRO—as a "subversive" political organization.[19]

Chapter 24

Man of the Year (January 1971)

Governors—from Connecticut up to Alaska, from South Dakota down to Texas—follow Rockefeller's IACRL-inspired lead by directing their law enforcement agencies to stop slurring Italian Americans by referring to organized crime as Mafia and Cosa Nostra. Mayor Lindsay, not to be outdone by his rival in the state's executive mansion, accepts an honorary League membership. So too does his deputy mayor, Dick Aurelio.[1]

"*Tri-Boro Post* Names Joe Colombo 'Man of the Year,'" trumpets the newspaper's first issue of the year in a page-1 headline announcing a $125-a-plate testimonial dinner planned for March at the Huntington Town House on Long Island. This is the first time the *Tri-Boro Post* identifies Joe in its pages as the founder of the Italian American Civil Rights League. Joe is also honored in the January issue of *New York* magazine by journalist Dick Shaap—along with Governor Rockefeller, Mayor Lindsay, and *New York Times* managing editor Abe Rosenthal—as one of the "Ten Most Powerful Men in New York."[2]

Steve Aiello appears before the city's Human Rights Commission, which is holding public hearings on charges of racial discrimination against New York City's Board of Education. Last July, HRC chair Eleanor Holmes Norton was the first government official to agree to the League's demand that city hall investigate allegations of defamation against Italians by local FBI offices. The current HRC hearings focus on education, and for the first time in anyone's memory they are not dominated by allegations of unfair treatment from Blacks and Puerto Ricans. "What was unique about these hearings," according to the *Tri-Boro Post*, "was the fact that, for the first time in its history, the Human Rights Commission was to hear the outraged cries of another minority people, the Italian-Americans."[3]

Aiello, whose credentials include his tenure as a public school teacher and his recent stint as head of IACRL's education task force, accuses the board of education of discrimination against Italians. Specifically, he testifies that while almost a quarter of the city's high school population is Italian American, only one among the ninety-two high school principals is an Italian—and he's retiring in June! Of the 1,600 assistant principal positions in the school system, only ninety are occupied by Italians. And it's been years since there has been an Italian on the board of examiners, the powerful body responsible for testing and licensing teachers and administrators in city schools.[4]

The HRC hearing energizes Aiello. He knows, however, that his efforts will come to naught if the League doesn't continue to apply pressure. He consults Joe. Headquarters for the Central Board of Education is in Brooklyn. He suggests that the League set up pickets on the sidewalk in front of the building. The action will be a new use of the successful tactic deployed by the League last year outside FBI headquarters. Joe signs off on the new pickets.

Aiello also teams up with Anthony Colombo to ghostwrite the League vice president's missives. This one is dated January 28, 1971.

> Mr. Robert Evans
> Vice-President—Prod. Dept.
> Paramount Pictures
> 1 Gulf & Western Plaza
> New York, N.Y. 10023
>
> Dear Mr. Evans:
>
> The book, "The Godfather," although fiction, is a spurious and slanderous account of the Italian-American. Therefore, we feel the filming of this book is, if you will permit us poetic license, "the straw that broke the Italian American's back." We feel you should do everything in your power to delete the words "Mafia" and "Cosa Nostra" and the characterization of Italians being "gangsters" from this movie. The Italian American Civil Rights League's officers, captains, and members are prepared to publicly demonstrate, and use all legal means at our command to stop

this blatant affront on the integrity, heritage and values of the Italian American people. We would appreciate an answer from your office as soon as possible concerning our humane demands.

Yours in Unity,

Anthony Colombo
Vice President, Italian American Civil Rights League
New York, N.Y.[5]

The League sends out a form letter, composed by Steve and signed by Anthony, to every elected official in Washington requesting action be taken to stop production of the movie. It's not long before Evans is inundated with protest mail from US congressmen as well as from New York State legislators, judges, civic leaders, and business leaders.[6]

Chapter 25

Hollywood Deal (February)

When Hollywood makes a movie with controversial content, letter writing campaigns on behalf of those offended are routine. But the League's opposition to *The Godfather* is anything but routine. It falls to Albert S. Ruddy, the movie's producer, to fix the problem for Paramount studios. He's heard rumblings about not enough Italians being cast in the film; he's heard rumors of union walkouts, work stoppages, and boycotts; and he's now being told that shooting locations in and around New York City, where director Frances Ford Coppola insists on filming, can't be secured because the locals refuse to cooperate. He even receives a death threat.[1]

Ruddy goes straight to Joe Colombo for help. He invites Joe to a meeting in his Manhattan office. Joe accepts the offer and is accompanied to the meeting by his lawyer Barry Slotnick and his son Anthony.

Joe surprises Ruddy, who had half expected to be the victim of a shakedown but instead finds himself participating in a back-and-forth business negotiation. Ruddy promises that the movie will not defame Italian Americans.

Joe doesn't trust him. He knows a guy from Hollywood will say anything to get his movie made. Joe hands Ruddy a list of League demands. Ruddy sets the list aside for the moment and asks Joe, "Why don't you take a copy of the screenplay with you and read it and then get back to me about what you think?"

On the drive back to Brooklyn, Joe assigns Anthony and Barry the task of reading the script. Anthony pulls out a red pen. He crosses out the two times where the word "Mafia" appears, and passes the script to Barry. "I found the phrase 'Jew Congressman,'" Barry says to Joe. "That's offensive to me."[2]

"That's not the deal," Joe says.

***

Slotnick is back in court. He's defending Joe Jr. in front of a jury on the coin melting charge, which was the catalyst for launching the League last April. The government has spent the last ten months building its case against Joe Jr. and his accomplices around the testimony of Richard W. Salomone, a coin dealer.

Today, in a startling twist, Salomone recants his grand jury testimony. The prosecution's key witness now claims to have invented "a story" to satisfy the FBI, which, he contends, reneged on "promises" made in exchange for his false testimony. Specifically, Salomone tells the judge that FBI agents have withdrawn their agreement that they would reinstate his permit to carry a firearm and recover $50,000 lost in a business transaction.[3]

The judge throws out the charges. Case dismissed. Pandemonium breaks out in the courtroom. Someone hurls a threat at a Department of Justice prosecutor ("How do you want to get it, with a knife or a fist?"). The judge tries to calm his courtroom, "I don't have remind anyone about threats to Federal officers." From the gallery, a woman shouts, "What about vice versa?"

Figure 25.1. Joseph Colombo Jr. exits the Brooklyn Federal Courthouse alongside his mother Lucille "Jo-Jo" and his father Joseph Sr., after being acquitted in the coin melting conspiracy case on February 21, 1971. *Source:* New York Daily News/Getty Images. Used with permission.

Hollywood Deal (February) | 157

Standing in the lobby of the courthouse (Fig. 25.1), twenty-four-year-old Joe Jr. tells the press: "I feel that justice was done. This will advance the cause of the Italian-American Civil Rights League. This proves that it was a frame-up and there was no basis for arresting me."

His father agrees, saying that "the only good that came out of all this is the birth of the Italian-American Civil Rights League."[4]

The dismissal of the government's case against Joe Jr. serves to escalate the FBI's determination to criminalize the Italian American Civil Rights League. The Bureau leaks incriminating information about the organization to *Staten Island Advance* journalist Everett R. Harvey. An article with Harvey's byline appears in the *Advance* that reveals, without disclosing its source, a federal investigation into the League. A grand jury was convened last December, after the FBI seized Joe's briefcase containing a list of IACRL members and its contributions. "It is speculated," Harvey reports, "that primary among the aims of the grand jury probe will be an attempt to determine the extent of the intimidation mob muscle exercised in the signing up of members, store owners, businessmen and, currently, a drive to sign up the 15,000 membership of the International Longshoremen's Association headed by Anthony Scotto."[5]

At a raucous bimonthly meeting in the Park-Sheraton ballroom on February 25, fifteen hundred League members vote on a motion to resume picketing in front of the FBI building in Manhattan. An overwhelming voice vote approves the action, which includes mounting IACRL pickets at the headquarters of the *Staten Island Advance*.[6]

Nat Marcone, League president, introduces the next order of business. "You heard of the most controversial book in this country in the past century," Marcone begins. "It's a successful book. It sold a lot of copies. And now there's plans for a movie."

Joe, perched at the far end of the dais, looks on.

"Tonight," Marcone continues, "we have with us Al Ruddy, producer of *The Godfather*, who will explain, speak to you, and if you have questions, please ask him. Mr. Al Ruddy."[7]

The thirty-six-year-old Hollywood producer has been sitting near the podium at the center of the dais, waiting patiently for his turn to speak. Ruddy stands, lanky tall, and moves to the podium. He wears a black turtleneck and bellbottom corduroys supported by a wide belt. League executives seated along the dais wear conservative suits and ties. His loafers are Italian.

"Thank you, ladies and gentlemen," Ruddy begins. "As we say in Hollywood, these are very hard acts to follow." He glances down at the men sitting on the stage. "These are very bright, exciting, effective people."

Grumblings from the audience. Some can't hear what he's saying; others are put off by the Hollywood tone of voice. A woman from the floor interrupts, "Louder!"

The mic hasn't been properly adjusted. It barely reaches his chest. Ruddy steps back and releases an "Ugh" as someone sitting next to the podium reaches up and raises the mic to his chin. He takes a breath and restarts. "I'm going to try my best to follow the people who have come up, who I have a great deal of respect for, who are very bright, exciting people that we're looking forward to working with on *The Godfather*."

Ruddy rattles off his points with raised voice. "OK. Let me say first, before we go into any discussion of the film, that it is not my intent nor Paramount's intent in any way, shape, or form to do *The Godfather* as a film that can be construed by anybody as an anti-Italian film. It will not happen. You have my word. You have the word of Paramount Pictures. And you also have the word of the people from your organization that we have been working with. Now, we have been in touch with the Italian American Civil Liberties Union . . ."

Marcone, sitting nearby, can be heard on Ruddy's mic correcting him. Ruddy nods apologetically in Marcone's direction, "'Civil Rights,' excuse me." He continues with a promise: "We're going to delete any reference to 'Mafia' or 'Cosa Nostra.' I think it is something we'll all be proud of. We would like all of your enthusiasm. We are working closely with your organization to get ultimately the result that I want, that Paramount wants, and that you all want."

Reserved applause from the audience mixed with a few boos. It's a tough crowd.

The podium is yielded to Anthony Colombo, who steps in front of the mic and confirms Ruddy's statement. Anthony is also pleased to announce that Paramount has sweetened the pot in its negotiations with the League. "The Studio has volunteered to donate the proceeds of the movie's premiere to the League's hospital fund."[8]

Enthusiastic applause from the floor. The mood in the room is shifting in Ruddy's favor.

Anthony returns to his seat. Joe moves to the podium. He wastes no time making his point. "Let me say that I couldn't care less if they gave us $2 million." Ruddy is caught off guard. He's not sure what to make of

Joe's statement. Didn't they have a deal? Joe looks at Ruddy and raises his voice. "No one can buy the right to defame Italian Americans."

The audience erupts with cheers.

Ruddy raises his hand like a schoolboy asking for permission to speak. Joe yields. Ruddy leans forward and pivots to his best Brooklynese, "This will not be a schlock gangster movie." The audience remains restless. He pleads, "Look who's playing roles."

Before Ruddy can rattle off the names of the movie's A-list actors, like Marlon Brando, Joe interjects, "How about a good kid from Bensonhurst?"

Nicholas Pileggi, working on assignment for *The New York Times*, observes from the back of the ballroom. A knowing smile appears on Ruddy's face. Joe grins and points to League photographer Joe Labella snapping photos from the front row. Now the audience is cheering. Ruddy nods in agreement, making mental notes about hiring bit players and extras, such as Labella, who will appear as the photographer who lines up the Corleone family in the movie's opening wedding scene.[9]

Joe raises his hand. The audience goes quiet. He speaks solemnly. "I assure you that, what he says, I think he will go along with, because we will not be fooled. So, let us see. He has come here in good faith. What he has said, we will see that he will do. And then we will go on and get a good relationship."[10]

Joe walks over to Ruddy, who stands up. Joe inserts a captain's pin in his lapel, making the Paramount producer an honorary member of the League.

Ruddy receives a standing ovation.

Fists are raised. Fingers point to the sky. Chants echo, "*One! One! One!*"

The meeting is adjourned.

Pileggi's *New York Times* piece is an exclusive for the Sunday Magazine section. Prior to the movie's release, most Hollywood insiders, even those at Paramount, assume *The Godfather* won't rise above playing as just another gangster picture. When the *Times* offers to do a pre-release feature on the making of *The Godfather* film in exchange for the studio agreeing not to give any other news outlet access to the movie set, Paramount—eager to get free promotional publicity from a prestigious publication with a large circulation—accepts the terms. The studio also cuts a deal with *Life* magazine. The weekly gets exclusive rights to photograph Marlon Brando in full makeup as Don Vito Corleone in exchange for putting the star on its cover during the week of the movie's nationwide release.

Chapter 26

No-Show (March)

The deal between IACRL and Paramount Picture Studios is formally announced at a news conference held in the League's Madison Avenue office suite. Al Ruddy sits before a crowd of reporters and TV cameras. He declares that all references to Mafia and Cosa Nostra have been removed from *The Godfather* shooting script. "We omitted the words," Ruddy explains to the press. He emphasizes that "what the movie is really about: an indictment against society and not just one group." He concludes by announcing that proceeds from the movie's premiere will be donated to IACRL's hospital fundraising campaign. The next day, a photo of Ruddy flanked by Nat Macone and Anthony Colombo at the press conference appears alongside a three-column headline on the front page of *The New York Times* (Fig. 26.1).[1]

Coverage of another League activity, which occurs the same day as the Ruddy-League news conference, is buried on page 34, at the very end of the same *Times* article. "Yesterday," paragraph 26 of the story begins, "the league and other Italian-American organizations demonstrated outside the Board of Education headquarters building at 110 Livingston Street in Brooklyn from 11 A.M. to 1 P.M." Although the *Times* does not describe it as such, the protest—organized by IACRL and led by Steve Aiello and joined by Joe Colombo—is a first.

Over the last few years, Blacks and Puerto Ricans have staged demonstrations in front of school headquarters but never before have Italian Americans. Hundreds of League pickets are joined on the sidewalk by members of the Columbia Association of Italian American Teachers.[2]

Their signs read:

ITALO-AMERICANS NOT REPRESENTED ON B.O.E.

WHY NO ITALIAN AMERICAN HIGH SCHOOL PRINCIPALS?

STOP DEFAMING ITALIANS IN SCHOOL TEXTBOOKS

ITALIAN STUDENTS DEMAND BILINGUAL EDUCATION

Carlo Gambino, Joe's staunchest supporter among high-ranking Mafiosi, is a no-show at Joe Colombo's Man of the Year tribute dinner. Gambino attended the Frank Sinatra–headlined Madison Square Garden benefit last

Figure 26.1. News conference, IACRL headquarters, Manhattan, March 1971; back to front, Nat Maricone, IACRL president; Al Ruddy, producer of *The Godfather* movie; Anthony Colombo, IACRL vice president. *Source:* New York Times/Redux. Used with permission.

November. However, ever since December, when the FBI found his name on the list of IACRL contributors in Joe's briefcase, Gambino has cooled to the League.[3]

Adding to Joe's troubles, "Crazy" Joey Gallo—a rouge gangster who spent the last nine years locked up on an extortion charge—has recently been released from jail.

In 1961, during the Profaci war, Joey Gallo kidnapped Joe Colombo and other members of Profaci family leadership in an attempt to extract a more equitable split of income from Joe Profaci in Gallo's South Brooklyn neighborhood of Red Hook. After reaching a deal with Profaci, Gallo released Colombo and the others. However, before the year was over, Gallo was convicted in federal court on extortion and sent to prison.

A few years later, around the same time Joe Colombo was elevated to boss of the Profaci family (renamed the Colombo family) and Colombo and Larry Gallo were hatching their plan to launch the American Italian Anti-Defamation League, word leaked out that "Crazy" Joey was engaged in a civil rights action of his own inside prison. As disclosed in The New York Times, *Attica State Prison inmate Joey Gallo had charged the New York Department of Correction with subjecting him to "cruel and unusual punishment" because he had "attempted to break down color barriers" in jail. Gallo's petition to the State Supreme Court alleged that his mistreatment by Attica corrections officials began "when he permitted a Negro barber to cut his hair." The deputy corrections commissioner responded to Gallo's charge by labeling him "an agitator and belligerent prisoner."*[4]

Rumors circulate that Joey Gallo, back on the streets of South Brooklyn, is insisting that Joe Colombo hand over all franchises promised to him before he went to prison, including vending machine companies, loan shark operations, and policy banks.

Joe refuses, saying, "That was years before I became boss. Those aren't my debts."[5]

Joe is much less worried about Joey Gallo than he is about the threat posed by law enforcement. Slotnick has kept Joe out of jail, but state and federal indictments—on charges of perjury, tax evasion, and criminal conspiracy—continue to rain down. At the Man of the Year ceremony, Joe takes a minute to speak with a reporter from *Time* magazine. "The Attorney General hates our guts," he begins, adding, "I think the President is behind it." Joe's plan: "I want to make the league the greatest organization in the country, the greatest organization in the world, so that people will be proud of us no matter what we do, where we are, even if we are in prison."[6]

On the evening of March 22, fifteen-hundred people attend the Huntington Town House black-tie affair saluting the IACRL founder's humanitarian efforts, raising $150,000 earmarked to purchase land for the League hospital. Nat Maracone, as IACRL president, stands before the gathering and salutes Joe for "restoring dignity, pride and recognition to every Italian." He presents Joe with a fourteen-carat-gold plaque, reading: "He is the guiding spirit of Italian-American unity." The presentation is followed by a five-minute standing ovation.[7]

That night, Al Ruddy not only attended Joe's Man of the Year dinner but bought a table at the ceremony to demonstrate his goodwill toward IACRL initiatives.[8]

The following morning, Ruddy's support for the League pays off as *The Godfather* begins its first day of filming. It is not uncommon for movie productions in New York to be disrupted by harassment from local toughs or shakedowns from unions or corrupt cops. However, in the case of *The Godfather*, the once-threatened sabotage, pickets, and work stoppages vanish overnight.[9]

When Hollywood's hometown newspaper, the *Los Angeles Times*, announces shooting on *The Godfather* has begun, it reports that the IACRL is readying sections of New York City "to give the movie people a cordial reception." Nat Marcone secures a location not far from his Staten Island home for staging *The Godfather's* compound. League captains canvass neighborhoods to mollify residents suspicious of outsiders.[10]

The first day's shooting takes place on the sidewalk outside Best and Company department store on Fifth Avenue at Fifty-First Street. *The Godfather* ensemble is untouchable. Joe's power is everywhere, notes Nicholas Pileggi, who stands on the edge of the set. He observes a security contingent made up of off-duty sanitation workers—not wiseguys but real bruisers nonetheless. Wiseguys watch the goings-on but hang back.

The shoot is not far from League headquarters on Madison Avenue, and Joe, energized by last night's celebratory dinner, drops by the set after lunch. Ruddy immediately recognizes him and walks over to the street corner where Joe stands with a group of men.

Earlier in the day, Joe received a call from League "vocalist" Tony Darrow. Darrow informed him that he didn't get the part of the movie's Sinatra-like singer after auditioning for it. Joe doesn't mention this to Ruddy, who had already indulged Joe's "suggestion" that League loyalist and aspiring actor Gianni Russo play Carlo Rizzi, Don Corleone's obstinate son-in-law, a part that had yet to be cast.[11]

"Can you find me a Luca Brasi?" Ruddy says, half-joking. Joe's read the novel and knows the character. The author describes Luca as "a dangerous man" and "an animal" but also as Don Vito Corleone's most trusted killer.

Joe looks around and eyes Lenny Montana, a Colombo crime family bodyguard who stands over six-feet and weighs about three hundred pounds and who once worked as a pro wrestler. "There's your Luca Brasi," Joe says to Ruddy while nodding in Lenny's direction.

Ruddy sees that Montana gets a shot at the part not because he feels pressure from Joe but because Joe never asks anything for himself.[12]

Off the set, Ruddy runs into unexpected trouble in the press. He opens the morning paper and sees that he's taken a tongue-lashing on *The New York Times* editorial page, which condemns *The Godfather* producer for following IACRL's "deplorably misguided" efforts "in fighting not the Mafia but all references to its existence." The ellipsis in the March 23 editorial's title—"Yes, Mr. Ruddy, There Is a . . ."—draws attention to the studio's complicity with censorship as well as its unspoken partnership with mobsters.[13]

On the same afternoon that the censure of the Paramount-League alliance appears in the *Times*, Anthony Colombo holds another press conference to publicize additional IACRL victories. ABC-TV, Anthony announces, has agreed to refrain from using slurs against Italians in its popular detective series *The F.B.I.* He explains that this was the result of the League appealing directly to Lee Iacocca, president of Ford Motor Company, the show's sponsor. Ford responded to the League's request with the following statement: "The producer, Quinn-Martin Productions of Hollywood, does not intend to use the words 'Mafia' or 'Cosa Nostra' in the future."[14]

Anthony also makes a point of saying that IACRL's anti-defamation campaign is not limited to censoring the words "Mafia" and "Costra Nostra." By way of illustration, he discloses that the League has reached an agreement with Miles Laboratories, producer of Alka Seltzer, which will remove its popular "Magadini's Meatballs" commercial from the airwaves. Anthony points out that although the "Magadini's Meatballs" ad doesn't contain offending words, it nonetheless defames Italians. The ad, created by the Madison Avenue firm of Doyle Dane Bernbach, features a mustached man repeating, in broken English, "Mama mia, datsa soma spicy meatball."[15]

That evening, the annual International Broadcasting Award ceremony is hosted in Hollywood by the Radio and Television Society. Publicity surrounding Miles Laboratories' agreement with the League—that is, to retire the Alka Seltzer commercial—is amplified when the "Magadini's Meatballs" spot is bestowed the year's top honor in advertising.[16]

As the month comes to a close, Mary Sansone finally wins approval for a large-scale CIAO-sponsored South Brooklyn daycare center, the first of its kind serving the Italian American community. "After two years and 180 attempts," reports Pileggi in the pages of *New York* magazine, "the Congress of Italian-American Organizations, one of the city's only social-action Italian coalitions, received city approval to sponsor day-care centers and after-school and senior-citizen programs in predominantly low-income Italian neighborhoods."[17]

The New York Times, in its coverage of CIAO's ambition to open its first childcare facility, identifies eleventh-hour resistance among Community Planning Board 6 members concerned that the sponsor of the Carroll Gardens center will limit service to children of Italian background. Mary is adamant that this will not happen. While CIAO is interested in the welfare of Italian Americans, she promises that "every child of any color, race or creed will be welcome."[18]

Chapter 27

Park-Sheraton Slap (April)

News of Mary's success in procuring city funding for a CIAO-sponsored community center in Italian South Brooklyn reaches Joe. He decides it's time to double down on winning Mary's favor, and by doing so, he hopes to secure an alliance between CIAO and the League. He phones Mary, offers his congratulations, and asks if she'd like to come to an IACRL meeting in the Park-Sheraton at the end of the month. She can use the occasion to tout CIAO's accomplishments and promote the organization's future plans.

Mary is intrigued by the invitation but remains, for the moment, noncommittal. After she hangs up, she calls Nick Pileggi. "Joe Colombo contacted me again," she says. "Now he's asked me to speak about CIAO at a League meeting."

"Go," Nick says, offering to help Mary with her speech. "What have you got to lose?"[1]

The Italian American Civil Rights League publishes the inaugural issue of its new mouthpiece, *Unity News*, which contains an editorial reading, "Never in the history of the mass media, whether radio, television or the motion picture industry, has an ethnic group, or anyone else for that matter, been able to change a line in the production of a film. But the Italian American Civil Rights League has done just that."[2]

Readers of *Unity News* find little difference in font or format between it and the *Tri-Boro Post*, which has suddenly ceased circulation. Photo credit is still given to Joe Bruno, son of former *Tri-Boro Post* publisher Lou Bruno. Articles are written in the same style and tone—although now all are published without bylines and with exclusive focus on League activities. Additionally, no one is identified as the paper's editor. Instead, the editorial page lists the names of IACRL's four officers—below the name of its "founder," Joseph A. Colombo Sr.

Unity News signals a new IACRL strategy, bold but perhaps imprudent—maximum feasible exposure for Joe. The publication not only identifies Joe as League founder on its masthead but displays, on its first cover, a blown-up photo of Joe in black tie at his testimonial dinner and surrounded by IACRL officers. Beneath the photo is a headline referring Joe Jr.'s February acquittal: "The Jury Says, 'Not Guilty' and the League Wins 'Vindication.'"[3]

Joe now makes appearances in front of TV news cameras to promote the League. He gets an offer to be a guest on ABC's *The Dick Cavett Show*, a late-night TV talk fest taped in New York City that runs opposite NBC's *Tonight Show Starring Johnny Carson*. On the evening of April 14, Joe, his son Anthony, and Steve Aiello appear on *Cavett*. During the first segment, Cavett interviews Joe alone. He asks Joe what he does for a living. Joe says he works in real estate, adding that he "owns a piece of a funeral home." The host's eyes light up. The studio audience releases a nervous laugh. Joe, undaunted, describes himself as "honest and sincere business man" who is falsely accused of being a Mafia boss. There is a government conspiracy targeting him orchestrated by the FBI, he claims, which is also harassing his wife and children.

After a commercial break, Anthony Colombo and Steve Aiello join Joe onstage along with an earlier guest, Washington socialite Barbara Howar (Fig. 27.1). Anthony talks about League accomplishments and ongoing projects, such as the fundraising campaign to build a hospital. Aiello, who is the IACRL Education Task Force director, describes himself as a teacher who is concerned about the demeaning stereotypes of Italian Americans found in school textbooks.

To fight the defamation, Aiello insists that Italians must join forces with other minorities who have been maligned. "The Italian-American must learn to identify with the causes of all who are being oppressed," he says, including "the cause of Angela Davis." He finishes with a proclamation: "Power unchecked is power corrupted."[4]

IACRL's militant message is precisely what draws forty-year-old artist Aldo Tambellini to the League. Ever since he appeared alongside Mary Sansone on New York public television's *Newsfront* last July, Tambellini has been an outspoken proponent of the League's aggressive anti-defamation stance.

Figure 27.1. *The Dick Cavett Show*, April 1971; left to right, Barbara Howar, Joseph Colombo Sr., Anthony Colombo, Dick Cavett, and Steve Aiello. *Source:* ABC Photo Archives/Getty Images. Used with permission.

In the summer of 1959, Tambellini arrived on the Lower East Side, which was undergoing slum clearance in the name of "urban renewal." The gutted carcasses of buildings reminded Tambellini of his early teens in Italy, when his hometown of San Concordio was destroyed by bombings during World War II before being liberated by "Buffalo Soldiers," an all-Black infantry in the Army's Ninety-Second Division. Tambellini's civilian exposure to the horror of war caused him to suffer posttraumatic stress, but his introduction to African Americans as liberators at war's end would shape his adult understanding of art as well as freedom.

Born in Syracuse, New York, Tambellini left for Italy with his family when he was an eighteen-month-old child, and he didn't return to his country of birth until after World War II. Back in the US, Tambellini, who spoke English with a heavy Italian accent, aspired to be an artist but struggled to fit into the burgeoning commercial artworld. In the early 1960s, he found a home in New York City's kinetic underground counterculture, where he organized public art events in nontraditional venues, including the first loft show in an area soon to be known as SoHo. By the mid-1960s, Tambellini had started painting directly on film, an innovation that pioneered the video art movement. At the same time, he was developing close ties with Black artists, including N. H. Pritchard and Ismael Reed, members of the African American Umbra Collective. This was the context in which he created his *Black Film Series*, within which he produced *Black TV*, an intermedia installation that won the 1969 International Gran Prix at the Oberhausen Film Festival.

In Tambellini's eyes, Joe Colombo is Italian America's Malcolm X. After watching Joe on *The Dick Cavett Show*, Tambellini decides he must attend a League meeting. He arrives at the Park-Sheraton wearing Lower East Side counterculture couture: black beret, turtleneck, and jeans. Entering the crowded ballroom, Tambellini thinks to himself: I've been thrown into an Edward G. Robinson picture. He takes a breath. The air is heavy with Aramis. The chandeliers give off a moldering dimness. Middle-aged men in double-breasted, wide lapelled blue serge suits walk the aisles. Women wearing bouffant hairdos cluster in the back (Fig. 27.2).

The next day, Tambellini phones the League. He gives his name and asks the receptionist how he can get permission to videotape IACRL activities. He's told someone will look into it and call him back. The next morning, he receives a call inviting him to League headquarters on Madison

Figure 27.2. Joe Colombo stands and speaks from behind a lectern at the front of the ballroom inside midtown Manhattan's Park-Sheraton Hotel, where IACRL members and nonmembers gather to discuss the organization and its activities, 1971. Seated next to Joe Colombo on his left is his son Anthony; Steve Aiello sits three seats to Joe Colombo's right. *Source:* Anthony and Carol Colombo Family Archive. Used with permission.

170 | Rebel Girl and the Godfather

Avenue that afternoon. He arrives at the scheduled time and is escorted to a conference room where Joe sits, eyeglasses in hand, sifting through a pile of papers. Aides scurry around the table and almost appear to bow toward Joe in peasant supplication.[5]

Tambellini observes the acolytes from just inside the door frame. Joe looks up and asks without prompting, "Why should we let you record the League?"

Tambellini is caught off guard. In a halting Italian accent, he replies, "I am an artist. I am Italian American. I've felt prejudice because I'm Italian—as an artist."

"You might be surprised," Joe says, "but other artists have come to me and said to me the same story." Leaning forward, he asks, "Who do you work for?"

"No one. I am independent. I am an artist. I believe in your cause—in what you are doing."

Without fanfare, Joe gives Tambellini his blessing.

Nicholas Pileggi stands on the corner of Mott and Grand Streets in Little Italy waiting for filming to begin on the set of *The Godfather* movie. It's almost noon. Earlier in the morning, he witnessed Nat Marcone, IACRL president, deploy League captains to knock on doors of the narrow, tenement-lined street to make sure residents knew to cooperate. He also watches as hired security for Paramount strong-arm and remove a photographer from the *Daily News* trying to sneak a picture of Marlon Brando in full Vito Corleone makeup.[6]

This afternoon, Coppola is filming the scene where gang rivals of an aging Vito Corleone attempt to murder him. Loud shots hammer the streets as the godfather's assassins fire their guns. An overturned vegetable cart spills bright fruit across gray pavement, where the victim is sprawled.

Pileggi eyes the edge of the set. He jots notes he'll use to write his *New York Times Sunday Magazine* feature. "The people of Mott Street watched in silence from tenement windows, fire escapes and rooftops as the gunmen slipped away. Then, to spontaneous applause, the grim site tableau came to life, and the old man—the godfather, Marlon Brando—lifted himself slowly from the ground, smiled at the cheering crowd and bowed."[7]

The natives can't believe a movie is being made about them. Pileggi's focus is interrupted by the wiseguy standing next to him on the corner. "They hold pieces like flowers," he says by way of instructing Pileggi on the finer points of authentic gangsterdom. "A man of that stature," he continues, pointing to Brando, "would never wear a hat like that. They never pinched in the front like that. Italian block, that's the way they wore them, Italian block."[8]

For the remainder of the day, Pileggi's attention is turned toward the edge of the set, where a wiseguy runs back and forth between the street corner and Ferrara's on Grand. There, Carlo Gambino sits—holding court and drinking coffee—while receiving updates on the shoot.

At the end of the month, Mary attends an IACRL meeting at the Park-Sheraton. League regulars are wary of Mary. It's rumored that she rebuffed IACRL's offer to form an alliance with CIAO. Some are put off by what they perceive to be Mary's superior attitude. Many are simply not comfortable with a woman who takes charge in public.

Mary wears a white dress with modest embroidery. She is ushered to her chair on the dais. She looks out at the sea of faces and recognizes Rose, who set up the meeting with Joe Colombo back in November and who worked out of Mary's basement on the Procaccino mayoral campaign.

Mary is the featured speaker at tonight's meeting. She waits while others onstage speak before she gets her turn. Finally, Mary rises from her seat and moves toward the podium to lukewarm applause. She reaches up to adjust the microphone but before she can pull it down to her chin, a man standing at the floor mic says, "Mrs. Sansone, we've got a few questions to ask you." Mary, startled, looks up. She doesn't recognize her inquisitor.[9]

She glances at League leadership sitting on either side of her on the dais. She turns back to the audience, looks directly at the man at the microphone, and says in a firm voice, "I wasn't aware that I was invited to an interrogation."

The room is on edge.

The man says, "I have two questions. Are you affiliated with Ralph Salerno, and are you associated with Nick Pileggi?"

Mary looks back at him. "I don't have to answer that." Speaking to everyone in the room, "But I will. I am not associated or affiliated with Ralph Salerno or Nick Pileggi," she says, before adding, "We're just friends and I admire what they do."

Grumblings can be heard from the audience.

The room settles and Mary begins. She explains that her remarks tonight are drawn from a CIAO report and its findings, specifically on the topic of the relationship between the Italian poor and the city's failing schools. Mary tells the audience that CIAO is collaborating with the CUNY-Richmond Center for Migration Studies, located in Dongan Hills on Staten Island, which is led by two dynamic Scalabrini priests, Silvano Tomasi, who holds a doctorate in sociology from Fordham University, and his brother, Reverend Lydio Tomasi. CIAO is working with the center to complete a statistical analysis of Italian communities across the five boroughs.[10]

"Did you know," Mary begins, "that the poverty areas in New York containing fifty percent or more first- and second-generation Italians are all in Brooklyn? I'm talking about neighborhoods where many of us live. Bushwick, Coney Island, South Brooklyn, Williamsburg.

"In these poverty areas, the high school dropout rate among Italian youth is over fifty percent. That means half the Italian kids in the neighborhoods where many of us live are dropouts. That leads to unemployment and drug abuse.

"If you look at Italian neighborhoods in New York, our kids on average complete only the first year of high school. The average for all the other ethnic groups in the city is three years. That's two more years of high school for non-Italian youth. This disparity in education for our children is not acceptable.

"How can we bring down the Italian dropout rate? We can start by demanding that City Hall fund bilingual education for our children in elementary school. There are over 4,000 children in New York City for whom Italian is their first language, which means when they enter school they struggle to learn because classes are taught in English. Many of these kids end up dropping out, and that's just the beginning their problems—and ours."

Mary times her presentation for twenty minutes. She's mindful not to reference Mafia or Cosa Nostra or crime of any kind in her presentation, but when she's finished, she looks up and sees the man who asked the earlier question about Ralph Salerno and Nick Pileggi standing once again behind the floor mic.

"Mrs. Sansone," he says, "we have proof that you testified as an expert before the crime commission."

This guy is like a dog with a bone, Mary thinks. "I never testified as an expert before a crime commission," she states delusively (she is not a crime expert even if she did testify before a crime commission), "so I don't know where you got your phony proof from." Finally, she declares, "I'm not an authority on crime."

Chaos ensues. Anthony Colombo, sitting on the stage, breaks in. He tries to explain. "Mrs. Sansone, you insulted us and we didn't insult you."

Michael Pesce, a young Legal Aid Society lawyer from Carroll Gardens and a member of CIAO's executive board, stands up from his seat in the audience and shouts, a calm but lone voice in a sea of agitated faces, "What did she say that's so bad? I know Mary Sansone. Nobody fights harder for our community on behalf of the Italian poor than this woman."

"Well," Anthony says, "she said *she's* not an authority on crime." He pauses. "Meaning *we* are."

Mary speaks. "That's not true. I said, 'I, Mary Crisalli Sansone, am not an authority on crime.' I didn't mention anyone else."

Another man, well-dressed and heavy-set, steps up to the mic and asks a question. "Mrs. Sansone, is it true that you can't become a member of CIAO unless you got a PhD?"

A rough voice from the back of the room shouts, "What's a PhD?"

The large man standing at the mic answers, "It's a degree."

"Well," the rough voice cracks, "even a thermometer's got a degree, and you know what you can do with that!"

Laughter erupts from the room.

The man at the floor mic continues. "Mrs. Sansone, I never heard of CIAO before tonight, and I live in Bensonhurst."

"From the looks of you, sir, you don't need CIAO." Mary's retort elicits angry howls from the audience. It's after one o'clock in the morning and Mary has heard enough, but she's determined to have the last word. "Dear friends, I came here to talk to you about CIAO. Apparently, some of you are not interested in the welfare of the poor. Thank you and good night."

She walks away from the podium, but instead of returning to her seat she heads toward the steps at the edge of the stage. Joe, who has been standing at the corner of the dais and observing, intercepts her path to the stairs.

Mary pauses in front of Joe. The ballroom holds its breath.

"Mrs. Sansone," Joe declares in a loud and magnanimous voice, "thank you for coming tonight."

Joe holds a League pin between his fingertips. "In appreciation . . ."

But before Joe can pin her, Mary slaps his hand away, slips by him, and races off the stage.

Boos rain down from the audience. Mary pushes through the noise, clearing a path for herself with the resolve of a Sherman tank. Above the din, a woman's voice trails her out the door, taunting, "Kill her! Kill her!"[11]

Chapter 28

CIAO Coalition (May)

At the next IACRL meeting at the Park-Sheraton, Mary Sansone and CIAO are the target. Joe, dressed conservatively in a dark suit and tie, stands behind the podium. The floor mic is open, and he calls on League member Rose to address the room. "I'm very nervous because I've kept quiet for so long but I couldn't keep quiet anymore. I will do my best to make my point, which is this. Mary Sansone is crooked."[1]

Rose, a middle-aged woman who wears large medallion earrings crowned by a tight black bouffant, is dressed in a form-fitting outfit accented with a white stripe down the left side. She crosses her arms in a defensive posture, clears her throat, and continues: "I've known Mary Sansone for a long time. I worked with her on the Procaccino campaign in Brooklyn. I worked with her for two years on CIAO. But no more."

Rose recites Mary's alleged transgressions. "Whatever money CIAO made went right into Mary Sansone's pocket. Nothing was ever done for the people. If someone ever went to her for a job, she would send them to an employment agency. CIAO had dances and luncheons and she never gave an account of any of the money. This woman has taken $25,000 out of CIAO and no one knows where it goes. She never did anything for anyone other than bring the money to the bank."

Rose warns the gathering of Mary's ambition. "She's having a big dinner Friday night. She has now organized a new coalition. This man is coming from Washington. This man will be at her dinner. She's going to do what she wants because she doesn't care for anyone. She never says the good that Mr. Colombo does, but she will say the good that she does. And what Joe Colombo has done for the League, we need a hell of a lot more men like him."

Rose's rant is met by raucous applause. Others in attendance rise and take their turn testifying to Mary's affront to the League's cause. Joe, for the moment, refrains from addressing the matter of Mary Sansone. Instead, he attacks, for the first time in public, the organization that he covertly started—Americans of Italian Descent—and its current president, former US Congressman Alfred Santangelo.

"You all have heard of the organization called AID. I want to tell you something. AID has never done anything for the Italian people."

Joe takes a breadth before restarting. "I'm going to tell you a little story I've never told before. AID has spent $550,000 that we, the people, went and raised. We gave the concert in Madison Square Garden. We brought Sammy Davis there. We sold memberships. AID hasn't done anything. And the President of AID right now doesn't even know who funded his organization. Doesn't know where it's coming from."

Joe references the Liuni adoption case in his attack on AID. "And when a little girl from Upstate . . ." Anger rises from his voice. "The judge says: she has blue eyes, blond hair, could not be adopted by Italian people because she couldn't be Italian (my mother's got blue eyes!), that we are bastards.

"I said to AID, 'Please, get out there and fight this.' They said, 'Wait, we gotta think, we got a lot of judges, we got a lot of congressmen. We gotta walk very careful.'"

Next, Joe attacks AID's newspaper. "In this paper, *The Challenge*, which we bought for $25,000. *We* bought it. Mr. Santangelo didn't buy it. *We* raised the money for that paper. He doesn't even know where the money came from.

"We went out, store to store, door to door, and signed members. And do you know until today a lot of people don't know who AID is and they confuse it with us? Everything that we do he prints in his paper. He takes credit for it."

Joe turns his attention from AID to CIAO.

"Getting back to CIAO, let me tell you something." While speaking, Joe thrusts his index finger repeatedly at the audience to reinforce his point. "Now you're fighting a different thing. It's not willful ignorance. It's divide and conquer. The Nixon Administration is worried that this organization, the Italian American Civil Rights League, is fighting for the rights of people. I want you to know that Ralph Salerno is on the board of directors of CIAO.

"I want you to know that they have a tax-exempt stamp," Joe continues. "I want you to know that, if anything, they are political. We are not political. I want you to know that they get anything they want.

"Why? Only because they want to stop this League. But believe me when I tell you, and listen to me close, they have the Administration, they have the people who have never done anything. We have God on our side. He's there. He'll be there. He'll not turn His face on the work we're doing. Our work is sincere, it's just, it's good, it will continue that way."

Joe finally takes direct aim at Mary.

"And Mrs. Sansone, who got on the radio program and said, 'The Italian American Civil Rights League is militant . . .' " Joe lowers his voice. "It's not militant, hasn't been militant," his voice rises, "but she'd better pray to God we never do get militant!" Joe brings the audience to its feet.

Mary receives threats from anonymous phone callers.[2]

Nick Pileggi tries to put Mary's mind at ease. "Number one," he says, "Colombo won't go after a woman. Number two, he knows your connection to Ralph Salerno and me. Three, a thousand people saw what happened."

Friends phone her with words of encouragement. One call, from Uncle Joe, her mother's kid brother, Mary can't shake from her mind.

"I heard what happened at the League meeting. Everybody's talking about it."

"I've already moved on."

"Mary, you stood eight feet tall that night!"

Silence.

"Mary, I don't want you to worry."

"I'm not worried."

"Still, I don't want you to. You know Joey Gallo?"

"Isn't he in jail?"

"He's back in the old neighborhood. I ran into him on President Street. He says to me, 'I heard all about what Mary did. Tell your niece not to worry about anything because Colombo is gone.' "

Mary finds an excuse to hang up. She knows there's bad blood between Colombo and Gallo. But she stays as far away from their feud as possible.

She's having a big dinner Friday night.

On Friday, May 14, the Congress of Italian American Organizations holds its fourth annual dinner dance in Bensonhurst at the Cotillion Terrace banquet hall.

Figure 28.1. Program cover for the annual CIAO dinner dance event, Bensonhurst, May 1971. *Source:* CIAO. Author's collection.

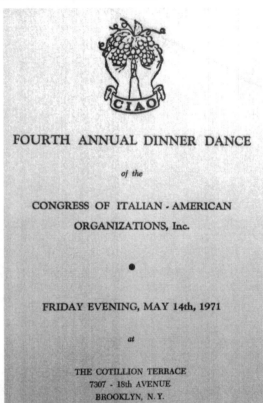

Several hundred guests honor Rev. Tomasi from the Center for Migration Studies as CIAO's Man of the Year. Behind a microphone, Mary presents the award to the reverend, proclaiming, "Father Tomasi's life is dedicated to God and his fellow man." She admires the reverend, who, like Mary, has the gall to call out the *prominente* in public. He does so, for instance, in Brooklyn's *National Italian-American News.* "Old empty balloons claiming to be the leaders of the American Italian communities have simply talked and talked and talked," Tomasi chastises. "They have talked about the defamation of Italians, of the need to build monuments, and on the necessity of parades, with the only result being that they have pocketed the meager treasury collected for those purposes."[3]

Rev. Tomasi thanks Mary and her social-action organization for the award and for the work they do. Mary returns to the podium to update those in attendance about CIAO's collaboration with Tomasi's Center for Migration Studies on the first demographic study of Italians in New York City. Mary remains at the mic and reflects on the road CIAO has traveled to get here tonight. "In the years to come," she begins, "we will look back on the last twelve months as the year we took the giant step forward—going from the planning stage to the actual implementation of those social, civic and educational programs envisioned five years ago. The going couldn't be described as smooth. We were on our own all the way. We were not funded and there were no models in the Italian-American community we could turn to as examples to emulate."[4]

Everyone in attendance knows that without Mary's optimism and tenacity there would be no CIAO. "City Hall," Mary says looking at Mayor Lindsay, who attends the annual event for the first time in CIAO's history, "has singled out CIAO to operate two daycare centers for pre-school children of working parents in communities Italian-American in character. The city's Department of Social Services has granted CIAO the exclusive mandate to come up with other areas where Italians are heavily concentrated and in need of such services, such as after-school and senior citizen's programs. Our demographic study will help us make this determination."

She never says the good that Mr. Colombo does, but she will say the good that she does.

Joe is boxed out. Only CIAO, not the League or any other Italian American organization, has been awarded antipoverty funding from the city.

CBS News cameras roll as Mary introduces the mayor (Fig. 28.2). Nicholas Pileggi attends the fête. Writing in *New York* magazine, he reports, "When introduced by its president, Mary Sansone, who like many of the 500 attending the dinner had supported Procaccino in the last campaign, Lindsay was surprised to hear himself being cheered."[5]

Lindsay has boxed out Meade Esposito. As Democratic Party boss, Esposito wants the patronage jobs that come with community development projects like Mary's. By throwing the support of city hall behind Mary—who has never had a strong allegiance to either major political party and who despises clubhouse politics—Lindsay maneuvers to build his own base of power among the city's white ethnic voters.

This man is coming from Washington. This man will be at her dinner.

The New York Times coverage of CIAO's dinner dance focuses not on the mayor's first-time appearance at the event but on the attendance of

Figure 28.2. New York City Mayor John Lindsay and CIAO President Mary Sansone honoring the Rev. Silvano Tomasi as Man of the Year at the annual CIAO dinner dance event, Brooklyn, May 1971. *Source:* Charles Frattini/New York Daily News. Used with permission.

Washington insider named Ralph J. Perrotta, a thirty-seven-year-old ethnic affairs specialist for the National Urban Coalition.

She has now organized a new coalition.

According to the *Times* coverage of the dinner dance, Mary makes public a "new alliance" between CIAO and the Washington-based Urban Coalition "to bring ethnic Americans and minority groups together" to deal with the problems "facing both the white working class and the black poor." The Urban Coalition assigns Perrotta to run the New York Project within its Manhattan office, which is funded by a civic-religious-business-labor alliance originally launched in the aftermath of the 1967 summer riots by Mayor Lindsay. CIAO will team with the New York Project to promote interracial cooperation via neighborhood development throughout the city.[6]

Joe's lawyer, Barry Slotnick, calls his client to cancel their morning meeting. This afternoon, another Slotnick client, Rabbi Meir Kahane, is going before a judge at the federal courthouse in Brooklyn. Slotnick is worried that the judge is likely to set the bail too high for Kahane to pay, and he explains to Joe that he needs more time to prepare Kahane's case. Joe doesn't know Kahane personally but he knows about the rabbi's organization, the Jewish Defense League. In fact, on December 31 last year, Joe joined three hundred members of the Italian American Civil Rights League in support of a JDL-sponsored rally to protest the Soviet Union's unjust treatment of its Jewish population.[7]

At the time, an FBI agent dispatches a memo, filed under "92-12264: ITALIAN AMERICAN CIVIL RIGHTS LEAGUE," to Washington headquarters detailing individuals "representing selves as members of captioned organization join[ing] members of Jewish Defense League in demonstration at Foley Square. Among individuals observed participating were LCN boss Joseph Colombo, ———, Nat Marcone, Rocco Miraglia and Caesar Vitale. New York news media provided coverage of this demonstration."[8]

Today, when Slotnick enters the Brooklyn Federal Courthouse for Kahane's arraignment, who does he see seated in the first row of the gallery? Joe Colombo.

"What are you doing here?"

"You told me the rabbi is in trouble," Joe says.

During the courtroom proceedings, Kahane is arraigned with several of his JDL followers on conspiracy charges under the 1968 Federal Gun Control Act. The judge sets bail at $45,000 for Kahane and his accomplices.

Joe puts up the bail.

Kahane is lifted onto the shoulders of JDL supporters. Held aloft, Kahane holds Joe's hand in a sign of unity as he's swept out of the courthouse.

An impromptu press conference is held in front of the building. Colombo and Kahane announce an alliance between IACRL and JDL. "Conspiracy is synonymous with frame," Joe asserts. "The federal government is using provocateurs and framed charges to harass the League."[9]

Joe connects the League's struggle to JDL's. "There is a conspiracy in this country against Italians and the same tactics are now being used against Rabbi Kahane." Joe says that Kahane "is fighting for his people in Russia and we're fighting for our people here. If they need our support, we will give it."[10]

Kahane returns the favor, saying, "We would picket the offices of the F.B.I. if Mr. Colombo asks our help."[11]

The media frenzy surrounding the IACRL-JDL alliance rivals the publicity generated in February when Paramount Pictures announced its concessions to the League. In the next day's *New York Times*, a four-column page 1 headline reads, "Kahane and Colombo Join Forces to Fight Reported U.S. Harassment." Below the headline is a photo of Kahane and Colombo, standing in front of the federal courthouse, smiling at one another.[12]

Joe, once IACRL's engine, is now its anchor. Even prominent supporters of the League are increasingly skeptical about the long-term viability of the organization whose public face is a mob boss. Before the month is out, Meade Esposito meets privately with Joe "to discuss ways of ridding the League of any image of underworld connections and molding it into a powerful political force," according to an anonymous source quoted in the *Daily News*.[13]

In 1958, when Esposito was fifty-two years old, he saw himself as a New Deal Democrat who understood the importance of building coalitions with Brooklyn's powerful Jewish voting blocs. During his successful insurgent campaign, Esposito captured the endorsement of New York reform movement leaders Herbert H. Lehman and Eleanor Roosevelt. As Daniel Bell explained in 1953, urban machine operatives had a history of embracing liberal causes, including FDR's New Deal and Truman's Fair Deal, and concluded, "The basic measures of the New Deal, which most Americans today agree were necessary for the public good, would not have been possible without the support of the 'corrupt' big-city machines."[14]

Esposito was streetwise. He quit Manual Trades High School at the age of fourteen and went into the bail bonds business, where he freely acknowledged that some of his clients were mobsters, "including," he said, "Joe Colombo, Jimmy Napoli, and Apples McIntosh."[15]

He founded the Thomas Jefferson Democratic Club in Canarsie to challenge the Irish incumbent in Brooklyn's Fifth District. "This guy called me a guinea bastard," Esposito later said of the former district leader. "He said you could buy an Italian with a beer. He said that behind my back. I decided to get him."[16]

Esposito did just that. He campaigned not only by knocking on doors in his district but by asking residents if they had any parking tickets they needed "taken care of." His opponent, informed of the scheme, alerted the police so that Esposito would be arrested as soon as he tried to put the "fix" in. On the hook for thousands of dollars' worth of tickets, Esposito out-maneuvered his opponent by paying off his debt with savings he accrued while working as a bail bondsman.[17]

By 1969, Esposito had shed all pretense to being a reform politician when he rose from district to county leader of the Democratic Party, the largest and *most powerful big-city patronage machine this side of Chicago.* The New York Times *profiled the new boss as a self-educated man who spoke three languages and read "everything from Mickey Mouse to Plato."* Asked about his agenda for his new position, Esposito still expressed progressive ideals by highlighting *"his plans to involve more Brooklynites, especially young people, in party activities and to involve his organization more deeply in community activities."*[18]

Esposito asks Joe to step away from the League.

At the last IACRL meeting of the month, Joe explains his predicament to a gathering packed inside the Park-Sheraton ballroom. "I met with a man," Joe begins, without referring to Esposito by name, "that I would say is one of the finest Italians that we have—quiet, strong, and has come a long way, and his voice is very loud, far and powerful. He said, 'Joe, if you were not with the League, I believe many, many, many big politicians would step-in in one minute and come forth for this League and join this League.'"[19]

"And my answer to him was, 'All you gotta do is sit down with me and show me these people that will let me know and let me see that they have this League's interest at heart and that they would continue to do the work that the League has been endeavoring to do and to keep working for the people, *for the people*. Then I will call the press conference, and I will say that I will just step down.'

"But I've heard them words with AID. I heard the same thing. 'Joe, step to the back and don't worry, we can do it, you've done enough, you'll see the job we'll do.' And, lo and behold, I didn't see any job but I did see a lot of money go down the drain that was worked so hard for, and I've seen so many wonderful, wonderful people that got discouraged and have now been embittered.

"I asked this man if it was possible that the same thing is happening now that happened before with AID. He said, 'Joe, I can't answer that. I couldn't honestly say that wouldn't happen.'

"I said to him, 'Well, until that happens, then Joe Colombo will be right here. Joe Colombo will be watching over the League, fighting for the League, doing everything I can for the League. And as long as God wants me here, nobody can take me away.'"

"A camp for underprivileged kids," according to news coverage, "is Colombo's lifelong dream." Right now, it's also a distraction for Joe, who pays a steep price for his defiance. To alleviate the stress, Joe attends to readying Camp

Unity, an upstate summer retreat for inner city youth, in time to open immediately after next month's Unity Day rally. He tells a reporter, "Just think, 3,000 kids will get out of New York and see what the country is like. They will be able to breath unpolluted air, swim, eat." The camp will be free and open to all children, he adds, regardless of race or religion.[20]

The League allocates $280,000 to purchase 266 acres of land in an isolated part of Ulster County near Rosendale, New York. It's not far from Joe's Blooming Grove estate. IACRL also spends thousands of dollars rehabilitating the property, most recently the home of Schroeder's Mountain Lake Resort, which contains an old camp and two large lakes. Two swimming pools, one with access for people with disabilities, are installed. A small army of carpenters, bricklayers, plumbers, electricians, and engineers make improvements to the facilities, which include twenty-two refurbished bungalows soon to house 250 kids every week of the summer. Each bungalow has a rustic plaque nailed to its front door and engraved with the name of a celebrated Italian American. The honorees range from FBI founder Charles Bonaparte and America's first saint, Frances Xavier Cabrini, to Hollywood entertainer Frank Sinatra and Democratic Party leader Meade Esposito.[21]

Preparations for the second annual Unity Day event increasingly consume Joe's attention. The mayor dispatches his assistant, Urban Task Force leader Barry Gottehrer, to work with the League on logistics. Gottehrer will also be the mayor's representative at this year's Unity Day. Like last year, the rally is scheduled for the last Monday in June, although city hall anticipates an even larger gathering in Columbus Circle. This year, however, Sammy Davis Jr. will be the headliner, and according to Harlem's *Amsterdam News*, Aretha Franklin will perform if her tour of Italy doesn't delay her return to the States.[22]

Police officials worry about crowd control for the event and want it held in an area that is easier to secure. Gottehrer arranges for League officers to meet with the deputy commissioner of Parks, Teddy Mastroianni, who suggests that the rally be held in Sheep Meadow, an area in the southwest corner of Central Park. Officers from the League inspect the site. Large trees block unobstructed views of where the city proposes to locate the stage. League officers insist on removing the trees.[23]

"Those are 100-year-old maples," a stunned Parks official says, adding, "You can't go around cutting down trees in Central Park."

"Don't worry," a League official says. "I'll send some boys around late tonight. They'll take care of it. Nobody will notice a thing."[24]

Columbus Circle is back in play. Joe, in a reprise of last year's performance, is invited to NYPD Centre Street headquarters to discuss details. Gottehrer arrives at a second-floor conference room. Twenty top police officials are sitting around a conference table with Joe Colombo. The scene is surreal, Gottehrer thinks. Police negotiating with a reputed Mafia boss on how he can stage a protest rally against the FBI.

An IACRL official has set up audiovisual equipment on the table and, on Joe's command, starts the show. An architect's rendering of the Columbus Circle stage appears on the wall. Gottehrer watches as diagrams of the positions of hot dog vendors, a schedule of events, and a breakdown of costs fly by to the sound of a musical score. *A veritable off-Broadway production*, Gottehrer thinks. He surveys the room. Decorated officers, apparently impressed by Joe's pitch, green-light the League's Unity Day plans.[25]

"Mafia, what's the Mafia?" Joe retorts, responding to this media question for the umpteenth time. "There is not a Mafia," he explains to the reporter. "Am I the head of a family? Yes. My wife and four sons and a daughter. That's my family."[26]

The Mafia—fact or fiction? Paradoxically, Joe's unrelenting denial of its existence coupled with the League's successful censorship campaign keeps the word in the public eye. Louis Harris and Associates polling company, which produces surveys that are syndicated in newspapers across the county, takes notice. To measure public opinion on the topic, Harris polls 1,508 households nationwide in the spring of 1971. The results of the survey, along with commentary by Louis Harris, appear on page 1 of the May 17 edition of the *Chicago Tribune*. The article's title, "Most Believe There's a Mafia," signposts the article's conclusion—"The survey would indicate that the protestations of Colombo and his group simply do not hold water with most Americans."

The figures Harris uses to support his conclusion include evidence that a majority of Americans surveyed believe, by a margin of 17 to 78 percent, that "there is a secret organization engaged in organized crime in this country which is called the Mafia." When IACRL officials see the same figures, they interpret the evidence differently. Isn't it possible that these same data can be used to confirm the League's contention that Americans are conditioned to believe spurious national myths, such as the one about an omnipresent Mafia?

According to Harris, the survey also demonstrates that citizens, by a 24 to 57 percent margin, reject the assertion that the Mafia is exclusively Italian. "Thus," Harris concludes, "the claims of some alleged leaders of the Mafia that . . . charges of a secret criminal organization are part of a pattern of ethnic prejudice, appear to have left large numbers of the American people unimpressed." IACRL officials wonder why these same data aren't evidence of the success of the League's year-long campaign to abolish the defamatory association between Italians and crime in the minds of Americans.[27]

Chapter 29

Scorpio (June)

"No one can be certain just when the Italian-American revolution began," opens Nicholas Pileggi's *New York* magazine cover story, which appears in anticipation of this month's second annual Unity Day.

Figure 29.1. Cover of *New York* magazine, June 7, 1971, featuring Nicholas Pileggi's report on the rise of "Italian Power" in New York City. *Source:* New York Magazine/Vox Media. Used with permission.

Taking the pulse of Italian Power, Pileggi finds that "no matter how disreputable its leader," Joe Colombo's League "has activated New York's traditionally disenfranchised working-class Italians" to an extent previously unimaginable. The buzz created by Joe and his civil rights outfit is foregrounded in the piece, but Pileggi makes a point of crediting Mary Sansone for the inroads she's made into city hall on behalf of CIAO. While Joe and the League make headlines, Mary has been leading what Nancy Seifer, the mayor's twenty-seven-year-old ethnic affairs aide, identifies as another kind of revolution: "a quiet revolution . . . in white working class communities . . . which will enable the poor to form coalitions."[1]

Nancy Seifer was an idealist. In the immediate aftermath of Martin Luther King Jr.'s assassination, she was impressed by John Lindsay's ability to do what no other big-city mayor had done: defuse racial tensions in Black ghettos by showing compassion. A former Peace Corps worker, Seifer had been accepted into Columbia University's School of Journalism and was set to begin classes in the fall of 1969 when, at the start of summer, she decided to volunteer on Lindsay's reelection campaign. Her youthful vivacity on display, she was quickly put in charge of organizing the campaign's "special committees," which were made up of doctors, lawyers, teachers, and social workers. As summer turned to fall, Seifer—fearing a Procaccino victory—withdrew from graduate school rather than abandon the campaign.[2]

As a reward for her loyalty and hard work, Seifer was offered employment in the second Lindsay administration. She accepted a position that complemented her interest in journalism: director of the City Hall Neighborhood Press Office under Press Secretary Tom Morgan. Seifer and her staff of four spent part of each day scouring the city's two hundred-plus ethnic and foreign-language newspapers, a list that included the Colombo-financed Tri-Boro Post. *They did so in order to locate problems that needed to be addressed but that, in the past, had gone unnoticed by Lindsay officials. Seifer's office collected information in the form of newspaper clippings on everything from potholes to policing and then advocated on behalf of neighborhoods by bringing their concerns directly to the appropriate agencies within city hall.*[3]

With the new fiscal year fast approaching at the month's end, Mayor Lindsay and Governor Rockefeller hammered out an eleventh-hour city budget. The outcome was a "retrenchment" in city hall, where a number of agencies, including the Neighborhood Press Office, were sacrificed in the name of austerity. Seifer, who had been running a year-long memo writing campaign inside city hall advocating on behalf of white ethnic communities, was reassigned to work under Chief of Staff Jay L. Kriegel. Her new title: aide to the mayor for ethnic affairs. She remained one of the few women in the Lindsay administration and the only female mayoral aide.

In her new capacity as an aide to Mayor Lindsay, Nancy Seifer attends a CIAO-sponsored meeting one evening in Little Italy. She's heard of Mary Sansone but this is the first time Seifer has an opportunity to see Mary in action. Mary informs residents about CIAO's proposal to build a neighborhood senior center on Mott Street and then solicits feedback on the plan from her audience. Seifer is impressed by Mary's energy, ideas, and performance. In a memo addressed to her former boss, Press Secretary Tom Morgan, Seifer urges him "to have the mayor mention CIAO . . . headed by Mary Sansone" at his next opportunity. "Until yesterday," she continues, "I had only heard about the things they were doing . . . last night, I really saw. . . . They [older people] couldn't believe they were getting anything. This was the first time."[4]

Seifer's memo also details the "total commitment" on the part of city hall's Human Resources Administration ("Sugarman's office") to building CIAO's Little Italy senior center facility. She highlights the fact that Mary "made clear that while sponsored by an Italian group, the Center is for everyone in the area—that it would be open to Chinese, Puerto Rican and Blacks as well." Her memo addresses how residents in attendance respond to Mary's pitch. "The people were delighted (the meeting was interrupted several times by applause), although some were somewhat skeptical, due to constant disappointments in the past."[5]

Seifer's memo reports that "the most interesting aspect of the meeting was the fact that 2 Blacks" accompanied Mary on the dais. One was there "to explain" how city hall would provide jobs for people living in Little Italy; the other, "to tell all those who were poor and wanted a college education, with remedial help, for their children, to call him" at Brooklyn's Long Island University. "The waves at the meeting were beautiful," the memo closes. "There was no hint of racism anywhere. Only tremendous appreciation on the part of old, young and middle-aged Italians—hundreds of them—in the audience."[6]

Among Lindsay's inner circle, Nancy Seifer becomes Mary's number-one advocate.

At 176 Elizabeth Street—a block south from where Bayard Rustin happened to live less than a decade earlier and a block north from the site of CIAO's proposed senior center—lives Little Italy resident Jerome Addison Johnson, a twenty-four-year-old Black man who shares a one-room apartment with his pet monkey. His possessions are few: a book on the origins of Christianity titled *Fragments of a Faith Forgotten*, a picture of Adolf Hitler, a stash of pornographic photos, a gold and maroon cape, a serape, a black cane, a riding crop, a curved Indian sword, a 7.65-mm. Menta, and a box of cartridges.[7]

On occasion, he resides at other addresses in the area, including the Chelsea Hotel and Hotel Christopher, the latter of which houses a tawdry after-hours club operated by the Gambino crime family. Johnson is known to hang around the club, called Christopher's End, described in John Paul Hudson's recently published *Gay Insider* as "a bar that goes beyond tacky to truly trashy."[8]

Johnson was a seeker and a survivor, a dreamer and a degenerate. Born in Waycross, Georgia, he moved to New Brunswick, New Jersey, at age nine. A 1963 graduate of New Brunswick High School, he arrived in Los Angeles as an aspiring filmmaker just before the Watts riots. People close to Johnson, including Italian American playwright Joseph Tuotti, almost never saw him without a camera during his six years in southern California.

Tuotti, when he first met Johnson, had recently authored Big Time Buck White. *The play became the first production to open at the Frederick Douglass Theater in Watts. A smash hit in Los Angeles, it had a short run on Broadway, where the lead was played by Muhammad Ali (billed as Cassius Clay), who had been recently stripped of his Heavyweight Champion boxing title for refusing the wartime draft. During this period, Tuotti and Johnson engaged in deep conversations "exploring reactions to racism against Italian Americans and blacks." Their connection, as characterized by Tuotti, went "much further than friendship." It bordered on "mystical."*[9]

Johnson's Hollywood break never materialized, and he turned to petty crime. According to Los Angeles police records, Johnson was first arrested in the summer of 1966 for "soliciting sales without a license." A year and a half later, he received three-month's probation for possession of marijuana. In August 1968, he was charged with rape and burglary. Both cases were dropped. A year later, in September 1969, another charge of burglary was reduced to trespassing and he was given ninety days in county jail.

While in the penitentiary, Johnson cut a cellmate with a razor and was charged with assault with the intent to commit murder. The charge was reduced to assault with a deadly weapon, and according to the Los Angeles Times, "he was released on probation so that he could return to New Jersey."[10]

According to LA County Probation Department reports, Johnson sometimes went by the aliases Jerome Rand or Addison Rand. Johnson also "admitted having homosexual tendencies."[11]

Back in New Jersey by the summer of 1970, Johnson quickly gained a reputation on the campus of Rutgers University as a natty dresser and a spellbinding conversationalist who, according to a police report, put on a skit about Scorpio and death that "first fascinated, but then frightened" some of the co-eds. "He'd say he was the Pisces man as a way of picking up chicks," one said. Johnson, in fact, was born under the sign of Cancer. A student filed a sexual assault case against him. When questioned by campus police about his occupation, Johnson listed "playwright and astrologer." Soon after the student complaints, he drifted away before turning up in New York City during the first months of the year.[12]

Johnson is a street hustler. He preys on women, particularly white prostitutes. He still dreams of directing Hollywood movies, although lately he's turned his attention to making stag flicks.

This life is kept secret from friends and family in New Brunswick, including his cousin Richard Garvin, director of the Department of Community Services at Rutgers. Johnson visits Garvin in his office, asking to borrow the department's tape recorder. He's also looking for some money to rent a camera. Garvin asks what it's for.

"I made a score in New York working for the Italian American Civil Rights League," Johnson tells his cousin. "I'm getting in on the Italian American movement while it's young." He explains further that he plans to document IACRL activities through photographs, tape recordings, and filmstrips. "I'm going to be recording in Columbus Circle on June 28. Hopefully, this will turn in to a full-time gig working for the League."

"Why do you care so much about Italian power?" Garvin asks. "Why not concentrate on Blacks?"

"Italians are discriminated against too, you know," Johnson's replies.

June 28 is not only Italian American Unity Day but also the seven-year anniversary of the founding of the Organization of Afro-American Unity in the Audubon Ballroom by Malcolm X. Garvin doesn't mention that. He knows all about his cousin's ambition to be a filmmaker. He hands him the Sony tape recorder and some cash.[13]

Joe's eye catches the camera staring up at him from the floor. Without looking away from the Sony Portapak, he continues speaking from behind the podium to the audience inside the Park-Sheraton ballroom. "You see Mr. Tambellini here today?" Joe says, sounding like a proud papa. "He's an artist."

Joe is in a self-reflective mood tonight. He returns to a subject he introduced at last month's League meeting: the origins of IACRL in AID, and his role in starting AID. "I said five years ago, 'Our people need leaders and they need them so bad.' "[14]

"I spoke to a man, and this man, who's an entertainer, he says, 'You can lead our people and take them out of the woods.' " The unnamed entertainer is Frank Sinatra. Joe continues, saying he told the entertainer, " 'I can't. They brainwashed the public. They told many a story. They made me a monster. I can't come out.' "

Joe makes a promise to the entertainer. " 'I'll fight. I'll do anything. But I'll always be honest and sincere. And I'll never do anything wrong. And believe me when I tell you, if you get a dollar, it will be by check. It will be honest money. And hard earned. Don't be ashamed of it. There's nothing bad about it. They only did this to indoctrinate our minds.' "

Joe pivots to founding AID. "It started and that was your organization, AID," he says in a soothing tone before allowing his voice to rise. "The politicians took it and destroyed it."

Joe addresses his critics. "And those of you who sit here and think I lie, I never lied in my life. I die of cancer if I gotta lie. Remember one thing, when you wanna fight, you gotta get out and fight and face them. And don't fear. They're nothing."

Joe riffs on government corruption. "But I don't blame you because they are a big organization who have been brainwashing the people for many a year. And they've got all our money to spend."

Joe addresses the problem of troubled youth. "And where they cut back on a narcotics program for the needs of our kids, and where they would appropriate the money to send for bombs to kill innocent kids"—Joe's voice cracks with sorrow—"that don't even know why they're fighting over in Vietnam."

Joe returns to the topic of his role as leader of IACRL. "I give you my word. When I can't help this League, then I'll walk away from this League faster than you would want me to. If I would hurt this League, then I want to die, I wouldn't want to live anymore."

Joe Colombo sits for another interview, this one with a new youth-oriented political tabloid called the *Herald*. "There is a conspiracy in this country against every Italian-American," he tells the reporter before asking, "Why should they label any one particular group of people, one ethnic group of people, and label them to be crime?"[15]

To be crime.

In the *Herald* interview, Joe treats a wide range of liberal-left issues beyond the criminalization of America's immigrants. He endorses the League's "active support . . . for anti-war candidate Bella Abzug in her Manhattan race for Congress in November." He offers his opinion on the Vietnam War and the response to it at home. "I'm for the peace groups a million percent," to which he adds that if he wasn't born "Joseph Colombo," he would "be in Washington and would be honored to be arrested for the peace movement."

On the evening of June 19, two hundred Vietnam War veterans encamp in the Long Meadow section of Brooklyn's Prospect Park, where they hold overnight memorial services for Indochinese and US war casualties. Food is served to the vets from a portable kitchen supplied by the IACRL.[16]

The following day, under a sunny sky, IACRL is joined by more than seventy-five war veteran, civic, political, and labor groups in the Coalition to Take Brooklyn Out of the War, a month-old organization created to broaden participation in the peace movement and "show other Americans that in the pursuit of peace there could be no generation gap."

Congresswoman Bella Abzug and Brooklyn Borough President Sebastian Leone, who have shared an IACRL stage in the past and who are outspoken critics of the war, make speeches to the crowd.

Abzug, a veritable hurricane under a hat, rallies the troops. "If only we learn to put the power together," she rasps, "this coalition is going to change the system."

"Let us get Brooklyn out of the war today," Sam Leone intones. "Let us dedicate our national funds and energies to give Brooklyn new housing and transportation."

More than three thousand people attend the day's events, which, beyond speechifying, include music and theater. The rally, according to news coverage, has "almost a festive air" as children scamper around booths manned by coalition members while two rock bands play "music for peace." In between songs, another band, set up a few yards away, plays martial tunes as a counterpoint. At the end of the set, a group of vets calling themselves "the raiders" rush the stage and enact a "search-and-destroy" operation, which receives "thunderous applause" from onlookers.[17]

June 28 is fast approaching. Unity Day plans are put in place. The *New York Daily News* reports that the League is making a concerted effort to give the event an "ethnic-umenical" twist by posting Unity Day signs "in Polish meat markets, Chinese laundries, Jewish bakeries." The press quotes IACRL

Vice President Anthony Colombo declaring that "this year the rally will be held for all persecuted ethnic groups." He underscores his claim that among the League's two thousand captains, two hundred are Jewish and ninety are Black. As if to demonstrate this point, a handful of Black and Puerto Rican activists from Brooklyn's Brownsville-East New York section, site of NYC's worst slum, are invited to a League Park-Sheraton ballroom meeting. The men stand together behind the open floor mic and take turns endorsing IACRL activities in the context of organizing their own community.[18]

League captains canvass neighborhoods across the five boroughs. They ask merchants to hang signs in their windows and close on Unity Day. In a reprise of a controversy that flared during the run-up to last year's rally, rumors circulate throughout the city that shop owners who decline to shut down for Unity Day face harassment. A *New York Times* reporter contacts FBI headquarters in Manhattan. "He advised," the FBI report begins, "*Times* has received complaints from merchants in Brooklyn area that pressure was being exerted upon them to close their businesses on June twenty-eighth next in honor of IACRL Unity Day."[19]

The FBI communication, addressed to the director in national headquarters, adds that the *Times* reporter stated that the League issued a denial "but subsequently called him and alleged that an FBI agent named ——— and two other men had been going around today removing IACRL signs from store windows and destroying them." The memo assures the director that the agent "categorically denied" engaging in any such activity. At the bottom of the FBI document—filed under "92-12264: ITALIAN AMERICAN CIVIL RIGHTS LEAGUE" on "6/24/71"—is what appears to be J. Edgar Hoover's handwritten initial beneath the scrawl, "*Keep pressure on Colombo.*"[20]

Rocky Miraglia, Joe's driver, walks the streets of South Brooklyn. He carries an armful of Unity Day signs he seeks to post in shop windows. Joey Gallo, residing in his hometown of Red Hook since being released from jail, intercepts Miraglia exiting a storefront. According to accounts appearing in *The New York Times*, Gallo "personally" removes League posters from South Brooklyn storefronts and rips them up while his "two black bodyguards" rough up Miraglia before running him out of the neighborhood.[21]

Joe Colombo is much less worried about Joey Gallo than he is about angering Carlo Gambino. To the surprise of some, Gambino doesn't seem too concerned by Gallo's act of insubordination toward Colombo. To no one's surprise, Gambino is losing patience with Joe. Anti-defamation victories won by the League have boomeranged. They are now outweighed by pressure from law enforcement on Gambino family operations in retaliation for IACRL activism targeting the Bureau. This has to stop, Gambino tells Joe.

> On 6/15/71, informant [Gregory Scarpa] . . . advised that it was now official that not only will CARLO GAMBINO discontinue his support of COLOMBO but is now withdrawing any of his previous support.[22]

The League's FBI pickets—resumed in February after the twin revelations that the government's key witness against Joe Jr. was bought off by the feds and that a grand jury has convened to investigate allegations of a criminal conspiracy perpetrated by IACRL—are suddenly shut down.[23]

In another unexpected development, one of IACRL's four officers, lead organizer Joe DeCicco—on loan from Gambino—suddenly resigns from the League's executive board. An IACRL publicist cites "health reasons" for DeCicco's departure. FBI informant Scarpa links the decision to Gambino.

> —— pointed out that JOE DE CICCO, LCN member in the GAMBINO family who had been a paid organizer for COLOMBO's IACRL was told to resign from the League and not to have further dealings with COLOMBO.

Gambino also takes aim at deflating Unity Day. He refuses to grant ILA Vice President Anthony Scotto permission to give Local 1814 workers time off to attend Monday's rally.

> —— also observed that ANTHONY SCOTTO's longshoremen were being instructed not to attend the Columbus Day [sic] rally as well as other groups who are loyal to the GAMBINOs.[24]

On the Friday before Unity Day, Anthony Scotto publicizes his regrets. "I think the cause is a great one," he tells *The New York Times*, "but I've got other commitments."[25]

Joe's devotion to his cause is unwavering.

***

In the days leading up to the rally, rumors of IACRL's imminent demise reach the leaders of *prominente*-led organizations, who begin circling the League like sharks in the water. On June 25, Italian American leaders representing twenty of the city's civic, fraternal, and church groups assemble to discuss defamation and discrimination and the prospect of forming a new coalition. The meeting is held in the Manhattan office of the New York State's Human Rights Commission and convened by Assistant Commissioner Dominic R. Massaro.

In 1971, at just thirty-two years of age, Dom Massaro had already been knighted by both Italy's president and the Pope. Born and raised in the Bronx, Massaro held a bachelor's in economics, a master's in government, and a degree in law. In 1963, he was appointed national director on public relations by the Supreme Venerable Order Sons of Italy (OSIA) in America. In 1964, the United States Jaycees named him an Outstanding Young Man of America. The following year, he received his first government appointment as the "Italian" representative on John Lindsay's City Commission on Human Rights. Although he would turn against Lindsay by the end of the mayor's first term, that began Massaro's decade-long commitment to government service, for which he was rewarded with a string of Republican Party appointments in the administrations of New York Governors Nelson Rockefeller and Malcolm Wilson and in the administrations of United States Presidents Richard Nixon and Gerald Ford.[26]

Back in September 1967, Massaro, in his capacity as OSIA's national director for public relations, assisted Mary Sansone in organizing the CIAO-sponsored New York City meeting of the Italian American National Federation.[27]

The Congress of Italian American Organizations is not represented at Massaro's meeting, although former CIAO President Joe Valletutti, estranged from Mary since last summer, is in attendance. The most conspicuous absence, however, is representation from the IACRL, whose Unity Day is just around the corner. The press in attendance can't help but notice, and one reporter follows up with a question for the assembled, "What about the Civil Rights League success in banning words like 'Mafia' and 'Cosa Nostra' from Hollywood movies and newspapers?"[28]

"*We* did it," scolds Alfred Santangelo, president of AID. "You people are giving credit where credit is not due."

Another representative from AID explains, "You've got to see that our organization is like the NAACP while the league is more like the Black Panthers."

For Massaro, fighting defamation, whether through legislation or street protests, may not be the primary aim of the anticipated coalition. As a political insider who operates across the municipal, state, and federal levels, he is aware that large sums of government money will soon be made available to white ethnics, whose community organizations have, until now, been shut out from War on Poverty funding.

When someone raises his voice to propose that the twenty groups form an alliance, Santangelo—who, along with Massaro, holds membership in the Sons of Italy's Vince Lombardi Lodge 2091 on Bruckner Boulevard in the Bronx—invites the participants to join his organization, AID, in exchange for a guarantee that those present will be awarded a seat on AID's board of directors.

"Why join his board of directors?" a participant tells a reporter. "I got a nice board of directors of my own."

Journalist Nicholas Pileggi notes that attendees at the June 25 meeting seem "far more interested in projecting themselves as the city's *real* Italian Americans leaders" than in helping poor and working people in their community.

It's the last League meeting in the Park-Sheraton prior to the annual Unity Day. Joe, standing with his hands resting on either side of the podium while holding a pair of black-framed glasses between thumb and forefinger, delivers an impassioned speech. "I don't think there's a man or a woman alive," he begins, "that hasn't in some way done something that they feel that someone in this country could put them in jail for. I talk about the President of the United States. If they dig into Nixon, they'll put him in jail."[29]

Guffaws from the ballroom floor. Joe holds up one hand and says, "Don't laugh. I'm serious."

He starts again. "There's an article in the paper about Hoover, J. Edgar Hoover, who is the head of the FBI, and Jack Anderson wrote it, and how much money he's absconded with already. And if they go through this, they'll have to give him a hundred years in jail." Laughter again from the audience, but Joe ignores it.

"It's a serious thing because, while you're doing nothing, they're appropriating your own money to put you in jail."

The audience sobers up. "So don't be in fear. Remember one thing. If you're right and you're just, God will never turn his face on us."

Joe takes a moment to allow his words to sink in. "And you keep saying, 'Why does a man like Joe Colombo keep saying God so much?'" Joe's voice becomes a whisper, "'Could God be on *his* side?'"

Joe's voice rises. "He's there. He's making everything happen. There is nothing that happened in our League that He hasn't made possible coming."

Full volume: "And for those of you who don't believe in Him, better you believe in Him. He's there. Better you believe that He'll turn the arrows around. Better you believe that He's got an umbrella so big over this League that nobody could touch it."

He concludes: "I don't care who they are. Nobody's gonna hurt this League. And this League very well may—and we say it very openly—save this country, help this country."

A standing ovation. League supporters are getting what they want. But is it what they need? Cheers echo through the hotel lobby and spill out on to Seventh Avenue.

Chapter 30

Columbus Circle (June 28)

Day 424. The second Unity Day is scheduled to kick off at noon. Temperatures in the city rose over the weekend, but today, Monday, the sun struggles to break through morning clouds. Plastic tatters, gaily festooned, bedeck Columbus Circle. At eight o'clock, Joe arrives to oversee last-minute preparations. He's riding high.

According to an FBI memo, Colombo speaks to FBI informant Scarpa shortly after he arrives.

```
COLOMBO advised that although GAMBINO was not
furnishing him any support for this rally
that he had assured GAMBINO this would be his
"swan song" and that in the future he would
take a back seat to all the IACRL activities
devoting himself to the humanaritan [sic]
causes such as boys camps, hospitals and the
like and would refrain from fighting the FBI.[1]
```

At nine o'clock, *New York Post* reporter Judy Michaelson arrives on the scene. A yellow League-authorized Special Event press badge is pinned to the left shoulder of her orange V-neck blouse. Joe wears the colors of the Italian flag: dark green pants, a red windbreaker, and a white short-sleeved shirt. He's easy to spot. Michaelson trails Joe, first at a distance, because he makes it plain to her that he doesn't like being followed. Everyone recognizes Joe, and within an hour, he's become more relaxed and Michaelson is allowed to shadow him. One minute Joe is barking orders to workers; the next, he's cracking jokes with reporters. He hustles everyone along.[2]

"I need an electrician," he shouts to men standing on the north side of the circle.

"Joe," yells a middle-aged woman behind a food stand, "I'll die in the sun without an awning."

Joe turns to a League captain standing by his side. "See that she gets an awning."

When the police, who number 1,500 patrolman and 250 officers for today's event, are slow to close off the surrounding streets, Joe grabs a bullhorn.[3]

"Caesar, tell the people to move into the streets if the cops won't close it. Get 'em into the streets."

"Move into the streets," Vitale shouts, arms waving.[4]

Joe walks past a group of boys occupying a row of folding chairs. He stops and turns. "Those are for your mothers. Stand. You're young." The boys are quick to obey.[5]

The eleven o'clock hour approaches. Joe enters an area in front of the viewing stand restricted to League officials, police, and credentialed press. Across from the stage, a Teamsters Benevolent Association banner is prominently displayed. Joe eyes it approvingly. "Beautiful, beautiful," he says to no one in particular.[6]

Michaelson notices Joe's mood souring. NYPD Deputy Chief Inspector Arthur O'Morgan is informing him that the League can't bar regular Central Park vendors access to Columbus Circle during the rally.

"Barry!" Joe shouts.[7]

Barry Slotnick, standing nearby, walks over to Joe, who asks the chief inspector to explain the situation again, which he does.

Joe turns to Slotnick. "That wasn't the deal."

Joe says to the inspector, "Look, if you allow those other guys in, it will destroy us." The inspector shrugs. Joe tries a different tack. "You're risking a confrontation."

The inspector looks at Slotnick, who chimes in. "Just say a health and safety hazard will occur if they come in."

Joe walks away confident that his lawyer will fix it.

During the exchange between Joe, Barry Slotnick, and the chief inspector, a Black man holding a movie camera approaches the restricted area. A camera bag hangs from his shoulder. The area is cordoned off with wooden horses except for an opening. Thomas Nestro, the League's public relations director, monitors the entrance. Nestro studies the press credentials of "Jerome A. Johnson." They're detailed and professional but they don't include the Special Event Unity Day press pass.

"Alright, but get the Special Event pass *in advance* next time."

"I will," Johnson promises.[8]

About one hundred feet from the statue of Columbus, Joe slips through a throng of police and press. He passes a young Black woman wearing an afro. She calls, "Hiya, Joe." Joe slows and swivels to return the greeting. Johnson, gripping a 16-mm. Bolex in front of his face, steps out from behind the woman. Caught in the eye of the camera, Joe freezes for a moment before turning away.

Figure 30.1. Jerome Johnson seen behind a movie camera moments before Joseph Colombo Sr. (front) is shot during Italian American Unity Day, Columbus Circle, Manhattan, June 1971, in a photo obtained by the *New York Daily News* "from a film clip given to police." *Source:* New York Daily News.

Without dropping the Bolex, Johnson reaches with his left hand into the camera case and pulls out the 7.65-mm. Menta. He steps behind Joe, raises the German automatic and—in an instant—three shots smash into the back of Joe's head.[9]

An FBI report in Joe Colombo's file reads,

> On June 28, 1971, at approximately 11:20 AM, as a small crowd . . . gathered in anticipation of the Unity Day Rally to start at twelve noon, COLOMBO was shot three times by one JEROME A. JOHNSON, FBI Number 185 112 G, a Negro male, date of birth July 16, 1946. JOHNSON was immediately shot and killed by as-yet unidentified individual, whom police know only to be an associate of COLOMBO. COLOMBO was immediately rushed to Roosevelt Hospital, New York City, where a five-hour operation was performed and he remains in very critical condition and in a coma.[10]

Another Bureau report, this one in Greg Scarpa's file and dated June 30, 1971, contains two entries, one for each of the prior two days.

> On June 28, 1971, subject [GREGORY SCARPA] was observed by Bureau Agents at Columbus Circle, New York City, during Italian American Unity Day. The subject was observed in the area at the same time that JOSEPH COLOMBO was shot.
>
> On June 29, 1971, Detective —— Brooklyn District Attorney's Office, advised Special Agent —— that subject [GREGORY SCARPA] was acquitted in Kings County Court for his October 8, 1969 arrest for Possession of Stolen Property.[11]

Part Four

Stayin' Alive

Italian, Black, and Puerto Rican teens pose in front of a graffiti-tagged wall on a vacant lot where the NYPD Seventy-Second Precinct Station House once stood, South Brooklyn, 1977. *Source:* Larry Racioppo. Used with permission.

Chapter 31

Nowhere Man (1971)

As ambulances raced Joe Colombo and Jerome Johnson to Roosevelt Hospital, TV cameras in Columbus Circle crowded around *New York Post* reporter Judy Michaelson, who was by Joe's side when he was shot. A newsman asked, "Did you have the feeling that maybe you were in the middle of *The Godfather*?"[1]

"No," Michaelson snapped with a sideways glance at her colleague, "I had the feeling I was in the middle of gunfire and I wanted to get the hell out."

From the start, Joe Colombo the social activist and the civil rights organization he founded were destined for trouble. In the wake of the Columbus Circle shooting, as Joe lingered in a hospital bed on life support, the League collapsed. The near-fatal shooting of Colombo, like the gangland murder of his father before him, made front-page headlines coast to coast.

Two weeks into the news cycle, the cover of *Time*, America's most popular weekly news magazine, staged a red-framed close-up photo of Joe pointing a finger at the camera to match his glare. He also sported a League pin in his left lapel. The yellow tape cutting across the top of Joe's head cautioned "The Mafia at War."

At the same time as Joe's stare appeared on newsstands across the country, Mayor John Lindsay received a missive typed on League letterhead from IACRL Vice President Anthony Colombo. It began, "On behalf of myself, my family and the entire Italian American Civil Rights League, I wish to extend our appreciation for all your cooperation and the efforts of the Police Department at a time such as this," and concluded: "Please do not hesitate to contact us if there is any matter in which we can be of assistance to you."

Before forwarding the letter to his deputy mayor, Richard Aurelio, Lindsay penned a notation across the top—"RA F.Y.I. JVL"—and then, in the margins alongside the concluding sentence, jotted "!!"[2]

Press coverage of the Columbus Circle shooting reinforced the connection between the Italian American Civil Rights League and organized crime. So too did the police investigation into Joe's would-be assassin. Who was Jerome Addison Johnson, and more importantly, what was his motive for shooting Joe? The most widely circulated theory, vigorously pursued by law enforcement as well as the press, was that the mob had put out a contract on Joe. If true, who hired Johnson? The main suspects were Mafia kingpin Carlo Gambino and rouge gangster Joey Gallo. Prior to the Unity Day rally, word on the street was that mob bosses, wary that League operations were threatening their underworld fiefs, had withdrawn their support. Gambino ordered Joe to step down but his refusal made Joe vulnerable in the underworld from which he had well-nigh emerged.

A big hole in the Gambino theory was that there was scant evidence of the Mafia ever hiring an outsider—perhaps especially an African American—to perform a job of this magnitude. The only gangster plausibly capable of hiring a Black man to assassinate Joe Colombo was "Crazy" Joey Gallo. While serving time, Gallo had reportedly taken up the civil rights causes of African American co-prisoners. He also had a beef to pick with Colombo over his boss's refusal to return illicit enterprises to Gallo upon his recent release from jail. But no one was ever able to establish a connection between Gallo and Johnson.[3]

League supporters without Mafia ties—ranging from IACRL insiders like Anthony Colombo and Rev. Louis Gigante to outsiders like Aldo Tambellini and Ti-Grace Atkinson—gravitated toward conspiracy theories connecting clandestine government operatives to the shooter. At the time, this paranoia was buttressed by a seeming tsunami of revelations regarding government covert operations and cover ups. These disclosures included FBI malfeasance in the form of COINTELPRO programs, in operation through 1971, designed to infiltrate and disrupt domestic organizations deemed subversive; evidence of police involvement in the assassinations of Black revolutionaries, including Malcolm X in 1965 and Fred Hampton in 1969; and the suspicion, confirmed decades later through documents obtained through the Freedom of Information Act, of the "conversion" of notorious hit man Greg Scarpa as an FBI Top Echelon informant. Scarpa provided the bureau with confidential information on the League as well as on his boss and Colombo crime family operations, and the Top Echelon classification gave him a license to commit crimes, including murder, with apparent immunity from government prosecution.

Jerome Addison Johnson remains an enigma. As an assassin, he perhaps resembles no one so much as Lee Harvey Oswald. It's enough to make the amateur Mafia-ologist resign himself to the hollow conclusion—all-too-familiar to the weary JFK assassination buff—that the shooter was a lone gunman.

Chapter 32

Cellar to Suite (1971)

The fact that Joe Colombo's would-be assassin, Jerome Johnson, was African American inevitably made race a factor in the shooting and its aftermath. Minutes after Colombo and Johnson were shot, a Black bystander in Columbus Circle was attacked by angry whites in attendance. Within an hour of the assault, the Associated Press received an anonymous message, which turned out to be fraudulent, from a someone claiming "credit" for the hit on Colombo on behalf of a "black revolutionary attack team." "Madness in Columbus Circle" howled a headline on the next day's *New York Times* editorial page, which began by vilifying Colombo as someone who "appealed to a kind of chauvinism that . . . threatens to pit Italian-American against Negro" and ended by condemning "organized racial assaults" by a "black revolutionary group."[1]

The same day's *New York Post* coverage offered a more generous assessment of Colombo's civil rights legacy in light of the Columbus Circle melee, opening with the statement: "The racial amity Joseph Colombo sought to promote seemed shakier than ever." Harlem's *Amsterdam News* reported that "only thru the cool heads of those who are respected and listened to in the Italian-American Civil Rights League was a calamity averted." IACRL's coolest, most respected and listened to voice, according to the *Amsterdam News*, was Sammy Davis Jr., whose "decision . . . to visit the critically wounded League founder, the day after he was shot, did a lot to ease the building tension." According to the *New York Post* reportage, the mayor's office reached out to Bayard Rustin for his advice on how city hall should respond to the shooting. Rustin called for calm by appealing to racial tolerance, adding: "I certainly hope that this will not be permitted to deteriorate into a conflict between blacks and Italians."[2]

To cool racial tensions, Mayor Lindsay also needed an assist from Rustin's friend Mary Sansone, who had been working closely with antipoverty organizer Ralph Perrotta from the Urban Coalition since May. On the Friday after Joe Colombo was gunned down, a reporter for *The New York Times* interviewed Mary alongside Perrotta, who described the shooting as "a human tragedy, because a lot of people's hopes were riding on him; for a lot of people, he (Colombo) was their voice." The article opened with the acknowledgment that for years the Urban Coalition in New York had ministered "almost exclusively to the needs of blacks and Puerto Ricans." Now, however, with the New York Urban Coalition joining forces with CIAO, it "embarked on a new project—organizing Italian Americans." The piece concluded by noting that "Mayor Lindsay has assigned one of his aides, Nancy Seifer"—who had already begun championing Mary Sansone inside city hall—"to work with Mr. Perrotta."[3]

Seifer's mission was to move city hall toward an enlightened approach to serving poor and working-class ethnic whites, including Italian Americans. Rather than allow racial polarization and fear to fester in New York, she lobbied the mayor to support progressive groups, most notably CIAO, who actively engaged inter-ethnic and cross-racial cooperation. During July 1971, Seifer wrote a memo to her new boss, Jay Kriegel, updating him on a CIAO-sponsored meeting. "Re: July 11th meeting of JVL and Italian community leaders (Mary Sansone, Ralph Perrotta, Sara Ricchio, Rich Leotta, Norma DeGandido and Nick Pileggi). The meeting was enthusiastically hailed a success by all present. It was viewed with great optimism as the beginning of a 'new relationship' between City Hall and the Italian American communities." The memo described CIAO's primary concerns (lack of representation in city hall, high school dropout rates, drug addiction, lack of senior care, etc.) and the mayor's commitments (most importantly, super-agency administrator meetings but also Little Italy and South Brooklyn walking tours).[4]

The key to CIAO's success was the organization's willingness to work across racial lines. "We're the only group that can deal with blacks and Puerto Ricans," said Mary, "because they know we're not taking away from them but are merely sharing." By fall, CIAO had been awarded a $52,400 Human Resources Administration contract from the city "to develop a plan for the establishment of three senior citizens multi-service centers in South Brooklyn, Corona-East Elmhurst in Queens, and Lower East Side, Manhattan."[5]

Mayor Lindsay sent Mary a congratulatory letter, dated October 26, 1971, celebrating her pioneering efforts on behalf of Italian Americans. He also welcomed CIAO's headquarters to city hall's Park Row neighborhood.

Dear Mary,

I was delighted to have had the opportunity to participate in the groundbreaking ceremony for the first day care center to be sponsored by CIAO. It was an important milestone in CIAO's history, and a significant accomplishment for the City's Human Resources Administration, as well.

I was also extremely pleased to learn that the meeting we had in my office in July resulted in a planning grant to enable CIAO to begin to respond to the needs of senior citizens in Italian communities . . .

Now that CIAO's headquarters are moving from your basement to Park Row, we will be neighbors and I will expect to be kept well-informed of your activities.

With best regards,

John V. Lindsay
MAYOR[6]

Chapter 33

Button Men (1971–72)

The Italian American Civil Rights League imploded after the attempt on Joe Colombo's life in Columbus Circle. Less than a month later, FBI Top Echelon informant Greg Scarpa appeared before a US Senate subcommittee investigating stolen securities. Scarpa—whose reputation as a hit man for the Colombo crime family after the Columbus Circle shooting would earn him the nickname "the Grim Reaper"—didn't say much during the hearing but he wore a menacing smile. Chain smoking, he pleaded the Fifth Amendment sixty times, even when questioned twice, by two different committee members—Senator Charles Percy and Chairman John McClellan—about the League pin in his left lapel (Fig. 33.1).

> SENATOR PERCY: Just one observation, Mr. Chairman. When a man gets up in the morning and dresses, he puts on jewelry, decorations, whatever it may be, of his own choice. I presume that the button you are wearing, Mr. Scarpa, is something that you are proud to have on. Would you care to describe what the association or organization is that stands behind that button?
>
> MR. SCARPA: I respectfully decline to answer the question on the grounds it may tend to incriminate me.
>
> SENATOR PERCY: I would presume that the button is readily identifiable as a Joe Colombo unity button. If you are proud to wear it, wouldn't you care to at least describe the organization that you belong to? Many, many people belong to it. It is well-known to the public.

MR. SCARPA: I respectfully decline to answer the question on the grounds it may tend to incriminate me.

Pursuing his colleague's line of inquiry, Senator McClellan pressed Scarpa again about the IACRL pin.

CHAIRMAN MCCLELLAN: You asked him [Scarpa] a while ago, Senator [Percy], about the pin he is wearing. Is that the badge or the pin of the organization that Joe Colombo organized? The name of it, I believe, is the Italian American Civil Rights League.

MR. SCARPA: I respectfully decline to answer the question on the grounds it may tend to incriminate me.

CHAIRMAN MCCLELLAN: Did you know Joe Colombo?

Figure 33.1. Colombo crime family member Gregory Scarpa, wearing an IACRL pin in his left lapel, testifies at a United States Senate organized crime hearing, Washington, DC, July 1971. *Source:* Bettmann Archive/Getty Images. Used with permission.

Mr. Scarpa: I respectfully decline to answer the question, Senator, on the ground it may tend to incriminate me.

Chairman McClellan: Are you a member of the Colombo family?

Mr. Scarpa: I respectfully decline to answer the question.

Chairman McClellan: Was it through his organization that you did this work on fencing stolen goods?

Mr. Scarpa: I respectfully decline to answer the question, Senator, on the ground it may tend to incriminate me.

Chairman McClellan, visibly vexed, finally asked the witness, "Do you regard yourself as dangerous?"

Scarpa, suddenly *sans* smile, shot back: "Do you, Senator?"[1]

Ten months after the shooting in Columbus Circle, "Crazy" Joey Gallo was gunned down on his forty-third birthday. Gallo was sharing an early morning meal with his family at Umberto's Clam House in Little Italy when he was spotted by a Colombo crime family associate, who shot him dead. When Greg Scarpa's FBI handler questioned Scarpa about the killing and insinuated that Scapa knew something about Gallo's murder, he referred to the League in his defense and then made a point of praising its outreach efforts on behalf of the community.

> SCARPA stated that when something like this happens, automatically people blame the Italians, and this is one reason why the Italian-American Civil Rights League was formed. He pointed out the good work the Italian-American Civil Rights League is doing, such as Camp Unity for neglected children.[2]

According to witnesses, while Gallo was trying to dodge a hail of bullets, he stumbled out of Umberto's and collapsed in the gutter next to his car. The vehicle was plastered with "Americans of Italian Descent" bumper stickers. Days before he died, Gallo had begun working as a "recruiting representative" for AID. The job was the result of negotiations he had had with AID President Alfred Santangelo. "I'm not interested in money," Gallo told Santangelo. "I don't want to collect it. I don't want to hold it. I don't want to handle it like Colombo."[3]

Santangelo, perhaps still harboring enmity toward Joe Colombo, accepted Gallo's offer to work for him, but Gallo's career as an AID activist was over almost before it began. Santangelo, now embarrassed by the publicity surrounding Gallo's demise, used AID's monthly newspaper, *The Challenge*, for which he was executive editor, to issue a denial. Gallo "never worked or was associated with AID in any way, either officially or otherwise," the paper lied, "Nor was AID feuding with any other Italian-American organization, least of all with the Civil Rights League."[4]

Joey Gallo's end played out like a scene from *The Godfather*, which had been released in theaters a month earlier. The film, which the League had a hand in making, turned out to be one of the most critically acclaimed and commercially successful Hollywood movies of all time. However, with Colombo near death and the League in disarray, Paramount Pictures reneged on Ruddy's promise to donate the proceeds from the movie's premiere to the League's hospital fund. Instead, according to an ad in *The New York Times* appearing two days before the film's March 14 premiere, its beneficiary would be the Boys' Club of New York.[5]

On the same day, March 12, the League's contribution to the making of *The Godfather* was recognized in the paper's Arts and Leisure section by *Times* movie critic Vincent Canby, whose advance review of the film was the first to be published anywhere. Tempering what was otherwise a rave, he deferred to "the members of the Italian American Civil Rights League" who protested mobsters receiving "much more publicity than they ever honorably deserved." Adhering to the spirit of the League, Canby's review is remarkable for the words not used: Mafia and Costa Nostra. While identifying the experiences of the movie's main characters as "exotic" and "unique," Canby was careful to describe the characters themselves not as Italian but instead as "one small group of first and second generation Americans" who, the reviewer demurred, "I'm not qualified to discuss."[6]

At the start of 1972, veiled references to the League found their way into episodes of *All in the Family*, TV's biggest hit. In its second season, *All in the Family* had an audience every week of more than fifty million people, or 60 percent of all viewers. In an episode aired on the last Saturday in January, the League appeared under the pseudonym Pro-Italia Society. The episode begins with Archie Bunker, having witnessed a mugging, failing his civic duty to provide the police eyewitness testimony. When his family learns of Archie's inaction, they accuse him of being a bad citizen. Archie defends himself by fabricating a story he believes will give him cover. He claims the crime was committed by the Mafia, which he says prohibits him from alerting authorities lest he too become their victim. "Them Sicilians is famous for two things," he rants, "spaghetti and revenge." The other members of Archie's family, keepers of society's moral compass, insist he do the right thing and go to the police. Begrudgingly, he visits the local precinct, where he makes a false statement about Mafia involvement in the crime. In the next day's paper, to his surprise, his false eyewitness account is repeated in the form of a tabloid headline: "Mafia Execution Attempt."[7]

The sensational headline, with its use of the M-word, rouses the attention of a local chapter of the civil rights group Pro-Italia. Someone from the organization phones Archie to inform him that they plan to pay him a friendly visit at his home. The call heightens Archie's anxiety. Reassurances from his family, that "it's just an Italian anti-defamation group," fall flat: "It's another cover name for the Mafia," he retorts. Archie's family is indifferent, to which he answers his own question—"Don't you know what that means?"—by stating, "The guy'll be probably coming over here to give me one of them eternal kisses." Archie's family, unpersuaded, dismiss his fears by telling him, "You're seeing too many movies."

There's a knock at the door. Archie opens it and finds a member of the Italian American anti-defamation league who matter-of-factly drapes his arm over Archie's shoulder and disavows the existence of the Mafia. "I just dropped by to tell you that that organization which you mentioned this morning in the paper, it don't exist," adding in coarse Brooklynese, "It's defunc-it." He cautions Archie, "We don't say that word. It's not a very nice word." He ticks off examples of the prohibition, which are drawn from actual IACRL victories. "You see, even in this movie, *The Godfather*, which is about that defunct organization, even they don't use that word." He puts a bow on it: "Even the FBI don't use that word."

With childlike malapropisms and double negatives, Archie promises the anti-defamation league representative: "Words like 'kosher nostras' or that 'mmm' word, I ain't never gonna use them words no more." By episode's end, order is restored in the Bunker household only after Archie learns a heartfelt lesson. Archie isn't really evil; he's just ignorant. In producer Norman Lear's TV universe, empathy and repentance are a balm for tribalism and intolerance.

In another episode of *All in the Family*, aired just a few weeks later, the League was cast in a very different shadow. IACRL stalwart Sammy Davis Jr.—who, the day after the Columbus Circle shooting, was the most notable public personality to make an appearance at Roosevelt Hospital in support of the critically wounded Colombo in an effort to ease racial tensions caused by the melee, and who, more recently, announced he would headline the League's June 1972 Madison Square Garden fundraiser—appeared on *All in the Family* as his real-life self.[8]

The "Sammy's Visit" episode is etched in TV immortality mainly due to its finale, when the guest star—at the exact moment he's being photographed standing next to Archie by an adoring fan—plants an eternal kiss on TV's super-bigot. For Archie, celebrity transcends Blackness, which allows him to treat Sammy with what passes for respect rather than with bigotry. Archie's hospitality toward his special guest extends to offering his chair to Sammy, the only person so honored during the show's nine seasons (Fig. 33.2). Sammy, however, is hip to his host's intolerance. Sitting on Archie's throne, Sammy undermines his host's inarticulate assumptions about white superiority through a barrage of hilarious indirect gibes, which—while they delight the liberal-minded youth in the room (his daughter, son-in-law, and their Black next-door neighbor)—exceed Archie's comprehension.[9]

Throughout his virtuoso performance, Sammy Davis displays in his left lapel a pin. It pairs the American and Italian flags. Close inspection reveals that the Stars and Stripes is wed to the tricolor by the number 1, which is inscribed with the letters IACRL (Fig. 33.3).

The camera never zooms in on Sammy's lapel and—without a close-up—the League never quite shares the guest star's spotlight.

The inconspicuous pin, perceptible only to the most devoted eye, turned out to be fitting. Just as the mark of the League goes all but unnoticed during the "Sammy's Visit" episode of *All in the Family*, any contribution IACRL might have made to era's civil rights campaigns was all but eclipsed by Jerome Johnson's shooting of Joe Colombo in Columbus Circle nine months earlier, the circumstances behind which would forever remain a mystery.

Figure 33.2. Guest star Sammy Davis Jr., IACRL pin in his lapel, sitting in Archie Bunker's chair, *All in the Family*, February 1972. *Source:* All in the Family/Sony Pictures Television. Used with permission.

Figure 33.3. IACRL lapel pin displaying the American and Italian flags, which are connected by the number "1." *Source:* Italian American Civil Rights League. Author's collection.

Chapter 34

Wobbly and Quaker (1971–72)

In March 1972, the Congress of Italian American Organizations acknowledged the achievements of its executive director by honoring Mary Sansone at its annual dinner dance. Held at the Commodore Hotel on Forty-Second Street in Manhattan, it was quite a step up from Bensonhurst's Cotillion Terrace, where Mayor Lindsay had been honored by CIAO the year prior. Feted by *The New York Times*, the Commodore event drew over six hundred attendees, including Lindsay, who during the ceremonies "presented a city certificate of appreciation for distinguished service to Mrs. Sansone."[1]

Two days later, on March 15, CIAO held its fourth annual symposium at the Statler-Hilton, a hotel located across the street from Penn Station and Madison Square Garden. The symposium topic, "ethnic communities and the challenge of urban life," brought together more than three hundred "ethnic leaders—Italians, Blacks, Puerto Ricans, Jews and others," according to *New York Times* coverage. Mary offered the welcome and Ralph Perrotta gave the closing remarks. Msgr. Geno Baroni, director of the National Center for Urban Ethnic Affairs, delivered the keynote. Baroni, who was the Catholic Church's coordinator for the 1963 March on Washington, today appealed for "a new American dream—the urban ethnic pluralistic society"—to enable "diversity to become an asset instead of a liability" in the United States.[2]

The symposium's panels were a who's who of urban ethnic activists and thinkers and included Professor Michael Novak, whose *The Rise of Unmeltable Ethnics*, the movement's emotional treatise, was set to be released; newspaper columnists Jimmy Breslin and Pete Hamill; Corona 69 lawyer Mario Cuomo; New York City Human Rights Commissioner Eleanor Holmes Norton; International Longshoremen's Association Vice President Anthony Scotto; nationally recognized community organizers Barbara Mikulski (Baltimore) and Steve Adubato (Newark); and the American Jewish Committee's Urban

Projects director Irving M. Levine, arguably the first public intellectual to articulate an agenda for the fledgling movement.[3]

The featured speaker at CIAO's 1972 symposium was Mary's old friend Bayard Rustin, the director of the A. Philip Randolph Institute, which coordinated the AFL-CIO's campaign for civil rights and economic justice. The symposium was the culmination of a recent collaboration between Bayard and Mary, which was launched a year earlier in Mary's cellar, a confab covered by *The New York Times*. "Bayard Rustin had a homemade Italian meal served on paper plates in Mrs. Mary Sansone's finished basement in Boro Park, Brooklyn," the *Times* story began. The article, headlined "Ethnic Leaders Attempt a Coalition," described the forty attendees as a "mix of mainly middle-class people . . . chosen by Mr. Rustin and Mrs. Sansone, who is chairman of CIAO."[4]

Sitting on medal folding chairs but "warmed by red wine and chicken caciatore [*sic*]," invited guests were led by what the observer characterized as Bayard's soft touch. "Let's not formalize things too quickly," he said. "Let's

Figure 34.1. Bayard Rustin, director of the A. Philip Randolph Institute, addressing a CIAO symposium, Statler-Hilton Hotel, Manhattan, March 1972. *Source:* Jack Manning/New York Times/Redux. Used with permission.

have affection." Mary chimed in: "I go into the communities and find Italians happy and willing to join with blacks and Puerto Ricans once they discover what they have in common." The *Times* coverage concluded that after "two hours of some of the more unusual, hard-boiled dialogue heard in recent times," the evening ended in song. This too was led by Bayard, an accomplished tenor who sacrificed a singing career to devote his life to political activism, but who was currently preparing to record a live album, *Bayard Rustin Sings Spirituals, Work & Freedom Songs*. Still, some of Mary's guests were surprised when Bayard offered an affective rendition of "Una Furtiva Lagrima," from the second act of Donizetti's *L'Elisir d'Amore*. It was an aria he had been performing, in Italian, since high school. Before he began, however, Bayard turned to Mary and asked her to sing "The Rebel Girl," a union song written by IWW organizer Joe Hill.[5]

The Congress of Italian Amercian Organizations was hailed by crusading journalist Jack Newfield (who, together with Jeff Greenfield, a former Lindsay speechwriter, had just published *A Populist Manifesto: The Making of a New Majority*) as "the closest thing to an authentic populist movement in New York." Newfield saluted CIAO's "founder and moving spirit . . . Mary Sansone, whose husband is a longshoreman on the Brooklyn docks, and whose father was an organizer for the IWW." In the early seventies, the A. Philip Randolph Institute worked closely with CIAO to find ways to bring ethnic groups together to solve common problems. "I urge Italians not to make the mistake many black people have made," Bayard warned, maintaining that "the most serious problem facing America today is the economic problem." "Everywhere in the world," he admonished, "people are substituting ethnicity for the solution of problems."

Mary agreed with Bayard that economic justice was the most pressing issue facing the city's dispossessed. And she understood that appeals to Italian American identity could lead to tribalism. However, she also understood that—coming out of the 1960s—claiming ethnic entitlement would be the most politically efficacious means for poor Italians to gain access to government programs that until recently were made available only to racial minorities. Reducing polarization among the city's working class required building racial coalitions that encouraged whites and Blacks and Latinos to join together to fight mutual enemies, whether they be school boards or mortgage brokers.[6]

By the spring of 1972, the Congress of Italian Amercian Organizations was going like gangbusters. It began publishing a monthly newsletter, *CIAO*

Reports. In its second issue, *CIAO Reports* announced that Joseph R. Erazo, New York City commissioner of manpower and career development—and the highest-ranking Puerto Rican in city hall—had joined Mary Sansone and Bayard Rustin to lead biweekly dinner discussions in Mary's basement with ethnic leaders from the community. In a May meeting, Mary pointed out to her guests that Brooklyn College sponsored institutes for Afro-American studies, Puerto Rican studies, and Judaic studies but not for Italian American studies, despite the fact that Italians were the largest ethnic group in the borough. Commissioner Erazo agreed to work with Mary to remedy the omission. He committed $10,000 from his agency on a plan to start an Italian American research center at Brooklyn College, an amount to be matched by the city's Board of Higher Education. Erazo also assigned his staff adviser, Richard Leotta, to work with Mary on the proposal.[7]

On the back page of the same issue of *CIAO Reports*, a joyous announcement appeared. "Mary and Zachary Sansone and Frances Leotta celebrated the marriage their children Carmela and Richard on June 24th at the Plaza Hotel." The gala Midtown Manhattan wedding brought CIAO and city hall even closer together. Mary, eager to expand the organization's political reach and financial footing beyond the city, appointed her new son-in-law "CIAO representative" to New York State's Comprehensive Health Planning Agency.[8]

That summer, Mary committed the organization's resources to backing Michael Pesce, an immigrant turned activist lawyer and a member of CIAO, in a bruising Democratic Party state assembly primary campaign against the incumbent, a longtime Meade Esposito crony. The insurgent candidate, who *The New York Times* editorial page endorsed as having "enlightened views on social issues in sharp contrast the incumbent," won the Fifty-Second District seat handily.[9]

Chapter 35

New League Retreat: Canarsie's Busing Crisis (1972–73)

Shortly after Joe Colombo was shot, the Italian American Civil Rights League, unable to pay the fat rental on its Madison Avenue headquarters, retreated to Bensonhurst. Not all was lost. The next summer, New York City awarded the League money to organize community activities through a youth employment program. In 1972, its first year of city funding, the organization received $20,000 from the Youth Services agency to create sixty-five Neighborhood Youth Corps summer jobs. The award was split between IACRL's two most prominent remaining chapters—4, Joe's "mother chapter," and 8, Meade Esposito's Canarsie chapter—in the amount of $9,850 and $9,050, respectively. The fact that the chapters' summer funding fell just short of $10,000—the amount that would automatically trigger board of estimate scrutiny prior to approval—went almost unnoticed in the press.[1]

In the fall of 1972, however, when forced busing came to Canarsie schools, Canarsie became headline news. With a population of eighty thousand, Canarsie had been home to a predominantly Italian community for fifty years. More recently, Jews from Brownsville and East New York, fleeing an influx of poor Blacks and Puerto Ricans into their neighborhoods, resettled in Canarsie, a community of modest one- and two-family homes described, at the time, in bucolic terms by *The New York Times*: "The trees, the frame houses, the families out for a walk on a cool evening, the dim and infrequent street lights give the neighborhood a small-town air." Canarsie's Black residents numbered only four thousand and mostly lived in two public housing projects on the eastern and southern edges of the community.[2]

On October 11, 1972, less than a month into the school year, New York City's Education Chancellor Harvey B. Scribner "ordered" thirty-one Black children from the Samuel J. Tilden Houses, a low-income housing development in nearby Brownsville, bused to John Wilson Junior High in Canarsie. Scribner's decision was based the fact that Black and Puerto Rican student population at the Tilden children's former school, East Flatbush's Meyer Leven Junior High, had recently crept over the 50 percent mark and was thus deemed in imminent danger of "tipping."

Racial tipping was a controversial concept deployed by some education experts in an attempt to determine the point at which a certain percentage of minority student enrollment in a school would precipitate white residential flight from surrounding neighborhoods. More specifically, according to proponents of the tipping theory, a school was in danger of tipping when it reached a ratio of 70 percent white and 30 percent black. When measured against the tipping theory, Scribner's busing plan was destined to fail because John Wilson Junior High had already reached the benchmark 70/30 split between whites and Blacks. Canarsie parents with students at Wilson Junior High argued that busing threatened the precarious racial balance in *their* school.

On the following Monday, October 16, after Scribner announced he would not reverse his decision, two hundred white parents stormed Wilson Junior High to prevent staff and pupils from entering. For three days, two dozen Canarsie mothers staged a lockout they dubbed a "sleep-in"—an around-the-clock occupation of the school gymnasium. Tilden Houses parents couldn't help notice a racial double standard. One month earlier, when they staged a sit-in at the local board of education office in Canarsie to protest unequal treatment of Black children in education, they were removed within hours and charged with criminal trespassing. "If that was us," said one of the Tilden mothers, referring to the Canarsie women, "we'd take it over at 7 A.M. and by 9 A.M. we'd be at Rikers Island."[3]

On the third day of their sleep-in, Canarsie housewives were joined by a local resident, Carl Cecora, head of Chapter 8 of the IACRL, and other members of his organization.

A thirty-two-year-old bachelor and a high school dropout, Cecora drove a truck delivering electric light bulbs for a company owned by his brother. He wore tattoos on each arm: "Mother and Father" on his right; the name of school buddies on his left. He had been active in the League since the Canarsie chapter opened its doors at 9229 Flatlands Avenue in the fall of 1970 with the backing of Meade Esposito, Joe Colombo's childhood friend and an early, behind-the-scenes supporter of the League (Fig. 35.1).

A year later, Cecora attended Unity Day in Columbus Circle as an event "captain." He stood only steps away when Joe was gunned down. His vivid account of that moment—specifically of a "colored girl" sporting an afro, who caught Joe's attention just before Jerome Johnson drew his weapon and who then fled "over the barricade before anyone realized" what was happening—was featured on the evening's TV news and in the next day's papers. Cecora's eyewitness testimony became a seed from which a hundred Columbus Circle conspiracy theories bloomed.[4]

In September of 1972, just prior to the Canarsie busing crisis, IACRL Chapter 8 was struggling for relevancy. It had recently moved local headquarters from Flatland Avenue to a cramped plywood house on Avenue L, which happened to be just around the corner from the Thomas Jefferson clubhouse, where Meade Esposito held court.

A month later, the busing crisis made the League—*sans* Joe Colombo— relevant again. By adding "Canarsie schools for Canarsie kids" to the

Figure 35.1. Carl Cecora, chairman of Chapter 8 of the IACRL, Canarsie, Brooklyn. By the end of 1973, Cecora had been named president of the "New League" and Chapter 8 had become IACRL national headquarters. *Source:* Terrence McCarten Family Archive. Used with permission.

224 | Rebel Girl and the Godfather

national organization's "Unity in Community" motto, Cecora's Chapter 8 seized the moment and led the fight against the city's attempt to desegregate its schools. Chancellor Scribner's first concession to anti-busing Canarsie parents was to change his plans for the thirty-one Tilden Houses children who he had initially sent to Wilson Junior High. Scribner revised his plan by deciding that Tilden Houses children would instead be bused to Irving Bildersee—another Canarsie junior high but one that was 98 percent white.[5]

Only days later, the city's Central Board of Education overruled Scribner's revised plan. Prominent liberal advocates of racial integration expressed outrage over the chancellor's capitulation to Canarsie parents. Kenneth B. Clark, the only African American on the state board of regents, although friends with Scribner, repeatedly denounced the chancellor's flip-flop. In a hand-delivered letter to Scribner, he accused him of engaging in "another compromise with racism where the interests of minorities are consistently subordinated to the passions and prejudices of whites." The board of education, siding with Clark's sentiments, overruled the chancellor's order and directed the thirty-one Tilden Houses seventh graders back to John Wilson Junior High, where they had previously been barred from entering by protesting white parents. On October 27, the day the Brownsville students were bused back to John Wilson, local news showed 150 police in riot gear clearing a path to shield Black students from more than a thousand sneering whites. The following day, Clark appeared on WCBS-TV's "Man in Office" program and made public his charge that racism, "conscious or unconscious," was the real issue in the busing dispute. He said that the scene at John Wilson, where Black students had to be escorted into school by police, was a "reflection of profound sickness in this nation that is exploited by people seeking high office." He followed with criticism of Mayor Lindsay, who he accused of remaining silent on "the crime in Canarsie."[6]

The showdown in Canarsie was, for Clark, a watershed event. At the time, he was president of the Metropolitan Applied Research Center (MARC), an organization advocating on behalf of the poor and powerless in American cities "by mobilizing trained intelligence" to influence public policy. Eighteen years earlier, Clark's famed "doll" experiments, conducted alongside his wife Mamie, were key to persuading the US Supreme Court justices to rule in favor of overturning segregation in public schools in the landmark *Brown v. Board of Education* decision. But by the early 1970s, school integration was not merely stalling but losing ground in the face of white opposition. Clark warned that a decision in favor of Canarsie parents "would provide the most effective way for Northern and Southern communities to evade and make a mockery of all of the Federal court decisions which require and demand desegregation of our public schools," concluding, "This cannot be permitted to happen."[7]

The Canarsie crisis took the form of community-wide school boycott, which began October 27, forced six schools to close for two weeks, and kept more than nine thousand Canarsie students at home. At the same time, two hundred riot-equipped police officers guarded the thirty-one Tilden Houses pupils as they entered John Wilson Junior High. Behind the "white" barricades, a forty-four-year-old longshoreman and IACRL block captain named Louis Colonna tried to keep the peace. "We don't want anybody to get hurt. If you can't keep calm, go home and stay there," he said to a gang of white toughs on the morning of the boycott's third day. During a moment of calm, Colonna approached Rev. William B. Miller, a Black leader of the Tilden parents.

"I'll keep my boys away from here tomorrow," Colonna told him, "if you keep yours away."

"Now we're rapping," Rev. Miller said. "This is one of the best things I've heard."[8]

Police took advantage of what the *New York Post* described as the presence of IACRL "peacekeepers" among white parent leaders. Inspector

Figure 35.2. Louis Colonna of the IACRL exchanges views on the Canarsie school busing crisis with Rev. Wilson Miller, Tilden Houses parent leader, November 1972. *Source:* Barton Silverman/New York Times/Redux. Used with permission.

James Meehan, speaking to a *New York Times* reporter, explained the NYPD tactic. "We had a guy in front of the school, a big, beefy guy with an Italian-American Civil Rights League badge and," the inspector added with a smirk, "every time I saw him I wasn't sure he was one of our guys."[9]

This was a button-wearing crowd. Tiny American flag pins and Nixon reelection buttons were plentiful. Nixon's 1972 campaign had appropriated Alabama Governor George C. Wallace's anti-busing pledge as its own; in addition, some influential Black celebrities and athletes—including James Brown, Jim Brown, and most ingloriously, Sammy Davis Jr.—publicly embraced Nixon's reelection bid. "But the biggest button and the only badges are of the Italian-American Civil Rights League," reported the *New York Post*. "Many, too, sport the button that proclaims: 'I was there on Unity Day.'"[10]

Roberta Gratz, reporting from behind the white barricades for the *New York Post*, overheard an exchange between two Canarsie mothers. "Our families voted liberal all their life and look where it got us," one of them said to no one in particular. Then she turned to her friend, raised a finger, and said, "You know, you're Jewish and I'm Jewish and you know as well as I know that the only place to buy a home in this city is in an Italian neighborhood because the Italians have more guts than the Jews." The sentiment perhaps helped explain why, at the time, Jews accounted for over 40 percent of League membership in Canarsie's Chapter 8.[11]

"There are people in Canarsie," opened a *Village Voice* article published during the school busing crisis, who "call the Civil Rights League the 'Mafia,' they call its members hoodlums, who threaten parents and children not boycotting the schools. They talk about the Canarsie trailer. But they don't say these things publicly." The "trailer" was a stealth reference to the screaming headlines about the discovery of a Five Family Mafia command post in a Canarsie junkyard.[12]

On October 17, *The New York Times* ran a pair of front-page stories on Canarsie, neither particularly flattering to the Brooklyn community. One, headlined "Protests by White Parents Shut 2 Canarsie Schools," chronicled the street melee surrounding the first day's anti-busing sit-in at John Wilson Junior High. The other, headlined "Grand Jury Writs Served on Hundreds of Members of 5 Mafia Families Here," was accompanied by a photo showing a dingy forty-by-fifteen-foot trailer in a Canarsie junkyard and captioned "summit headquarters," a derisive reminder of the infamous meeting that took place almost exactly twenty-five years earlier at Joseph Barbara's upstate mansion.

While the Apalachin summit was allegedly held to reorganize Mafia family holdings in the wake of the assassination of Murder Inc. boss Albert Anastasia, Canarsie "summit headquarters," according to *The New York Times*, was located in "the area where Murder, Inc., once dumped the bodies of many of its victims." For the past six months, according to Brooklyn District Attorney Eugene Gold, the trailer had been under electronic surveillance from a police perch hidden inside Nazareth High School, on the edge of East Flatbush, just across the street from the Canarsie junkyard. Information gleaned from surveillance—36,000 feet of color film, 54,000 still photos, and 1.6 million feet of tape from wiretaps—was the linchpin in "the most massive investigation of organized crime in the history of this country."[13]

Brownsville parents of the bused Tilden Houses students were, first and foremost, concerned about the safety of their children. A rumor circulated among them that all-white Irving Bildersee Junior High was under Mafia protection. Alternatively, John Wilson Junior High, "which has a history of integration," according to *The New York Times*, "seemed more likely to provide a safe and receptive welcome to the new minority-group pupils." Brownsville parents were more than likely pleased by the Central Board of Education's decision to reverse Chancellor Scribner's directive and instead sent their children back to John Wilson.[14]

The two-week John Wilson boycott ended after a hastily called November 7 meeting in the American Legion Hall attended by six hundred Canarsie parents, who, as described in the press, "appeared to agree to accept the 32 black children . . . but only if they were assured that there would be no further transfer of Brownsville children into the district." At the assembly, the parents also launched a new organization called Concerned Citizens of Canarsie, whose Jewish president, Alan Erlichman, was a dues-paying member and an outspoken supporter of the IACRL. Later that evening, at a meeting a block away from the American Legion Hall at Meade Esposito's Thomas Jefferson Democratic Club, representatives of fifty-two local community organizations formed the United Canarsie Council under the leadership of Nat Marcone, identified in the *Times* as IACRL "international chairman." The council, which included participants from the public assembly in American Legion Hall, "pledged full support" for the "effort to rezone the school district at the direction of the Central Board of Education."[15]

"We're not against the Central Board," said Carl Cecora, chairman of the League's Chapter 8. "We felt we had to make a stand," he continued in reference to the white parent protest. "We can see the need for integration in our society," he conceded. "We're not even asking the [Tilden Houses] children . . . to get out. We're just asking for no *more*." *New York Post* columnist Pete Hamill summed up Canarsie parents' concerns this way: "They are not afraid of black people or Puerto Rican people *per se*. They *are* afraid of what happens when racial balance is tipped in a school."[16]

The Canarsie busing crisis dragged on into the winter of 1973 while the board of education debated the issue. During this period, Kenneth Clark committed nearly two-thirds of his MARC staff to monitoring on-the-ground conditions in Canarsie schools while attempting to persuade the Central Board to find a solution in keeping with federal guidelines for desegregating schools "with all deliberate speed." By the beginning of March, Canarsie parents—fed up with what they deemed "stalling" by the board of education—reinstated their IACRL-led community-wide school boycott. By the end of the first week of the month, 8,440 of the area's 9,736 elementary and junior high school pupils had stayed away from classes. "We'll get thousands out here," said a man wearing an IACRL lapel button to a *New York Times* reporter. "They'll come from all over the city. We won't give up until we win."[17]

On March 30, the Central Board of Education unanimously adopted a plan to phase out the busing of Tilden Houses children. Under the approved plan, beginning in September, no first-grade pupils from Brownsville would be permitted to enroll in Canarsie elementary schools. The Central Board's decision was based on what it characterized as its continuing commitment to "quality integrated education *to the extent feasible*."[18]

In the end, Carl Cecora and Alan Erlichman—head of the local chapter of the IACRL and the Concerned Citizens of Canarsie, respectively—hailed the central board's decision as "a total victory for Canarsie." Kenneth Clark slammed the Central Board's final decision. A MARC press release, dated May 2, 1973, criticized it as a duplicitous mechanism for institutionalizing the fear of so-called tipping schools and more generally for fostering "racial exclusion in the guise of integration." In addition, Clark took a direct swipe at an unnamed "individual" working for the board of education: "This individual must be viewed either in the prime role as one of the leaders or a direct advisor to the primary leaders of the illegal boycott of the white parents."[19]

Clark was alleging a conspiracy, with its origins in the aftermath of the 1971 shooting of Joe Colombo, between the Central Board, led by Brooklyn representative Dr. Seymour P. Lachman, and the IACRL. "Two years ago," Clark said through a MARC spokesman, "Dr. Lachman had the foresight to appoint as his Assistant for Community Relations a functionary of the League who praised Joseph Colombo Sr. as 'a truly marvelous man.'" The unnamed "functionary of the League," who currently worked on the board as Lachman's assistant and who had made the foolhardy statement about Colombo, was Steve Aiello, head of IACRL's education task force. It was common knowledge that Seymour Lachman, although appointed to the Central Board by Brooklyn Borough President Sam Leone, owed his position to Aiello's mentor Meade Esposito.[20]

On August 29, 1971, a few months after the shooting in Columbus Circle and a day after Joe Colombo was released in a semi-comatose state from Roosevelt Hospital to convalesce at his Dyker Heights home, Lachman hired the League's twenty-eight-year-old education director as a staff assistant at the behest of Esposito. Steve Aiello's "main duty," according to Lachman, "would be maintaining liaison with community school boards and citizen groups in Brooklyn." According to *The New York Times*, Lachman had been impressed by Steve Aiello, a liberal educator, who in March 1971 "helped lead a league demonstration at board headquarters in Brooklyn against what the league called 'discriminatory practices' in the school system." The *Times* reporter added, "Another participant in the demonstration was Joseph A. Colombo Sr., a reputed Mafia leader."[21]

Even during the League's darkest days following the shooting at the second Unity Day rally, Steve Aiello refused to renounce IACRL's founder. As a result, when on the evening of August 29 his qualifications for the position on Lachman's staff were being vetted by the Central Board, Aiello was vigorously denounced by Dr. Mary E. Meade, the seventy-three-year-old representative from Staten Island. Dr. Meade, a retired school administrator and the only woman on the Central Board, had been described in the *Amsterdam News* as "an arch-conservative" who "is reportedly against any form of community control, particularly where blacks have it." A self-described "proponent of decentralization," Aiello sided with African American parents who pressed for greater community control of schools during the contentious New York City Teachers' Strike of 1968. During the debate over Aiello's hiring, Dr. Meade caused an uproar when she protested that she wanted nothing to do with "bringing on this gangster!"[22]

At the meeting's conclusion, after Steve Aiello was approved by a majority of the Central Board, *New York Times* reporter Myron A. Farber phoned Aiello to ask for his comment on the raucous debate over his hiring. He responded by praising Joe as "a truly marvelous man," adding: "I may be naïve but I never met a person more dedicated to his ethnic group—and with no ulterior motive. I would ask other Italian-Americans: Where were they when they were needed?"[23]

Lachman assigned Aiello to run his community relations staff. His job was to go into neighborhoods and deal directly with Brooklynites—students, parents, and local boards—on behalf of the Central Board. On the first day of the Canarsie boycott, Aiello was there talking to people on both sides of the issue. Throughout the busing crisis, his behind-the-scenes negotiation with local League officials was key to suppressing the spread of violent protest among Canarsie's whites.

Before the close of 1973, Chapter 8 Chairman Carl Cecora maneuvered to take charge of the national organization of the IACRL. Riding a wave of support after the forced busing crisis in Canarsie was put to bed—and while the original IACRL president, Nat Marcone, languished in jail on a tax evasion conviction—he made his move. Cecora arranged a sit-down with a half dozen League chairmen from chapters as near to Canarsie as Middle Village, Queens, and as far away as Youngstown, Ohio, at which he was anointed the group's president. In turn, he pronounced Canarsie's Chapter 8 national headquarters. Finally, having unceremoniously scrubbed all evidence of founder Joe Colombo from IACRL, Cecora dubbed what remained of the organization "the New League."[24]

Chapter 36

"A Model for All New Yorkers" (1973–75)

In November 1972, at the height of the Canarsie busing crisis, the New York City's Human Rights Commissioner Eleanor Holmes Norton named Mary Sansone, along with Corona 69 lawyer Mario Cuomo, to a commission seeking "ways to remove polarization among the city's various ethnic groups, such as resulted from the Canarsie schools dispute." Norton knew that Mary had allocated CIAO resources to educational reform in an effort to address the needs of the city's Italians alongside other underrepresented groups. A month later, in December, one of these reform efforts bore fruit when the city's Board of Higher Education gave the go-ahead to establish a Center for Italian American Studies at Brooklyn College. In January 1973, City University of New York announced that the center—"the first of its kind in the City University system"—was "being organized with the cooperation of CIAO." Mary was quoted as stating, "The Congress of Italian-American Organizations, committed as it is to multi-ethnic cooperation, believes that the programs of Italian American studies at the university level will contribute to the mutual understanding of various ethnic groups in New York City." By summer, the new center—"the only one of its kind in New York," according to Harlem's *Amsterdam News*—"officially opened its doors at Brooklyn College."[1]

Over the years, Mary gained a well-deserved reputation among city officials as one of the few community activists capable of advancing interracial cooperation at a moment when ethnic divisions were being stoked and making headlines. Creating harmony between the races was at the heart of CIAO's mission: "When I develop programs in an Italian community, we're getting the Italians to work with other ethnic groups too." HRC Commissioner Norton—who, as a twenty-six-year-old member of the Student Nonviolent Coordinating Committee, worked under Bayard Rustin's leadership when he organized the 1963 March on Washington—concurred:

"CIAO is a model for all New Yorkers of how to work effectively on behalf one's own group while insisting that equal rights be accorded to all." CIAO's programs, Norton added, "unselfishly help all the poor, the aged, and others in need in the neighborhoods," which is why the organization is "one of the strongest forces in the city for coalition building."[2]

On February 21, 1973, the CIAO realized its goal of operating a large-scale facility dedicated to its service delivery mission when it opened the Multipurpose Center at 5901 Thirteenth Avenue in Boro Park. When two years earlier the city pledged funding to build CIAO's center, it marked the first time any Italian American group was awarded antipoverty money. New York City's antipoverty structure had originally been established in 1966, during the first Lindsay administration, as the Human Resources Administration—a super-agency charged with funneling welfare, job training, and antipoverty programs into New York City's poor Black and Puerto Rican communities. Poor inner-city whites in New York, as elsewhere, were not eligible to receive War on Poverty funds targeting racial minorities. Five years later, in 1971, CIAO was identified in *The New York Times* as "the first Italian group to sponsor a city-supported day-care center."[3]

At the grand opening of CIAO's Multipurpose Center, a Roman Catholic priest delivered the invocation and a Hasidic rabbi gave the benediction. Conversations could be overheard in Yiddish and Italian as well as in English as attendees savored Italian sausages and knishes. "The center is open to all ethnic groups from the community," reported the *Times* despite the fact that, as Mary explained, CIAO was called "anti-Italian" by other Italian groups who opposed the organization "because we wanted to deal on a multi-ethnic basis." Support of CIAO, Mary stated, came from Mayor Lindsay. "He was the only one to extend one hand and then the other," she said. Mary's fiercest opponents were powerful Italian American machine politicians, such as James V. Mangano, profiled in *The New York Times* in 1970 as "the leader of the Mazzini Democratic Club in South Brooklyn for 30 years and [US Congressman John] Rooney's most dependable producer of votes." In that same year, 1970, local community leaders affiliated with the Italian-American Business and Professional Men's Association named Mangano its "Italian-American Man of the Year."[4]

CIAO was committed to empowering the community it served by allowing those enrolled in the center's programs to serve on advisory committees, which consisted of senior citizens and the parents of children enrolled at the facility. Mary organized 180 senior volunteers to assist with center activities, including a daycare program serving one hundred children, an after-school program accommodating forty children, a family daycare program with seventy-five preschoolers placed in provider homes, and a senior citizen program for which five thousand people sixty-five-years and older were registered. In addition, the center sponsored evening adult courses, art exhibits and performances, community health services, and drug prevention and treatment. Brooklyn residents Anna Shaw and Santa Salvo, attending the opening, called it "one of the most wonderful events we have been to in a long time. We heard the story of how a woman with a dream fought for eight years, fighting against politicians who laughed at her. She was like a voice crying in the wilderness."[5]

Less than four months after the Fifty-Ninth Street Center began operating, CIAO launched a second daycare center at 292 Court Street in South Brooklyn in a building that formerly housed a movie theater. Opening CIAO's Court Street Center was personally gratifying for Mary. This was the neighborhood where she grew up, and in order to win approval for the daycare center, she overcame fierce opposition from South Brooklyn district leader Mangano and his cronies. It was a sweet victory for Mary, and she celebrated it by honoring her father. In what the June 1973 issue of *CIAO Reports* characterized as a "moving ceremony," Mary—standing alongside her sisters Millie and Josie and her brother Joe—dedicated the Court Street Center to Rocco Crisalli. There, Mary saluted Rocky as a man "who devoted his life to aiding all people in their struggle for social justice."[6]

Mary, like her father, didn't trust powerful men to give a damn about the poor unless it was a means to lining their own pockets or increasing their political power. While running CIAO, she was committed to doing whatever was necessary to run a clean organization capable of thwarting hostile takeover bids from racketeers, politicians, and the *prominente*. Under these circumstances, the only practical way Mary could see to keep CIAO's day-to-day operations corruption-free was to hire family and friends. These were the only people she felt she could truly trust. CIAO's Fifty-Ninth Street Center, for instance, was under the directorship of Amy Bogin, daughter of Josie Del Mastro, Mary's sister. Mary's other sister, Millie, was on staff as a teacher's aide at the Court Street daycare center. Mary's adult children along with their cousin organized a CIAO-operated summer recreation program enrolling more than a hundred boys and girls, ages eight to thirteen, out of a Boro Park storefront at 5609 New Utrecht Avenue.[7]

By 1975, CIAO claimed to have 650 affiliated groups under its umbrella. Mary soon encountered one of CIAO's biggest challenges: opening storefronts and daycare centers in boroughs outside Brooklyn. At the start of 1975, when the organization was on the verge of finally planting its flag in Manhattan's Little Italy, Mary crossed the Verrazano Bridge into Staten Island for the same purpose. At a widely advertised meeting with a Rosebank parent group, she spoke about the organization's mission to solve the problems of the neediest in their community. Before leaving the meeting, she was confronted by a small group of residents in attendance. "You just said CIAO would help any Italian group," one of them said before asking: "Would you help the Civil Rights League or the Italian American Coalition?" Mary was indignant. The League and Italian American Coalition were run by those she considered "Colombo's people." She responded to the question by stating, "I didn't say every group, I said most every group." Her reply didn't go over well with this crowd, and they strongly advised her not to return.[8]

Mary was not inclined to back down from a fight, but she soon learned that the Staten Island contingent was threatening an eleventh-hour effort to block plans to build the CIAO senior center on Mott Street in Little Italy. As Mary was preparing for an appearance before the board of estimate to receive final contract approval for the Mott Street Center, she received a call from the Staten Island borough president, who was determined to thwart CIAO's effort to make inroads on his turf. He told her, "I will approve your contract to open in Little Italy on one condition: that you agree never to bring CIAO into my borough without first getting permission from me."[9]

Mary was incredulous. "Why the condition?" she asked.

"The Italians in Staten Island want it that way."

The Little Italy project was close to Mary's heart. It was her husband Zachary's dream to retire from the docks and direct a senior care facility not unlike the one he had designed thirty years prior, when he was mayor of Sant'Antonio Abate. Mary would do just about anything for Zach, and she knew she needed the vote of the borough president from Staten Island to get the Mott Street Senior Center approved. The borough president was, in Mary's estimation, a political hack beholden to racketeers, so she simply told him what he wanted to hear. "Not only will I give you a verbal commitment, but I'll send you a written commitment." What she didn't tell him was that she made two copies of the letter, one for herself and one for reporter Nicholas Pileggi, who always had her back. At the time, Mary acknowledged Pileggi's support on the Christmas-themed "Special Thanks" page in the December 1975 issue of *CIAO Reports*. "And, last but not least, CIAO's long standing and 'behind the scenes' consultant and friend, Nick Pileggi."[10]

Mary was determined to return to Staten Island over the opposition of a machine politician. By late 1975, she had done just that by maneuvering to open a pair of CIAO chapters on Staten Island. To achieve this goal, however, Mary had to compromise by allowing these chapters to function less like service delivery operations and more like fraternal orders. Unlike CIAO chapters in other boroughs, which were labeled according to location (e.g., Court Street Center in Brooklyn, Mott Street Center in Manhattan, Ozone Park Center in Queens), the Staten Island chapters followed the naming conventions of Sons of Italy by taking the moniker of famous Italians. One was called CIAO's Dante Chapter. The other dubbed itself CIAO's Meucci Chapter, in celebration of the borough's renowned Italian inventor. CIAO's Staten Island chapters focused their outreach efforts on cultural heritage rather than service delivery. As the country's two-hundred-year anniversary approached, they launched a bicentennial multimedia project celebrating Italian Americans' contributions to the nation. According to *CIAO Reports*, the project was coordinated by Peter L. Vale, who worked closely with Meucci Chapter President Eugene Cutolo. In the same issue of the newsletter that commended the Staten Island chapter's bicentennial programming, Vale was identified as chairman of CIAO's newly constituted Italian American Committee for Public Relations and Special Projects.[11]

Even as overseeing CIAO's operations became like conducting a three-ring circus, Mary's focus remained fixed on finding ways for the organization to serve the poor. On February 5, 1975, CIAO scored its biggest public relations victory: the organization's first press conference, held in its Park Row headquarters, where Mary announced the release of CIAO's demographic study, *A Portrait of the Italian-American Community in New York City*. CIAO's report, the first of its kind, was financed by an Office of Economic Opportunity grant, the only OEO funding CIAO had ever received. It drew upon 1970 US census statistics and data from the city's health and education departments. The study set out to prove, once and for all, the dogged fact that—as a result of years of neglect by government officials and disavowal by local community leaders—Italian Americans living in the city were subject to high rates of poverty while receiving a disproportionately small share of public assistance in employment, education, drug treatment, childcare, and senior care.[12]

"It is marvelous to see that the Italian community is learning a lesson the black community learned long ago," declared Bayard Rustin, who sat by Mary's side at the CIAO news conference. "Very simply," Bayard said, "it is that the squeaky wheel gets greased." Also flanking Mary at the news conference were two women—Gladys Harrington and Nancy Seifer—who, along with Joe Erazo, were Mary's biggest champions inside city hall. Together, Harrington and Seifer (who had left city hall before the end of the Lindsay administration) were responsible for shepherding Mary's programs through the municipal bureaucratic maze.[13]

On the occasion of the news conference, Mary sported a new look as CIAO's president. Gone were the bouffant and the floral dress. In their place: relaxed hair (by way of a "liberated" haircut, according to Ms. Sansone) and a smart pantsuit ("middle-aged Mary Richards," the look said, rather than "risqué" a la feminist and fashion icon Gloria Steinem). Mary stepped up to the microphones and addressed the press. "The disclosures in this study are unpleasant—and shocking," she stated flatly. "There are Italian Americans who are poor."

Figure 36.1. CIAO press conference, Manhattan, February 1975; left to right, Gladys Harrington, commissioner of New York City Human Resources Administration; Harrison Goldin, comptroller; Josephine Casalena, lead author of CIAO's demographic study *A Portrait of the Italian-American Community in New York City*; Mary Sansone; Bayard Rustin; and Nancy Seifer, director of the American Jewish Committee Center on Women and American Diversity. Source: Joan Roth. Used with permission.

"A Model for All New Yorkers" (1973–75) | 237

In New York City census tracts with more than 50 percent Italian population, 41 percent of all individuals living without family were below poverty level in 1970, but only 9 percent received government aid.

"There are Italian Americans who are dropouts."

During the 1973–74 school year, only 823 of 11,000 Italian-speaking school children with English language difficulties were receiving any bilingual instruction.

"There are Italian Americans who need assistance."

One-third of the Italian elderly classified as poor did not receive social security benefits because of lack of awareness or stigma, or because some of their work history was in Italy.

"Our study offers concrete evidence that government has been blatantly insensitive to the needs of the Italian American community. We are going to fight for our share of the pie."[14]

Newspapers from as far away as Honolulu reported on CIAO's February press conference with headlines like "City's Italian Poor Suffer in Silence, A Survey Shows." Soon after, CBS TV news broadcast a three-part segment on the plight of poor Italian Americans, buttressed by data gleaned from CIAO's report "on the poor, the neglected elderly, and school drop outs in New York's Italian communities." *Washington Post* coverage of CIAO's press conference, titled "Study Adds Italians to New York's Disadvantaged Minorities," drew the attention of US Senator Hubert Humphrey, chairman of the powerful Joint Economic Committee. How could he forget Mary Sansone, who he met at the outset of his 1968 presidential campaign on the occasion of her inauguration as president of the National Federation of Italian American Organizations?[15]

After getting hold of the CIAO study, Humphrey contacted the OEO to ask why Mary's organization wasn't receiving federal funding for programming to address the problems raised by its report. OEO's New York regional office responded that an Italian American group *was* receiving an OEO grant for programming targeting New York City's Italians. The funded group went by the name Italian American Center for Urban Affairs, which was a nonprofit subsidiary of an organization called Italian American Coalition. It was led by Dom Massaro, a New York State Republican Party appointee, who was the coalition's chairman. The executive director of the coalition's nonprofit subsidiary, IACUA, was Dr. Joseph Valletutti, disgruntled former president of CIAO. Italian American Coalition–affiliated organizations consisted of the usual suspects—Sons of Italy, UNICO, Americans of Italian Descent—groups led by men who were more likely to promote careerism alongside Italian heritage rather than working on behalf of the neediest in their neighborhoods.[16]

IACUA was seeking to renew its initial round of federal funding when, at the bequest of Senator Humphrey, officials from the Office of Economic Development were dispatched to take a closer look center's programming. Upon arrival, the Washington contingent was taken by local OEO staff on a tour of programs assumed to be operated by IACUA. During the tour, the group ran into Mary Sansone, who, surprised to see OEO officials on-site, introduced herself as the program's executive director. The Washington contingent told her how impressed they were with her programming and encouraged her to apply for "continued funding."[17]

Continued funding?

Mary smelled a rat. She phoned OEO's New York regional director Angel F. Rivera and asked, "How come the people from Washington thought they were touring programs paid for with federal funding? CIAO runs on city money." When the dust settled, Mary was told, "Somebody in the government didn't want to be embarrassed." It turned out that local OEO officials escorted the Washington delegation to see programs run by CIAO to avoid embarrassment. If the OEO Washington delegation had visited IACUA headquarters in Midtown Manhattan, what would they have seen? According to a Jack Newfield expose, they would have entered a "garish office" suite containing "zebra-striped sofas, wall-to-wall carpeting, a bar, and a stereo." Worse, IACUA's headquarters was furnished to the tune of $40,000 from the OEO federal grant.[18]

In January 1975, OEO's New York office conducted a "confidential" review of the Italian American Center for Urban Affairs programming and discovered that the lease on IACUA headquarters cost nearly double the rent allotment allowed by the OEO grant. IACUA's extravagant spending was just one illustration of the organization's failure to comply with grant guidelines. According to the OEO review, IACUA's board was made up of "elected officials, judges, lawyers, clergy, businessmen and Presidents of Fraternal Orders." It lacked representation from the ranks of the poor, which thereby placed IACUA in violation of the federal government's "maximum feasible participation" mandate.[19]

After Mary raised a red flag over the local OEO's attempt to use her programs to conceal IACUA negligence, OEO headquarters initiated a site visit. In January 1976, OEO dispatched its Washington officials back to New York. The investigators concluded that there was "too much emphasis placed on the Italian-American cultural aspect of . . . ethnic heritage" and "not enough emphasis placed on identifying the problems of the poor and working towards upgrading the standard of living for the poor." The site visit "recommendation" to OEO headquarters: "That the project not be refunded and that an immediate audit be initiated." A February 12 letter from regional director Rivera to Valletutti dealt IACUA—and by extension the Italian American Coalition—a death blow. It informed the executive director that IACUA would receive a $39,966 five-month close-out grant, after which the center would no longer be eligible for OEO funding.[20]

Mary turned IACUA's breach in her favor. With the help of Hubert Humphrey, she procured federal government funding for CIAO. The timing couldn't have been better. In October 1975, while President Gerald Ford was vowing to deny New York City a federal bailout to spare it from plunging into bankruptcy—resulting in the unrivaled *Daily News* headline "Ford to City: Drop Dead"—OEO was awarding $110,000 to Mary's coalition. The demographic report turned out to be not only a pioneering study of Italians in need. It was also a major contributor to CIAO's organizational growth, which now included a community service storefront on Eighteenth Avenue and Sixty-First Street in the heart of Bensonhurst. If so-called community leaders and the political bosses who backed them blamed Mary for Italian American Coalition's demise, she couldn't have cared less.[21]

By the mid-1970s, Mary had garnered considerable media attention. Her personal story, in the form of a forty-five-page autobiographical testimonial, appeared as the lead chapter in *Nobody Speaks for Me! Self-Portraits of American Working-Class Women*, authored by Nancy Seifer, former ethnic affairs aide to Mayor Lindsay, and published by Simon and Schuster. She was profiled as "the pint-sized dynamo" in Hope Macleod's *New York Post* Daily Closeup column. She was the featured interviewee on an hour-long WBAI radio program called *Ethni-city and the American Dream*, a broadcast produced by Gail Pellett, the station's news and public affairs director. Whether in print and over the air, Mary could be heard tallying a near decade's worth of achievements in community development. The metropolitan press never tired of prompting Mary to recount her run-in with Mafia boss Joe Colombo and the rivalry between CIAO and the League. Mary, for her part, never shied away from telling the tale of the confrontation that turned her into veritable legend and an inspiration to many Italian Americans, particularly women.[22]

Chapter 37

A League of Their Own: Williamsburg's Neighborhood Women (1974–77)

In the second half of WBAI's *Ethni-city and the American Dream* program, aired in November 1975, Gail Pellett transitioned from an in-depth interview with Mary Sansone to a lively roundtable with members of another female-led social action organization, the newly-formed National Congress of Neighborhood Women. NCNW was located in Williamsburg, a weather-beaten, industrial village on Brooklyn's Northside described in the 1970s by *The New York Times* as "one of the back-muscle neighborhoods of the city, tough and crucial, and unknown to people in places of greater power—Manhattan to the west, the suburbs to the east."[1]

Pellet kicked off the NCNW roundtable with the captivating voice of Sally Martino-Fisher, a lifelong Italian American resident of Williamsburg who identified herself as "Director of the Italian American Civil Rights League, Chapter 23." Other NCNW roundtable participants, a mix of Poles and Blacks as well as Italians, chronicled their community activism, but Pellett continually returned to Martino-Fisher, who—married, a mother of four, and a bingo banker at Saint Sabino Church—was "pleased" to announce that yesterday, for the first time in her thirty-one years, she was "arrested for disorderly conduct" in an NCNW-sponsored demonstration "protesting the cuts to antipoverty programs." Martino-Fisher divulged that her arrest for civil disobedience was in defiance of League directives issued by the all-male board of Chapter 23, where, she irreverently explained, "I'm sort of held down because of the fact that I'm a woman."[2]

Martino-Fisher, stout and tomboyish, had ten aunts and uncles on her mother's side and ten aunts and uncles on her father's side, all of whom called Withers Street in Williamsburg home. A dynamo, Martino-Fisher had been politically active in Williamsburg since 1971, when she was elected as a District 14 representative to the Greenpoint-Williamsburg school board, where the student population was 60 percent Puerto Rican and 25 percent Black. "I am for all the children, regardless of color," she told a *New York Times* reporter at the time of her election.[3]

Earlier that year, in the spring of 1975, Martino-Fisher was determined to see IACRL Chapter 23—which had, like many chapters, gone dormant in the wake of Joe Colombo's shooting but which Martino-Fisher had almost single-handedly resurrected—live up to its motto: "Unity in the Community." However, when, at League meetings, she promoted ideas for how Chapter 23 could serve not just Italian Williamsburg but the entire Northside community, her proposals were ignored or, at best, met with indifference.

Martino-Fisher found a way to leverage control inside the League's Chapter 23 by allying with a neighborhood outsider named Janice Peterson, an antipoverty community organizer who shared with Martino-Fisher a

Figure 37.1. IACRL Chapter 23 storefront, Williamsburg, Brooklyn. *Source:* Eugene Gordon/New York Historical Society. Public domain.

can-do spirit. Peterson had recently informed Martino-Fisher that she was putting together a big grant for funding outreach programs on the Northside through the federal government's new Comprehensive Employment and Training Act. CETA decentralized War on Poverty job training programs by giving block grants to state and local governments to help alleviate unemployment by funding jobs inside nonprofit organizations. CETA funding would allow Peterson to launch the NCNW, an ambitious working-class women's organization. According to a 1975 profile in the *Amsterdam News*, NCNW, headquartered in Williamsburg, would be "a heterogeneous organization involving Black, Puerto Rican, Italian, Polish and Irish neighborhood women" and tasked with tackling "such problems as housing, education, health and employment."[4]

The NCNW funding proposal was just one of a number of local initiatives sponsored by Jan Peterson's Northside CETA grant. Martino-Fisher worked with Peterson to generate a funding proposal that would transform IACRL Chapter 23 into a social action organization with the resources to reach the wider Williamsburg community. In the summer of 1975, Peterson's CETA initiative was awarded a $3-million pilot contract to fund more than a dozen Northside nonprofit organizations. One of those nonprofits was the Italian American Multi-Service Center, a tax-exempt legal arm Peterson helped Martino-Fisher create in order to make Chapter 23 eligible to receive public funds. The $3-million award called for Martino-Fisher's IAMSC and Peterson's NCNW to be awarded twenty-five CETA jobs each. One IACRL Multi-Service Center slot was designated for Martino-Fisher, who be responsible for hiring and managing office staff and social workers as the center's director.[5]

By 1975, poverty was rampant among New York City's growing West Indian population, and Martino-Fisher resolved to address the problem by deploying IAMSC assets to the Williamsburg's predominantly Puerto Rican southside. This led Martino-Fisher to make her most unorthodox CETA hire. In March, an application for CETA employment crossed her desk from a woman named Kellie Everts, who currently rented a sixth-floor walk-up on the southside and whose plight had very recently been publicized in a local newspaper called the *Greenpoint Gazette*. Readers of the *Gazette*, perhaps particularly Greenpoint's Poles, would have been familiar with a story such as Kellie Everts's, which chronicled a postwar Eastern European childhood. Born Rasa Sofija Jakstas in a German refugee camp to Lithuanian parents fleeing Soviet occupation, she and her parents, devout Roman Catholics, emigrated to the United States and settled in New Jersey.[6]

A free-spirited teenager, Everts dropped out of high school in the early 1960s and ran off to Hollywood to become a model. The *Greenpoint Gazette* profile was silent on this period of her life, which began to resemble something ripped from the pages of a tabloid magazine. During the first few years after arriving in Los Angeles, Everts wed, got pregnant, and had a baby girl. She was raped by a different man, which resulted in a second pregnancy and a trip across the border into Tijuana for an abortion. Everts's husband, refusing to believe his wife's rape story, became physically abusive. To protect herself and her child, Everts left her husband and moved into a nearby motel with her infant daughter. Soon after, she learned that her husband had developed an aggressive form of cancer. He died within the year.[7]

Everts, a widowed mother struggling to make ends meet, was in possession of a statuesque figure measuring 44-18-38. Hollywood photographers pictured her as a pinup rather than as a fashion model, and by decade's end, Everts was working as a stripper when not winning Miss Body Beautiful competitions or performing in B-movie biker flicks. Everts suffered severe depression during this period of life but found spiritual healing in a non-denominational New Age sect out of San Bernardino called One World Light. By the early 1970s, she was ordained a minister by the church's founder, Verna Talbot, who never asked her to give up stripping. In fact, Talbot encouraged Everts to find ways to use her unique gifts to shepherd others toward the light of God. With Talbot's blessing, Everts went back east with her ten-year-old daughter, which is where the 1975 *Greenpoint Gazette* profile resumed.

While stripping was Kellie Everts's profession, the ministry was her calling. She told the *Gazette* reporter that "she found nothing incompatible" about the unlikely combination of vocations. Years before sex-positive feminism had a name, Everts was "preaching" shameless radicalism from her pulpit at Follies Burlesk Theater on Forty-Sixth Street in Times Square, where she was billed as "the Most Beautiful Body in the World." She earned the titled after winning Dan Lurie's annual Miss Body Beautiful USA Body Builders of America competition, an award that was the result of more than a decade of weight training begun during her first pregnancy.[8]

The *Gazette* reporter was stunned not just by Everts's discernible beauty but also by "her dignified and quiet manner . . . she is also quick witted and surprisingly very evolved on the mental state." Everts announced in the *Gazette* profile that she was currently pursuing "a major part of her ministry in Williamsburg close to Grand Street and South Street where she lives." Accompanying the article were four photos of Everts, each registering a discrete pose. A pinup pose, where she lounges on a pedestal, mouth open, head thrown back in ecstasy, exposed cleavage, bare legs, high heels. A prayer card pose, where her eyes and mouth are closed, her hands clasp a cross, and her arms are covered by black sleeves. A domestic angle pose, where she stands in her living room, her smiling eyes cast down on the delighted reporter, who is framed by Everts and her towering Miss Body Beautiful USA trophy. Finally, a street preacher pose, where she stands on the corner of a busy intersection, hands clasping Bible, surrounded by sixteen boys and girls.[9]

It was the last photo, captioned "Rev. Kellie Everts on Grand Street and South 1st Street with youngsters in the neighborhood," that would have pricked the interest of an activist like Sally Martino-Fisher, someone committed to addressing the needs of racial minorities. The best way to do that on Williamsburg's southside, where a growing number of Hispanics resided, was to recruit an organizer who lived there. Martino-Fisher hired Kellie Everts, who suspended her career in burlesque. For the next couple years, Everts devoted herself to full-time social work for the Chapter 23's IAMSC. She counseled troubled kids and organized youth activities.[10]

Everts had two additional venues for community outreach. She currently appeared every Friday night on cable TV, where she preached the Gospel on a program called *One World Light*. And, beginning in April 1975, her byline regularly appeared in a *Greenpoint Gazette* column under the banner Let There Be Light, where she explained why she was not ashamed of stripping ("God gave me a beautiful body and I don't see anything wrong with exhibiting it"). However, she did feel exploited by the men who controlled the business—so much so that she claimed to be in the process of forming a labor organization called The Nude Models and Nude Dancers Union ("Every girl I've talked to wants to join. The girls have no representation. . . . The way they're treated, it could destroy them"). As Everts told a reporter for the *San Juan Star*, a Puerto Rican English-language newspaper, the IAMSC's CETA job in Spanish Williamsburg was an opportunity for her to fulfill a calling to "work in the ghetto and bring the Light to the poor people."[11]

In November 1975, a week before Sally Martino-Fisher appeared on WBAI's *Ethni-city and the American Dream* broadcast, Jan Peterson persuaded Martino-Fisher to join a demonstration on the Williamsburg Bridge to protest government cuts of up to 30 percent to antipoverty programs. The proposed cuts would not directly impact League Chapter 23 IAMSC funding, but Martino-Fisher thought, What if next time they come for our programs? "Today it's theirs, tomorrow ours," she proclaimed to *Woman's Day* magazine. "It's the same fight." Determined to publicize the League's commitment to helping the poor by participating alongside Peterson's NCNW protest, Martino-Fisher poached the large Italian American Civil Rights League banner hanging in Chapter 23's office and carried it with her to the action.[12]

On Tuesday, November 18, thousands of demonstrators marched through the streets of New York. At an entrance to the Triborough Bridge in the Bronx, Rev. Louis Gigante, currently a city councilman, rallied a crowd of noisy protesters. According to *The New York Times*, he told the gathering that this was "a great demonstration of the will for survival of the people of New York." The *Times* also reported that, in Brooklyn, four hundred protesters assembled on the Williamsburg Bridge ramp at the start of afternoon rush hour "but the police were able to cordon them off and keep traffic over the bridge moving." One police officer, who recognized Martino-Fisher standing behind the unfurled IACRL banner, told her, "Go home. This isn't your fight." Martino-Fisher refused the officer's admonishment and, along with protesters from the NCNW, was arrested on charges of obstructing traffic. As she was dragged into a paddy wagon, bystanders could hear Martino-Fisher holler, "Let me out! I have to pick up my kids from day care! I have a PTA meeting tonight!"[13]

"Mother in the paddy wagon, waving her banner and calling out instructions about her kids, might well serve as an emblem of the NCNW style," observed *Woman's Day* magazine. It was, however, at odds with Chapter 23's manner, which did not endorse disobedient women who waved the League banner en route to Brooklyn's Ninetieth Precinct for booking. "There was always a man there," Martino-Fisher said of her experience as director of the Italian American Multi-Service Center inside the League's Chapter 23, "like a toothache."

Martino-Fisher, having outgrown the New League, had had enough. During the early months of 1976, she plotted with Peterson on an exit strategy from the IAMSC that would allow her, under CETA guidelines, to be "outstationed" to another nonprofit. By March, Peterson was negotiating with Thomas Guidice, chairman of IACRL Chapter 23, who signed off on sending Sally Martino-Fisher's Chapter 23 CETA line to the NCNW office, where she would work as the executive assistant for the employment and training program.[14]

One week before the nation's bicentennial, Brooklyn's NCNW held its first national conference. Billed as Neighborhood Women: A Call for Action, the three-day confab was assembled at East Flatbush's Nazareth High School. Martino-Fisher led a workshop called Women as Community Leaders. Keynotes were delivered by Jan Peterson along with Nancy Seifer and Msgr. Geno Baroni. The press described conference attendees as a diverse group of ordinary women ("working class women of varied ethnic and racial backgrounds . . . most of whom were mothers and housewives," according to the *Amsterdam News*). CIAO's Mary Sansone was a featured speaker along with a who's who of the most prominent progressive women activists at mid-decade, including Bella Abzug, Shirley Chisholm, Barbara Mikulski, and Gloria Steinem.[15]

Brooklyn's Northside bicentennial parade featured IAMSC-CETA worker Kellie Everts as the "Unofficial Queen" of the *Greenpoint Gazette* float. Standing and waving to the crowd watching the parade along Metropolitan Avenue, Everts sported a bikini, cape, and crown. The outfit matched what she wore a year earlier in a July 1975 *Esquire* magazine spread. In the spring of 1975, *Esquire*'s art director Jean-Paul Goude contacted bodybuilding entrepreneur Dan Lurie seeking what at the time was considered a rarity among oddities—a female bodybuilder. Lurie sent him to Kellie Everts, who, having won Miss Body Beautiful USA in September 1974, appeared on the front cover of the December *Muscle Training* magazine, an issue that featured an Italian sheet metal worker from Brooklyn named Lou Ferrigno—a.k.a. "Mr. America trained by Dan Lurie"—on the back cover. Everts agreed to work with Goude, and she ultimately appeared in *Esquire* modeling a red-and-white-striped bikini for a photo essay with a Spanish title, "Viva Machisma!"

The *Esquire* piece covered a half dozen pages and included eight pictures of Everts flex-posing across a two-page spread. The rest was a mix of glossy bodybuilding photos and provocative conversation, prefaced by words meant to reassure the audience for a men's magazine: "Her name is Kellie Everts. She lives in the Williamsburg section of Brooklyn. She is an intelligent, cooperative woman, happy to answer an assortment of questions, each one respectfully posed." In the Q&A, Everts insisted that muscles on a woman were not unfeminine ("Muscle development make a woman look vibrant and healthy") and that although training never interfered with her love life, her religion did (she had taken a vow of celibacy since becoming a One World Light minister). The article concluded with Everts commenting on her ambitions: "In 1976, Kellie Everts plans to run for Congress. 'Let's face it. Eventually I'm going to have to give up the body stuff. I'd like to be in a position to do some good. . . . A woman body builder would be a better congressman than these lawyers are. At least I'm not so conservative.' "[16]

Although Everts never realized her dream of running for Congress, she did campaign on behalf of her CETA boss Sally Martino-Fisher, who was running for reelection as a Greenpoint-Williamsburg's District 14 school board representative. In the *Greenpoint Gazette*, Everts wrote that she was giving Martino-Fisher's candidacy her "full support" and attested to the fact that "while working under her at the Italian American Multi-Service Center, Chapter 23, Sally did everything in her power to see to it that through our office we helped the youth of the community. I, personally, spent much my time under Sally in my effort to help the Puerto Rican youth of Williamsburg, and made great progress in this field, because Sally

Figure 37.2. IACRL Chapter 23 annual Christmas charity event, Williamsburg, December 1975; left to right, Rosanne Mirando; Gloria Garglulo; Sally Martino-Fisher, IAMSC director; Kellie Everts. *Source:* Greenpoint Gazette.

did care and did want me to do this work. I too note that Sally often sent workers out into schools and day care centers when the need arose, and she kept in touch with all the schools and the problems they were having."[17]

Everts's political endorsement was published after Martino-Fisher left IAMSC for NCNW. Meanwhile, Everts remained employed as a social worker with IACRL Chapter 23. By the year's end, the *Greenpoint Gazette* was covering a new emphasis in Everts's outreach efforts—the well-being of young women. "Daughters of the Light is a new religious social club started by Rev. Rasa Kellie Everts," the article began. "It consists of fifteen girls ages nine to sixteen who have been meeting almost daily in Rev. Kellie's house for the last seven weeks." The reporter went on to describe how the girls were initially brought together to listen to Everts speak about the Light of God (what the girls called "Doing the Light") but had more recently begun to focusing on "other studies and diversions," including learning about "martial arts and women's liberation" along with "gymnastics and nutrition."[18]

Just after the release of *Pumping Iron* in January 1977, graphic artist Jean-Paul Goude appeared once again at Everts's door to pitch a second collaboration. *Pumping Iron* was a surprise pop culture sensation, and it was making an Austrian immigrant named Arnold Schwarzenegger famous. The documentary cast his bodybuilding rival, Brooklyn's Lou Ferrigno, as a muscle-headed variation on Victor Frankenstein's monster as imagined by novelist Mary Shelley—namely, the piteous victim of a maniacal Italian father. Schwarzenegger, the movie's jaunty star, played the part of the irresistible villain.

Goude wanted to capitalize on the buzz surrounding *Pumping Iron* by reshooting Everts's *Esquire* bodybuilding spread in the pages of *Playboy* magazine. Kellie Everts was perfectly comfortable posing nude, something she had done for a living since modeling as a teenager. Cashing in on the *Pumping Iron*–fueled fitness craze was even more enticing. While the documentary pulled back the curtain on "underground" bodybuilding subcultures stretching from Brooklyn's Sheepshead Bay to LA's Venice Beach, it failed to question the absence of women from the sport. Everts, more than any female bodybuilder of her generation, had firsthand experience of being brushed off inside bodybuilding circles and locked out of competition prize money. She was eager to get a piece of the action.

Everts's X-rated pictorial burlesqued *Pumping Iron* not merely as striptease but also as a playful mockery of bodybuilding's fragile hypermasculinity. On the first of a three-page spread in *Playboy*'s May 1977 issue, Goude photographed Everts inside a drab Brooklyn gym with walls stained by graffiti and illuminated by a bare bulb hanging from the ceiling. A group of Hispanic-looking young men, who sit on a nearby bench curling small black dumbbells, are distracted from their pump by Everts's conspicuous presence in their cave. Everts—perched on stiletto heels and crowned by bleached spikes—pauses mid-lift while holding a silver barbell beneath a confident, open-mouthed smile. She wears a red string bikini, which covers her privates but otherwise reveals her glistening, spray-tanned body. "The lady you see here is Kellie Everts," the caption begins. "As you can see, she's also a weight lifter." The reader is reassured that weightlifting doesn't make women's muscles "into magic mountains like Arnie Schwarzenegger's. It can make their muscles look like those on Kellie Everts." On the second page, Everts is outside the camera's frame. The reader sees only the weightlifting men, who stare off camera, mouths open, jaws—like the small dumbbells they lift—dropped. On the final page, Everts completes her burlesque. Holding a triumphant grin, she hoists the heavy barbell above her coiffed hair. The denouement: Under the pressure of her expanding muscles, top and bottom bikini strings snap, becoming live wires that merge with the wall graffiti and give off a neon-electric glow illuminating Kellie Everts's fully naked figure.[19]

When the *Playboy* pictorial hit newsstands, tongues wagged in Williamsburg. No longer shielded by her ex-boss Sally Martino-Fisher inside the Italian American Multi-Service Center, Everts faced the scorn of IACRL Chapter 23 leadership. She sought refuge, like Martino-Fisher had before her, at the National Congress of Neighborhood Women. Before the end of the first week of May, Chapter 23's newly appointed president, Frank Guidice (brother of Tom), had penned a perfunctory letter to Christine Noschese, NCNW's director, stating, "Please be advised that your request for Kellie Everts to be outstationed at your office has been approved . . . effective May 9, 1977."[20]

The pay for a community organizer under the Northside CETA contract was a meager $150-a-week. Even while living in a southside Williamsburg ghetto apartment, Everts could barely support herself and her daughter on a yearly salary of less than $8,000. Beyond financial hardship, Everts was burned out. She had dedicated herself to counseling (by her count) six hundred neighborhood children over the past few years as an IACRL Chapter 23 social worker. Some of these kids were classified as "troubled youth," which made Everts's job that much more challenging and stressful.[21]

"Finally, I knew I had to find another way to serve God," Everts told the *San Juan Star* a few months after she found her new calling at the

NCNW. "The *Playboy* spread spoiled my work [at the IAMSC] . . . I was persecuted, not by the Puerto Ricans, but by the Italians, who are more conservative about those things." That was also the end of Kellie Everts's collaboration with Jean-Paul Goude. He had moved on to the equally statuesque but even more exotic Grace Jones, a Jamaican-born model turned pop singer for whom he would fashion an iconic visual style.[22]

Chapter 38

Requiem and Redemption (1977–79)

In the fall of 1977, the *New York Daily News* ran an article with the title "What Ever Happened to Joe Colombo?" As reported, Joe's condition had not improved since his shooting. For six years, he lingered in a vegetative state. In assessing the current state of the organization Colombo founded, the *Daily News* sought out IACRL Chapter 23 President Frank Guidice, whose Multi-Service Center continued to operate under the federal contract awarded on the basis of Sally Martino-Fisher's CETA grant. Guidice, a former corrections officer, was hesitant to align himself with a mobster but conceded, "You have to give Colombo credit—he did organize the Italian people. I like the concept of what he started." Rev. Louis Gigante, also quoted in the article, was more reverent. "Joe Colombo gave us our ethnic consciousness," the League's chaplain maintained. "With him came the first swelling of Italian-American pride in America."[1]

In the spring of 1978, surrounded by his family at his Blooming Grove estate, Joe Colombo died at age fifty-five. At a requiem high mass at St. Bernadette's Church in Bensonhurst, he was eulogized by Father Gigante. "I would like everyone to remember that the Italian community was not Joe's only concern," he began. "Joe was concerned for the rights of all people, the little people especially, whom he helped to stand up for their rights against oppressive governmental agencies." Under the bells of St. Bernadette's, pallbearers carried Joe's gold casket out of the red brick church. Rev. Gigante stood on the steps and told the cameras, "People began to realize their dignity as Italian Americans because of him. That you right what is wrong in society even to the extreme—that you die for it."[2]

The reverend was not alone in his steadfast belief that Joe Colombo was a martyr and that the social justice organization he founded, the Italian American Civil Rights League, was no hoax. The summer before Joe passed, when a reporter asked Steve Aiello whether his feeling about the man had changed since the shooting, Aiello said his support was unshaken. Joe Colombo, he believed, should be remembered as the leader of a massive grassroots movement. Aiello conceded, however, that "had the devil himself initiated a movement to wake up Italian-Americans in this country, I probably would have been part of it."[3]

Loyalty to Joe continued to pay dividends for Steve Aiello. A year after the Canarsie school busing crisis was settled, Seymore Lachman stepped down as Brooklyn's representative to the city's Central Board of Education. Borough President Sam Leone appointed—no doubt with the blessing of Leone's benefactor Meade Esposito—Lachman's community relations aide to the post. At age thirty-one, Aiello was the youngest member of the education board. In 1977, he ascended to president of New York City's Central Board of Education and became, at age thirty-four, the youngest person ever to lead the nation's largest public school system.[4]

The organization Joe founded didn't receive a widely publicized reprieve until two years later, when it found absolution in, of all places, a *New York Times* editorial—the same space where Frank Sinatra, in 1967, was pilloried for his role as national chairman of earlier Colombo-backed organization, AIADL, and where Paramount Pictures producer Al Ruddy, in 1971, was taken to task for seeking to accommodate the League's anti-defamation demands while making *The Godfather* movie. On the last Sunday of October 1979, the *Times* editorial page did an about-face. The paper's editors conceded that "the now-defunct Italian-American Civil Rights league, an association founded by the late Joseph Colombo Sr., a reputed organized crime figure . . . pursued the legitimate purpose of combating reckless slanders against Americans of Italian descent."[5]

The reassessment of Colombo's League was the result of the *Times*' interest in advocating on behalf of Steve Aiello, who was being considered for an appointment as special assistant for ethnic affairs to the president of the United States. The campaign to approve the federal appointment had been initiated by Aiello's mentor, Meade Esposito. The Brooklyn Democratic County chairman asked New York Lieutenant Governor Mario Cuomo, head of President Carter's reelection campaign in the state, to forward Aiello's nomination to the White House. Inside the beltway, behind-the-scenes maneuvering was performed by longtime League supporter Bronx Congressman Mario Biaggi. An FBI background check had, however, put

Aiello's nomination in jeopardy. According to the *Times*' editorial, it "judged him guilty—of association." The editorial protested the Bureau's assessment. "Mr. Aiello . . . belonged to the same, noncriminal organization as a reputed criminal." Echoing a familiar IACRL talking point, the *Times* concluded, "Guilt by association is something fair-minded Americans remain unwilling to pronounce."[6]

By the first day of November, with the president's reelection campaign moving into high gear, the Carter administration—well aware that no recent candidate had won the White House without winning the Catholic vote and that the vast majority of so-called white ethnics were Catholic—overruled FBI objections. Mr. Aiello was on his way to Washington.[7]

Chapter 39

The Machine Strikes Back (1977–79)

With Steve Aiello in the White House, Williamsburg native Irene Impellizzeri succeeded him as Brooklyn's representative on the New York City Board of Education. A couple years earlier, in the spring of 1977, Midge Costanza, special assistant to newly elected President Jimmy Carter, attended the Congress of Italian American Organizations' tenth annual dinner dance, where she presented CIAO's first-ever Woman of the Year Award to Impellizzeri, dean of the School of Education at City University of New York's Brooklyn College, where Mary had spearheaded the founding of the first-ever Italian American research center. Costanza, the first female assistant to a US president, was tasked with facilitating inclusiveness inside the Carter administration toward women, minorities, and gays—groups traditionally without a voice inside the White House. At the CIAO event, Costanza was accompanied by her aide Janice Peterson, who, before moving to Washington to work for Costanza, turned over leadership of the National Congress of Neighborhood Women to Christine Noschese.[1]

CIAO's dinner dance was held at the Queens Terrace on Roosevelt Avenue, a gala establishment that Joe Colombo once operated as a silent partner and where ten years earlier he booked an extravagant *ricevermento* for his son Anthony and his bride, the former Miss Carol O'Brien. The CIAO event drew nearly six hundred attendees, including a list of notable 1970s New York liberals—Congresswoman Bella Abzug, Human Resources Commissioner Gladys Harrington, New York Secretary of State Mario Cuomo, New York City Mayor Abraham Beame, and Deputy Mayor John Zuccotti. Beame's administration, like Lindsay's, had been very good to CIAO.

To raise money for CIAO, a signed screenprint by painter Ralph Fasanella was auctioned off at the dinner dance. Fasanella was a labor organizer and a longtime friend of Mary's. In 1972, after twenty-five years of exhibiting his paintings in churches and union halls, Fasanella finally gained renown as a self-taught artist of working-class city life when he appeared on the cover of *New York* magazine next to the caption "This man pumps gas in the Bronx for a living. He may also be the best primitive painter since Grandma Moses." The feature inside the magazine was authored by Nicholas Pileggi. The painting auctioned at the CIAO event was *Feast of San Gennaro* (1976), a dense and colorful composition that captured Mott Street during the *festa*. At the end of the evening, the winning bidder bequeathed Fasanella's painting to CIAO's Little Italy Senior Center, where it hung on the wall inside the facility's newly renovated building at 180 Mott Street.[2]

At heart, Mary remained Rocky Crisalli's daughter. She was in the midst of leading a lobbying effort to persuade city hall to proclaim August 27, 1977, "Sacco and Vanzetti Day." That date was the fiftieth anniversary of the execution of Nicola Sacco and Bartolomeo Vanzetti, the immigrant anarchists convicted, on the basis of inconclusive and prejudicial evidence, of killing two men in a payroll holdup outside Boston. When, in August, McGraw Hill published historian Roberta Strauss Feuerlicht's *Justice Crucified*—a comprehensive account of the Sacco and Vanzetti case that was receiving favorable reviews in newspapers nationwide—the featured blurb accompanying the book's promotional campaign was from CIAO's executive director. "Their [Sacco and Vanzetti's] fate is a part of immigrant history, because it symbolizes the fate of every unwanted alien and dissident in America." Following Mary's blurb was another, this one from her friend Bayard Rustin, A. Philip Randolph Institute president, who touted the book's portrayal of Sacco and Vanzetti "as real human beings, capturing their dignity and courage without treating them as cardboard figures in a morality play."[3]

New York City Mayor Beame joined Massachusetts Governor Michael Dukakis in agreeing to honor Sacco and Vanzetti, but the day before he was scheduled to give the proclamation in city hall's Blue Room—a ceremony organized by Mary—Beame called it off. The reason: The mayor was up for reelection and he couldn't afford to be seen as soft on crime. Beame had recently buttressed his crime-fighting bona fides by endorsing capital punishment. Aligning his name with convicted murders Sacco and Vanzetti might undermine that pledge in the mind of voters. These election-year decisions were made in the immediate aftermath of a perceived collapse of law and order in New York City. On a hot summer night in July, a Con Edison power blackout plunged New York into darkness and resulted in rioting, looting, and arson in Black sections of the city. Almost four thousand people were arrested and property damage was estimated at $100 million.

During the same month, New York City was put on edge and then sent into hysteria when police disclosed that a mystery serial killer was on the loose who called himself Son of Sam.[4]

Those two events traumatized the city. They damaged the mayoral campaign not only of incumbent Abe Beame but of liberal candidates, such as Bella Abzug and Mario Cuomo, while they benefited Edward Koch, a neoconservative Democrat. Koch was a political opportunist of the first order. He began his political career as a reform candidate during the 1960s, defeating machine boss Carmine DeSapio for the position of Democratic Party district leader in Greenwich Village in 1963 (and again in a 1965 rematch) before winning, in 1969, Manhattan's "Silk Stocking" congressional seat once held by liberal Republican John Lindsay. With his finger to the wind, Koch soon tacked rightward. By the early 1970s, Koch recognized that a fear of Black crime was exasperating the white backlash. He exploited that fear in 1972 when he became a leading opponent of a Forest Hills "scatter site" public housing project, which threatened to bring poor Blacks into a Jewish section of Queens. As a compromise, Corona 69 lawyer Mario Cuomo, at the behest of Mayor Lindsay, brokered a housing plan only half the size of the original proposal. The pushback against the project, however, became a lasting symbol of white middle-class resistance to residential integration in New York City.[5]

By November, the campaign for mayor was essentially a two-man race between Congressman Koch and Mario Cuomo. Koch was the Democratic Party candidate, having won the party's primary election; Secretary of State Cuomo ran on the Liberal line. Earlier in the year, during the first of two Democratic primaries, Mary endorsed the reelection of her unwavering ally in city hall. Once Beame bowed out of the race, Mary eagerly joined Cuomo's campaign.

During the Democratic Party runoff, Koch's handlers mercilessly attacked Cuomo as soft on crime by targeting his refusal to support the death penalty. How, then, had Cuomo received enough votes to force Koch into a runoff? "Biaggi . . . Biaggi . . . Biaggi—that's how he got into the runoff," ranted David Garth, Koch's TV campaign adviser. Garth's tirade insinuated that without the endorsement of the city's most popular law-and-order politician Mario Biaggi, Cuomo would not have had a strong showing in the primary.[6]

Mario Cuomo was an unreconstructed New Dealer who was popular with Italians ever since, as the lawyer for the city's first neighborhood preservation "cause" the decade prior, he led the Fighting Corona 69 into battle with city hall. In addition to being the Liberal Party candidate during the general election, Cuomo placed his name on the Neighborhood Preservation line, a newly created party that appealed to dissident Democrats and independent voters. The Neighborhood Party harnessed the energy of an evolving national "neighborhood" movement that, in the second half of the 1970s, was refocusing its outreach on to white ethnics in urban America. CIAO member Mike Pesce, for whom Mary also vigorously campaigned, had won reelection to the New York State Assembly with the backing of South Brooklyn's Independent Neighborhood Democrats. The reform party's platform called for implementing good governance, such as streamlining communication between local community boards and municipalities, as well as backing progressive initiatives that embraced environmentalism and historic preservation while opposing blockbusting by realtors and redlining by banks.[7]

Congressman Biaggi abandoned candidate Cuomo during the general election campaign, abruptly switching his allegiance to the frontrunner Ed Koch. Why did Biaggi change horses just when the mayoral election entered the home stretch? Cuomo, rather than berate Biaggi for his betrayal, accused

Figure 39.1. A 1977 New York City mayoral campaign poster. *Source:* Yanker Poster Collection/Library of Congress. Public domain.

Koch of making "arrangements," "deals," "accommodations," and "political contracts" with "various people." Journalist Jack Newfield investigated Cuomo's charges and discovered that Koch had engaged in a secret meeting with Kings County leader Meade Esposito, who, along with Biaggi, was a longtime Italian American Civil Rights League loyalist.[8]

According to Newfield's sources, after the September runoff, Koch and his handlers made their way to Esposito's mother's house in the Ocean Hill section of Brooklyn for a meatball dinner. After getting hopelessly lost, they finally arrived at Felicia Esposito's, where they were joined by Meade and his protégé, district leader Anthony Genovesi. During the sit-down, Esposito made no demands on the candidate in exchange for his support except one: "I want to know you will return all my phone calls." Koch agreed to the demand on the condition that Esposito keep his endorsement out of the news. Chairman Meade was no doubt pleased, knowing that his tacit endorsement of Koch was proof of one of his favorite maxims: "Today's reformer is tomorrow's hack."

In public, according to *The New York Times*, Meade Esposito "professed neutrality" in the election. Although the Democratic Party boss went so far as to acknowledge that he had talked to Koch since the initial primary, he was quick to add that Cuomo "didn't even call." Apparently, Cuomo insulted Esposito by refusing to even ask for his support. Esposito retaliated for the slight by dispatching Genovesi to run the machine's Koch for Mayor campaign. Two days before the election, an article broke in the *Village Voice* under the title "Clubhouse Confidential." The *Voice* reporter observed, "In Brooklyn, you can't find a more fervent Koch backer than Anthony Genovesi, whose first allegiance is to the Democratic boss Meade Esposito, whom Genovesi hopes to succeed when Meade steps down next year."[9]

Mary Sansone went door to door in Brooklyn for the Cuomo campaign. The weekend before the general election, polls showed Koch's once commanding lead over Cuomo had shrunk to just 4 points. Meade Esposito sought out Mary Sansone, catching up with her at a Cuomo campaign rally. He pulled her aside and told her that it would be in her best interest to switch her allegiance to Koch. She turned to walk away. He got angry.[10]

"You forget I'm county leader," Esposito called after her.

"You forget I don't give a damn," she said without looking back.

Mary was a veteran of Brooklyn's tribal feuds, and CIAO was a product of them. For the past five years, CIAO had emerged victorious, untouched by scandal, and by 1977 the benefactor of $3 million in federal, state, and local funds with 285 employees who provided welfare services to poor Italians and other ethnic minorities across the city. By the end of the year, CIAO's community outreach programs assisted 5,500 Italian Americans and low-income minorities, primarily African Americans and Puerto Ricans, in every borough but the Bronx. Funding for CIAO's service delivery operations, however, flowed primarily through city hall. The organization's survival was largely predicated on Mary's ability to maintain the mayor's favor. It was the key to Mary's unrivaled success during the second Lindsay administration and vital to sustaining CIAO's programming during the city's fiscal crisis at mid-decade, when Lindsay's predecessor, Brooklyn's Abe Beame—an old friend of Mary's dating back twenty years—served as mayor.[11]

Ed Koch's November 1977 victory in the New York City mayoral election changed everything. On election day, voter exit polls gave his challenger, Mario Cuomo, a 15 percentage-point margin over Koch as the more independent candidate. Nevertheless, Meade Esposito's machine delivered Brooklyn to Koch, who prevailed in the election.[12]

To give the appearance of independence, Mayor Koch immediately installed screening panels to ensure that job candidates for top posts in his administration were vetted for their competency rather than appointed though the patronage trough. However, Koch promptly bypassed his advisory committee's recommendation when he appointed Anthony Ameruso, an Esposito crony, as transportation commissioner. The panel, which had rejected Ameruso as unqualified, publicly protested the mayor's brazen decision.[13]

Koch's response was to disband his advisory committee and attack his critics rather than reconsider Ameruso's qualifications. The new mayor, while attending a dinner at Cotillion Terrace honoring Meade Esposito, used red-meat rhetoric to denounce his former screening panel as Manhattan elitists. From behind the podium, Koch asked the assembly of fourteen hundred mostly Italian attendees, "What would you think of a committee that doesn't want an Italian commissioner in this city?" and was greeted with a wave of boos. When he followed up the question with another—"What do you think of a mayor who does?"—the boos turned into a cascade of cheers. Soon after, Transportation Commissioner Ameruso found himself entangled in a series of ethical lapses that would eventually land him in jail.[14]

Another prominent theme from Koch's 1977 mayoral campaign was the candidate's race-baiting promise to root out "poverty pimps" and "pledge to deny funds to any program that was 'ripping off the public." The pejorative "poverty pimps" was repeatedly used by Koch to criticize self-appointed minority leaders who, according to the candidate, failed to act on behalf of the poor while benefiting financially from the political arrangement. In interviews just before he took office, Koch told *The New York Times* that "one of his first priorities would be a restructuring of the antipoverty program," specifically the Human Resources Administration and its $4 billion annual budget, believed to be the largest municipal agency in the United States.[15]

Hardest hit by the Koch administration's HRA reorganization were African American employees, for whom it was a purge. According to Harlem's *Amsterdam News*, while "the ten top white HRA administrators" were retained by Koch's newly appointed HRA Commissioner Blanche Bernstein, she fired the four Black upper-tier agency managers. Gladys Harrington, Mary Sansone's longtime ally inside the agency, was one casualty of Koch's anti-antipoverty crusade.[16]

During both the Lindsay and Beame administrations, Harrington maneuvered to ensure that CIAO won approval for service delivery contracts. For instance, when approval was required for Mary's husband Zach to be hired to run CIAO's Mott Street Center, Harrington pushed it through over objections raised by those who resented CIAO's "most-favored status" inside city hall. Back in 1973, when readers opened *CIAO Reports*, they were greeted by Mary's Thanksgiving message, which included a short list of "special people" who enabled the organization's success. First on the list was "Gladys Harrington of HRA, who taught me how to deal with city bureaucracy."[17]

The removal of Mary's supporters inside city hall, combined with the new mayor's dubious relationship with Meade Esposito, spelled trouble for CIAO, and Mary knew it. Here's what she didn't know: New members of CIAO's board of directors, who hailed from the recently launched Staten Island chapters, were plotting her demise. At a CIAO executive meeting on November 15, exactly one week after Koch's mayoral election, board members Peter Vale and Eugene Cutolo—affiliated with the Meucci Chapter and identified in *The New York Times* as low-level HRA employees—blindsided Mary at an organization meeting when they accused her of "nepotism and corruption."[18]

Less than a week later, on November 21, Peter Vale sent a confidential letter to Congressman Mario Biaggi that outlined charges against Mary and alluded to the discovery of Mary's wrongdoings. "About two months ago," Vale wrote to Biaggi, "I received an anonymous letter, containing allegations of nepotism and corruption in the administration of the various programs run by C.I.A.O. in New York City." Vale wrote that after receiving the anonymous tip, he consulted "some Project Directors employed by C.I.A.O." in order to corroborate the allegations. Vale also described the November 15 organization meeting where he initially "confronted" Mary with "facts given to me by said Project Directors." Vale expressed shock that the executive director refused to immediately respond to charges made by his anonymous source. "Mary Sansone seemed determined to continue doing 'business as usual,'" Vale wrote. For good measure, Vale's letter borrowed from the newly elected mayor's smear campaign. "I feel that we should not tolerate in our midst any 'poverty pimps,'" he wrote in reference to Mary, "who would give a bad name to all of us Italian Americans."[19]

Vale's confidential letter to Biaggi was the first in a series of missives implicating Vale and his accomplices in a conspiracy to topple Mary, even at the cost of laying waste to the Congress of Italian American Organizations. Vale's letter to Biaggi was written on letterhead from an organization called the Italian American Committee for Public Relations and Special Projects. The letterhead identified Vale as its chairman and as "Director of Public Relations, CIAO." The letterhead's sidebar listed other officers and board members, including current US Congressman Biaggi (the letter's addressee). Directly beneath Vale's name on the letterhead's sidebar was Dominic R. Massaro, who had joined the organization in August and was listed as general counsel. Massaro had reentered private law practice after a string of recent Republican Party executive branch defeats at the federal and state levels. He was also linked to Biaggi through the now-defunct Italian American Coalition. Massaro had led IAC as its chairman; Biaggi had served as IAC vice president. While running for mayor in 1973 (Fig. 17.1), Biaggi resigned from IAC's board to avert a scandal over IAC's cozy relationship with the Italian American Civil Rights League, whose president, Nat Marcone, had recently been jailed on IACRL-tainted loan fraud and tax bribery charges.[20]

On the same date Mario Biaggi received the confidential letter from Peter Vale outlining the charges against Mary Sansone—November 21—Dom Massaro also received a letter from Vale on the same letterhead. Unlike Biaggi's missive, however, Vale's designation as CIAO's director of public relations had been scrubbed. In the text of his letter to Massaro, Vale explained, with conspiratorial undertones, that the erasure was the result of their November 17 phone conversation. "With regard to my listing on our letterhead ("Director of P.R., CIAO") I think that you are right, i.e., we must delete it."[21]

The accusations made against Mary by Peter Vale and Eugene Cutolo at CIAO's November 15 meeting precipitated a split inside the organization's board reminiscent of the breach that nearly sank CIAO in the summer of 1970, when a Joseph Valletutti–led faction tried to persuade the board to vote with Joe Colombo's League. Currently, some board members, following

Vale and Cutolo, thought the charges against Mary were worth pursuing in the name of good governance. Others believed them to be little more than a politically motivated mugging. Mary tried to squelch the dissent by brushing aside the accusations against her. But the insurgents, with a friend in city hall, would not be silenced. Immediately after Koch's January 1978 inauguration, they took their case to the press, where they charged Mary with everything from "petty corruption" to "tyrannical rule." She denied the charges, of course, countering, "I'm a woman, and the men that are fighting me are very chauvinistic and very conservative," and concluding with an understatement: "They find me a little too liberal to do what I do."[22]

The accusation causing the biggest stir was not the false allegation that CIAO was drowning in bureaucratic waste or deliberate fraud, or even that its leader was a despot. The charge that gained traction was that Mary ran CIAO like a family business by giving preferential treatment in hiring to blood relations. "Italian-American Group's Board Levels Charge of Wide Nepotism" screamed *The New York Times* headline for the article that broke the story. Paragraph after paragraph profiled a total of ten CIAO employees, paid and volunteer, who had family connections to Mary. Her husband directed the Mott Street Senior Center; her daughter operated the Bay Ridge Child Counseling Program; she appointed her son to CIAO's executive board. Near the article's end, the reporter buried a seemingly significant concession, legally speaking: "Investigators familiar with the situation say that there are apparently no laws against nepotism."[23]

It was a fate all too familiar to Italian Americans—live by the family, die by the family. Mary never tried to hide the fact that she hired family and friends to work for CIAO. "I feel secure with them," she freely admitted in a February press interview. "During the early days, when some undesirable Italian American organizations wanted [to] take us over, they were the only ones I knew I could trust. Now that I'm more secure, I can't kick my relatives out." Her husband and daughter were each paid annual salaries of $18,000 while her son worked gratis. Longtime board member Buddy Scotto was quoted in the paper as saying that CIAO benefited from city agencies "eager to identify a white ethnic group that would be eligible to share in antipoverty financing." He claimed firsthand knowledge of HRA administrators telling Mary that "it was O.K. to hire her daughter, son, whoever—officially."[24]

Rival factions on CIAO's board could not reach an agreement on what, if anything, Mary had done wrong and what, if anything, should be done about it. Mary's supporters hit back at Peter Vale and Eugene Cutolo, the board members who made the allegations of corruption against Mary. They contended that because Vale and Cutolo were HRA employees, they were guilty of an ethical "conflict of interest" by holding simultaneously positions on CIAO's board and jobs inside the agency (HRA) primarily responsibility for administering the city's antipoverty public assistance programs, including CIAO's.

Blanche Bernstein, Koch's newly appointed HRA commissioner, assigned Reuven Savitz, deputy administrator for intergovernmental relations, to oversee the city's investigation of CIAO. Savitz was profiled in *The New York Times* as having "strong ties" to a "Brooklyn Democratic organization." According to the *Village Voice*, Savitz was "a clubhouse crony of [Anthony] Genovesi," from whom Savitz had been bequeathed "a patronage job with HRA."[25]

By December 1978, HRA Deputy Savitz announced that CIAO's contracts would be terminated on January 1 and turned over to an interim ninety-day sponsor (Catholic Charities of the Archdiocese of New York) "until a new sponsor can be selected." According to the *Times*, Savitz based his final decision on an unreleased New York State Comptroller audit, which found that "many of the community groups" CIAO claimed to represent "were nothing more than paper entities."[26]

Mary reacted to the news by attacking the Koch administration move as a hostile "takeover" orchestrated by Savitz and Bernstein to allow the mayor to "establish a political base." She believed that Koch had made a backroom deal with Meade Esposito to funnel CIAO's programming—and the jobs that went with it—into the Brooklyn machine's patronage trough. The decision to wrest control of CIAO away from Mary still had to be approved by the board of estimate, where during what *Newsday* described as "an emotional four-hour hearing," Mary vigorously defended CIAO against charges of mismanagement. In a split vote, the board of estimate, persuaded by Mary's testimony, declined to allow HRA to remove city contracts from CIAO.[27]

Mary's victory was short-lived. Koch had seen enough. Determined to separate CIAO from its city contracts—and in doing so oust Mary Sansone's influence inside city hall—he attended the next board meeting, which was the last of the year. This time, however, he deployed a procedural maneuver to ensure a vote in his favor, after which, according to coverage of the meeting in *The New York Times*, the mayor found himself "heckled and booed" by more than two hundred angry, mostly Italian, CIAO supporters.[28]

Jack Newfield, writing in the *Village Voice*, reported that the city funds for CIAO service pacts were "turned over to a Genovesi group." The following year, the Internal Revenue Service completed its audit of CIAO, which was required by law due to charges brought against it by the city. Mary was exonerated. The IRS even allowed CIAO to keep its tax-exempt status as a nonprofit organization. At the time, Mary claimed to have been sent a letter from federal auditors expressing their sympathy for the loss of the CIAO's programs, which they had determined were remarkably free from fraud or waste.[29]

Mary refused to give up. She packed up CIAO's Park Row headquarters and returned to Boro Park, where she set up her organization's operation in the familiar surroundings of her wood-paneled basement. Unbowed at age sixty-three, she crowed that the Congress of Italian American Organizations "is very much alive." Her next move was to open a storefront at Fifty-Ninth Street and New Utrecht Avenue in Brooklyn. Although CIAO no longer received financial support from federal, state, or local agencies, the organization nonetheless recommitted itself to service delivery. It offered a modest range of programming, funded by charitable donations, from assisting youth with special education needs to fighting eviction cases for elderly tenants. Mary was a survivor, someone who refused to succumb to despair even when her life's work was being ripped away. "I've never been a quitter," she said in the midst of the battle with the Koch administration over CIAO's programs, "and I'm ready to fight now."[30]

Coda

In the winter of 1972, *The New York Times* convened a roundtable on "ethnic roles" with a spirited group of up-and-coming Italian New Yorkers, including City Youth Board Director Frank Arricale, Center on Migration Studies Director Rev. Silvano Tomasi, and State Human Rights Assistant Commissioner Dom Massaro. Some of the participants, such as League Education Director Steve Aiello and CIAO Executive Board Member Mike Pesce, were known to have chosen sides in the rivalry between Joe Colombo and Mary Sansone. The *Times* correspondent, having listened to the discussants debate ethnic identity, concluded that the roundtable could only come to a consensus about one thing related to the Italian American experience. "Everyone seemed to agree that self-hatred was indeed a problem."[1]

Fast-forward a decade. Mario Cuomo, running for New York governor in the fall of 1982, vanquished New York City Mayor Ed Koch in the Democratic Party primary by 10 points before going on to win the general election. The following spring, a *New York Times Sunday Magazine* cover appeared with the celebratory headline "Italian-Americans: Coming into Their Own." The accompanying story, authored by journalist Stephen Hall, a resident of Brooklyn, featured a present-day study of Italian American identity. "A recent survey of 213 third-generation Italian-Americans in their early 30's, all of whom had grown up in the heavily Italian Bensonhurst neighborhood of Brooklyn, revealed overwhelmingly positive feelings about their Italian roots. To the question 'Would you change your ethnic identity?' not a single person in the sample said yes—a possibility almost inconceivable a generation ago." Said the study's author—Mary Sansone's daughter, Carmela—to the *Sunday Magazine*, "This is a group that has come a long way."[2]

Notes

Preface

1. On Rev. Martin Luther King Jr.'s praise for Bayard Rustin's "expertness and commitment" in the "method of nonviolence," see King's letter to Edward P. Gottlieb, March 18, 1960, in *The Papers of Martin Luther King, Jr.*, vol. 5, *Threshold of a New Decade: January 1959–December 1960* (University of California Press, 2005), 390; on Sammy Davis Jr.'s fundraising acumen for the civil rights movement, see Gerald L. Early, *This Is Where I Came In: Black America in the 1960s* (University of Nebraska Press, 2003), 45.

Chapter 1

1. Maria Forte, Tape 157, New York Immigrant Labor History Project Oral History Collection, Robert F. Wagner Labor Archives, New York University, qtd. in Jennifer Guglielmo, *Living the Revolution: Italian Women's Resistance and Radicalism in New York City, 1880–1945* (University of North Carolina Press, 2010), 115.

2. Hope Macleod, "Daily Closeup: Sharing and a Share," *New York Post*, March 13, 1975; Nancy Seifer, *Nobody Speaks for Me! Self-Portraits of American Working Class Women* (Simon and Schuster, 1976), 47.

3. "Ex-Convict Slain with Woman in Car," *New York Times*, February 7, 1938, 32.

4. "Ex-Convict Slain with Woman in Car."

5. Macleod, "Daily Closeup"; Seifer, *Nobody Speaks for Me*, 50–51; Joe Hill, "The Rebel Girl" (1915), the lyrics for which first appeared in the 1916 edition of the IWW's *Little Red Songbook*.

6. Seifer, *Nobody Speaks for Me*, 51; Guglielmo, *Living the Revolution*, 68, 91, 244, 250.

7. Don Capria and Anthony Colombo, *Colombo: The Unsolved Murder* (Unity Press, 2015), 10–13, 39, 71.

8. Capria and Colombo, *Colombo*, 16, 20; Judith Michaelson, "The Vigil at the Hospital," *New York Post*, June 29, 1971, 3; Wesley F. Gill, "Joe Loves Golf, Doesn't Smoke," *Evening News (Newburgh, NY)*, June 30, 1971, 8D.

9. Macleod, "Daily Closeup"; Seifer, *Nobody Speaks for Me*, 52; Philip S. Foner, "The IWW and the Black Worker," *Journal of Negro History* 55 (January 1970): 48; letter from Bayard Rustin to Joseph Beam, April 21, 1986, in *I Must Resist: Bayard Rustin's Life in Letters*, ed. Michael G. Long (City Lights, 2012), 460.

10. Capria and Colombo, *Colombo*, 21–25; Michaelson, "The Vigil at the Hospital"; Douglas Robinson, "Mafia Believed Behind the Italian-American Protests Over 'Harassment,'" *New York Times*, July 19, 1970, 57.

11. "Brooklyn Mafia Chief: Joseph Colombo," *New York Times*, March 25, 1970, 40.

12. Seifer, *Nobody Speaks for Me*, 45.

13. Macleod, "Daily Closeup"; Seifer, *Nobody Speaks for Me*, 53–54.

14. Seifer, *Nobody Speaks for Me*, 52.

15. Seifer, *Nobody Speaks for Me*, 55.

16. "Rosie and Vic Return from Truman Visit," *Brooklyn Eagle*, May 18, 1948, 3.

17. "Happenings Around the Borough," *Brooklyn Eagle*, September 13, 1947, 3; *Brooklyn Eagle*, September 18, 1947, 3.

Chapter 2

1. "Costello's Help Called Vital In 1949 New York Mayoralty," *Washington Post*, March 13, 1951, 1.

2. Meyer Berger, "3 Go to Trial Here as Atom Spies," *New York Times*, March 7, 1951, 1; "'Space Ship' Spying Bared," *Chicago Tribune*, March 13, 1951, 1.

3. William R. Conklin, "Atom Bomb Secret Described in Court," *New York Times*, March 13, 1951, 1.

4. Jack Gould, "Costello TV's First Headless Star," *New York Times*, March 14, 1951, 1; "Frank Costello Dies of Coronary at 82," *New York Times*, February 19, 1973, 21.

5. *Meet the Press*, NBC, Washington, DC, March 25, 1951, Motion Picture Division, Library of Congress.

6. *Meet the Press*, NBC, Washington, DC, April 1, 1951, Motion Picture Division, Library of Congress.

7. Estes Kefauver, *Crime in America* (Doubleday, 1951), 21.
8. Daniel Bell, "Crime as an American Way of Life," *Antioch Review* 13 (Summer 1953): 143.
9. Bell, "Crime as an American Way of Life," 144.
10. Walter Winchell, "Costello's Solution: Legalized Gambling," *Miami Herald*, April 2, 1951, 1, 4.

Chapter 3

1. Seifer, *Nobody Speaks for Me*, 56–57.
2. Seifer, *Nobody Speaks for Me*, 81.
3. Capria and Colombo, *Colombo*, 33; "Brooklyn Mafia Chief: Joseph Colombo," 40.
4. Capria and Colombo, *Colombo*, 37.
5. Charles Grutzner, "Mafia Steps Up Infiltration and Looting of Businesses," *New York Times*, September 14, 1965, 1; Nicholas Gage, "Colombo: The New Look in the Mafia," *New York Times*, May 3, 1971, 1.
6. Capria and Colombo, *Colombo*, 44–46.
7. Seifer, *Nobody Speaks for Me*, 51, 58–59.
8. Seifer, *Nobody Speaks for Me*, 56.
9. Seifer, *Nobody Speaks for Me*, 44.
10. Capria and Colombo, *Colombo*, 57–60; "Drive on Crime Pressed," *New York Times*, December 25, 1958, N2.
11. Capria and Colombo, *Colombo*, 51–52; "Joe Joined Country Club Listed as 'Chicken Farmer,'" *Evening News (Newburgh, NY)*, June 30, 1971, 8D.
12. Capria and Colombo, *Colombo*, 52, 63.

Chapter 4

1. "Emanuel Perlmutter, "Powell Charges Touch Off Raids," *New York Times*, January 6, 1960, 1; "Negro Rackets Get Raw Deal, Solon Charges," *Henderson, NC Times News*, January 3, 1960, 5.
2. Daniel Patrick Moynihan, "The Private Government of Crime," *The Reporter*, July 6, 1961, 16–17.
3. Adam Clayton Powell Jr., Commencement Address, Howard University, May 29, 1964; Kenneth B. Clark, interview with Walter Goodman, "'Just Teach Them to Read!'" *New York Times*, March 18, 1973, SM64.
4. "Powell Raps N.Y. Gambling Rackets," *Chicago Daily Defender*, January 14, 1960, 2.
5. U.S. Congress, House, 106th Cong. Rec., January 13, 1960, 439–40.

6. "Adam C. Powell Apologizes for Racial Remark," *Charleston SC News and Courier*, January 18, 1960, 13.

7. Kennett Love, "Italian-American Group Assails Gangster Stereotypes in Shows," *New York Times*, January 23, 1960, 39; Walter Winchell, "Broadway Beat," *Sarasota Journal*, January 15, 1960, 11.

8. Advertisement, *Los Angeles Times*, October 29, 1959, 12.

9. Winchell, "Broadway Beat," 15.

10. William Federici, "Joe Colombo: OK, I'll Be a Mafioso for Good," *New York Daily News*, July 3, 1970, 3.

11. Marin A. Gosch and Richard Hammer, *The Last Testament of Lucky Luciano* (Little, Brown, 1975), 424; Paul S. Meskil, *The Luparelli Tapes* (Playboy Press, 1976), 151–52; Peter Diapoulos and Steven Linakis, *The Sixth Family* (Dutton, 1976), 46.

Chapter 5

1. Meskil, *The Luparelli Tapes*, 152.
2. Bob Williams, "On the Air," *New York Post*, March 10, 1961, 95.
3. "Power Plays Topple Fall Lineup," *Broadcasting*, March 20, 1961, 27–28; Val Adams, "Miss Ball Views Desilu from Top," *New York Times*, November 20, 1962, 54.
4. "They Want Full Surrender," *Broadcasting*, March 20, 1961, 27–28.

Chapter 6

1. Elisabeth Bumiller, "A Godmother of Politics for Giuliani," *New York Times*, January 17, 1996, B1.
2. Seifer, *Nobody Speaks for Me*, 62–63, 76; "Johnson to Appear Here," *New York Times*, April 16, 1962, 8; "Anfuso to Run Again in New 14th District," *New York Times*, May 1, 1962, 30; "Anfuso Takes Up Fight of Minorities," *New York Amsterdam News*, November 11, 1961, 5; Joseph Hearst, "Women May Fly in Space," *Chicago Tribune*, July 16, 1962, 1.

Chapter 7

1. Simon Anekwe, "Dockers Give CORE $1300," *New York Amsterdam News*, May 25, 1963, 26.
2. Tom Brooks, "New Shape-Up on Bush Four," *New York Herald Tribune New York Magazine*, March 1, 1964, 5–6; John P. Callahan, "Former Politics Student Heads Largest Local in I.L.A. at 28," *New York Times*, April 13, 1963, 30.

3. John P. Callahan, "Racial Picketing Idles Freighter," *New York Times*, October 11, 1963, 58; "Stevedores Refuse to Unload S. African Ship," *Chicago Daily Defender*, October 16, 1963, 6.

4. Simon Anekwe, "Dockers Give CORE $1300," 26.

5. Brooks, "New Shape-Up on Bush Four," 5–6.

6. U.S. Department of Justice, Federal Bureau of Investigation, memo, March 20, 1962, SAC, NYC, to Director, FBI, Gregory Scarpa, Bureau File NY 92-2657, p. 3.

7. U.S. Department of Justice, Federal Bureau of Investigation, memo, June 6, 1962, SAC, NYC, to Director, FBI, Gregory Scarpa, Bureau File NY 92-2657, p. 1.

8. U.S. Department of Justice, Federal Bureau of Investigation, memo, November 20, 1962, SAC, NYC, to Director, FBI, Gregory Scarpa, Bureau File NY 92-2657, p. 5.

9. U.S. Department of Justice, Federal Bureau of Investigation, memo, December 16, 1963, SAC, NYC, to Director, FBI, Gregory Scarpa, Bureau File NY 92-2657, p. 14.

10. Craig R. Whitney, "Realty Man Denies He Knew of Employe's Alleged Link to Mafia," *New York Times*, January 24, 1970, 14; Gage, "Colombo," 1.

11. Miriam Ottenberg, "U.S. Crime Kingdom Is Bared By Convict," *Boston Globe*, August 4, 1963, 1, 7; Emanuel Perlmutter, "Valachi Accuses Mafia's Leaders at Senate Inquiry," *New York Times*, September 28, 1963, 1.

12. Peter Kihss, "Valachi Hearing Stirs Hostility," *New York Times*, October 4, 1963, 25.

Chapter 8

1. U.S. Department of Justice, Federal Bureau of Investigation, memo, May 4, 1964, SAC, NYC, to Director, FBI, Gregory Scarpa, Bureau File NY 92-2657, p. 7.

2. U.S. Department of Justice, Federal Bureau of Investigation, memo, June 3, 1964, SAC, NYC, to Director, FBI, Gregory Scarpa, Bureau File NY 92-2657, p. 3.

3. Gage, "Colombo," 1.

4. Tim Weiner, *Enemies: A History of the FBI* (Random House, 2012), 211–12; Richard Harwood, "J. Edgar Hoover: The Librarian with a Lifetime Lease," *Washington Post*, February 25, 1968, D1.

5. Curt Gentry, *Hoover: The Man and the Secrets* (W. W. Norton, 1991), 533.

6. Peter Maas, *The Valachi Papers* (G. P. Putnam, 1968), 36.

7. Richard Barr and Cyril Egan Jr., "Mural Is Something Yegg-stra," *New York Journal-American*, April 15, 1964, 3.

8. John Giorno, *You Got to Burn to Shine* (High Risk, 1994), 127–28.

9. Sam Blum, "To Get the Bars Back on Their Feet," *New York Times*, September 27, 1964, SM84.

10. Victor Bockris, *The Life and Death of Andy Warhol* (Bantam, 1989), 150; Mark R. Levy and Michael S. Kramer, *The Ethnic Factor: How America's Minorities Decide Elections* (Simon and Schuster, 1972), 165; Rainer Crone, *Andy Warhol*, trans. John William Gabriel (Praeger, 1970), 30.

11. Anthony Villano with Gerald Astor, *Brick Agent: Inside the Mafia for the FBI* (Quadrangle, 1977), 90–93.

12. Charles Grutzner, "Dimes Make Millions for Numbers Racket," *New York Times*, June 26, 1964, 1; Malcolm X, "Speech on the Founding of the Organization of Afro-American Unity," June 28, 1964, https://malcolmxfiles.com/collection/oaau-founding-rally-june-28-1964/.

13. Fred Powledge, "Mulberry Street Is Angered Over CORE Pickets," *New York Times*, July 24, 1964, 8; "Relative Calm Is Restored to Riot-Torn Areas Here," *New York Times*, July 24, 1964, 1.

14. "Teen-Agers Throw Eggs at CORE Unit Picketing the Police," *New York Times*, July 22, 1964, 19; Nicholas Pileggi, "Little Italy: Study of an Italian Ghetto," *New York*, August 12, 1968, 23.

15. Nicholas Pileggi, "Risorgimento: The Red, White and Greening of New York," *New York*, June 7, 1971, 34.

Chapter 9

1. Hugh A. Mulligan, "Chronicler Makes Honest Living Monitoring the Mob," *Los Angeles Times*, August 30, 1988, 1.

2. Mario Puzo, *The Fortunate Pilgrim* (Atheneum, 1965), 73.

3. Mario Puzo, Preface to *The Fortunate Pilgrim* (Random House, 1997), x; Mario Puzo, "The Making of *The Godfather*," in *The Godfather Papers and Other Confessions* (G. P. Putnam's Sons, 1972), 25, 27.

Chapter 10

1. Charles Grutzner, "Colombo Is Given 30-Day Jail Stay," *New York Times*, April 8, 1966, 58.

2. "13 Seized in Queens In 'Little Apalachin,'" *New York Times*, September 23, 1966, 1; Charles Grutzner, "$1.3-Million Bail Frees 13 Of Mafia," *New York Times*, September 24, 1966, 1; "Sketches of 13 Seized in Queens Raid," *New York Times*, October 1, 1966, 18.

3. U.S. Department of Justice, Federal Bureau of Investigation, memo, July 20, 1967, SAC, NYC, to Director, FBI, Joseph Colombo, Bureau File NY 92-1965, p. 1.

4. Paul Hoffman, "New Body Decries Slurs on Italians," *New York Times*, November 23, 1966, 41.

5. Hoffman, "New Body Decries Slurs on Italians," 41; "Lashback," *Chicago Defender*, December 6, 1966, 34; William Fulton, "Report from New York," *Chicago Tribune*, December 20, 1966, B8.

6. U.S. Department of Justice, Federal Bureau of Investigation, memo, n.d., SAC, NYC, to Director, FBI, Joseph Colombo, Bureau File NY 92-5449-356, p. 11; also see U.S. Department of Justice, Federal Bureau of Investigation, memo, July 14, 1967, SAC, NYC, to Director, FBI, Joseph Colombo, Bureau File NY 92-1965, pp. 5–6.

7. U.S. Department of Justice, Federal Bureau of Investigation, report, n.d., SAC, NYC, to Director, FBI, Joseph Colombo, Bureau File NY 92-1965.

8. Josephine Casalena, *A Portrait of the Italian-American Community in New York City*, vol. 1 (Congress of Italian American Organizations, 1975), 63.

9. Memorandum from Robert E. Helm, Executive Chambers, State of New York to Richard E. Stewart, Subject Liuni Adoption Case: Facts, November 16, 1966, in Nelson A. Rockefeller Papers at Rockefeller Archive Center.

10. Charles Grutzner, "B'nai B'rith Anti-Defamation League Threatens Suit Over a Similar Name," *New York Times*, May 18, 1967, 36; "Appeal to Be Heard Today in the Liuni Adoption Case," *New York Times*, November 18, 1966, 30; "Ethics and Ethnics," *Washington Post*, November 27, 1966; Richard L. Madden, "Governor Orders Liuni Case Study," *New York Times*, November 29, 1966, 45.

11. Leroy F. Aarons, "Liuni Adoption: Notoriety Arouses Sleepy Catskills County," *Washington Post*, December 11, 1966, 1; "5 Bills Propose Easier Adoptions," *New York Times*, January 18, 1967, 31; "County Drops Its Opposition to Liuni Adoption," *Washington Post*, January 13, 1967, 1.

Chapter 11

1. "Image in a Curved Mirror," editorial, *New York Times*, May 5, 1967, 37.

2. "The News of the Day," *Los Angeles Times*, May 5, 1967, 2; Grutzner, "B'nai B'rith Anti-Defamation League Threatens Suit Over a Similar Name," 36.

3. U.S. Department of Justice, Federal Bureau of Investigation, memo, n.d., SAC, NYC, to Director, FBI, Joseph Colombo, Bureau File NY 92-5449-356, p. 11.

4. "Image in a Curved Mirror," 37; Charles Grutzner, "An Odd Group Held as Plotters in Case," *New York Times*, December 19, 1967, 1; Edith Evans Ashbury, "De Sapio Is Guilty on Three Counts at Bribery Trial," *New York Times*, December 14, 1969, 1.

5. Pileggi, "Risorgimento," 32; Gay Talese, "Frank Sinatra Has a Cold," *Esquire*, April 1966, 94; Mario Puzo, "The Italians, American Style," *New York Times*, August 6, 1967, SM183.

6. "Sinatra Warns New York Kids Against Racism," *New York Times*, November 3, 1945, 3; Harry Stathos, "Show Biz Aids Integration Bid," *Chicago Daily Defender*, February 4, 1961. 1.

7. Peter Kihss, "Sinatra to Head Antibias Group," *New York Times*, May 4, 1967, 1; Paul Hofmann, "Italo-Americans Hold Rally Here," *New York Times*, October 20, 1967, 58.

8. "It's Bay Ridge Day at the White House," *Bay Ridge Home Reporter and Sunset News*, October 2, 1964, 1; Charles Grutzner, "Scotto Is Called Captain in Mafia," *New York Times*, August 21, 1969, 1.

9. Hofmann, "Italo-Americans Hold Rally Here," 58; "18,000 Hail Sinatra at Garden Rally," *New York Post*, October 20, 1967, 20; Murray Kempton, "Rallying Around Frankie, *New York Post*, October 20, 1967, 52; Robert Mayer, "Frank Sinatra's Ethnic Joke," *Newsday*, October 20, 1967, 1; "Sinatra at Rally of Italian-Americans," *Los Angeles Times*, October 21, 1967, 16; "Sammy Sees the Light," *Afro-American (Baltimore)*, September 30, 1967, 4.

10. "League Protests Slurs on Italians," *Toledo Blade*, October 20, 1967, 2.

11. Charles Grutzner, "City Police Expert on Mafia Retiring from Force," *New York Times*, January 21, 1967, 37.

12. President's Commission on Law Enforcement and Administration of Justice, *The Challenge of Crime in a Free Society* (Washington, DC: U.S. Government Printing Office, 1967), 192.

13. Yvette Scharfman, "Political Patter," *City Courier*, May 13, 1967.

14. Scharfman, "Political Patter."

Chapter 12

1. *Report of the National Advisory Commission on Civil Disorders* (E. P. Dutton, 1968), 1, 278–82.

2. Vincent J. Cannato, *The Ungovernable City: John Lindsay and His Struggle to Save New York* (Basic Books, 2001), ix, 204–8; Edward Schreiber, "Shoot Arsonists: Daley," *Chicago Tribune*, April 16, 1968, 1; Thomas A. Johnson, "Scattered Violence Occurs in Harlem and Brooklyn," *New York Times*, April 5, 1968, 1; John Kifner, "City Keeps Slum Task Force," *New York Times*, April 20, 1968, 35.

3. Nicholas Pileggi, "Barry Gottehrer's Job Is to Cool It," *New York Times*, September 22, 1968, SM28.

4. Hugh A. Mulligan, "Chronicler Makes Honest Living Monitoring the Mob," *Los Angeles Times*, August 30, 1988, 1.

5. Mary O'Flaherty, "Interethnic Group to Aid Kids," *New York Daily News*, October 13, 1968, B2; "Italian Americans Tackle a Problem," *The Tablet*, November 14, 1968.

6. Paul Hofmann, "Italian-Americans Agree to Back a Federation of their Groups," *New York Times*, December 25, 1967, 34.

7. "First National Conference of the National Federation of Italian American Organizations, Willard Hotel, Washington, DC, April 29–May 1, 1968," in Order Sons of Italy, National Office Records, Box 25, Folder 12, Immigration History Research Center, University of Minnesota.

8. "Launch Federation," *Fra Noi*, May 1968, 1.

9. Advertisement, *New York Times*, August 23, 1968, 37.

10. Grutzner, "B'nai B'rith Anti-Defamation League Threatens Suit Over a Similar Name," 36; "Italian Group Yields Claim to 'Anti-Defamation League,'" *New York Times*, March 28, 1968, 42; *New York Times*, April 3, 1968, cited in Donald R. Cressey, *Theft of the Nation: The Structure and Operations of Organized Crime in America* (Harper and Row, 1969), 11.

11. Herb Lyon, "Tower Ticker," *Chicago Tribune*, April 17, 1968, 23; Joyce Haber, "Sinatra Concerts to Aid Humphrey," *Los Angeles Times*, May 16, 1968, C16; Lawrence E. Davies, "Sinatra Supports Slate Competing with Kennedy's," *New York Times*, May 5, 1968, 42.

12. Nicholas Gage, "Sinatra's Pals," *Wall Street Journal*, August 19, 1968, 1; "Convention Date Off for Sinatra," *Los Angeles Times*, August 25, 1968, F7; "Sinatra Sends His Regrets, Won't Sing at Reception," *Wall Street Journal*, August 26, 1968, 10.

13. Roscoe Drummond, "Former Pennsylvania Governor Vice Presidential Possibility," *Observer-Reporter (Washington, PA)*, August 7, 1968, 5.

14. Seymour Korman, "San Francisco's Mayor Alioto Puts Humphrey in Nomination," *Chicago Tribune*, August 29, 1968, 8; Carl Rowan, "San Francisco Mayor Humphrey Seen Choice," *Evening News (Newburgh, NY)*, August 8, 1968, 7; Roscoe Drummond, "Former Pennsylvania Governor Vice Presidential Possibility," *Observer-Reporter (Washington, PA)*, August 7, 1968, 5.

15. Warren Weaver Jr., "Humphrey Shops for Running Mate to Bolster Ticket," *New York Times*, August 27, 1968, 1.

16. Seymour Korman, "Alioto's Star Ascends as He Waits in Wings," *Chicago Tribune*, August 22, 1968, 27.

17. Jack Anderson, "Some from U.S. Favor Thieu Hard Line," *Washington Post*, September 15, 1969, B11; Richard Carlson and Lance Brisson, "The Web That Links San Francisco's Mayor Alioto and the Mafia," *Look*, September 23, 1969, 17.

18. Korman, "Alioto's Star Ascends as He Waits in Wings"; Richard Bergholz and Carl Greenberg, "Mayor Alioto Facing a Test of Tolerance," *Los Angeles Times*, September 14, 1969, 1.

19. Carlson and Brisson, "The Web That Links San Francisco's Mayor Alioto and the Mafia," *Look*, 17; "Magazine Links Alioto to Mafia," *New York Times*, September 6, 1969, 1; Daryl Lembke, "Article Links Alioto and Mafia Leaders," *Los Angeles Times*, September 6, 1969, 1.

20. "Alioto's Odyssey," *Time*, November 13, 1972, 24; "Tunney Charges Justice Dept. With Alioto Leaks," *Los Angeles Times*, March 18, 1971, 1; also see Wallace Turner, "Look Trial Hears of Source in F.B.I.," *New York Times*, May 1, 1970, 31.

21. Ken W. Clawson, "U.S. Opposes Curb on Data Gathering," *Washington Post*, March 10, 1971, 1.

22. William Chapman, "Wiretaps in Crimes Resumed," *Washington Post*, February 12, 1969, 1.

23. Jack Anderson, "Hoover Helps Mitchell Fight the Mafia," *Washington Post*, January 22, 1970, D23.

24. Steve Ostrow, *Live at The Continental: The Inside Story of the World-Famous Continental Baths* (Xlibris, 2007), 88–93.

25. James Patterson and Benjamin Wallace, *The Defense Lawyer: The Barry Slotnick Story* (Little, Brown, 2021), 65–66, 102–3.

26. *Village Voice*, July 3, 1969, 1.

Chapter 13

1. Albert A. Seedman and Peter Hellman, *Chief! Classic Cases from the Files of the Chief of Detectives* (A. Fields Books, 1974), 350–52; Jerome Charyn, "Officer Reilly He's Not," *New York Times*, September 19, 2004, CY1; Peter Hellman, "It's Very Hard to Smile at Albert Seedman When He Is Not Smiling at You," *New York Times*, April 30, 1972, SM14.

2. Seedman and Hellman, *Chief*, 350–52.

3. "How Joe Bonanno Schemed to Kill—And Lost," *Life*, September 1, 1967, 18; Gage, "Colombo," 1.

4. U.S. Department of Justice, Federal Bureau of Investigation, memo, January 14, 1970, SAC, NYC, to Director, FBI, Joseph Colombo, Bureau File NY 92-1965.

5. "Brooklyn Mafia Chief: Joseph Colombo," 40; Gage, "Colombo," 1.

6. "How Joe Bonanno Schemed to Kill—And Lost," 18.

7. Dave Smith, "Did Former Agent Instigate Bonanno Blast? FBI Is Silent," *Los Angeles Times*, August 20, 1969, 25; Adam Clymer, "Tucson Gangland Bombings Believed Work of FBI Agent," *Boston Globe*, June 2, 1971, 2.

8. Robert M. Smith, "The Case of the F.B.I. Man and Bombing of the Mafia," *New York Times*, June 11, 1971, 16.

9. Smith, "The Case of the F.B.I. Man and Bombing of the Mafia," 16; Clymer, "Tucson Gangland Bombings Believed Work of FBI Agent," 2; "Was There an FBI Plot?" *Boston Globe*, February 12, 1978, F7.

10. U.S. Department of Justice, Federal Bureau of Investigation, memo, July 19, 1966, W. C. Sullivan to C. D. Deloach, "'Black Bag' Jobs;" John Crewdson, "Seeing Red," *Chicago Tribune*, March 2, 1986, H15–16.

11. Smith, "The Case of the F.B.I. Man and Bombing of the Mafia," 16; Gay Talese, "The Bombing of Joe Bonanno," *Esquire*, October 1971, 141.

12. Talese, "The Bombing of Joe Bonanno," 141–42.

13. "Was There an FBI Plot?," F7; Clymer, "Tucson Gangland Bombings Believed Work of FBI Agent," 2.

14. Smith, "The Case of the F.B.I. Man and Bombing of the Mafia," 16.

15. "Was There an FBI Plot?," F7.

16. Talese, "The Bombing of Joe Bonanno," 234; Eric Volante, "FBI Jumps, Then Shuts Down Probe," *Arizona Daily Star*, February 3, 2004; "Bombing By 'F.B.I. Agent,'" *San Francisco Chronicle*, August 21, 1969, 10; "Officials Call for Investigations," *Prescott Evening Courier*, August 15, 1969, 13; Smith, "The Case of the F.B.I. Man and Bombing of the Mafia," 16.

17. "Bombing By 'F.B.I. Agent,'" 10.

18. Paul Dean, "When Will the FBI Defend Itself and Erase Those Gnawing Doubts?," *Arizona Republic*, August 18, 1969, 23; Talese, "The Bombing of Joe Bonanno," 238.

19. Gay Talese, *Honor Thy Father* (World Publishing, 1971), 308–10.

20. Hamilton E. Davis, "White Ethnics Ignored?," *Providence Evening Bulletin*, December 12, 1971.

21. Pete Hamill, "The Revolt of the White Lower Middle Class," *New York*, April 14, 1969, 28; Robert Mason, *Richard Nixon and the Quest for a New Majority* (University of North Carolina Press, 2004), 46.

22. Nicholas Pileggi, "The More the Mario," *New York*, April 14, 1969, 34; Tom Buckley, "Answering November's Big Question: What Is a Mario Procaccino?," *New York Times*, August 19, 1969, SM62.

23. Richard Reeves, "Lindsay Introduces New Party Whose Aim Is to Re-Elect Him," *New York Times*, August 1, 1969, 31; "Promotion Group Is Named by Mayor," *New York Times*, May 29, 1966, S20.

24. Homer Bigart, "New Unit to Push Job Redevelopment," *New York Times*, March 26, 1966, 13.

25. Nicholas Pileggi, "Inside Lindsay's Head," *New York*, January 4, 1971, 44; Martin Tolchin, "U.S. Moves to Sell Navy Yard to City for $22.5-Million," *New York Times*, June 25, 1969, 1; Nan Robertson, "U.S. Will Lease Army Base to City to Create Jobs," *New York Times*, June 10, 1969, 1.

26. Jean Heller and Mark Brown, "Labor Leader, Labeled as Mafia Figure, Linked with Lindsay," *Nashua (NH) Telegraph*, January 27, 1972, 15.

27. A. H. Raskin, "Everyone's Got Muscle but the People," *New York Times*, June 13, 1971, E1; Paul L. Montgomery, "Tough Dock Leader: Anthony Michael Scotto," *New York Times*, February 9, 1970, 16.

28. Charles Grutzner, "Scotto Is Called Captain in Mafia," *New York Times*, August 21, 1969, 34.

29. William E. Farrell, "Lindsay Camp Asserts It Won't 'Run Out' On Scotto," *New York Times*, October 14, 1969, 34.

30. Alan L. Otten, "Politics and People: The Selling of the Mayor," *Wall Street Journal*, November 6, 1969, 18l; William E. Farrell, "Dr. King's Widow Supports Lindsay," *New York Times*, October 12, 1969, 47.

31. Peter Kihss, "Rich and Poor, Not Middle-Class, The Key to Lindsay Re-Election," *New York Times*, November 6, 1969, 37; Jean Heller and Mark Brown, "Labor Leader, Labeled as Mafia Figure, Linked with Lindsay," *Nashua (NH) Telegraph*, January 27, 1972, 15.

32. Martin Tolchin, "Lindsay Looks for City Gains in 1970," *New York Times*, December 25, 1969, 1.

33. Nathan Glazer and Daniel Patrick Moynihan, introduction, *Beyond the Melting Pot: The Negroes, Puerto Ricans, Jews, Italians, and Irish of New York City*, 2nd ed. (MIT Press, 1970), lxvi.

Chapter 14

1. U.S. Department of Justice, Federal Bureau of Investigation, memo, July 9, 1970, SAC, NYC, to Director, FBI, Gregory Scarpa, Bureau File NY 92-2657.

2. Morris Kaplan, "Jury Told of Plot to Melt Silver," *New York Times*, February 17, 1971, 31; Norma Abrams and Stephen Brown, "Mafia Chief Organizes a Picket at the FBI," *New York Daily News*, May 1, 1970, 12.

3. "Klein Confirms Appointment," *New York Times*, August 16, 1951, 35.

4. U.S. Department of Justice, Federal Bureau of Investigation, memo, May 5, 1970, SAC, NYC, to Director, FBI, Gregory Scarpa, Bureau File NY 92-2657. Also see Joseph Cantalupo and Thomas C. Renner, *Body Mike: An Unsparing Exposé by the Mafia Insider Who Turned on the Mob* (Villard, 1990), 97.

5. Craig R. Whitney, "Italians Picket F.B.I. Office Here," *New York Times*, May 2, 1970, 35.

6. U.S. Department of Justice, Federal Bureau of Investigation, memo, May 5, 1970, SAC, NYC, to Director, FBI, Gregory Scarpa, Bureau File NY 92-2657.

7. Norma Abrams and Stephen Brown, "Mafia Chief Organizes a Picket at the FBI," *New York Daily News*, May 1, 1970, 12.

8. Abrams and Brown, "Mafia Chief Organizes a Picket Line at the FBI," 12.

9. Patterson and Wallace, *The Defense Lawyer*, 69.

10. Whitney, "Italians Picket F.B.I. Office Here," 35.

11. Tom Buckley, "The Mafia Tries a New Tune," *Harper's*, August 1971, 47.

12. U.S. Department of Justice, Federal Bureau of Investigation, memo, May 5, 1970, SAC, NYC, to Director, FBI, Gregory Scarpa, Bureau File NY 92-2657.

13. U.S. Department of Justice, Federal Bureau of Investigation, memo, July 2, 1970, SAC, NYC, to Director, FBI, Gregory Scarpa, Bureau File NY 92-2657.

Chapter 15

1. Abrams and Brown, "Mafia Chief Organizes a Picket Line at the FBI," 12; U.S. Department of Justice, Federal Bureau of Investigation, memo, July 7, 1970, SAC, NYC, to Director, FBI, Gregory Scarpa, Bureau File NY 92-2657.
2. Villano with Astor, *Brick Agent*, 226.
3. "FBI Accused of Harassment," *Long Island Post*, May 7, 1970, 2.
4. "Italian-Americans Picket the FBI," *The Challenge*, May 1970, 1, 6–7.
5. "June 29th, Proclaimed Italian Unity Day," *Long Island Post*, June 4, 1970, 2.
6. "Priest to Demonstrators: 'My Brother was Framed,'" *Long Island Post*, May 21, 1970, 2.
7. Sonia Sotomayor, *My Beloved World* (Alfred A. Knopf, 2013), 105.
8. David K. Shipler, "Tenants Assail Rent Proposals," *New York Times*, May 27, 1970, 1.
9. "Priest to Demonstrators," 2.
10. Whitney, "Italians Picket F.B.I. Office Here," 35; John Mullane, "Colombo Defends FBI Pickets," *New York Post*, June 6, 1970, 2.
11. "Protest: Italian Power," *Newsweek*, June 22, 1970, 22.
12. Fred Ferretti, "Italian-American League's Power Spreads," *New York Times*, April 4, 1971, 64; Nicholas Pileggi, "The Goons, the Mob, and The School-Bus Strike," *New York*, March 12, 1979, 46.
13. U.S. Department of Justice, Federal Bureau of Investigation, memo, July 2, 1970, SAC, NYC, to Director, FBI, Gregory Scarpa, Bureau File NY 92-2657; Charles Grutzner, "Dispute Over 'Mafia,'" *New York Times*, September 5, 1970, 19.
14. U.S. Department of Justice, Federal Bureau of Investigation, memo, July 2, 1970, SAC, NYC, to Director, FBI, Gregory Scarpa, Bureau File NY 92-2657.
15. Fred J. Cook, "Hard-Hats: The Rampaging Patriots," *The Nation*, June 15, 1970, 718; Don Oberdorfer, "Nixon Meets 'Hard Hat' Supporters," *Washington Post*, May 27, 1970, 1.
16. U.S. Department of Justice, Federal Bureau of Investigation, memo, July 2, 1970, SAC, NYC, to Director, FBI, Gregory Scarpa, Bureau File NY 92-2657.
17. Mullane, "Colombo Defends FBI Pickets," 2.

Chapter 16

1. Lou Benton, "Anti-Discrimination Drive Grows," *Long Island Post*, May 14, 1970, 2; "June 29th, Proclaimed Italian Unity Day," *Long Island Post* June 4, 1970, 2; Ferretti, "Italian-American League's Power Spreads," 64; U.S. Department of Justice, Federal Bureau of Investigation, memo, July 2, 1970, SAC, NYC, to Director, FBI, Gregory Scarpa, Bureau File NY 92-2657.
2. Pete Hamill, "The Pickets," *New York Post*, June 10, 1970, 57.

3. Lou Benton, "Pete Hamill Tells It Like It 'Ain't,'" *Long Island Post*, June 18, 1970, 2.

4. Craig R. Whitney, "Reputed Mafia Figure Linked to Picketing of F.B.I.," *New York Times*, June 9, 1970, 51; Paul L. Montgomery, "Italians to Hold Rally Tomorrow," *New York Times*, June 28, 1970, 34.

5. Capria and Colombo, *Colombo*, 167.

6. Lou Benton, "Judge Tells the FBI Pickets," *Long Island Post*, June 18, 1970, 2.

7. U.S. Department of Justice, Federal Bureau of Investigation, memo, July 1, 1970, SAC, NYC, to Director, FBI, Gregory Scarpa, Bureau File NY 92-2657.

8. Ferretti, "Italian-American League's Power Spreads," 64.

9. Montgomery, "Italians to Hold Rally Tomorrow," 34; "Unity Day & Italian Business," *New York Post*, June 17, 1970, 24.

10. U.S. Department of Justice, Federal Bureau of Investigation, memo, July 2, 1970, SAC, NYC, to Director, FBI, Gregory Scarpa, Bureau File NY 92-2657.

11. U.S. Department of Justice, Federal Bureau of Investigation, memo, July 2, 1970, SAC, NYC, to Director, FBI, Gregory Scarpa, Bureau File NY 92-2657.

12. Montgomery, "Italians to Hold Rally Tomorrow," 34.

13. U.S. Department of Justice, Federal Bureau of Investigation, memo, July 2, 1970, SAC, NYC, to Director, FBI, Gregory Scarpa, Bureau File NY 92-2657.

14. "Post Publisher's Letter to Son Explains His Fight for Italian Unity," *Long Island Post*, June 25, 1970, 2.

15. *New York Times*, June 28, 1970, 42.

16. *New York Daily News*, June 28, 1970, 18.

17. U.S. Department of Justice, Federal Bureau of Investigation, memo, July 2, 1970, SAC, NYC, to Director, FBI, Gregory Scarpa, Bureau File NY 92-2657.

18. Anthony Scaduto, "80,000 Italians in Protest," *New York Post*, June 29, 1970, 4; Paul L. Montgomery, "Italian Americans Ready for Colorful Unity Day," *New York Times*, June 29, 1970, 40.

19. U.S. Department of Justice, Federal Bureau of Investigation, memo, October 30, 1970, SAC, NYC, Gregory Scarpa, Bureau File NY 92-2657. pp. 1, 3.

20. John Marchi, guest editorial in *New York Daily News*, June 30, 1970, 43; Pileggi, "Risorgimento," 33.

21. Pileggi, "Risorgimento," 31.

Chapter 17

1. Michael T. Kaufman, "In Brooklyn's Italian Section, Businesses and Mouths Are Closed," *New York Times*, June 30, 1970, 28.

2. Roger Wetherington and Gene Spagnoli, "The Italians Rally Draws 100,000," *New York Daily News*, June 30, 1970, 28.

3. Scaduto, "80,000 Italians in Protest," 4.

4. Paul L. Montgomery, "Thousands of Italians Here Rally Against Ethnic Slurs," *New York Times*, June 30, 1970, 1.

5. U.S. Department of Justice, Federal Bureau of Investigation, memo, July 2, 1970, SAC, NYC, to Director, FBI, Gregory Scarpa, Bureau File NY 92-2657.

6. U.S. Department of Justice, Federal Bureau of Investigation, memo, July 2, 1970, SAC, NYC, to Director, FBI, Gregory Scarpa, Bureau File NY 92-2657.

7. Nicholas Pileggi, "Italian Americans Today: The Ties That Unbind," *New York*, July 12, 1976, 34.

8. Scaduto, "80,000 Italians in Protest," 4.

9. The speech by Anthony Colombo at the Unity Day rally is transcribed from *NBC News*, NBC, New York, 29 June 1970.

10. Wetherington and Spagnoli, "The Italian Rally Draws 100,000," 28.

11. Ferretti, "Italian-American League's Power Spreads," 64; Richard Reeves, "An Ex-Cop Makes His Move to Take Over the City," *New York*, December 11, 1972, 42.

12. Buckley, "Biaggi Tells His Listeners: I, Too, Have Worked Hard," *New York Times*, March 19, 1973, 37.

13. Buckley, "Biaggi Tells His Listeners," 37; Reeves, "An Ex-Cop Makes His Move to Take Over the City," 48.

14. Wetherington and Spagnoli, "The Italians Rally Draws 100,000," 28; Montgomery, "Thousands of Italians Here Rally Against Ethnic Slurs," 1.

15. Anthony Mancini, "Italian Day Organizers: It's Only the Beginning," *New York Post*, June 30, 1970, 2.

16. Scaduto, "80,000 Italians in Protest," 4; Mancini, "Italian Day Organizers," 2.

17. Wetherington and Spagnoli, "The Italian Rally Draws 100,000," 28; Mancini, "Italian Day Organizers," 2.

18. Margaret Crimmins, "Lower Manhattan's Bella Abzug Rasps It Like It Is," *Washington Post*, July 5, 1970, G1.

19. Montgomery, "Thousands of Italians Here Rally Against Ethnic Slurs," 1.

20. "Powell to Form New Party for Election Bid," *Washington Post*, June 29, 1970, 20.

21. Thomas A. Johnson, "A Man of Many Roles: Adam Clayton Powell, Former Harlem Representative, Dies," *New York Times*, April 5, 1972, 30; the speech by Adam Clayton Powell Jr. at the Unity Day rally is transcribed from *NBC News*, NBC, New York, 29 June 1970.

22. The speech by Anthony LaRosa at the Unity Day rally is transcribed from *NBC News*, NBC, New York, 29 June 1970.

23. The speech by Joseph Colombo Sr. at the Unity Day rally is transcribed from *NBC News*, NBC, New York, 29 June 1970.

24. *Long Island Post*, July 2, 1970, S4.

25. Montgomery, "Thousands of Italians Here Rally Against Ethnic Slurs," 1.

26. William Federici, "Joe Colombo, 23 Indicted by L.I. Grand Jury," *New York Daily News*, July 1, 1970, 3.

27. U.S. Department of Justice, Federal Bureau of Investigation, letter, June 30, 1970, Director, FBI, to John J. Marchi, Italian American Civil Rights League, Bureau File 92-12264.

Chapter 18

1. U.S. Department of Justice, Federal Bureau of Investigation, memo, July 2, 1970, SAC, NYC, to Director, FBI, Gregory Scarpa, Bureau File NY 92-2657.

2. Federici, "Joe Colombo: OK, I'll Be a Mafioso for Good," 3.

3. *Newsfront*, "The Ethnic Syndrome," aired July 9, 1970, on WNDT-TV (Channel 13), on Tape 5988-001, Aldo Tambellini Archive, ZKM Center for Art and Media, Karlsruhe, Germany.

4. Seifer, *Nobody Speaks for Me*, 87.

5. *The Challenge*, November 1970, 8; *The Challenge*, January 1971, 5; Edwin McDowell, "Italian-American Group's Board Levels Charge of Wide Nepotism," *New York Times*, January 27, 1978, 15.

6. Rudy Garcia, "Rights Chief Probing Italian Bias Charges," *New York Daily News*, July 19, 1970, M4.

7. Lesley Oelsner, "Police-Crime Link Is Under Inquiry," *New York Times*, July 24, 1970, 18.

8. Garcia, "Rights Chief Probing Italian Bias Charges," M4.

9. Ronald J. Ostrow, "Mitchell's Softer Line Credited to New Aide," *Los Angeles Times*, July 22, 1970, 12; "FBI Told to Shun Use of Mafia Name," *Washington Post*, July 24, 1970, 7; "'Mafia' Loses Its Place in Federal Vocabulary," *New York Times*, July 24, 1970, 28; "Dailies Do It Anyway," *Long Island Post*, July 30, 1970, 4.

10. U.S. Department of Justice, Federal Bureau of Investigation, memo, July 24, 1970, Director, FBI, to Tolson.

11. Grutzner, "Dispute Over 'Mafia,'" 19.

12. "Mitchell Says the Term for Mafia Is 'Syndicate,'" *New York Times*, July 30, 1970, 21.

13. Smith, "The Case of the F.B.I. Man and Bombing of the Mafia," 16.

14. Logan McKechnie, "Judge Says Ex-FBI Man Caused Tucson Bombings," *Washington Post*, July 25, 1970, 1.

15. McKechnie, "Judge Says Ex-FBI Man Caused Tucson Bombings," 1; reprinted as "The FBI, Bonanno & Bombs," *New York Post*, July 25, 1970, 3, and as "Tucson FBI Bomb-Throwers," *The Challenge*, December 1970, 6.

16. Logan McKechnie, email to the author, 2012: "'So-called' is a term I have used for years, but I'm sure the desk—the Washington Post copy editors—would have made the call to use the quote marks around Mafia. Don't see me doing that and don't see a copy editor allowing them to stay in the story unless that was part of the overall style at the time."

17. Robinson, "Mafia Believed Behind the Italian-American Protests Over 'Harassment,'" 57.

18. "Italian Unit Picketing the Times," *New York Post*, July 30, 1970, 28; "Times Is Picketed by Protest Group," *New York Times*, July 31, 1970, 27.

19. "Times Is Picketed by Protest Group," 20.

20. Patterson and Wallace, *The Defense Lawyer*, 69.

Chapter 19

1. Letter from Italian American Civil Rights League to Editor, August 27, 1970, *Tri-Boro Post*, September 3, 1970, 6.

2. U.S. Department of Justice, Federal Bureau of Investigation, memo, July 2, 1970, SAC, NYC, to Director, FBI, Gregory Scarpa, Bureau File NY 92-2657.

3. Letter from Governor Nelson Rockefeller to Editor, August 26, 1970, *Tri-Boro Post*, September 3, 1970, 6.

4. "'Mafia' Now a No, No," *New York Daily News*, August 28, 1970, 30.

5. Patterson and Wallace, *The Defense Lawyer*, 73–75; "Bomb Criminal Lawyer's Office," *New York Daily News*, August 25, 1970, 5; "Blast Rips Office of Attorney," *News and Courier (South Carolina)*, August 25, 1970, 9.

6. "Law Offices Blasted by a Pipe Bomb Here," *New York Times*, August 25, 1970, 32; "Bomb Rocks Office of Gangsters' Lawyer," *Washington Post*, August 25, 1970, 2.

7. "Bomb Criminal Lawyer's Office," 5.

Chapter 20

1. "Italian-American Civil Rights League Holds Membership Drive," *Tri-Boro Post*, September 3, 1970, 8; U.S. Department of Justice, Federal Bureau of Investigation, memo, July 2, 1970, SAC, NYC, to Director, FBI, Gregory Scarpa, Bureau File NY 92-2657.

2. Alfonso A. Narvaez, "Adams Bolts Democrats to Endorse Rockefeller," *New York Times*, September 12, 1970, 14; *Tri-Boro Post*, November 24, 1970, 1; "A Governor Joins the Italian-American Civil Rights League," *Tri-Boro Post*, September 17, 1970, 4.

3. "An Ethnic Manifesto," *Village Voice*, June 6, 1974, 8.
4. Levy and Kramer, *The Ethnic Factor*, 165.
5. Jack Newfield, "Crushing of Corona by A Plastic Glacier," *Village Voice*, November 19, 1970, 1.
6. Murray Schumach, "Neighborhoods: 69 Homes in Corona at Stake," *New York Times*, August 11, 1970, 35.
7. "Corona Residents May Be Evicted," *New York Times*, September 5, 1970, 13.
8. "Battista Visits Wall St. With Elephant, Monkey," *Wall Street Journal*, July 28, 1965.
9. "Italian-American Civil Rights League Joins Eviction Fight," *Tri-Boro Post*, September 17, 1970, 3.
10. "Discrimination Sparks Violence at City Hall," *Tri-Boro Post*, October 1, 1970, 1.
11. Maurice Carroll, "Protesting Groups Scuffle at City Hall," *New York Times*, September 20, 1970, 34.
12. "Italian-American Civil Rights League Joins Eviction Fight," 3; Carroll, "Protesting Groups Scuffle at City Hall," 34; "Discrimination Sparks Violence at City Hall," 1.

Chapter 21

1. Pileggi, "Risorgimento," 29.
2. "5th Avenue Columbus Parade Draws Crowds and Candidates," *New York Times*, October 31, 1970, 37; Gene Spagnoli, "Chris Has His Day—with a Dash of Red Paint," *New York Daily News*, October 13, 1970, 5; *Tri-Boro Post*, October 15, 1970, 1, 6.
3. "Another Local Chapter," *Tri-Boro Post*, October 22, 1970, 6.
4. *(Official Song of) The Italian-American Civil Rights League*, 1970, Sanfris Records SP74A, 45 rpm.
5. "Another Local Chapter," 6; Stanley Penn, "Colombo's Wounding Also Crippled Group That Fought 'Slurs,'" *Wall Street Journal*, June 2, 1972, 1.
6. Anthony Colombo, "Speaking Out," *Tri-Boro Post*, October 29, 1970, 11; Edward Ranzal, "Leone Is Elected to Succeed Stark," *New York Times*, September 10, 1970, 52.
7. Anthony Bruton, "Bella Vows She Won't Just Sit Around Down in D.C.," *New York Daily News*, November 5, 1970, 6; Suzanne Brawn Levine and Mary Thom, *Bella Abzug* (Farrar, Straus and Giroux, 2007), 92–93.
8. Eric Pace, "Italian-American League Is Beset by Woes," *New York Times*, June 6, 1972, 45; Vincent Colombo, "Speaking Out," *Tri-Boro Post*, November 2, 1970, 11.

9. Nicholas Pileggi, "Why They Had to Shoot Colombo," *New York*, July 12, 1971, 8.

10. Robinson, "Mafia Believed Behind the Italian-American Protests Over 'Harassment,'" 57.

11. Pileggi, "Risorgimento," 32.

Chapter 22

1. Letter from Mary C. Sansone to Mayor John V. Lindsay, November 27, 1970, in Mayor John V. Lindsay Collection, New York City Municipal Archive.

2. Seifer, *Nobody Speaks for Me*, 64; Peter Kihss, "More Whites Here Going on Relief as Jobs Dry Up," *New York Times*, November 29, 1970, 1; Juan M. Vasquez, "Day-Care Centers to Get City Help," *New York Times*, November 6, 1970, 39.

3. Pat Patterson, "Long Island Sounds," *New Pittsburgh Courier*, December 31, 1960, 3; "Church to Enlist Catholics Here for Capital Civil Rights Rally," *New York Times*, August 11, 1963, 1.

4. Seifer, *Nobody Speaks for Me*, 69, 82; Rudy Johnson, "Day-Care Center Wins in Brooklyn," *New York Times*, March 28, 1971, BQ85.

5. Davis, "White Ethnics Ignored?"

6. Seifer, *Nobody Speaks for Me*, 72.

7. Macleod, "Daily Closeup;" Seifer, *Nobody Speaks for Me*, 72–73.

8. Capria and Colombo, *Colombo*, 220–21.

9. "IACRL to Sponsor Gala Concert at Felt Forum," *Tri-Boro Post*, November 12, 1970, 2.

10. U.S. Department of Justice, Federal Bureau of Investigation, memo, December 22, 1970, SAC, NYC, to Director, FBI, Gregory Scarpa, Bureau File NY 92-2657.

11. *New York Times*, November 15, 1970, B2.

12. "Italian-Americans Contribute $500,000 at a Charity Show," *New York Times*, November 21, 1970, 27.

13. "A Gala Festival," *Tri-Boro Post*, November 26, 1970, 6.

14. "Unwilling Witnesses Recalled in Loan-Shark Inquiry," *New York Times*, April 1, 1971, 33.

Chapter 23

1. Ti-Grace Atkinson, "The Political Woman," February 1970; repr. in *Amazon Odyssey* (Links Books, 1974), 90–91.

2. Marylin Bender, "The Feminists Are on the March Once More," *New York Times*, December 14, 1967, 78.

3. Robert Miraldi, "Equal Pay for Work," *Staten Island Advance*, March 7, 1976, 1.

4. Ti-Grace Atkinson, "On 'Violence in The Women's Movement,'" August 1971, reprinted in *Amazon Odyssey*, 201.

5. Ti-Grace Atkinson, Press Release, Human Rights for Woman Inc., 1972, box 81, folder 15, Ti-Grace Atkinson Papers, Schlesinger Library, Radcliffe Institute, Harvard University.

6. David Hilliard and Lewis Cole, *This Side of Glory: The Autobiography of David Hilliard and the Story of the Black Panther Party* (Little, Brown, 1993), 339–40. It is worth noting that the popularity and influence of *The Godfather* narratives among African Americans extended well beyond the Black Panther Party's study of Mario Puzo's 1969 novel. Hollywood industry surveys estimated that Black audiences made up as much as 35 percent of filmgoers for the first *Godfather* movie. Released in 1972, *The Godfather* was a blockbuster that also contributed to the rise of blaxploitation films focusing on Black crime bosses who could beat "the man" (the white establishment) at their own game. Showman James Brown, who recorded the soundtrack for *Black Caesar*, began billing himself "the Godfather of Soul" immediately after the movie's 1973 release. See James Monaco, *American Film Now: The People, the Power, the Money, the Movies* (Oxford University Press, 1979), 193; Dennis Hunt, "Brown: Still Working Hard," *Los Angeles Times*, April 17, 1973, D10.

7. Ti-Grace Atkinson, Press Release, Human Rights for Woman Inc.

8. Joan Kron, "Radical Chick," *Philadelphia*, February 1971, 48–53.

9. Tom Wolfe, "Radical Chic," *New York*, June 8, 1970, 28.

10. The "alleged Mafia chiefs and/or relatives" from the IACRL referenced by Ti-Grace Atkinson in her press release were not exclusively or even mostly "of Sicilian descent." Joe Colombo's ancestry was, like many of his associates, Calabrian.

11. Gloria Steinem, Review of Joan Didion's *Play It as It Lays*, *Los Angeles Times*, July 5, 1970, O1.

12. Jurate Kazickas, "Joseph Colombo and the Feminists," *Long Island Press*, August 21, 1974, 28; Ti-Grace Atkinson, "On 'Violence in The Women's Movement,'" 199, 207; Letter from Ti-Grace Atkinson to the Italian American Civil Rights League: Nat Marcone, Anthony Colombo, Caesar Vitale, Joseph diCicco, July 28, 1971, box 33, folder 7, Ti-Grace Atkinson Papers, Schlesinger Library, Radcliffe Institute, Harvard University.

13. "Italian-American Civil Rights League to Play Santa Claus for Needy Kiddies," *Tri-Boro Post*, December 17, 1970, 3.

14. Frank J. Prial, "Italian-American Defense League List is Seized," *New York Times*, December 18, 1970, 52.

15. U.S. Department of Justice, Federal Bureau of Investigation, Washington, DC, file No. 92-12264: Italian American Civil Rights League.

16. Fred J. Cook, "A Family Business," *New York Times*, June 4, 1972, SM 94.

17. U.S. Department of Justice, Federal Bureau of Investigation, Washington, DC, file No. 92-5509: Joseph Anthony Colombo.

18. Gage, "Colombo," 1.

19. Stanley Penn, "Colombo's Crusade," *Wall Street Journal*, March 23, 1971, 1; Pileggi, "Why They Had to Shoot Colombo," 8; COINTELPRO, an abbreviation derived from Counter Intelligence Program, was a Federal Bureau of Investigation covert operation that was conducted between 1956 and 1971, and that aimed at surveilling, infiltrating, discrediting, and disrupting domestic political organizations deemed subversive by the FBI.

Chapter 24

1. "Govs Respond to League's Request," *Unity News*, April 1971, 6; Fred Ferretti, "Italian-American Rights League Builds Strength in Several Major Cities," *New York Times*, May 16, 1971, 61; Letter from Deputy Mayor Richard R. Aurelio to Anthony Colombo, January 10, 1971, in Mayor John V. Lindsay Collection, New York City Municipal Archive.

2. "*Tri-Boro Post* Names Joseph Colombo 'Man-of-Year,'" *Tri-Boro Post*, January 14, 1971, 1; Dick Shaap, "The Ten Most Powerful Men in New York," *New York*, January 1971, 24.

3. Steve Aiello, "Politix," *Tri-Boro Post*, February 11, 1971, 5.

4. Aiello, "Politix," 5.

5. Letter from Anthony Colombo to Robert Evans, January 28, 1971, in *Unity News*, April 1971, 4.

6. *Unity News*, April 1971, 7; Harlan Lebo, *The Godfather Legacy* (Fireside, 1997), 42.

Chapter 25

1. Lebo, *The Godfather Legacy*, 43.

2. Patterson and Wallace, *The Defense Lawyer*, 71–72.

3. "Colombo Acquitted in Conspiracy Case," *New York Times*, February 27, 1971, 1.

4. "Colombo Acquitted in Conspiracy Case," 1; Robert Kappstatter, "Jury Clears Colombo Amid Threats & Scuffles," *New York Daily News*, February 27, 1971, 5.

5. Everett R. Harvey, "U.S. Probes Italian Rights Unit," *Staten Island Advance*, February 3, 1971, 1.

6. Morris Kaplan, "Jury Is Studying Italian Picketing," *New York Times*, March 4, 1971, 39.

7. The speech by Al Ruddy at the IACRL meeting is transcribed from *NBC News*, NBC, New York, February 25, 1971.

8. Fred Ferretti, "Corporate Rift in 'Godfather' Filming," *New York Times*, March 23, 1971, 28.

9. Nicholas Pileggi, "The Making of 'The Godfather'—Sort of a Home Movie," *New York Times*, August 15, 1971, SM45; Capria and Colombo, *Colombo*, 266.

10. The speech by Joseph Colombo Sr. at the IACRL meeting is transcribed from *NBC News*, NBC, New York, February 25, 1971.

Chapter 26

1. Grace Lichtenstein, "'Godfather' Film Won't Mention Mafia," *New York Times*, March 20, 1971, 1; "No Mafia in Movie," *Washington Post*, March 20, 1971, C7.

2. Bernard Bard, "Colombo Unit Pickets Bd. of Ed.," *New York Post*, March 19, 1971, 3.

3. Nicholas Pileggi, "Crazy Joey Gallo Was Expendable," *New York*, April 27, 1972, 36.

4. "Suit by Gallo Charges 'Unusual Punishment,'" *New York Times*, August 29, 1964, 9.

5. Pileggi, "Why They Had to Shoot Colombo," 8; Pileggi, "Crazy Joey Gallo Was Expendable," 36.

6. "A Night for Colombo," *Time*, April 5, 1971, 33.

7. "Colombo Honored at Dinner," *Tri-Boro Post*, March 25, 1971, 3; Emanuel Perlmutter, "Italian Rights Group Honors Colombo," *New York Times*, March 23, 1971, 46; "Colombo Honored at Dinner," *Unity News*, April 1971, 2.

8. "'Mafia' Lies Dead on the Cutting Room Floor," *New York Daily News*, March 28, 1971, 49.

9. Pileggi, "The Making of 'The Godfather,'" SM45.

10. "'Godfather' Film Shooting in New York," *Los Angeles Times*, March 25, 1971, G19; Pileggi, "The Making of 'The Godfather,'" SM45.

11. Tom Buckley, "The Mafia Tries a New Tune," *Harper's*, August 1971, 54; Patterson and Wallace, *The Defense Lawyer*, 71.

12. Lebo, *The Godfather Legacy*, 91.

13. "Yes, Mr. Ruddy, There Is a . . . ," editorial, *New York Times*, March 23, 1971, 36.

14. Fred Ferretti, "TV's 'F.B.I.' to Drop 'Mafia' and 'Cosa Nostra' From Its Scripts," *New York Times*, March 24, 1971, 40.

15. "Commercial Wins Award," *New York Times*, March 24, 1971, 40.

16. "Commercial Awards," *Washington Post*, March 25, 1971, C12.

17. Pileggi, "Risorgimento," 29.

18. Rudy Johnson, "Day-Care Center Wins in Brooklyn," BQ85.

Chapter 27

1. Bumiller, "A Godmother of Politics for Giuliani," B1.
2. *Unity News*, April 1971, 6.
3. *Unity News*, April 1971, 1.
4. U.S. Department of Justice, Federal Bureau of Investigation, memo, April 15, 1971, SAC, NYC, to Director, FBI, Italian-American Civil Rights League; Jimmy Breslin, "What's in an Italian Name? For Aiello It's Pride!" *New York Daily News*, October 18, 1979, 4.
5. *CBS Reports*, "An Essay on the Mafia," CBS, New York, June 25, 1972.
6. Frank Faso and Theo Wilson, "Marlon Makes Mott St. Scene," *New York Daily News*, April 20, 1971, 4.
7. Pileggi, "The Making of 'The Godfather,'" SM7.
8. Pileggi, "The Making of 'The Godfather,'" SM7.
9. Seifer, *Nobody Speaks for Me*, 73–75.
10. A CIAO-sponsored socioeconomic study of Italians across the five boroughs would be published in January 1975, under the title *A Portrait of the Italian-American Community in New York City*.
11. Seifer, *Nobody Speaks for Me*, 74.

Chapter 28

1. Tape 6010-023, Aldo Tambellini Archive, ZKM Center for Art and Media, Karlsruhe, Germany.
2. Seifer, *Nobody Speaks for Me*, 75.
3. S. M. Tomasi, "Nixon, McGovern and the Italian American Vote," *National Italian-American News*, November 1972, 3, Italian American Collections, Newspapers, Immigration History Research Center, University of Minnesota.
4. "Fourth Annual Dinner Dance Program, Congress of Italian-American Organizations, May 14, 1971."
5. Pileggi, "Risorgimento," 29.
6. "Urban Group Joins an Ethnic Alliance," *New York Times*, May 15, 1971, 12.
7. Patterson and Wallace, *The Defense Lawyer*, 77; "Demonstration in Foley Square," *Jewish Telegraphic Agency*, December 31, 1970, 1; Stephen Aiello, "Politix," *Tri-Boro Post*, January 7, 1971, 10.
8. U.S. Department of Justice, Federal Bureau of Investigation, Washington, DC, File No. 92-12264: Italian American Civil Rights League.
9. Morris Kaplan, "Kahane and Colombo Join Forces to Fight Reported U.S. Harassment," *New York Times*, May 14, 1971, 1.

10. Irving Lieberman and Jack Robbins, "Colombo and Kahane Establish an Alliance," *New York Post*, May 13, 1971, 5.

11. Kaplan, "Kahane and Colombo Join Forces to Fight Reported U.S. Harassment," 1.

12. Kaplan, "Kahane and Colombo Join Forces to Fight Reported U.S. Harassment," 1.

13. Sam Roberts, "Italo Group 'Purge' Sought," *New York Daily News*, May 30, 1971, 5.

14. Bell, "Crime as an American Way of Life," 150.

15. Jack Newfield, "Meade, the Mob, and the Machine," *Village Voice*, January 3, 1974, 23.

16. Hendrik Hertzberg, "'Hi, Boss,' Said the Judge to Meade Esposito," *New York Times*, December 10, 1972, SM33.

17. Denis Hamill, "My, How Times Have Changed," *New York Daily News*, March 24, 2011, 7.

18. Thomas P. Ronan, "New Brooklyn Leader: Meade Henry Esposito," *New York Times*, January 11, 1969, 34.

19. Tape 5996-009, Aldo Tambellini Archive, ZKM Center for Art and Media, Karlsruhe, Germany.

20. "Camp for Underprivileged Kids Is Colombo's Lifelong Dream," *Evening News (Newburgh, NY)*, June 30, 1971, 8D; Frank G. Coletti, "Joe Colombo Remembered," *Italo-American Times*, March 14, 1977, 6, in Italian American Collections, Newspapers, Immigration History Research Center, University of Minnesota.

21. "Italian Unit's Camp for Children Opens Upstate This Week," *New York Times*, July 4, 1971, 25; Coletti, "Joe Colombo Remembered," 6.

22. Les Matthews, "Hired Killer or Nut?," *New York Amsterdam News*, July 3, 1971, 1.

23. Phillip Greer and David C. Berliner, "Reputed Mob Boss Shot at N.Y. Rally," *Washington Post*, June 29, 1971, 1.

24. Barry Gottehrer, *The Mayor's Man* (Doubleday, 1975), 302.

25. Gottehrer, *The Mayor's Man*, 303.

26. Lawrence Van Gelder, "Colombo: A Man with Several Roles," *New York Times*, June 29, 1971, 20.

27. Louis Harris, "Most Believe There's a Mafia," *Chicago Tribune*, May 17, 1971, 1; Louis Harris, "Poll: Yes, There is a Mafia," *New York Post*, May 17, 1971, 4.

Chapter 29

1. Pileggi, "Risorgimento," 26, 33; Memorandum from Nancy Seifer, Mayor's Press Office, June 17, 1971, reproduced in *The Ordeal of Assimilation: A Documentary History of the White Working Class*, eds. Stanley Feldstein and Lawrence Costello (Doubleday, 1974), 456–457.

2. Seifer, *Nobody Speaks for Me*, 13–21.

3. Letter from Nancy Seifer, Director, Neighborhood Press Office, to Editor, *Tri-Boro Post*, December 17, 1970, 8.

4. Memorandum from Nancy Seifer to Tom Morgan, June 25, 1971, in Mayor John V. Lindsay Collection, Box 37, Folder 657, New York City Municipal Archive.

5. Memorandum from Nancy Seifer to Tom Morgan, June 25, 1971.

6. Memorandum from Nancy Seifer to Tom Morgan, June 25, 1971.

7. John D'emilio, *Lost Prophet: The Life and Times of Bayard Rustin* (Free Press, 2003), 12–13; Robert Daley, *Target Blue: An Insider's View of the N.Y.P.D.* (Delacorte, 1973), 202–4.

8. Fred Ferretti, "Suspect in Shooting of Colombo Linked to Gambino Family," *New York Times*, July 20, 1971, 1; Arthur Bell, "The After-Hours 28: Greetings from the Feds," *Village* Voice, December 23, 1971, 21.

9. Barbara Campbell, "Cousin Asserts Jerome Johnson Told of Job with Italian League," *New York Times*, July 1, 1971, 53.

10. Jim Stingley, "Slain Gunman Had Long L.A. Police Record," *Los Angeles Times*, June 29, 1971, 10.

11. Stingley, "Slain Gunman Had Long L.A. Police Record," 10.

12. Francis X. Clines, "Jerome A. Johnson Depicted by the People Who Knew Him," *New York Times*, June 30, 1971, 27; John Mullane and Ernest Johnson Jr., "The Triggerman's Past," *New York Post*, June 29, 1971, 2.

13. Campbell, "Cousin Asserts Jerome Johnson Told of Job with Italian League," 53.

14. Tape 6020-033, Aldo Tambellini Archive, ZKM Center for Art and Media, Karlsruhe, Germany.

15. Louis Sepersky, "Joe Colombo: New Civil Rights Activist," *Herald*, April 25, 1971, 1.

16. "Antiwar Rally Set for Next Weekend in Prospect Park," *New York Times*, June 13, 1971, BQ92.

17. "Rally in Prospect Park Asks That All Ages Protest War," *New York Times*, June 21, 1971, 4.

18. William Federici, "Add Final Touches for Unity Day's Rally," *New York Daily News*, June 27, 1971, 5; Ferretti, "Italian-American League's Power Spreads," 64; Tape 5999-012, Aldo Tambellini Archive, ZKM Center for Art and Media, Karlsruhe, Germany.

19. U.S. Department of Justice, Federal Bureau of Investigation, "Special Investigations Division," June 24, 1971, File No. 92-12264: Italian American Civil Rights League.

20. U.S. Department of Justice, Federal Bureau of Investigation, "Special Investigations Division," June 24, 1971, File No. 92-12264: Italian American Civil Rights League.

21. Cook, "A Family Business," SM 94; Nicholas Gage, "Informants Give Mafia reaction to Colombo Shooting," *New York Times*, June 30, 1971, 26.

22. U.S. Department of Justice, Federal Bureau of Investigation, memo, June 16, 1971, SAC, NYC, to Director, FBI, Gregory Scarpa, Bureau File NY 92-2657; Pileggi, "Crazy Joey Gallo Was Expendable," 36.

23. Nicholas Pileggi, "Merciful Heaven, Is This the End of Joe Colombo?," *New York*, June 14, 1971, 46.

24. U.S. Department of Justice, Federal Bureau of Investigation, memo, June 16, 1971, SAC, NYC, to Director, FBI, Gregory Scarpa, Bureau File NY 92-2657.

25. James F. Clarity, "Italian-American League Said to Pressure Shops," *New York Times*, June 26, 1971, 15.

26. "Names National Committees, Massaro Is National Deputy," *OSIA News*, November 1973, 1, 3, Italian American Collections, Newspapers, Immigration History Research Center, University of Minnesota; Dominic R. Massaro, Application for Membership, National Italian American League to Combat Defamation, May 8, 1967, Dominic Massaro Papers, Box 40, Folder 5, Immigration History Research Center, University of Minnesota; "News Report from State Senator John D. Calandra: Elect the Marchi-Massaro-Corona Team [1969]," Dominic Massaro Papers, Box 45, Folder 14, Immigration History Research Center, University of Minnesota.

27. Letter from Dominic R. Massaro to Miss Pedock, August 4, 1967, in Order Sons of Italy, National Office Records, Box 25, Folder 12, Immigration History Research Center, University of Minnesota; Letter Dominic R. Massaro to Worthy Venerable, September 13, 1967, in Order Sons of Italy, National Office Records, Box 25, Folder 12, Immigration History Research Center, University of Minnesota.

28. Pileggi, "Why They Had to Shoot Colombo," 8–9; "United Italo Groups Rap Pileggi's Story," *The Challenge*, September 1971, 9; Minutes, OSIA Northeast Bronx Lodge 2091, July 26, 1971, Dominic Massaro Papers, Box 22, Folder 18, Immigration History Research Center, University of Minnesota.

29. Tape 6020-033, Aldo Tambellini Archive, ZKM Center for Art and Media, Karlsruhe, Germany.

Chapter 30

1. U.S. Department of Justice, Federal Bureau of Investigation, memo, July 20, 1971, SAC, NYC, to Director, FBI, Gregory Scarpa, Bureau File NY 92-2657.

2. Judith Michaelson, "'I Was with Him,'" *New York Post*, June 28, 1971, 3.

3. Robert Daley, *Target Blue*, 190.

4. Michaelson, "'I Was with Him,'" 3.

5. Walter Anderson, *Courage Is a Three-Letter Word* (Random House, 1986), 155.

6. Gottehrer, *The Mayor's Man*, 304; Michaelson, "'I Was with Him,'" 3.

7. Michaelson, "'I Was with Him,'" 40.

8. Campbell, "Cousin Asserts Jerome Johnson Told of Job with Italian League," 53.

9. William E. Farrell, "Bullets Found at Johnson Home," *New York Times*, July 2, 1971, 28.

10. U.S. Department of Justice, Federal Bureau of Investigation, memo, n.d., SAS, NYC, to Director, FBI, Joseph Colombo, Bureau File NY 92-1965, p. 3.

11. U.S. Department of Justice, Federal Bureau of Investigation, memo, June 30, 1971, SAC, NYC, to Director, FBI, Gregory Scarpa, Bureau File NY 92-2657, pp. 1–2.

Chapter 31

1. *ABC News*, ABC, New York, June 28, 1971; Francis X. Clines, "News Policy of Police," *New York Times*, July 15, 1971, 35.

2. Letter from Anthony Colombo to Mayor John V. Lindsay, July 9, 1971, in Mayor John V. Lindsay Collection, New York City Municipal Archive.

3. Pileggi, "Why They Had to Shoot Colombo," 8; also see William Sherman, "The Mystery Man Who Shot Joe Colombo," *New York Daily News*, August 26, 1971, 68; and "Jerome Johnson: A Real Nowhere Man," *New York Daily News*, August 27, 1971, 40.

Chapter 32

1. "Madness in Columbus Circle," editorial, *New York Times*, June 29, 1971, 36.

2. Ralph Blumenfeld and Joel Dreyfus, "Anger Over Shooting Unleashed on Blacks," *New York Post*, June 29, 1971, 3; Billy Rowe, "Billy Rowe's Note Book," *New York Amsterdam News*, June 10, 1971, B6.

3. Ralph Blumenthal, "Urban Coalition to Help Italians," *New York Times*, July 5, 1971, 8.

4. Memorandum from Nancy Seifer to Jay Kriegel, July 20, 1971, in Mayor John V. Lindsay Collection, box 37, folder 658, New York City Municipal Archive.

5. Macleod, "Daily Closeup;" "Grant Finances Multi-Center Developments for Elderly," *New York Amsterdam News*, December 11, 1971, D4.

6. Letter from Mayor John V. Lindsay to Mary C. Sansone, New York City, October 26, 1971.

Chapter 33

1. U.S. Congress, Senate, Permanent Subcommittee on Investigations, *Organized Crime—Stolen Securities: Hearings before the Committee on Government*

Operations, 92nd Cong., July 21, 1972, 625, 630–31; "Senate Witness Tells of Payoffs," *Chicago Tribune*, July 22, 1971, 3.

2. U.S. Department of Justice, Federal Bureau of Investigation, June 8, 1972, SAC, NYC, Gregory Scarpa, Bureau File NY 92-2657.

3. Fred Ferretti, "Italian Group Got Gallo Aid for Day," *New York Times*, April 8, 1972, 34.

4. "Joseph Gallo Never an AID Member," *The Challenge*, April 1972, 12.

5. Advertisement, *New York Times*, March 12, 1972, D11.

6. Vincent Canby, "Bravo, Brando's 'Godfather,'" *New York Times*, March 12, 1972, D25.

7. Emily Nussbaum, "The Great Divide," *New Yorker*, April 7, 2014; *All in the Family*, "Archie Sees a Mugging," CBS, Los Angeles, January 29, 1972.

8. Rowe, "Billy Rowe's Note Book," B6; Penn, "Colombo's Wounding Also Crippled Group That Fought 'Slurs,'" 1.

9. *All in the Family*, "Sammy's Visit," CBS, Los Angeles, February 19, 1972.

Chapter 34

1. "Italian-American Congress Honors Executive Director," *New York Times*, March 14, 1972, 23.

2. Peter Kihss, "Ethnic Leaders Discuss the Assets of Diversity," *New York Times*, March 16, 1972, 49.

3. Program, Fourth Annual Symposium, Congress of Italian American Organizations, March 15, 1972; Michael Novak, *The Rise of Unmeltable Ethnics: Politics and Culture in the Seventies* (Macmillan, 1972). For an overview of the challenges faced by participants in CIAO's 1972 symposium "Ethnic Communities and the Challenge of Urban Life," see Perry Weed, *The White Ethnic Movement and Ethnic Politics* (Praeger, 1973).

4. Francis X. Clines, "Ethnic Leaders Attempt a Coalition," *New York Times*, October 16, 1971, 35.

5. D'emilio, *Lost Prophet*, 19.

6. Jack Newfield, "Lindsay's Latest Blunder," *Village Voice*, December 21, 1972, 3. Also see Jack Newfield and Jeff Greenfield, *A Populist Manifesto: The Making of a New Majority* (Praeger, 1972), 217; Kihss, "Ethnic Leaders Discuss the Assets of Diversity," 49.

7. *CIAO Reports*, June 1972, 1; Peter Kihss, "City Is Widening Its Help to Many Ethnic Groups," *New York Times*, September 8, 1972, 37; David Vidal, "Many Spanish Leaders, Disillusioned with Koch Policies, Seek New Paths to Progress," *New York Times*, May 13, 1979, 29.

8. *CIAO Reports*, June 1972, 3; *CIAO Reports*, August 1973, 4, in Italian American Collections, Newspapers, Immigration History Research Center, University of Minnesota.

9. "Legislative Primaries," editorial, *New York Times*, June 15, 1972, 40.

Chapter 35

1. *The Challenge*, April 1972, 1; Bernard Gavzer, "Italian League Claims Slaying Publicity a Help," *Los Angeles Times*, April 23, 1972, 86; Joseph P. Fried, "Inquiry Is Urged on a Youth Grant," *New York Times*, November 1, 1972, 49.

2. Amy Logan, "Around City Hall," *New Yorker*, November 11, 1972, 169; Hendrik Hertzberg, "'Hi, Boss,' Said the Judge to Meade Esposito," SM33; for a study of white ethnics living in the Canarsie section of Brooklyn in the second half of the 1970s, see Jonathan Rieder, *Canarsie: The Jews and Italians of Brooklyn Against Liberalism* (Harvard University Press, 1985); for the story of Boston's busing crisis in the decade following the assassination of Martin Luther King Jr., see J. Anthony Lukas, *Common Ground: A Turbulent Decade in the Lives of Three American Families* (Knopf, 1985).

3. Ronald Smothers, "But Blacks Contend Issue of Racism is Overriding," *New York Times*, October 22, 1972, 143.

4. Judith Michaelson, "The League Without Colombo," *New York Post*, June 1, 1974, 3; *NBC News*, NBC, New York, June 28, 1971; William E. Farrell, "Colombo Shot, Gunman Slain at Columbus Circle Rally Site," *New York Times*, June 29, 1971, 1; "Rivals Questioned in Colombo Shooting," *Berkshire Eagle*, June 29, 1971, 1. See, for example, Louis Gigante, "The Conspiracy of June 28, 1971," *Italo-American Times*, July 26, 1976, 1, in Italian American Collections, Newspapers, Immigration History Research Center, University of Minnesota.

5. Leonard Buder, "Protests by White Parents Shut 2 Canarsie Schools," *New York Times*, October 17, 1972, 1; Iver Peterson, "Canarsie Parents Block Black Pupils from Entering School for 2nd Day," *New York Times*, October 18, 1972, 1; Ivan Peterson, "Scribner Gets Writ to End 3-Day Sit-In at Canarsie School," *New York Times*, October 19, 1972, 43.

6. Leonard Buder, "Scribner Cast in a New Role," *New York Times*, October 25, 1972, 24; Ronald Smothers, "Canarsie Parents Press Their Boycott of Schools," *New York Times*, October 30, 1972, 25; Iver Peterson, "Canarsie: The Anatomy of a School Crisis," *Race Relations Reporter* 4 (January 1973): 9; Michael Meyers, "Canarsie: Study of an 'Integration' Plan," MARC, December 1973, 11 n.29, Box 388, Folder 6, Kenneth Bancroft Clark Papers, Library of Congress.

7. "Dr. Clark Calls for Board of Ed to Quit," *New York Amsterdam News*, May 5, 1973, 1.

8. Leonard Buder, "Eggs and Rocks Thrown as Boycott at Canarsie School Continues," *New York Times*, November 1, 1972, 1.

9. Jerry Capeci, "Portrait of a Peacemaker," *New York Post*, November 2, 1972, 3; Iver Peterson, "Policies of Police Help to Prevent Violence in Canarsie School," *New York Times*, November 12, 1972, 14.

10. Paul Delaney, "Black Supporters of President Under Fire," *New York Times*, October 17, 1972, 29; Capeci, "Portrait of a Peacemaker," 3.

11. Roberta B. Gratz, "Behind the White Barricades at 211," *New York Post*, November 2, 1972, 3.

12. Clark Whelton, " 'The People Are Coming to Us,' " *Village Voice*, March 22, 1973, 1.

13. *New York Times*, October 17, 1972, 1.

14. Clark Whelton, " 'The People Are Coming to Us,' " 1; Leonard Buder, "Board Reverses Scribner, Orders 32 Into J.H.S. 211," *New York Times*, October 27, 1972, 1.

15. Leonard Buder, "Canarsie Reports Attendance Gains," *New York Times*, November 9, 1972, 1.

16. Whelton, " 'The People Are Coming to Us,' " 1; Pete Hamill, "School Bus Named Desire," *New York Post*, November 1, 1972, 45.

17. Michael Meyers, "Canarsie: Study of an 'Integration' Plan," 21 n.61; Leonard Buder, "8,440, Most Since Fall, Out in Canarsie Boycott," *New York Times*, March 6, 1973, 50.

18. Leonard Buder, "Central School Board Decides to Shift Tilden Houses Pupils from Canarsie," *New York Times*, March 31, 1973, 39; M. A. Farber, "Clark Asks Ouster of City School Board," *New York Times*, April 28, 1973, 29.

19. Buder, "Central School Board Decides to Shift Tilden Houses Pupils from Canarsie," 39; "Dr. Clark's Charges Against Board of Ed," *New York Amsterdam News*, July 7, 1973, 1; Michael Meyers, "Canarsie: Study of an 'Integration' Plan," 6, 19.

20. "Board Bars Anti-Lachman Testimony," *New York Amsterdam News*, July 7, 1973, 1.

21. M. A. Farber, "Italian Rights Leader, 28, Named to Post at Board of Education," *New York Times*, August 30, 1971, 18; "Colombo Is Home with Two Guards," *Washington Post*, August 29, 1971, 14.

22. Benjamin W. Watkins, "Board Member No 'Token' Militant," *New York Amsterdam News*, September 20, 1969, 14; Gene I. Maeroff, "Decentralization Also Spreads Scandals Around," *New York Times*, December 22, 1974, E4.

23. Farber, "Italian Rights Leader, 28, Named to Post at Board of Education," 18.

24. Michaelson, "The League Without Colombo," 3.

Chapter 36

1. Robert Garrett, "Name Panel to Seek Ethnic Harmony," *New York Post*, November 2, 1972, 12; "College Gets Go-Ahead on Ethnic Study," *New York Daily News*, December 10, 1972; "Brooklyn to Offer Italian-American Studies," *The Reporter (Baruch College, CUNY)*, February 5, 1973, 1; J. Zamgba Browne, "Brooklyn Happenings," *New York Amsterdam News*, July 28, 1973, D10.

2. Robert Garrett, "Name Panel to Seek Ethnic Harmony," 12; *CIAO Reports*, April 1974, 3, in Italian American Collections, Serials, Immigration History Research Center, University of Minnesota.

3. Helen Drusine, "Center Crosses Ethnic Lines," *New York Times*, February 25, 1973, 93.

4. Mary Sansone, Tape 176a, New York Immigrant Labor History Project Oral History Collection, Robert F. Wagner Labor Archives, New York University; Helen Drusine, "Center Crosses Ethnic Lines," 93; Tom Buckley, "The Student Moves: Into the 14th C.D.," *New York Times*, June 21, 1970, SM10; "J. V. Mangano, 83, Brooklyn Politician, Dies," *New York Times*, October 12, 1988, 12.

5. *CIAO Reports*, March 1973, 2; *CIAO Reports*, May 1973, 2; *CIAO Reports*, June 1973, 3; *CIAO Reports*, August 1973, 2, in Italian American Collections, Serials, Immigration History Research Center, University of Minnesota; Rudy Johnson, "Day-Care Center Wins in Brooklyn," BQ85.

6. *CIAO Reports*, June 1973, 1, in Italian American Collections, Serials, Immigration History Research Center, University of Minnesota.

7. *CIAO Reports*, August 1973, 1, in Italian American Collections, Serials, Immigration History Research Center, University of Minnesota.

8. Seifer, *Nobody Speaks for Me*, 84; William Claiborne, "Study Adds Italians to New York's Disadvantaged Minorities," *Washington Post*, February 6, 1975, 4.

9. Seifer, *Nobody Speaks for Me*, 84–85; *CIAO Reports*, August 1973, 1, in Italian American Collections, Serials, Immigration History Research Center, University of Minnesota.

10. *CIAO Reports*, December 1975, 5; in Italian American Collections, Serials, Immigration History Research Center, University of Minnesota; Mary Sansone, interview by Gail Pellett, *Ethni-city and the American Dream*, WBAI, New York, 1975, in Pacifica Radio Archives.

11. *CIAO Reports*, October 1976, 3–4; in Italian American Collections, Serials, Immigration History Research Center, University of Minnesota.

12. Casalena, *A Portrait of the Italian-American Community in New York City*, 10. Sociologist John R. Logan's research on socioeconomic stratification among New York City's ethnic and racial groups, which also uses US census data from 1970, corroborates the findings in CIAO's *Portrait of the Italian-American Community in New York City*. I thank Professor Logan for sharing with me data from his unpublished

paper "How Many Years? The White Ethnic Hierarchy in New York, 1880–1970" (paper presented at the Conference on Immigrants' Economic Incorporation, Spatial Segregation, and Anti-Immigrant Sentiments, Madrid, Spain, Juan March Institute, October 2009).

13. Casalena, *A Portrait of the Italian-American Community in New York City*; Seifer, *Nobody Speaks for Me*, 69.

14. Macleod, "Daily Closeup"; "Statement by Mary C. Sansone, Executive Director, CIAO," press release, February 5, 1975, Congress of Italian American Organizations.

15. Mark Lieberman, "City's Italian Poor Suffer in Silence, A Survey Shows,'" *New York Daily News*, February 6, 1975; Diane Henry, "A Survey on Italian-Americans Finds Government Is Ignoring Their Needs," *New York Times*, February 6, 1975, 29; *CIAO Reports*, May 1975, 2, in Italian American Collections, Serials, Immigration History Research Center, University of Minnesota; Claiborne, "Study Adds Italians to New York's Disadvantaged Minorities," 4.

16. Joseph F. Valletutti, "First I-A Coalition Task Force Meeting," *The Challenge*, October 1971, 6, 10; *Italian-American Coalition Newsletter*, July 1972, 1, in Italian American Collections, Serials, Immigration History Research Center, University of Minnesota.

17. Seifer, *Nobody Speaks for Me*, 86.

18. Newfield, "Lindsay's Latest Blunder," 3.

19. Community Services Administration, "Program Overview," January 1975, 3, in Dominic Massaro Papers, Box 40, Folder 12, Immigration History Research Center, University of Minnesota.

20. Community Services Administration, "Project Manager Site-Visit," January 1976, 3, in Dominic Massaro Papers, Box 40, Folder 13, Immigration History Research Center, University of Minnesota; also see Letter from Angel F. Rivera to Anthony G. DiFalco, in Dominic Massaro Papers, Box 40, Folder 13, Immigration History Research Center, University of Minnesota.

21. Casalena, *A Portrait of the Italian-American Community in New York City*; Seifer, *Nobody Speaks for Me*, 86; "Ford to City: Drop Dead," *New York Daily News*, October 29, 1975.

22. Seifer, *Nobody Speaks for Me*, 42–87; Macleod, "Daily Closeup"; Mary Sansone, interview by Gail Pellett, *Ethni-city and the American Dream*.

Chapter 37

1. Francis X. Clines, "A Quiet Revolution in Northside," *New York Times*, January 21, 1978, 20; for a study of the multi-ethnic Williamsburg section of Brooklyn in the late 1970s, see Ida Susser, *Norman Street: Poverty and Politics in an Urban Neighborhood* (Oxford University Press, 1982); for a study of the National

Congress of Neighborhood Women, see chapters 3 and 4 in Tamar Carroll, *Mobilizing New York: AIDS, Antipoverty, and Feminist Activism* (University of North Carolina Press, 2015).

2. Sally Martino-Fisher, interview by Gail Pellett, *Ethni-city and the American Dream*, WBAI, New York, 1975, in Pacifica Radio Archives.

3. Barbara Grizzuti Harrison, "Hers," *New York Times*, May 22, 1980, C2; Gene I. Maeroff, "In Williamsburg, A School Board Dispute Simmers," *New York Times*, December 5, 1971, 17.

4. Harrison, "Hers," C2; Judith N. DeSena, *People Power: Grass Roots Politics and Race Relations* (University Press of America, 1999), 36; "Brooklyn Women Announce College Program and Goals," *New York Amsterdam News*, July 16, 1975, B6.

5. "Brooklyn Women Announce College Program and Goals," B6.

6. Ralph Carrano, "Local Stripper Becomes a Minister," *Greenpoint Gazette*, February 25, 1975, 3.

7. Kellie Everts's account of her life in 1960s Los Angeles can be found at https://kellieevertsistripforgod.com.

8. Carrano, "Local Stripper Becomes a Minister," 3; also see Kellie Everts, "Feminism in Theology," *Greenpoint Gazette*, February 22, 1977.

9. Carrano, "Local Stripper Becomes a Minister," 3.

10. Kellie Everts, Letter to the Editor, *Greenpoint Gazette*, March 8, 1977.

11. Bob McCoy, "Weight Lifting and Strip-Teasing Keeps Kellie Fit for the Lord," *San Juan Star (Puerto Rico)*, August 17, 1977, 1.

12. Fredelle Maynard, "Woman Power," *Woman's Day*, November 16, 1982, 171.

13. Frank J. Prial, "Marchers Here Protest Antipoverty Project Cuts," *New York Times*, November 19, 1975, 48; Maynard, "Woman Power," 171.

14. Maynard, "Woman Power," 171; Veronica Geng, "Requiem for the Women's Movement," *Harper's*, November 1976, 68; Memorandum from Sally Martino-Fisher, NCNW Coordinator, November 30, 1976, in Sophia Smith Collection, Smith College, National Congress of Neighborhood Women Papers, Box 15, Folder 16.

15. "Announcing N.C.N.W. Nat'l Conference, June 25–27, 1976," in Sophia Smith Collection, Smith College, National Congress of Neighborhood Women Papers, Box 30, Folder 31; "Working Women Get Together," *New York Amsterdam News*, June 31, 1976, B4.

16. *Greenpoint Gazette*, May 11, 1976; *Muscle Training Illustrated*, December 1974; "Viva Machisma!" *Esquire*, July 1975, 61–66.

17. Kellie Everts, Letter to the Editor, *Greenpoint Gazette*, March 8, 1977.

18. Dana Eden, "Daughters of the Light;" *Greenpoint Gazette*, February 10, 1977.

19. "Humping Iron," *Playboy*, May 1977, 167–69.

20. Letter from Frank Guidice, President, IACRL Chapter 23, to Christine Noschese, Director, NCNW, May 5, 1977, in Sophia Smith Collection, Smith College, National Congress of Neighborhood Women Papers, Box 42, Folder 33.

21. McCoy, "Weight Lifting and Strip-Teasing Keeps Kellie Fit for the Lord," 1; "Minister Is Back at 'Scene of Crime,'" *Long Branch (NJ) Daily Record*, August 21, 1975, 3.

22. McCoy, "Weight Lifting and Strip-Teasing Keeps Kellie Fit for the Lord," 1; Kellie Everts, "Feminism in Theology."

Chapter 38

1. Neal Hirschfeld, "What Ever Happened to Joe Colombo?," *New York Daily News*, October 14, 1977.

2. Pranay Gupte, "Colombo Is Eulogized as a Champion of Civil Rights," *New York Times*, May 27, 1978, 23; "Mafia Don Colombo Buried in New York," *Los Angeles Times*, May 27, 1978, 23.

3. Marcia Chambers, "New Head of Board of Education to Re-Evaluate Promotion Policies," *New York Times*, July 6, 1977, 46.

4. Leonard Buder, "State Investigators Widen School-Board Inquiry," *New York Times*, November 28, 1974, 26; Gene I. Maeroff, "Youngest Member of Education Board," *New York Times*, February 9, 1975, 93.

5. "Trial by Association," editorial, *New York Times*, October 22, 1979, 20.

6. "Trial by Association"; Marcia Chambers, "Aiello Is Still Under Consideration as Carter Aide, White House Says," *New York Times*, October 18, 1979, B3.

7. "White House Still Chooses Aiello," *New York Times*, November 2, 1979, B4. For an essay on white ethnic politics in the 1970s, see Joe Merton, "Rethinking the Politics of White Ethnicity in 1970s America," *Historical Journal* 55 (September 2012): 731–56.

Chapter 39

1. "Aiello's Seat on Board Going to College Dean," *New York Times*, February 5, 1980, B9; Karen De Witt, "Midge Costanza: The President's 'Window on the Nation,'" *Washington Post*, April 26, 1977, B14.

2. *CIAO Reports*, Fall 1977, 3, in Italian American Collections, Serials, Immigration History Research Center, University of Minnesota; Nicholas Pileggi, "Portrait of the Artist as a Garage Attendant in the Bronx," *New York*, October 30, 1972, 37–45.

3. *CIAO Reports*, Fall 1977, 3, in Italian American Collections, Serials, Immigration History Research Center, University of Minnesota; Frank Lynn, "Beame and Governor Split on Candidacy of Cuomo for Mayor," *New York Times*, April 15, 1977, 1; Advertisement, *Boston Globe*, August 28, 1977, 14.

4. "Beame Cancels a Plan to Honor Sacco, Vanzetti," *Boston Globe*, August 21, 1977, 79; "'Sacco-Vanzetti Day' Off," *New York Times*, August 21, 1977, 36.

5. Tom Buckley, "Players Lining Up for a Game Called Mayoralty," *New York Times*, August 2, 1972, 39.

6. Glenn Fowler, "Koch and Cuomo Seek Support for Runoff from Beaten Foes," *New York Times*, September 10, 1977, 1.

7. Glenn Fowler, "Cuomo Fleshes Out Second Ballot Line," *New York Times*, October 27, 1977, 29; for a study of neighborhood symbolism in the cultural politics of urban life in the United States after World War II, see Benjamin Looker, *A Nation of Neighborhoods: Imagining Cities, Communities, and Democracy in Postwar America* (University of Chicago Press, 2015).

8. Frank Lynn, "Koch, the Favorite, Matches Late Drive of 3 Mayoral Rivals," *New York Times*, November 6, 1977, 1; Fred Ferretti, "Cuomo Finds Race a Scramble for Money and Support," *New York Times*, September 15, 1977, 88; E. J. Dionne Jr., "Mayoral Candidates Sail Into Each Other," *New York Times*, October 8, 1977, 20; Jack Newfield and Wayne Barrett, *City for Sale: Ed Koch and the Betrayal of New York* (Harper and Row, 1988), 134.

9. Lynn, "Koch and Cuomo Backers Ignore Usual Alliances as Runoff Nears," 1; Newfield and Barrett, *City for Sale*, 133; Maurice Carroll, "Cuomo Tries to Stem Split on Ethnic Lines," *New York Times*, September 19, 1977, 46; Denis Hamill, "Clubhouse Confidential," *Village Voice*, November 7, 1977, 13.

10. Douglas E. Schoen and Mark J. Penn, "Koch's Narrow Win," *New York Times*, November 11, 1977, 26.

11. Jack Newfield, "Newfield's Annual Thanksgiving Honor Roll," *Village Voice*, November 23, 1982, 15; *CIAO Reports*, Fall 1977, 3, in Italian American Collections, Serials, Immigration History Research Center, University of Minnesota; Judith Cummings, "City Accepts a Proposal for Settling Dispute in Italian-American Unit," *New York Times*, July 5, 1978, B3; Judith Cummings, "Antipoverty Agency Losing Contracts Following Audit," *New York Times*, December 17, 1978, 45.

12. Schoen and Penn, "Koch's Narrow Win," 26.

13. Maurice Carroll, "Koch Disbands Panel in Dispute Over Role," *New York Times*, January 25, 1978, 1.

14. Newfield and Barrett, *City for Sale*, 145–46.

15. Charles Kaiser, "Koch's Suspends 2 Antipoverty Pacts," *New York Times*, January 19, 1978, B10.

16. H. Carl McDall, "Abandoning the Poor Thru Re-Centralization," *New York Amsterdam News*, May 13, 1978, 4.

17. *CIAO Reports*, November 1973, 1, in Italian American Collections, Serials, Immigration History Research Center, University of Minnesota.

18. *CIAO Reports*, February 1976, 4, in Italian American Collections, Serials, Immigration History Research Center, University of Minnesota; "Ouster of an Ethnic Leader Stalls," *New York Times*, February 4, 1978, 42.

19. Letter from Peter L. Vale to Mario Biaggi, November 21, 1977, in Box 108, Folder 12, Elizabeth Holtzman Papers, Schlesinger Library, Radcliffe Institute, Harvard University.

20. Letter from Peter L. Vale to Mario Biaggi, November 21, 1977, in Box 108, Folder 12, Elizabeth Holtzman Papers, Schlesinger Library, Radcliffe Institute, Harvard University; Letter from Peter L. Vale to Friends of Italian American Committee for Public Relations and Special Projects, C.I.A.O., August 10, 1977, in Dominic Massaro Papers, Box 42, Folder 18, Immigration History Research Center, University of Minnesota.

21. Letter from Peter L. Vale to Dominic R. Massaro, November 21, 1977, in Box 41, Folder 9, in Dominic Massaro Papers, Box 40, Folder 10, Immigration History Research Center, University of Minnesota.

22. Judith Cummings, "City Accepts a Proposal for Settling Dispute in Italian-American Unit," B3; McDowell, "Italian-American Group's Board Levels Charge of Wide Nepotism," 15.

23. McDowell, "Italian-American Group's Board Levels Charge of Wide Nepotism," 15.

24. Edwin McDowell, "Social Agency Chief Ousted on Nepotism," *New York Times*, February 22, 1978, B2; Cummings, "City Accepts a Proposal for Settling Dispute in Italian-American Unit," B3.

25. Marcia Chambers, "Hiring of 687 for Education Board Bypassed Rules on Qualifications," *New York Times*, January 28, 1980, 1; Newfield, "Newfield's Annual Thanksgiving Honor Roll," 15.

26. Judith Cummings, "Antipoverty Agency Losing Contracts Following Audit," 45.

27. Cummings, "Antipoverty Agency Losing Contracts Following Audit," 45; Dena Kleiman, "Board of Estimate Votes Against the Westway Plan," *New York Times*, December 22, 1978, B1; Joy Allen, "Board Goes on Record 6–4 Against Koch on Westway," *Newsday*, December 22, 1978, 4Q.

28. Dena Kleiman, "Koch Is Booed by 200 for Refusal to Renew Group's Contract," *New York Times*, December 29, 1978, B4; Joy Allen, "Catholic Charities Get OK to Run Centers," *Newsday*, December 29, 1978, 23Q.

29. Newfield, "Newfield's Annual Thanksgiving Honor Roll," 15.

30. Edwin McDowell, "Head of Italian-American Group Assails Her Critics," *New York Times*, January 28, 1978, 42.

Coda

1. John Corry, "9 Italian-Americans Mull Ethnic Roles," *New York Times*, February 5, 1972, 31.

2. Stephen S. Hall, "Italian-Americans: Coming into Their Own," *New York Times*, May 15, 1983, SM28.

Selected Bibliography

Abrams, Norma, and Stephen Brown. "Mafia Chief Organizes a Picket at the FBI." *New York Daily News*, May 1, 1970.
Anagnostou, Yiorgos. "'White Ethnicity': A Reappraisal." *Italian American Review* 3 (2013): 99–128.
Atkinson, Ti-Grace. "On 'Violence in The Women's Movement.'" August 1971. Reprinted in *Amazon Odyssey*. Links Books, 1974.
Bell, Daniel. "Crime as an American Way of Life." *Antioch Review* 13 (1953): 131–54.
Cannato, Vincent J. *The Ungovernable City: John Lindsay and His Struggle to Save New York*. Basic Books, 2001.
Capria, Don, and Anthony Colombo. *Colombo: The Unsolved Murder*. Unity Press, 2015.
Carroll, Tamar. *Mobilizing New York: AIDS, Antipoverty, and Feminist Activism*. University of North Carolina Press, 2015.
Casalena, Josephine. *A Portrait of the Italian-American Community in New York City*. Vol. 1. Congress of Italian American Organizations, 1975.
Claiborne, William. "Study Adds Italians to New York's Disadvantaged Minorities." *Washington Post*, February 6, 1975.
Daley, Robert. *Target Blue: An Insider's View of the N.Y.P.D.* Delacorte, 1973.
D'emilio, John. *Lost Prophet: The Life and Times of Bayard Rustin*. Free Press, 2003.
Early, Gerald L. *This Is Where I Came In: Black America in the 1960s*. University of Nebraska Press, 2003.
Federici, William. "Joe Colombo: OK, I'll Be a Mafioso for Good." *New York Daily News*, July 3, 1970.
Ferraro, Thomas. *Feeling Italian: The Art of Ethnicity in America*. New York University Press, 2005.
Ferretti, Fred. "Italian-American League's Power Spreads." *New York Times*, April 4, 1971.
Gardaphé, Fred. *From Wiseguys to Wise Men: The Gangster and Italian American Masculinities*. Routledge, 2006.

Gennari, John. *Flavor and Soul: Italian America at Its African American Edge.* University of Chicago Press, 2017.

Glazer, Nathan, and Daniel Patrick Moynihan. Introduction to *Beyond the Melting Pot: The Negroes, Puerto Ricans, Jews, Italians and Irish of New York City*, 2nd ed. MIT Press, 1970.

Gottehrer, Barry. *The Mayor's Man.* Doubleday, 1975.

Guglielmo, Jennifer. *Living the Revolution: Italian Women's Resistance and Radicalism in New York City, 1880–1945.* University of North Carolina Press, 2010.

Hamill, Pete. "The Revolt of the White Lower Middle Class." *New York*, April 14, 1969.

Jacobson, Matthew Frye. *Roots Too: White Ethnic Revival in Post-Civil Rights America.* Harvard University Press, 2006.

Kefauver, Estes. *Crime in America.* Doubleday, 1951.

Kihss, Peter. "Ethnic Leaders Discuss the Assets of Diversity." *New York Times*, March 16, 1972.

Kron, Joan. "Radical Chick." *Philadelphia*, February 1971.

Lebo, Harlan. *The Godfather Legacy.* Fireside, 1997.

Lukas, J. Anthony. *Common Ground: A Turbulent Decade in the Lives of Three American Families.* Knopf, 1985.

Macleod, Hope. "Daily Closeup: Sharing and A Share." *New York Post*, March 13, 1975.

"'Mafia' Loses Its Place in Federal Vocabulary." *New York Times*, July 24, 1970.

Michaelson, Judith. "'I Was with Him.'" *New York Post*, June 28, 1971.

Michaelson, Judith. "The League Without Colombo." *New York Post*, June 1, 1974.

Montgomery, Paul L. "Thousands of Italians Here Rally Against Ethnic Slurs." *New York Times*, June 30, 1970.

Newfield, Jack, and Wayne Barrett. *City for Sale: Ed Koch and the Betrayal of New York.* Harper and Row, 1988.

Novak, Michael. *The Rise of Unmeltable Ethnics: Politics and Culture in the Seventies.* Macmillan, 1972.

Ostrow, Steve. *Live at The Continental: The Inside Story of the World-Famous Continental Baths.* Xlibris, 2007.

Patterson, James, and Benjamin Wallace. *The Defense Lawyer: The Barry Slotnick Story.* Little, Brown, 2021.

Perlstein, Rick. *Nixonland: The Rise a President and the Fracturing of America.* Scribner, 2008.

Peterson, Iver. "Canarsie: The Anatomy of a School Crisis." *Race Relations Reporter* 4 (January 1973): 9–12.

Pileggi, Nicholas. "The Making of 'The Godfather': Sort of a Home Movie." *New York Times* Sunday Magazine, August 15, 1971.

Pileggi, Nicholas. "Risorgimento: The Red, White and Greening of New York." *New York*, June 7, 1971.

Puzo, Mario. *The Godfather*. G. P. Putnam's Sons, 1969.

Puzo, Mario. *The Godfather Papers and Other Confessions*. G. P. Putnam's Sons, 1972.

Raab, Selwyn. *Five Families: The Rise, Decline, and Resurgence of America's Most Powerful Mafia Empires*. St. Martin's, 2005.

Rieder, Jonathan. *Canarsie: The Jews and Italians of Brooklyn Against Liberalism*. Harvard University Press, 1985.

Seedman Albert A., and Peter Hellman. *Chief! Classic Cases from the Files of the Chief of Detectives*. A. Fields Books, 1974.

Seifer, Nancy. *Nobody Speaks for Me! Self-Portraits of American Working Class Women*. Simon and Schuster, 1976.

Susser, Ida. *Norman Street: Poverty and Politics in an Urban Neighborhood*. Oxford University Press, 1982.

Talese, Gay. *Honor Thy Father*. World Publishing, 1971.

Villano, Anthony, with Gerald Astor. *Brick Agent: Inside the Mafia for the FBI*. Quadrangle, 1977.

Weed, Perry. *The White Ethnic Movement and Ethnic Politics*. Praeger, 1973.

Acknowledgments

Years ago, I told my mother I was going to Brooklyn to talk to Italians of her generation in order to do research for a book. She responded by telling me a story from her north Jersey childhood. "On holidays, we'd be waiting around for relatives from Brooklyn to arrive. I'd get impatient and ask your grandmother, 'Ma, who's coming?' and she'd say, 'Brooklyn's coming!'" I waited for my mother to tell me the rest but apparently it wasn't that kind of story because she made no attempt to fill the silence that followed. Puzzled, I put aside what she said, or thought I had. Whenever I felt blocked while writing this book, my grandmother's words—*Brooklyn's coming*—moved this pen.

The time I spent researching this book in and around Brooklyn would not have been possible without the hospitality of my brother Glenn, a resident of Carroll Gardens, who welcomed me into his home for extended stays. I owe a great debt to those who, having lived through the events recounted in this book, gave generously of their time and trust in author interviews conducted between the years 2010 and 2019.

Stephen Adubato Sr.	Sally Martino-Fisher	Nicholas Pileggi
Stephen Aiello	Barbara Mikulski	Carmela Sansone
Ti-Grace Atkinson	Christine Noschese	Mary Sansone
Anthony Colombo Sr.	Michael Novak	Nancy Seifer
Carol Colombo	Michael Pesce	Barry Slotnick
Louis Gigante	Janice Peterson	Aldo Tambellini

There are, of course, challenges involved in interviewing people about events that happened fifty years ago. Sometimes people's recollections contradicted one another or the historical record I uncovered in my research.

I have done my best in this book to reconstruct what happened based on what I was told alongside what I discovered in the archive. I am especially indebted to Mary Sansone and Anthony Colombo Sr. for allowing me to interview them for many hours over many days over many years. Listening to their words—of pride and regret, sadness and hope—was deeply affective. Mary and Anthony, along with a number of others I interviewed, died before I even began writing the book, but their rebel spirit never left me.

I was introduced to Mary Sansone and the Congress of Italian American Organizations when I read Mary's autobiographical essay in Nancy Seifer's *Nobody Speaks for Me! Self-Portraits of American Working-Class Women*. In the piece, published in the mid-1970s, Mary acknowledges Nancy's important role in CIAO's success. Mary's endorsement motivated me to reach out to Nancy, a benevolent soul who agreed to speak with me and, in doing so, furnished nuanced insight into the operation of politics and influence inside city hall, where she once held the title of ethnic affairs aide to New York City Mayor John Lindsay.

I was introduced to Anthony Colombo Sr. through Ti-Grace Atkinson, a rebel spirit in her own right. Ti-Grace, with whom I shared long hours of earnest dialogue on the topic of Joe Colombo and the League, offered to put me in touch with Joseph Colombo's lawyer, Barry Slotnick. Barry not only allowed me to interview him on a couple occasions but helped me make contact with Colombo's son, Anthony Sr., another client of his. Anthony Colombo Sr.'s biography of his father, co-authored with Don Capria, made a significant contribution to my reconstruction of Joe Colombo's early life.

Aldo Tambellini's first-generation Sony Portapak videotape recordings of Joe Colombo at League events are illuminating, and all credit goes to Anthony Colombo's son, Anthony Jr., for providing funds to digitize them, as well as to Anna Salamone, Aldo's partner and the person responsible for protecting the integrity of Aldo's art, much of which—including Aldo's *sui generis* League tapes—have found a permanent home in Karlsruhe, Germany, at the ZKM Center for Art and Media. I'm also grateful for the unwavering support of Carol Colombo, Anthony Colombo Sr.'s charming wife. Thanks also to Carmine Gibaldi for helping to arrange my initial meet-ups with Mary Sansone, and to Mary's daughter Carmela for sharing.

I thank Gloria Steinem for responding to questions via email and putting me in touch with Janice Peterson, founder of the National Congress of Neighborhood Women. Jan not only allowed me to interview her but arranged for me to meet with former NCNW staff members Christine Noschese and Sally Martino-Fisher. Sally, who before joining NCNW was a high-ranking official in IACRL's Chapter 23, gave up several days to talk with me about her leadership experience in the "New League." One of Sally's Chapter 23 hires, Kellie Everts, has built a provocative website (www.kellieevertsistripforgod.com) that includes a treasure trove of local news clippings detailing her foray into community organizing for the Italian American Civil Rights League under Sally's direction.

Nicholas Pileggi's contemporaneous reportage on New York City's Italians and organized crime—which is where I first became aware of Joe Colombo and the IACRL—is the cornerstone upon which this book rests. I am forever beholden to Mary Sansone, who put me in touch with Nick, her dearest friend. Nick invited me into his home to discuss my project. It was in conversations with Nick that I committed to focusing the book's narrative on the rivalry between Mary and Joe Colombo. During one such visit, it was Nick's words of encouragement that finally gave me the confidence to stop researching and start writing.

From start to finish, I relied on UCLA's world-class libraries, particularly the Charles E. Young Research Library and its interlibrary loan department as well as its subscription to online historical newspaper databases. During on-site visits to archives outside my own university, I benefited immeasurably from the help of dedicated librarians at the Immigration History Research Center at the University of Minnesota, the Sterling Memorial Library Manuscripts and Archives at Yale University, the New York City Municipal Library, the New York Public Library, the Library of Congress, the Rockefeller Archive Center, the Schlesinger Library at Harvard University, and the Sophia Smith Collection at Smith College. Through Freedom of Information Act requests, I acquired confidential Federal Bureau of Investigation documents unavailable on the FBI's website (www.vault.fbi.gov). The book's illustrations were gathered in myriad ways but I'd be remiss if I didn't thank those who allowed me to reproduce photos from their private collections as well as acknowledge the efficacious assistance of Kevin Macdonald, head of photography at *New York Daily News*.

Travel funds for archival research as well as for conducting in-person interviews were generously provided by UCLA's executive vice chancellor and provost, its Division of the Humanities and the Department of English. On several occasions during research trips to New York City and New Haven, Fred Gardaphé (CUNY-Queens and Calandra Institute) and Matthew Frye Jacobson (Yale University) acted as barstool sounding boards. *Molte grazie* to Fred, who, a long time ago, encouraged me to pursue this passion project of ours and then solicited my manuscript for his Italian American series at State University of New York Press. At SUNY Press, I was guided by editor-in-chief James Peltz as well as Diane Ganeles, Jenn Bennett-Genthner, Julia Cosacchi, and Carly Miller. My editors indulged my design ideas for the book, including its cover, which was inspired by the artwork of Elena Civoli Brittain, who gifted me permission to spotlight her painting.

This project was fueled over the past twenty-five years by my participation in team-taught "cluster" courses at the University of California, Los Angeles. I owe much to the thousands of enrolled students, hundreds of graduate teaching assistants, and more than a dozen colleagues from departments across the humanities and social sciences with whom I participated in these classes. Vilma Ortiz, Min Zhou, and Brenda Stevenson (from the Interracial Dynamics in America cluster) and Lynn Vavreck, Robert Fink, and Eric Avila (from the America in the Sixties cluster) share my commitment to collaborative teaching and never fail to inspire within me the delight in learning. A special shout-out to Samantha Pinto (University of Texas at Austin), who offered cogent feedback on my book. I wish to single out two of my colleagues in UCLA's English Department, Eric Jager and Ali Behdad, for their magnanimity. Timely conversations with Eric about true crime and narrative nonfiction proved invaluable. Ali, a friend in the truest sense, helped me secure research travel funding without which I could not have launched this project.

My children, Maleka and Max, never cease to bring joy and affirmation to my life. Last but foremost, I could not have written this book without the loving support of my life partner Jenny Sharpe, whose curiosity knows no bounds. It's Jenny's wide world of travel and gourmet cooking, and I'm just the lucky guy who gets to share in it.

Index

ABC (television), 26–29, 165, 168–69, *169*
Abyssinian Baptist Church (Harlem), 25
Abzug, Bella, 193, 247, 255, 257; IACRL support for, 133, 135; as IACRL Unity Day speaker, 109, *110*; as NCNW conference speaker, 247
activism, xvii, xix, xxi. *See also* community organizing
Addonizio, Hugh, 82
ADL. *See* B'nai B'rith Anti-Defamation League
adoption. *See* Liuni adoption case; Sansone, Mary
Adubato, Stephen, Sr.: as CIAO conference speaker, 218
AFL-CIO, 30, 95, *112*; A. Philip Randolph Institute of, 219–20. *See also* American Federation of State, County and Municipal Employees
AFSCME. *See* American Federation of State, County and Municipal Employees
African Americans. *See* Blacks
Agnew, Spiro, 80
AIADL. *See* American Italian Anti-Defamation League

AID. *See* Americans of Italian Descent
Aiello, Stephen, 134, 137, *169*, *170*, 266; background of, 134–35; as Central Board of Education Assistant for Community Relations, 229–31; as IACRL American Political Unity Association chairman, 134–35; as IACRL Education Task Force director, 153–54, 161, 168, 230; relationship with Meade Esposito, 230; views on Joseph Colombo, Sr., 230–31, 253; views on NYC Teachers' Strike, 230; as White House Special Assistant for Ethnic Affairs, 253–54
Albany (NY State government), 34
Ali, Muhammad, 190
Alioto, Joseph, 66; smeared as Mafia attorney, 67–68, 74
All in the Family (television), 214, *217*; IACRL pseudonym Pro-Italia Society on, 215–16; Sammy Davis, Jr. guest stars on, 216–17
American Federation of State, County and Municipal Employees D.C. 37 (AFSCME), 80, 101, *112*
American Italian Anti-Defamation League (AIADL), 56, 64, 83; antidefamation advocacy by, 49;

311

American Italian Anti-Defamation League (AIADL) *(continued)* failure to combat anti-Italian prejudice, 53, 65, 83; Frank Sinatra fundraises for, 55–56; Frank Sinatra named national chairman of, 53–55, 66, 253; Joseph Colombo, Sr. fundraises for, 176; Joseph Colombo, Sr. originates, 30, 48–49, 163; Madison Square Garden fundraiser for, 55–56, 56; Mafia existence denied by, 79; mantra of, 56; membership in, 55–56; media coverage of, 49, 54; renamed AID, 65, 79; Sammy Davis, Jr. fundraises for, 55–56, 176; sued by ADL, 53, 65. *See also* Americans of Italian Descent

American Jewish Committee, 218–19, 237

American Jewish Congress, 142

American Relief for Italy (ARI), 9, 16, 56

Americans of Italian Descent (AID), 65, 88, 92, 119, 238; "antidefamation league" name dropped by, 65, 79; Joseph Colombo, Sr. fundraises for, 176; Joseph Gallo works for, 214; Mafia existence denied by, 79; relationship with IACRL, 102, 196, 214. *See also* American Italian Anti-Defamation League

Amerigo Vespucci Day, 30

Ameruso, Anthony, 260

Amsterdam News (Harlem). *See* New York Amsterdam News

Anastasia, Albert "Lord High Executioner," 46; assassination of, 27, 30, 46, 61, 228

Anastasio, Anthony "Tough Tony," 18; ILA boycott against communist Cuba organized by, 31, 34; ILA boycott against Liggett & Meyers organized by, 30–31; ILA medical clinic built by, 31; as Gambino crime family member, 30

Anderson, Jack, 67, 69, 197

Anfuso, Victor, 33, 65

Annunzio, Frank, 64

antibusing. *See* Canarsie busing crisis

anticlericalism, 18, 61

anticommunism, 14, 19, 31, 130

antidefamation, 27–30, 38, 48–49, 53–55, 57, 65, 83, 97, 106, 117, 124, 144, 153, 168, 186, 194, 196–97, 215, 253

antidiscrimination, 63, 97, 101, 106, 123, 145, 148, 153–54, 196.

antifascism, 61, 94

anti-Italianism, 27, 38–39, 51–52, 57, 101, 108–109, 117, 120, 129, 147, 190; Joseph Colombo, Sr. on, 72–73; Mary Sansone on, 57

anti-Mafia activists, 165; Adam Clayton Powell, Jr. as, 25–26; John Marchi as, 78–79; Malcolm X as, 44; Mary Sansone as, xxi–xxii, 10, 57–58, 61, 141–42, 173–74, 177, 235, 240; Pete Hamill as, 97; Ralph Salerno as, 56–58; Robert F. Kennedy as, 152; and Stonewall riots, 71. *See also* Kefauver Hearings; National Crime Commission Hearings; McClellan Hearings

Antioch Review (magazine), 14

antiracism, 7, 35

antiwar movement, 95–96, 109, 190, 193

Apalachin summit, 27–28, 28, 227–28. *See also* Canarsie summit; Little Apalachin summit; Mafia

ARI. *See* American Relief for Italy

Arizona Republic, 75–76, 121

312 | Index

Arricale, Frank, 117, 266
Atkinson, Ti-Grace, 144–50, 206; background of, 144–45, 146; relationship with Joseph Colombo, Sr., 149–50; sexual abuse and, 144; sexism and, 149; views on IACRL, 145–49; views on Joseph Colombo, Sr., 149–50; views on Mafia, 146–47; and Willis lawsuit, 145–46, 149
Atlanta Constitution, 4
Audubon Ballroom (Harlem), 191
Augello, Anthony, 95, 103
Aurelio, Richard, 81–82, 131, 142–43, 206; as honorary IACRL member, 153; as IACRL Unity Day speaker, 109–10; relationship with Mary Sansone, 118

Ball, Lucille, 30–31
Banana War, 74–75
Baptist Street Church Bombing (Birmingham, AL), 39
Barbara, Joseph "Joe the Barber," 27, 227
Baroni, Msgr. Geno, 117, 247; as CIAO conference speaker, 218
Bath Beach (Brooklyn), 105
Battista, Vito, 129, 131; background of, 129–30
Bayard Rustin Sings Spirituals, Work & Freedom Songs (album), 220
Beame, Abraham, 65, 256, 260–61
Beame Administration, 255, 255, 257, 261
Bell, Daniel: on machine politics, 182; on Mafia as "myth," 14–15
Bensonhurst (Brooklyn), xxi, 7, 18, 20, 22, 38, 46–47, 60–61, 88, 132, 134, 160, 174, 177, *178*, 218, 240, 252, 260
Benton, Lou, 97

Bernstein, Blanche, 261, 264
Beyond the Melting Pot (Moynihan and Glazer), 82–83
Biaggi, Mario, 257–58, 261–62; background of, 107–108; as IACRL hero, 107; IACRL supported by, 132, 253, 259; as IACRL Unity Day speaker, 107–109; as New York City mayoral candidate, *107*, 262
Bianco, Nicholas "Nicky," 89, 103, 127, *128*
Bicentennial, 236, 247
Big Time Buck White (play), 190
bilingual education, 162, 173, 238
black-bag jobs. See FBI
Black Caesar (movie), 286n6
Black freedom struggle. See civil rights movement
Black Panther Party for Self-Defense (Black Panthers), 146–47, 196, 286n6
Black Power, Black nationalism, 44, 48–49, 191, 220
Black Revolutionary Attack Team, 208
Blacks, Black Americans, 7, 25, 35, 44, 59, 62, *63*, 82, 110, 117, 139–40, 142, 147, 153, 161, 163, 169, 189–91, 201–202, *203*, 206, 208–209, 216, 218, 220–25, 230, 241, 257, 260–61, 286n6; criminal activity of, xxi, 25–26, 44, 48, 191, 206, 257
Black studies, 221
Blooming Grove (NY), 19, 21–22, 152, 184
B'nai B'rith Anti-Defamation League (ADL), 54; sues AIADL, 53, 65; supports CIAO, 63–64, 142; supports plaintiff in Liuni adoption case, 51–53, 55
Board of Education, Central Board of Education (NYC), 62–63, 106,

Board of Education, Central Board of Education (NYC) *(continued)* 109, 153–54, 161–62, 221–23, 225, 228–32, 236, 253, 255
Bob Chevy Orchestra, 105–106, 131
bodybuilding, 244–45, 247–50
Bogin, Amy, 234
bombing, bombs: FBI covert operations targeting Mafia results in, 74–77, 121–22; Barry Slotnick office, 125–26; KKK, 39; Vietnam War, 96, 192; World War II, 169
Bonanno, Joseph, 36, 40, 74–77, 121–22
Bonanno, Salvatore "Bill," 75, 77
Bonaparte, Charles, 184
Boro Park, Borough Park (Brooklyn), xxii, 20, 33, 50, 61, 118, 219–21, 233–34, 265
Boston Globe, 38
Boston, 103, 256, 295n2
Brando, Marlon, 160, 171–72
Brennan, Peter, 96
Breslin, Jimmy, 78; as CIAO conference speaker, 218
Broadcasting (magazine), 30–31
Bronx. *See specific places*
Brooklyn: Official Flag of, 105. *See also specific places*
Brooklyn Bridge, 17
Brooklyn Citizens for Procaccino, 140, 172, 175, 179
Brooklyn College, 80, 221, 232, 255
Brooklyn Eagle, 9
Brooklyn Federal Courthouse, 157–58, *157*
Brooklyn Navy Yard, 79–80
Brooks, Tom, 35–36
Brown, James, 227, 286n6
Brown, Jim, 227
Brown v. Board of Education, 225
Brownsville (Brooklyn), 222, 225, 229

Bruno, Lou, 101, 124, 167
Bufalino, Russell, 151
Buffalo Soldiers, 169
Bushwick (Brooklyn), 173
busing. *See* Canarsie busing crisis

Cabrini, Frances Xavier, 184
Cahn, William, 112–13
Calabria: immigrants from, 3, 17, 46; 'Ndrangheta crime syndicate in, 3
Calaceta, Ralph, 119
Camp Unity. *See* Colombo, Joseph, Sr.; IACRL
Canarsie (Brooklyn), 182, 222–32, 295n2; description of, 222
Canarsie busing crisis, 222–31, *226*, 232; IACRL participation in, 223–29; Irving Bildersee Junior High and, 225, 228; John Wilson Junior High and, 223, 225–28; Samuel J. Tilden Houses (Brownsville) and, 222–23, 226; school boycott by white parents during, 226, 228–29. *See also* "white flight"
Canarsie summit, 227–28. *See also* Apalachin summit; Little Apalachin summit; Mafia
Canby, Vincent, 214
Cantalupo Realty Company, 37–38, 47, 88
Capone, Alfonso "Al," 77, 152
Capone outfit, 27
Carey, Hugh, 80
Carlozzi, Angela, 50
Carnegie Hall, 55
Carroll, Diahann, 55
Carroll Gardens (Brooklyn), 62, 140, 166, 177
Carroll Gardens Association, 50
Carter Administration, 253–55
Carter, Jimmy, 253
Casalena, Josephine, *237*

Castro, Fidel, 31
Catholic Church, 18, 49, 61, 173, 218, 233; charities sponsored by, 20, 264; women in, xviii, 150, 184, 241
Catholics, 42, 67, 82, 111, 128, 244, 254
Cavett, Dick, 163, 168, *169*
CBS (television), 147, 179, 225, 238
Cecora, Carl, 223–24, *224*; background of, 223; Canarsie busing crisis participation of, 223–25, 229; as IACRL captain, 224; as IACRL New League president, 231; views on Joseph Colombo shooting, 224. *See also* IACRL headquarters; New League
Census (US), 236, 238, 297–98n12
Center for Migration Studies (CUNY-Richmond), 173, 178–79, 266
Central Investigation Bureau (NYPD), 21
Center for Italian American Studies (Brooklyn College), 221, 232, 255
Central Park, 99, 105, 111, 184–85, 200
CETA. *See* Comprehensive Employment and Training Act
Challenge, The, 92, 119, 121, 178, 214
Chamberlain, Wynn, 43
Chicago, 26, 59–60, 68, 75, 98, 146, 183
Chicago Daily Defender, 26, 35, 49
Chicago Daily News, 13
Chicago Sun-Times, 66–67
Chicago Tribune, 4, 49, 66, 185
child daycare centers, 139–40, 166, 179, 209, 233–34, 236, 263
Chinese Americans, 189
Chisholm, Shirley: as NCNW conference speaker, 247
Church of the Most Precious Blood (Little Italy), 45

CIA, 77
CIAO. *See* Congress of Italian American Organizations
CIAO Reports, 220–21, 234–36, 261
City University of New York. *See* CUNY
civil rights movement, xvii, 33, 35, 55, 61, 65–66, 98, 122, 208, 216, 219, 267n.1; southern US, 34–35, 38–39, 44–45, 140. *See also specific individual and organization names*
Clark, Kenneth: Canarsie busing crisis and, 225–26, 229–30; views on Adam Clayton Powell, Jr., 25–26
Clark, Ramsey, 68, 76
Clay, Cassius. *See* Ali, Muhammad
coalition politics, xviii, 233. *See also* CIAO; Mary Sansone
COINTELPRO. *See* FBI
Cold War, 14, 19, 31, 130
Colombo, Anthony (son of JC), xix, 8, 18, 21–22, 48, 88, 98–99, 101, 103, *112*, 123, 127, *128*, 131, 137, 142–43, 148–49, 154–56, 159, 161, *162*, 165, 168, *169*, *170*, 173–74, 194, 205–206, 255; as IACRL Unity Day speaker, 106–107, 112; as IARCL vice president, 96; wedding of, 255
Colombo, Anthony "Two-Gun Tony" (father of JC), 4–5, 7, 28, 205
Colombo, Carol (née O'Brien), 255
Colombo crime family, 89, 165, 207, 211–13; Americanization of, 40, 73–74; ancestry of, 286n10; associates in, 73, 87; machine politics and, xviii; IACRL membership from, 89, 137; income sources of, 73–74, 152; territories of, 73
Colombo, Joseph, Jr. (son of JC), 48, 138; arrest of, 87; acquittal of, 157–58, *157*, 168, 195

Index | 315

Colombo, Joseph, Sr., xvii, 28, *112*, *116*, *157*, *169*, *170*, *201*, 211; as AIADL founder, 48–49, 54; antidefamation advocacy by, 30, 48, 116, 192, 253; arrest of, 47, *48*; assassination attempt on, xviii, xxi–xxii, *201*; assimilation of, 48; background of, 3; Blooming Grove home of, 19, 21–22; civil rights activism of, 91, 122, 154, 161, 192, 195, 208, 230, 252–53; as Colombo crime family boss, 40, 47, 97, 113, 115–16, 125, 137, 164–65, 182, 230, 252–54; coma suffered by, 202, 205, 230, 252; as compared to Malcolm X, 170; conspiracy theories related to, 73, 103, 163, 168, 181, 206–207, 224, 295n4; death of, 192, 252; drops out of New Utrecht High School, 7; Dyker Heights home of, 22, 97, 230; as factory worker, 7; as a father, 21, 48–49, 185; FBI harasses family of, 87, 92, 94, 106, 113, 115, 151, 168, 192; feud with Alfred Santangelo and AID, 88, 92, 102–103, 176, 183, 191–92, 196; feud with Joseph Gallo, xxi–xxii, 116, 163, 194, 206; feud with Mafia bosses, xxii, 162–63, 194–95; feud with Mary Sansone and CIAO, xvii–xviii, xxii, 119, 139, 141–42, 167, 172–77, 240; as IACRL founder, 90, 103, 137, 168; as IACRL fundraiser, 138, 151, 192; as IACRL Unity Day speaker, 110–12; IACRL meeting speeches by, 111, 137–38, 159–60, 176–77, 183, 191–92, 197–98; as ILA member, 18; indictments of, 112–13; IRS investigation of, 152; and labor unions, 94–95, 100, 200; *Long Island Post* purchased by, 124; Mafia coup thwarted by, 36, 74; Mafia existence denied by, 185; as Mafia "sleeper," 47, 73; as Magliocco crime family capo, 37; media coverage of, 47, 91–92, 103, 115–16, 122, 138, 153, 168, 188, 252; nonviolence advocacy of, 95, 122, 177; NYPD harasses family of, 21; *omertà* broken by, xxii, 115–16, 168; Paramount Picture Studios negotiates with, 156, 159–60, 214; personality of, 7, 73, 88, 93–94, 115, 192, 195, 197, 199; as Profaci crime family capo, 22, 28–29, 37, 48; psychiatric evaluation of, 8, 18; reaction to arrest of Joseph Colombo, Jr. by, 87; as real estate salesman, 18, 38, 47, 152, 168; relationship with Carlo Gambino, 28, 47, 116, 162–63, 194–95, 199; relationship with Frank Sinatra, 53–54, 143, 192; relationship with Larry Gallo, 163; relationship with Mary Sansone, xviii, xxii, 140–42, 167; relationship with Meade Esposito, 182–83; relationship with Sammy Davis, Jr., 133, 176, 208, 216; relationship with Ti-Grace Atkinson, 145–46, 149–50; shooting of, xviii, xxi–xxii, 202, 205–206, 209, 211, 213, 216, 224, 227, 230, 242, 252–53, 295n4; as silent business partner, 18–19, 70–71, 168, 255; *Tri-boro Post* honors, 153, 164; *Untouchables* boycott masterminded by, 28–30; Upstate New York retreats of, 18–19, 22; views on AID, 88, 103, 176, 183; views on Camp Unity, 183–84; views on God, 73, 177, 197–98; views on IACRL, 89–90, 93–96, 121, 158, 177, 192; views on J. Edgar Hoover, 197; views on Liuni adoption case, 53, 176; views on Mafia, 115–16, 168, 192; views on narcotics trafficking, 73, 136, 192; views on Richard Nixon, 163, 197; views on Ti-Grace Atkinson, 150; views on Vietnam War, 192–93; wedding of, 8; WWII enlistment of, 8; WWII imprisonment of, 8, 18. *See also* Colombo crime family; FBI racketeering files; Scarpa, Gregory; IACRL

Colombo, Lucille "Jo-Jo" (née Faiello; wife of JC), 8, 18, 89, 138, 151, *157*; background of, 7

Colonna, Louis, 226, *226*

Columbia Association of Italian American Teachers, 161

Columbia University, 134, 188

Columbus Circle (Manhattan), 132; 1970 IACRL Unity Day at, 98–99, 104–12; 1971 IACRL Unity Day at, 184–85, 191, 195, 199–202. *See also* Colombo, Joseph, Sr.: shooting

Columbus Day, 132

Commodore Hotel (Manhattan). *See* CIAO, annual dinner-dance celebration

communism, communists. *See* Cold War; socialism

community organizations, xvii–xviii; multiethnic, 232–33; multiracial, xviii, xxii, 166, 180

community organizing, 19, 32, 60, 62, 64, 98, 117, 149–50, 194, 209, 242, 309

Community Services Administration. *See* Office of Economic Opportunity

Comprehensive Employment and Training Act (CETA), 243, 245–48, 250, 252

Concerned Citizens of Canarsie (CCC), 228–29

Coney Island, 7, 99, 173

Congress of Italian American Organizations (CIAO), xvii–xviii, xxii, 57–58, 139, 221, 265; ADL support for, 63–64; after-school programs of, 62, 179, 233; annual dinner-dance celebration of, 175, 177–80, *178*, 218, 255–56; antidefamation advocacy by, 57–58; art and culture programs of, 234, 236; Bicentennial multimedia project of, 236; Catholic Church alliance with, 173, 178–80, 233; Center for Italian American Studies initiated by, 221, 232; Center for Migration Studies partners with, 173, 178–79; chartered as nonprofit, 49–50, 265; crime-free reputation of, xxii, 50, 139, 234, 259; child daycare programs of, 139–40, 166, 233–34, 179, 209, 233–34, 236, 263; community service delivery operations of, 62–63, 77–78, 139, 167, 209–10, 233–34; demise of, 259–65; drug rehabilitation programs of, 62, 139, 209, 234, 236; Ethnic Communities and the Challenge of Urban Life conference sponsored by, 218–19; finances of, 139–40, 142, 209, 255, 259–61, 265; Irene Impellizzeri honored by, 255; IRS investigation of, 265; Italian American Committee for Public Relations and Special Projects, 236, 262; job placement programs of, 63, 175; labor unions endorsement of, 180; leadership of, 118–19, 174, 188, 261–64; Mary Sansone honored by, 218; Mary Sansone speaks to, 179; media coverage of, xxii, 179–80, 188, 209, 218–20, 233, 238; member organizations of,

Index | 317

Congress of Italian American Organizations (CIAO) *(continued)* 139, 234; multi-ethnic and -racial coalition facilitated by, xxii, 62, 180, 188, 218–20, 232–33, 240; multi-ethnic and -racial programming by, 62, 139, 166, 180, 189, 209, 233, 260; New York City funding of, 62, 77, 139–40, 179, 189, 209–10, 221, 233–35, 237, 239; New York Urban Coalition partnership with, 180, 209; OEO funding of, 236, 239–40; political candidates supported by, 221, 258; press conference organized by, 236–38, *237*; relationship with AID, 119; senior care programs of, 166, 179, 189, 209–10, 233–36, 256, 263; Silvano Tomasi honored by, 178–79; summer youth recreation program of, 234; symposia sponsored by, 63–64, 218–19; views of Eleanor Holmes Norton on, 232–33; views of Gladys Harrington on, 140, 237; views of Nancy Seifer on, 188–89, 209, 237; views of Nicholas Pileggi on, xxii, 103, 106, 137–38, 141, 160, 164, 166, 177, 179, 188; and women, 234, 240; and working class, 188, 220; Youth Services Agency partnership, 62, 63. *See also* Center for Migration Studies; CIAO facilities; New York Urban Coalition; Portrait of the Italian-American Community in New York City; Sansone, Mary

Congress of Italian American Organizations facilities, 260; Bay Ridge Child Counseling Program (Brooklyn), 263; Bensonhurst, 240; Boro Park Multipurpose Center, 233–34; Corona-East Elmhurst (Queens), 209; Court Street (Brooklyn), 209, 234; Dante chapter (Staten Island), 236; "Genovesi group" takeover of, 264; Greenwood (Brooklyn), 139; Meucci chapter (Staten Island), 236, 261; Mott Street (Manhattan), 209, 235, 256, 261; New Utrecht Avenue (Brooklyn), 265; Ozone Park (Queens), 236; Park Slope (Brooklyn), 62, *63*

Congress of Italian American Organizations headquarters: in Boro Park basement (Brooklyn), xxii, 32, 50, 58, 61, 172, 210, 219, 221, 265; on Park Row (Manhattan), 210, 236, 265

Congress of Racial Equality (CORE), 7, 34–35, 44–45, 140

Conservative Party (NY), 107

Continental Baths, The (Manhattan), 69–71

Cook, Fred, 96

Copacabana, 70, 133

Coppola, Francis Ford, 156, 171

CORE. *See* Congress of Racial Equality

Corona (Queens), 60, 209. *See also* Fighting Corona 69

Corso, Joseph R., 16

Costanza, Midge, 255

Costello, Frank "Prime Minister," *12*, 15, 73; background of, 15; Kefauver Hearings testimony of, 11–13, 27, 38

Cotillion Terrace (Bensonhurst), *178*, 180, 260. *See also* CIAO, annual dinner-dance celebration

Council on Port Development and Promotion (NYC), 79

crime, criminals. *See* FBI; organized crime; Mafia; racketeering; *specific individual and group names*

Crime in America, 14. *See also* Kefauver, Estes
Crisalli, Jimmy (paternal uncle of MS), 20; as Mafia "sleeper," 61; as racketeer, xxi, 3; relationship with Mary Sansone, xxi, 9–10, 18
Crisalli, Joseph (maternal uncle of MS), xxii, 177
Crisalli, Martha (mother of MS), 8; attitude toward marital status of daughter, 16, 18, 20; runs pastry shop, 3–4, 6, 9, 16–20
Crisalli, Mary. *See* Sansone, Mary
Crisalli, Rocco "Rocky" (father of MS), xxi, 8–10, 256; anticlericalism of, 18, 61; CIAO honors, 234; death of, 8; IWW organizer, 3, 5–7, 220
CUNY (City University of New York), 221, 232, 255
Cuomo, Mario, *258*; as CIAO conference speaker, 218; as Fighting Corona 69 lawyer, 129, 218; Human Rights Commission appointment of, 232; as New York City mayoral candidate, 257–60; as New York State governor candidate, 266; as New York State Lieutenant Governor, 253, 255
Cutolo, Eugene, 236, 264; views on Mary Sansone, 261–63; relationship with Peter Vale, 236, 261

"Daily Closeup: Sharing and A Share" (Macleod), 240. *See also* Sansone, Mary
Daley, Richard J., 59–60
Damone, Vic, 143
Darrow, Tony, 133, 164
Davis, Altovise, 133
Davis, Angela, 168
Davis, Sammy, Jr., xvii, 55, *56*, 70, *217*, 227, 267n.1; AIADL supported by, 55–56, 176; as *All in the Family* guest star, 216–17; IACRL supported by, xvii, 133, *134*, 143, 184, 208, 216–17; "Italian American Civil Rights League" sung by, 133; relationship with Joseph Colombo, Sr., 133, 176, 208, 216; views on AIADL, 56; views on Frank Sinatra, 55; views IACRL, 133
Days of Rage (Chicago), 146
Dean, Paul, 76–77
DeCicco, Joseph, 127, *128*, 13, 195; as IARCL lead organizer, 96, 146
Dellacona, Ralph, 129
Democratic National Convention (1968), 66–68
Democratic Party, Democrats, 31, 65–66, 79, 109, 133, 128, 179, 182–84, 221, 257–59, 266
Department of Justice (DOJ), 13, 27, 41, 69, 76, 120–21, 157
DeSapio, Carmine, 25, 54, 257
desegregation. *See* racial integration
Desilu studio, 26, 30–31
Detroit, 59, 75
Detroit Free Press, 4
Dick Cavett Show, The (television), 168, *169*, 170
Dillon, Denis, 152
DiLorenzo, Ross, 56
DOJ. *See* Department of Justice
Dongan Hills (Staten Island), 173
drug rehabilitation programs, 62, 139, 143, 209, 234, 236
Dukakis, Michael, 256
Dunbar, William, 74–76, 121
Durante, Tony. *See* Colombo, Anthony "Two-Gun Tony"
Dyker Heights (Brooklyn), 5, 22, 132, 141, 230

East Harlem, 31, 88, 105, 107, 135, 137

Index | 319

East New York (Brooklyn), 194
Eboli, Thomas, 151
economy, xxi, 6, 25, 78–80, 93, 173, 220, 240, 243
education reform, 62, 153–54, 173, 179, 221, 223, 225, 229, 232; school dropouts and, 62. *See also* school desegregation
election: 1960 US presidential, 55; 1964 US presidential, 43, 55; 1965 New York City mayoral, 60, 129; 1966 New York governor, 128; 1968 US presidential, 64–68, 78, 80; 1969 New York City mayoral, 77–82; 1970 New York governor, 127–28; 1970 US Congressional, 109–10, 135; 1972 US presidential, 227; 1973 New York City mayoral, *107*, 262; 1976 US presidential, 255; 1977 New York City mayoral, 256–61, *258*; 1980 US presidential, 253–54; 1982 New York governor, 265. *See also* machine politics; voter registration; *specific individual and organization names*
Elizabeth (NJ), 101
Ellis Island, 3
Erazo, Joseph, 221, 237
Erlichman, Alan, 228–29
Esposito, Amadeo "Meade," 54, *134*, 140, 179, 182–84, 221, 230, 259–61, 264; background of, 182–83; feud with Mary Sansone, 259, 264; IACRL supported by, 133, 222–23, 230, 253, 259; relationship with Joseph Colombo, Sr., 182–83; Thomas Jefferson clubhouse leader, 182, 224, 228; views on IACRL, 182–83. *See also* machine politics
Esquire (magazine), 54, 247–49
"Ethnic Communities and the Challenge of Urban Life" (CIAO symposium), 218–19

Ethni-city and the American Dream (radio), 240–41, 245
ethnicity, ethnics. *See* white ethnics; *specific individual and group names*
ethnic studies, 221
Evans, Robert, 154–55
Everts, Rev. Kellie, *248*; background of, 243–44; 299n7; as bodybuilder, 244–45, 249–50; burlesque performed by, 244–45, 249–50; as cable TV host, 245; campaign of Sally Martino-Fisher supported by, 248–49; CETA contract "outstationed" to NCNW, 250–51; as IAMSC social worker, 245, 248–50; personality of, 244, 247–48; media coverage of, 243–45, 247–51; as Miss Body Beautiful USA, 245, 247; as NCNW staff, 50; as newspaper columnist, 245, 248–49; as ordained New Age minister, 244–45, 248–49; pictorials of, 245, 247–51; sexual abuse and, 244; striptease performed by, 244–45, 249–50; sexism and, 250–51; women's liberation promoted by, 249

factory labor, 6–7, 88, 108. *See also* sweatshops
Failla, Victor, *64*
Fair Deal, 182
Farber, Myron, 231
Fasanella, Ralph, 255–56
FBI, 11, 69; 73, 81, 184, 199, 253–54; black-bag jobs of, 75; COINTELPRO, 152, 206, 287n19; covert operations by, 74–77; Mafia surveillance by, xviii, 121; Mississippi Burning case of, 44; racketeering files by, xviii; smear campaigns orchestrated by, 67–68, 73, 92, 106, 168; Top Echelon

Criminal Informant program of, xix, 37, 207, 211; Tucson bombings and, 74–77, 121. *See also* communists; organized crime; FBI racketeering files; Hoover, J. Edgar; Mafia; Top Echelon Criminal Informant program
FBI headquarters (Manhattan), 181; IACRL pickets, xix, *85*, 88–92, 94–96, 111–12, 158, 195
FBI racketeering files, xix; IACRL identified in, 99, 114, 151, 181 194; J. Edgar Hoover comments in, 113–14, 120, 194; Joseph Colombo, Sr. identified in, 37–38, 40, 48–49, 53–54, 100–101, 103, 106, 114, 143, 152, 181, 194–95, 199, 202; 253–54
F.B.I., The (television), 165
FDNY, 125
Feast of San Gennaro (Fasanella), 255–56
Feast of San Gennaro Festival, 127–28, *128*
Federal Bureau of Investigation. *See* FBI
Federation of Italian American Democratic Organizations (FIADO), 31
Federici, William, 115–16, *116*
Felt Forum. *See* Madison Square Garden Felt Forum
feminism, feminists. *See* women's movement
Ferrigno, Lou, 247, 249
FIADO. *See* Federation of Italian American Democratic Organizations
Fifth Amendment, 121, 211
Fighting Corona 69, 128–31, 257
First Amendment, 89
Foley Square United States Courthouse (Manhattan), 11–12, *12*, 151, 181
Ford Administration, 196, 240
Ford, Gerald, 240

Fordham University, 173
Forest Hills (Queens), 257
Formisano, Ronald, 117
Forte, Maria, 3
Fortunate Pilgrim, The (Puzo), 46
foster care. *See* Liuni adoption case; Sansone, Mary
Four Seasons, The (band), 55, 143
Francis, Connie, 55, 143
Frankenstein (Shelley), 249
Franklin, Aretha, 184
"Frank Sinatra Has a Cold" (Talese), 54
Freedom Riders, 34. *See also* civil rights movement
Frey, William, 121
Frinzi, Dominic, 26
"Furtiva Lagrima, Una" (song), 220

Gabor, Zsa Zsa, 127
Gage, Nicholas, 74
Gallo, Joseph "Crazy Joey": AID activism of, 214; associates with Black criminals, xxi, 194, 206; background of, 163; civil rights activism of, 206; feud with Joseph Colombo, Sr., xxi–xxii, 163, 206; imprisonment of, 163; murder of, 213; prison release of, xxi, 206; views on Mary Sansone, xxi–xxii, 177; views on IACRL, 194; views on Joseph Colombo, Sr., 214
Gallo, Larry: AIADL started by Joseph Colombo, Sr. and, 163
Gallo War. *See* Profaci-Gallo War
Gambino, Carlo "Carl," 47, 74; monetary contributions to IACRL by, 151; relationship with Joseph Colombo, Sr., 28, 36, 162, 194; views on IACRL, 101, 163, 195, 199
Gambino crime family, 18, 30, 34, 81, 96, 195

Index | 321

gambling, 8, 26, 69, 73, 135; in Harlem, 25, 48, 110
Garglulo, Gloria, *248*
Garth, David, 257
Gay Insider, The (Hudson), 190
Gay Pride movement, 71
gays. *See* homosexuality
Genovese crime family, 38, 93
Genovesi, Anthony, 259, 264
Georgetown University, 93
Gibson, Kenneth, 82
Gigante, Rev. Louis: background of, 93; civil disobedience activism of, 246; as elected NYC Councilman, 246; as IACRL chaplain, 93, 106, 137, 252; as IACRL Unity Day speaker, 111; relationship with Joseph Colombo, Sr., 93; views on Joseph Colombo, Sr., 111, 206, 252
Gigante, Vincent "the Chin," 93
Giorno, John, 43
Glazer, Nathan, 82–83
Gleason, Thomas "Teddy," 96
Godfather, The (movie), 154–56, 158–60, 164–65, 171–72, 214, 286n6. *See also* IACRL
Godfather, The (Puzo), 46, 77, 83, 107, 154, 158, 165, 205, 286n6
Gold, Eugene, 228
Goldin, Harrison, *237*
Goldwater, Barry, 75–76
Gotbaum, Victor, 80–81; IACRL supported by, 101
Gottehrer, Barry, 60, 184–85
Gottlieb, Inez, 147
Goude, Jean-Paul, 247, 249–51
Grand Concourse (Bronx), 60
Grand Council of Columbia Associations (NY), 108
Gratz, Roberta, 227
Gravesend Bay, 105
Great American Songbook, 55
Great Depression, xxi, 3–6, 108

Great Gatsby, The (Fitzgerald), 129
Great Society. *See* War on Poverty
Greenpoint (Brooklyn), 60, 242–43, 248
Greenpoint Gazette (Brooklyn), 243–44, 245, 247–49
Greenwich Village, 93, 257
Greenwood (Brooklyn), 139
Grutzner, Charles, 47
Guidice, Frank, 250; views on Joseph Colombo, Sr., 252
Guidice, Thomas, 246

hair styles, 21, 56, 65, 89, 170, 175, 224, 237, 250
Hale, David Olin, 74–77, 121
Hall, Stephen, 266
Hamill, Pete, 78, 97–98, 229; as CIAO conference speaker, 218; views on Joseph Colombo, Sr., 97. *See also* "Revolt of the White Lower Middle Class"
Hampton, Fred, 146, 206
hard hat riot (Manhattan), 95–96, 98, 117
Harlem, 25, 34, 44, 60, 110, 140, 191; organized crime in, 25–26, 48; riot in, 44
Harrington, Gladys, *237*; background of, 140; CIAO supported by, 255; Mary Sansone supported by, 140, 237, 261; relationship with Malcolm X, 140
Harris poll on "Mafia," 185–86
Hart Island (Bronx), 8, 18
Harvey, Everett, 158
Henning, Walter, 21
Herald (magazine), 192–93
heroin. *See* narcotics
Hell's Kitchen, 46
Hilliard, David, 146
Hill, Joe, 220
Hoboken (NJ), 101

homosexuality, homosexuals, 43, 69, 190, 255. *See also* Gay pride movement; Stonewall riot
Honolulu, 238
Honor Thy Father (Talese), 75
Hoover, J. Edgar, 23, 37, 41, 66, 75–77, 88–89, 97, 152, 197; consents to partnering with DOJ Organized Crime Strike Forces, 69; reacts to US government ban on use of word "Mafia," 120–21; relationship with John Rooney, 41, 81; views on IACRL, 113–14; views on Joseph Colombo, Sr., 194; views on Joseph Valachi testimony, 41
Hopkins, Linda, 70–71
Howar, Barbara, 168, *169*
Howard Beach (Queens), 92
HRA (NYC government). *See* Human Resources Administration
Hudson, John Paul, 190
Human Resources Administration (HRA), 139–40, 189, 209–10, 233, *237*, 255; backlash against, 260–62. *See also* War on Poverty; welfare services
Human Rights Commission (NY), 196
Human Rights Commission (NYC), 119, 153, 218, 232
Human Rights for Women (Washington DC), 145–46
Humphrey, Hubert, 64–67, *64*, 238–40; relationship with Frank Sinatra, 66; relationship with Mary Sansone, 65, 240
Huntington Town House (Long Island), 153, 164
Hunts Point (Bronx), 93

IAC. *See* Italian American Coalition
Iacocca, Lee, 165
IACRL. *See* Italian American Civil Rights League
IACUA. *See* Italian American Center for Urban Affairs
IAMSC. *See* Italian American Multi-Service Center
IASO. *See* Italian American Service Organization
ILA. *See* International Longshoremen's Association
ILGWU. *See* International Ladies' Garment Workers' Union
Immigration, immigrants, 3, 5, 17, 19, 50, 59, 73, 93–94, 107, 129, 134, 193, 221, 249, 256
Impellizzeri, Irene, 255
Imperiale, Anthony, 82; as IACRL Unity Day speaker, 109
Independent Neighborhood Democrats (Brooklyn), 258
Independent Party of New York City, 79–82
Industrial Workers of the World (IWW; Wobblies), xxi, *1*, 3, 5, 7, 62, 220
informants (FBI). *See* Top Echelon Criminal Informant program
integration. *See* racial integration
Internal Revenue Service, 13, 152, 265
International Ladies' Garments Workers' Union (ILGWU), 6; Italian Dressmakers Local 89, 6; Mary Sansone organizes on behalf of, xxi
International Longshoremen's Association (ILA), 96, 106; ABC headquarters picketed by, 30; Liggett & Meyers boycott by, 30–31; Local 1814 (Brooklyn), 18, 30, 34–36, *36*, 80, 158, 218
Irish Americans, 20, 43, 72, 79, 82, 120, 128, 182, 243; neighborhoods of, 129
Italian American Center for Urban Affairs (IACUA), 238; demise of,

Index | 323

Italian American Center for Urban Affairs (IACUA) *(continued)* 239–40; Manhattan headquarters of, 239, OEO funding of, 239; OEO investigation of, 238–40. *See also* Italian American Coalition

Italian American Civil Rights League (IACRL), xvii, 98, 226–27, 253; advertisements for, 101–102, *102,* 127, 143; antidefamation advocacy by, 168, 194, 216, 253; anti-Vietnam War advocacy by, 193; Black and Puerto Rican community organizers support for, 194; Board of Education picketed by, 154, 161–62, 167, 230; badges, buttons, pins, and banners of, 106, 127–28, 133, 136, 148–49, 160, *170,* 174, 200, 205, 211–21, *212,* 216–17, *217,* 227, 229, 246; Captains Oath of, 136; Camp Unity of, 183–84, 199, 213; Canarsie busing crisis participation of, 223–29; as compared to Black Panther Party, 196; demise of, 205, 222, 253; drug rehabilitation programs of, 143; Education Task Force of, 154, 168, 230; FBI classification as racketeering of, 99, 114, 151, 181, 194; FBI harassment of, 92–94, 109, 111, 121–22, 181–82; FBI headquarters picketed by, xix, *85,* 88, 91–92, 94–96, 111–12, 158, 195; as Feast of San Gennaro Festival patron, 127–28; federal grand jury investigation into, 152, 158; fundraising by Carlo Gambino for, 151–52; fundraising by Joseph Colombo, Sr. for, 137–38, 142–43, 151–52; fundraising for Italian American hospital by, 143, 168, 199, 214; fundraising for the poor by, 137–38; *Godfather* movie involvement of, 154–55, 161, 164–65, 158–60, 167, 171, 196, 214–15; interracial cooperation facilitated by, 168, 226–27; IRS investigation of, 152; Italian American Political Unity Association of, 134; JDL alliance with, 181–82; Jewish support for, 106, 144, 194; Joseph Colombo, Sr. honored by, 164, 168; Joseph Colombo, Sr. speaks to, 111, 137–38; leadership of, 96, 100, 103, 142, 149; "Mafia" and "La Cosa Nostra" censored by, 113, 120, 122, 124–26, 153–54, 156, 159, 161, 165, 196, 214–15; Mafia existence denied by, 97; Mafia hoax allegations against, 96–97, 101, 106–107, 152, 174, 185–86, 205–206, 227; Mafia support for, 95–96, 101, 115, 135, 138, 144, 158, 227; Mary Sansone speaks at meeting of, xxii, 172–76, 235; meetings in Park-Sheraton ballroom of, xxii, 136–38, 145, *150,* 158–60, 167, 170, *170,* 172–77, 182–83, 191–92, 194, 197–98; membership in, xxii, 127, 136, 144, 194, 206; merchants harassed by, 100, 194; militancy of, 168, 177; motto of, 224–25, 242; *New York Times* printing plant picketed by, 122; nonviolence commitment of, 95, 112, 177; Official Song of, 133; political candidates supported by, 106–11, 133–35, 227; Pro-Italia Society pseudonym for, 215–16; Sammy Davis, honored by, 133; school reform advocated by, 153–54; *Staten Island Advance* offices picketed by, 158; summer youth employment program of,

222; toy drives of, 151; views of Aldo Tambellini on, 168; views of Anthony Scotto on, 195; views of Gregory Scarpa on, 213; views of John Lindsay on, 206–207; views of John Marchi on, 103, 113, 117; views of Joseph Colombo, Sr. on, 93, 136–38, 141, 158–60, 176–77, 183, 191–92, 195, 197–98; views of Mario Biaggi on, 259; views of Meade Esposito on, 182–83; views of Meir Kahane on, 181–82; views of Nicholas Pileggi on, 103–104, 137–38, 160, 171, 187; views of Pete Hamill on, 97; views of Ralph Salerno on, 117; views of Sally Martino-Fisher on, 241–42, 246; views of Sammy Davis, Jr. on, 133; views of Ti-Grace Atkinson on, 145–49; violent threats by, 95, 100, 174, 194, 200; Willis lawsuit involvement of, 145–46, 149; women in, xviii, 89, 92, 136, 142, 148–51, *150*, 172, 241–43, 245–46. *See also* Cecora, Carl; Colombo, Joseph, Sr.; Colombo crime family; FBI racketeering files; IACRL chapters; IACRL headquarters; Madison Square Garden; New League; Martino-Fisher, Sally; Unity Day

Italian American Civil Rights League chapters, 99, 135–36, 231; Chapter 4 (Bensonhurst), 132–35, *134*, 140–41, 222; Chapter 7 (Greenwich Village), 135; Chapter 8 (Canarsie), 222–31; Chapter 23 (Williamsburg), 241, *242*, 246; IAMSC Chapter 23 facility, 243, 246–47, 249–52

Italian American Civil Rights League headquarters: in Bensonhurst, 222; in Canarsie (New League), *224*, 231; on Madison Avenue, 136, 145, 148, *162*, 164, 170, 222; in Park-Sheraton, 98–99, 136

"Italian American Civil Rights League, The (Official Song of)," 133

Italian American Coalition, 197, 235, 238–39; affiliated organizations of, 238; demise of, 240, 262. *See also* Italian American Center for Urban Affairs

Italian American Multi-Service Center (IAMSC). *See* Italian American Civil Rights League chapters

Italian Americans, 6, 9, 46, 54, *63*, 79, 94, 153–54, 168, 179, 188, *203*, 231, 233, 238, 257; criminal activity of, 25, 44, 54, 107, 111, 150, 185, 265; ethnic prejudice against, 51–52, 67, 72–73, 83, 117, 171, 176, 186, 190–91; as electorate, 82; families of, xvii, 263; neighborhoods of, xxii, 20, 60, 129, 222, 227, 256; political power of, 16, 25, 33, 49–50, 53–54, 82–83, 94, 96, 103, 106, 108, 118–19, 27, 137, 139–40, 147, 149, 153, 161–62, 164, 182–83, 187–88, 191, 197, 233, 248, 252, 260, 266; as poor, xviii, xxii, 3, 15, 19–20, 49, 77, 137–38, 173–74, 188–89, 220, 236–38, 240, 260; stereotyped as criminals, xvii, 26–28, 30–31, 38–39, 43, 49, 56–58, 93, 97, 108–109, 111, 117, 120–22, 129, 168, 186, 192, 215, 228, 231; and women, 6–7, 9, 50, 89, 92, 137–38, 177, 240–41, 246, 256. *See also specific individual and organization names*

Italian American Service Organization (IASO), 19

Italian American Studies. *See* Center for Italian American Studies

Italian Power, 106, 127, *127*,
187–88, *187*, 191, 203. *See also*
"Risorgimento of Italian Power"
Italian Welfare League, 50
IWW. *See* Industrial Workers of the World

JDL. *See* Jewish Defense League
Jewish Defense League (JDL): IACRL alliance with, 181–82
Jews, Jewish Americans, 6, 53, 63–64, 72, 79, 82, 87, 106, 117, 140, 142, 144, 156, 181–82, 194, 218, 222, 227–28; anti-Semitism and, 55; neighborhoods of, 20, 60, 129, 222, 227, 257. *See also individual and organization names*
Johnson Administration, 69, 75–76, 80
Johnson, Jerome, 189–91, 200–201, *201*; background of, 190–91; death of, 202; Lee Harvey Oswald compared to, 207; Little Italy residence of, 189; shooting of Joseph Colombo, Sr. by, xxi, 202, 205–208, 216, 224
Johnson, Lyndon (LBJ), 55, 75–76; visits Mary Sansone's home, 33
Johnson, Philip, 41, 44
John Wilson Junior High School (Canarsie). *See* Canarsie busing crisis
Jones, Grace, 251
Junior Wobblies. *See* Industrial Workers of the World
Justice Crucified (Feuerlicht), 256

Kahane, Rabbi Meir: IACRL supported by, 180–82
Kefauver, Estes, 11–15
Kefauver Hearings (televised US Senate Special Hearings), 11, *12*, 13–15, 27. *See also* Costello, Frank
Kelly, Paul, 113

Kennedy Administration, 38–39, 66, 140
Kennedy, John (JFK), 55, 81; assassination of, 207
Kennedy, Robert (RFK), 66; as US attorney general, 38–39, 41, 66, 152
Kent State shootings, 95–96
Kerner Commission report, 59–60
King, Coretta Scott, 81
King, Rev. Martin Luther, Jr., xvii, 34, 55, 59, 81, 188
King riots (1968). *See* race riots
Koch, Administration, 260–61, 264–65
Koch, Edward, 257–61, 263–64, 266; views on Mary Sansone, 264
Krauss, Michael, 117
Kriegel, Jay, 188, 209
Kron, Joan. *See* "Radical Chick"
Ku Klux Klan (KKK), 39, 44

Labella, Joe, 160
labor unions, xxi, 6–7, 15, 18, 31, 34–36, 59, 65, 80, 88, 94–95, 98, 100, 122, 145–48, 164, 180, 200, 245, 255; and strikes, 6, 230. *See also* AFL-CIO; American Federation of State, County and Municipal Employees; Teamsters
Lachman, Seymour, 230–31, 253
La Cosa Nostra (LCN), 48, 67, 76, 87, 101, 108, 116–17, 120–22, 124–26, 153–54, 159, 161, 165, 173, 196, 214–15; Joseph Valachi, definition of, 38. *See also* Mafia
La Guardia, Fiorello, 79, 107
LaGumina, Salvatore, 117
Lansky, Meyer, 87
LaRosa, Anthony: as IACRL Unity Day speaker, 111
LaRosa, Joseph, 21
Las Vegas, 54, 70, 156
League, The. *See* Italian American Civil Rights League; New League

Lear, Norman, 216
Lehman, Herbert, 182
Leone, Sebastian "Sam," 133–34, *134*, 193, 230, 253
Leotta, Richard, 209, 221
Levine, Irving: as CIAO conference speaker, 218–19
Liberal Party (NY), 130, 258
Licavoli, Peter "Horseface" Sr., 75
Life (magazine), 73
Lindsay Administration, 60, 79–80, 82, 93, 96, 117–18, 128–31, 139–40, 180, 188–89, 209–10, 233, 237, 260–61, 263
Lindsay, John, 59, 77–82, 96, 210, 225, 240, 255, 157, 260; as CIAO celebrant, 179, *180*, 218; as honorary IACRL member, 153; race riots thwarted by, 59; relationship with Mary Sansone, 179, 209–10; views on CIAO, 210; views on IACRL, 205–206; views on Mary Sansone, 60–62, 218; views on Meade Esposito, 179
Little Apalachin summit, 47, *48*. *See also* Apalachin summit; Canarsie summit; Mafia
Little Italy (Manhattan), 44, 127, *128*, 135, 171–72, 189, 209, 213, 235, 256. *See also* CIAO facilities: Mott Street; Feast of San Gennaro Festival; NYPD headquarters
Little Red Book (Mao), 147
Little Red Songbook (IWW), 5
Liuni adoption case, 50–53; views of Joseph Colombo, Sr. on, 53, 176; views of Mary Sansone on, 51. *See also* B'nai B'rith Anti-Defamation League; American Italian Anti-Defamation League
Logan, John, 297–98n12
Lomenzo, John, 127, *128*, 133

Long Island (NY). *See specific places*
Long Island Post, 91–92, 97, 101, 153; IACRL advertises in, 101–102; *102*; Joseph Colombo purchases, 124
Long Island University (Brooklyn), 189
Longo, Lucas, *63*
Look (magazine), 67–68, 74
Los Angeles, 75, 190, 244
Los Angeles Times, 4, 27, 66, 148, 164
Lowenstein, Allard, 109
Lower East Side (Manhattan), 109, 117, 169–70, 209
Luparelli, Joseph, 29–30
Lurie, Dan, 244, 247

machine politics, machine politicians, xviii, 16, 25, 182, 257; in Brooklyn, 33, 54, 81, 140, 183, 233, 259–61, 264. *See also* election; *specific individual and organization names*
Macleod, Hope, 240
Madison Square Garden Felt Forum, 56, 81, 218; AIADL fundraiser at, 55–56, 176; IACRL fundraiser at, 142–43, 151–52, 162, 176, 216
Mafia, 26–27, 45, 66–68, 79, 205–207, 228; *All in the Family* representation of, 215; as "Black Mafia," 44; bosses in, xvii–xviii, xxii; Commission for, 30, 36; gay bars controlled by, 43, 69–71; IACRL censors word, 165, 214; media coverage of, xxii, 28–29, 38, 47–49, 66–68, 91, 121–26, 165, 227–28; myth of, 15, 57, 79, 109, 117; *Godfather* novel original title as, 46; as familiar word in US, 14, 28, *28*, 108–109; as unfamiliar word in US, 13–14, 41; views of Joseph Colombo, Sr. on, 115–16, 168, 185; views of Mary Sansone on, xxi, 57, 117, 140; views on IACRL

Index | 327

Mafia *(continued)*
of, 89–90, 101, 115, 137–38, 158, 161–62, 195, 199; violence by, 27, 73, 97, 165, 202, 213; waterfront controlled by, 18, 20, 33, 61, 81, 101. *See also* anti-Mafia; La Cosa Nostra; Italian Americans; organized crime; Harris poll on "Mafia"
"Magadini's Meatballs" (advertisement), 165
Magliocco crime family, 37, 40
Magliocco, Giuseppe, 36
Mailer, Norman, 78
Malcolm X, 44, 140, 170, 191, 206. *See also* Organization for Afro-American Unity
Malito, Robert, 118
Manasseri, Lillian, 129
Mangano, James, 233–34
Manhattan. *See specific places*
MARC. *See* Metropolitan Applied Research Center
Marcantonio, Vito, 135
Marcello, A.A., 27
Marchi, John, 78–79, 81–82, 109–10; views on IACRL, 103, 113, 117
March on Washington for Jobs and Freedom (1963), xvii, 140, 218
Marcone, Natale "Nat," 88–89, 97–100, 159, *162*, *170*, 164, 181; background of, 88; criminal conviction of, 231, 262; as IARCL president, 96, 137, 158, 171; as United Canarsie Council leader, 228
Martin, Dean, 55
Martino-Fisher, Sally, *248*; background of, 241–42; CETA contract "outstationed" to NCNW, 246–47, 249; civil disobedience activism of, 241, 246; elected to Greenpoint-Williamsburg school board, 241, 248; IACRL Chapter 23 CETA grant proposal co-authored by, 243, 252; as IAMSC director, 243, 245–46, 248–49; Kellie Everts hired by, 245; as NCNW conference speaker, 247; as NCNW staff, 247; personality of, 241, 246; sexism and, 241, 246; views on IACRL, 241–42, 246. *See also* Ethni-city and the American Dream
Martin, Ross, 143
Massaro, Dominic, 197, 262, 266; background of, 196; as Italian American Coalition chairman, 238
Mastroianni, Teddy, 184
"maximum feasible participation." *See* War on Poverty
Mazzini Democratic Club, 233
McCarthy, Joseph, 14, 19
McClellan Hearings (televised US Senate Select Committee Hearings), 38, 41, 43. *See also* Valachi, Joseph
McClellan, John, 211–13
McIntosh, Hugh "Apples, 182
McKechnie, Logan, 121–22, 283n16
Meade, Mary, 230
Meehan, James, 226–27
Meet the Press (television), 13–14
Melchionne, Theresa, *63*
Metropolitan Applied Research Center (MARC), 225, 229–30. *See also* Clark, Kenneth
Miami, 80, 98, 136
Michaelson, Judith, 199–200, 205
Middle Village (Queens), 231
Mikulski, Barbara: as CIAO conference speaker, 218; as NCNW conference speaker, 247
Miller, Rev. William, 226, *226*
Minnish, Joseph, *64*
Miraglia, Rocco "Rocky," 151, 181, 194

328 | Index

Mirando, Rosanne, 248
Mitchell, John, 69, 76, 81, 120–21
Montana, Lenny, 165
Moore, Richard "Red," 120–21
Morgan, Tom, 188–89
Moses, Robert, 43
Motto, Daniel, 54
Moynihan, Daniel Patrick, 25, 82–83
"Mulberry Boys," 45
murder, 27, 44, 72, 74, 103, 207, 257; of Anthony "Two-Gun Tony" Colombo, 4–5, 8, 18; of Joseph Gallo, 213–14. *See also* Colombo, Joseph, Sr.: shooting; Sansone, Mary: mob shootings
Murder, Inc., 27, 30, 228
Murders of Chaney, Goodman, and Schwerner (Neshoba County, MS), 44. *See also* Scarpa, Gregory
Murrow, Edward, 14–15
Muskie, Edmund, 67

NAACP. *See* National Association for the Advancement of Colored People
Naples: immigrants from, 17, 93
Napoli, James "Jimmy Nap," 182
narcotics, 48, 73, 136, 192; narcs and, 73
National Advisory Commission on Civil Disorders. *See* Kerner Commission
National Association for the Advancement of Colored People (NAACP), 142, 196
National Center for Urban Ethnic Affairs (NCUEA), 117, 218
National Congress of Neighborhood Women (NCNW), xviii, 241, 255, 298–99n1; conference sponsored by, 247; job placement programs of, 247; media coverage of, 241, 243, 246–47; and Williamsburg Bridge demonstration, 246; Williamsburg headquarters of, 243
National Crime Commission Hearings (Washington, DC), 57, 173
National Federation of Italian American Organizations (NFIAO): founding of, 63–65, *64*; Mary Sansone elected interim president of, 64
National Italian-American News (Brooklyn), 178
National Organization of Women (NOW), 145
National Urban League (NUL), 142
Nazareth High School (East Flatbush), 228, 247
NBC (television), 121, 168
NCNW. *See* National Congress of Neighborhood Women
NCUEA. *See* National Center for Urban Ethnic Affairs
'Ndrangheta crime syndicate, 3
neighborhood movement, 257–58
"Neighborhood Women: A Call for Action" (NCNW conference), 247
Nestro, Thomas, 201
Newark (NJ), 59, 82, 101, 109, 218
New Deal, 182, 257
Newfield, Jack, 129, 220, 239, 259, 264
New Journalism, 147
New League (IACRL), *224*, 231, 246. *See also* Cecora, Carl; IACRL facilities; Martino-Fisher, Sally
New Left, 146
Newsday, 264
Newsfront (television), 116–18
newspapers, xviii, 13, 91–93, 96, 111, 122–24, 167–68, 188, 256; headlines of, 4, 28, *28*, 91–92, 121–22, 153, 165, 168, 182, 185, *187*, 205, 208, 215, 227, 238, 240,

Index | 329

newspapers *(continued)*
  253–54, 259, 263, 266. *See also specific newspaper names*
Newsweek (magazine), 94
Newton, Huey, 146–47
New Utrecht High School (Bensonhurst), 7
New York (magazine), 35, 107, 148, 153, 166, 179, 187, *187*, 256
New York Amsterdam News (Harlem), 34–35, 184, 208, 230, 232, 243, 247, 261
New York Building and Construction Trades Council, 96
New York Citizens for Humphrey, 65
New York City, xviii, xxii, 3, 9, 11, 26, 44, 46, 54, 59, 61, 78–79, 82–83, 113, 116–17, 124, 133, 119, 144, 156, 164, 169, 173, 202, 221–22, 230, 232–33, 236, 238, 240, 243, 246, 253, 255–61, 266
New York City antipoverty program. *See* HRA
New York City "blackout" (1977), 256
New York City Board of Estimate, 235, 264
New York City Council, 78, 246
New York City Fire Department. *See* FDNY
New York City Hall (government), 18, 34, 45, 49, 54, 60, 78, 93, 96–97, 110, 125, 129–31, 139–40, 153, 173, 179, 184, 188–89, 208–10, 218, 221, 237, 239, 256–58, 260–61, 263–64
New York City Police Department. *See* NYPD
New York City Teachers' Strike (1968), 230
New York Daily Mirror, 15
New York Daily News, 4, *28*, 62, 89, 102–103, 115, 118–19, 125–26,

132, 135, 137, 171, 182, 193, *201*, 240, 252; IACRL advertises in, 102; relationship with FBI, 91
New York Herald Tribune, 35
New York Journal-American, 42
New York Post, 94, 97–98, 100, 103, 121, 199, 205, 208, 226–27, 229, 240
New York State. *See specific places*
New York Times, 3–4, 11, 21, 34, 38, 47–49, 53–54, 56, 64–65, 67, 74, 79–80, 82, 94, 98, 101, 103, 107–108, 111, 120, 122–29, 137, 143–44, 153, 161, 163, 165–66, 170, 179–80, 182–83, 194–95, 208–209, 214, 218–20, 222, 227–31, 233, 241–42, 246, 259, 261, 263–64; AIADL editorials by, 53–54; IACRL editorials by, 165, 208, 221, 253–54, 266; Sunday magazine of, 43–44, 60, 79, 160, 171, 266
New York University, 134
New York Urban Coalition, 180
New York World's Fair (1964), 41–45, *42*
NFIAO. *See* National Federation of Italian American Organizations
Nixon Administration, 68, 76, 78, 96, 120–22, 135, 163, 176–77, 196
Nixon, Richard, 67, 78, 96, 163, 197
Nobody Speaks for Me! (Seifer), 240. *See also* Sansone, Mary; Seifer, Nancy
nonviolent civil disobedience, xvii, 34, 44, 95, 112, 232, 267n1
Northside (Brooklyn), xviii, 241–43, 247, 250. *See also specific places*
Norton, Eleanor Holmes, 119–20, 153; background of, 232; as CIAO conference speaker, 218; views on CIAO, 233

Noschese, Christine, 250, 255
Novak, Michael: as CIAO conference speaker, 218
NOW. *See* National Organization of Women
numbers. *See* gambling
NYPD, 21, 57, 72, 107, 202, *203*, 205, 226–27, 246; Centre Street headquarters, 44; corruption inside of, 71, 164; Joseph Colombo shooting investigated by, 206; Patrolmen's Benevolent Association of, 108; relationship with Joseph Colombo, Sr., 72–73, 98–99, 185, 200, 202; "Most Wanted" mug shots, 41–43

OAAU. *See* Organization for Afro-American Unity
Ocean Hill (Brooklyn), 259
O'Dwyer, Paul, 109, 133, *134*, 142–42
Office of Economic Opportunity (OEO), 236, 238–40
Oliveri, Christine, 4–5, 7
omertà (code of silence). *See* Colombo, Joseph, Sr.; Valachi, Joseph
Omnibus Control and Safe Street Act (1968), 68–69, 135
O'Morgan, Arthur, 200
O'Neill, Jimmy, 43
Organization for Afro-American Unity (OAAU), 44, 191
organized crime, xviii, 4, 11, 13–15, 18, 26–28, 36, 38, 44, 49, 56–58, 61, 69, 71, 74, 76, 79, 81, 87, 107–109, 113, 117, 120, 124–25, 144, 152, 185, 206, 228, 253
Organized Crime Strike Forces (DOJ), 69, 152
Ostrow, Steve, 69–71
Oswald, Lee Harvey, 207
Ottinger, Richard, 109

Our Lady of Peace Church (Gowanus), 8
Ozone Park (Queens), 236

Paramount Picture Studios, 154–56, 158–61, 165, 171, 182–83, 214, 253
Park Row (Manhattan), 125, 210, 236, 265
Parks Department (NYC), 104, 184
Park-Sheraton Hotel, 98, 136. *See also* IACRL, meetings; IACRL headquarters
Park Slope (Brooklyn), 62, 97, 139
Paterson, Basil, 133, *134*, 135
Patriarca, Raymond, Jr., 151
Pellett, Gail, 240–41
Percy, Charles, 211–12
Perrella, Rev. Robert, 45
Perrotta, Ralph, 180, 209; as CIAO conference speaker, 218
Persico, Carmine "the Snake," 22
Pesce, Michael, 221, 258, 266; views on Mary Sansone, 174
Peterson, Janice, 242–43, 245–46, 255; as NCNW conference speaker, 247
Philadelphia (magazine), 247
Pileggi, Nicholas, 45–46, 54, 60, 79, 95, 172–73, 187, 197, 209, 256; background of, xxi–xxii, 61; relationship with Mary Sansone, xxi–xxii, 60–61, 141, 167, 172–73, 177, 188, 235; relationship with Ralph Salerno, 60; views on *Godfather* movie production, 160, 164–65, 171–72; views on CIAO, xxii, 166, 179, 188; views on IACRL, 103–104, 137–38, 160, 171, 187; views on Joseph Colombo, Sr., xxii, 103, 106, 137–38, 141, 160, 164, 167, 177, 179, 188; views on Mary Sansone, xxi–xxii, 60–61. *See also* "Risorgimento of Italian Power"

Pileggi, Nicola, 46, 61
Pileggi, Susan, 46
Playboy (magazine), 249–51
Play It as It Lays (Didion), 148
Plaza Hotel (Manhattan), 221
Polish Americans, 20, 67, 128, 193, 241; neighborhoods of, 60, 243
politics. *See* coalition politics; election; machine politics
polls. *See* Harris poll on "Mafia"
Pope, Fortune, 132
Populist Manifesto, A (Newfield and Greenfield), 220
Portrait of the Italian-American Community in New York City, A (CIAO), 236, 289n10, 297–98n12
poverty, 59, 93, 173–74, 236, 238, 243; and "poverty pimps" smear, 262. *See also* HRA; War on Poverty
Powell, Adam Clayton, Jr., 25–26; as IACRL Unity Day speaker, 110–11
Procaccino, Mario, 78–79, 81–82, 109–10, 130, 140, 172, 175, 179, 188; background of, 78; as IACRL Unity Day speaker, 109. *See also* Brooklyn Citizens for Procaccino
Profaci crime family, 29, 37, 47, 163
Profaci-Gallo War, 163
Profaci, Joseph, 28, 30, 36
Progresso Italo-American, Il, 132
Prohibition era, 40
Pro-Italia Society. *See* All in the Family
Proletario, Il, 3
prominente, 88, 102, 132, 178, 198, 234
Prospect Park (Brooklyn), 193
prostitution, 27, 73, 191
Puerto Ricans, 20, 60, 62, 63, 82, 93, 111, 117, 130, 139–40, 153, 161, 189, 194, *203*, 209, 218, 220–23, 229, 233, 242–43, 245, 248. 251, 260

Pulaski, Theodore, 133
Pumping Iron (movie), 249
Puzo, Mario, 46, 77; views on Frank Sinatra, 54–55. *See also* Fortunate Pilgrim, Godfather

Quakerism, Quakers, 7
Queens. *See specific places*
Queens Terrace (Queens), 255. *See also* CIAO, annual dinner-dance celebration

race riots, 59, 180; King assassination riots, 59–60; in Newark, 82; in Watts, 80
Racketeer Influence and Corrupt Organizations Act (RICO), 152
racketeering, racketeers, xviii, xxi, 3, 5, 9, 13, 16, 18, 21, 25–26, 37, 47, 50, 54, 57, 69, 73, 87, 103, 140, 234; FBI classifies IACRL as, 114, 152
racial integration, 26, 56, 62, 98, 225–26, 229, 257. *See also* Canarsie busing crisis
racial segregation, 34–35, 44, 55, 80–81, 225
racism, 7, 35, 45, 67, 78, 87, 117, 153, 188–90, 208–209, 216, 220, 223, 225, 229, 257
"Radical Chic" (Wolfe), 147
"Radical Chick" (Kron), 147–49
Rand School of Social Science (Manhattan), 6, 19
Reagan, Ronald, 67–68
"Rebel Girl, The" (song), 5, 220, 267n5
Red Cross (Brooklyn), 7–8
Red Hook (Brooklyn), 18, 62, 163, 194
Red Scare, 19
Rehnquist, William, 68

332 | Index

Republican National Convention (1968), 80
Republican Party, Republicans, 13, 16, 43, 67–68, 75–76, 79–82, 103, 107–10, 117, 125, 128–30, 196, 238, 257, 262
"Revolt of the White Lower Middle Class, The" (Hamill), 78–79
Ricchio, Jennie, 105
RICO. *See* Racketeer Influence and Corrupt Organizations Act
Riddle, Nelson, 27
Rikers Island, 223
Rise of Unmeltable Ethnics, The (Novak), 218
"Risorgimento of Italian Power" (Pileggi), *187*
Rivera, Angel, 239–40
Rivisto, Michael, *64*
Robinson, Edward G., 170
Rockefeller Administration, 108, 128, 196
Rockefeller, Nelson, 43, 52; as honorary IACRL member, 127–28, *128*, 153
Rodino, Peter, *64*
Rooney, John, 9, 33; relationship with J. Edgar Hoover, 41, 81; Mazzini Democratic Club support for, 233
Roosevelt, Eleanor, 182
Roosevelt Hospital, xxi, 202, 205, 216, 230
Rosemary (IACRL member), 140–42, 172, 175–76
Rosenberg Trial, 11
Rosenthal, A.M. "Abe," 122–23, 153
Rowen, Carl, 66–67
Rubinelli, Mario, *64*
Ruddy, Albert, 158, 159–61, *162*, 214, 253; views on Joseph Colombo, Sr., 159, 164–65

Russo, Frank: as IACRL Unity Day speaker, 109
Russo, Gianni, 164–65
Rustin, Bayard, xvii, 7, *237*, 140, 208, *219*, *237*, 232, 267n1; as CIAO conference speaker, 219; CIAO supported by, xvii, 62, 236–37; "Furtiva Lagrima" sung by, 220; Little Italy residence of, 189; Quakerism of, 7; relationship with Eleanor Holmes Norton, 232; relationship with Mary Sansone, 7, 60–62, 209, 219–21, 256; views on CIAO, xxii, 236; views on Joseph Colombo shooting, 208
Rutgers University, 191

Sacco and Vanzetti Memorial Day (1977), 256
Sacco and Vanzetti Trial, 5, 256
Sacramento (CA), 67–68
Salerno, Ralph, 56–58, 61, 69, 109, 117, 172–73, 176; background of, 56; relationship with Mary Sansone, 57, 60, 141, 172–73, 177; relationship with Nicholas Pileggi, 60; views on IACRL, 117
Salomone, Richard, 157
Samuel J. Tilden Houses (Brownsville). *See* Canarsie busing crisis
San Francisco, 66–68, 74, 146
San Francisco Chronicle, 68
San Francisco Examiner, 4
San Gennaro Festival (Manhattan). *See* Feast of San Gennaro Festival
San Juan Star, 245, 250
Sansone, Carmela (daughter of MS), 19–20, 65, 234; Italian American identity study by, 266; wedding of, 221
Sansone, Mary (née Crisalli), xvii, xix, *63*, *64*, 139, *180*, *237*, 256–

Index | 333

Sansone, Mary (née Crisalli) *(continued)* 57, 259–65; ancestry of, 3, 17; anticlericalism of, 18; antidefamation advocacy by, 51, 57–58, 117; as ARI fundraiser, xxi, 9, 16; background of, 3; Boro Park home of, 20, 32, 60–62, 219–21; Center for Italian American Studies facilitated by, 221, 232, 255; as CIAO conference speaker, 218; as CIAO founder, 49–50, 220; CIAO mismanagement accusations against, 175; City Hall honors, 218; civil rights movement supported by, 61–62; as community organizer, 32, 62, 232; as community service provider, 77, 179–80; cooking reputation of, 33, 219; death threats against, 174, 177; election campaigning, 16, 33, 76, 79, 140, 172, 175, 179, 257–59; feud with CIAO board members, 118–19, 196, 238, 260–64; feud with IAC/IACUA, 239–40, 262; feud with Jimmy Crisalli, xxi, 9–10, 16, 18; feud with Joseph Colombo, Sr. and IACRL, xvii–xviii, xxii, 119, 139, 141–42, 167, 172–77, 240; feud with Meade Esposito, 140, 259; as a foster parent, 20–21, 32, 50–51; Henry Street home of, 9–10, 17; as housewife, xvii, xxi–xxii, 19–20, 32–33, 60–61; Human Rights Commission appointment of, 232; as IACRL meeting speaker, xxii, 172; IASO founded by, 19; as ILGWU organizer, xxi, 6; interracial coalitions facilitated by, 7, 62–63, 118, 139–40, 166, 180, 188–89, 209, 219–20, 232; as Junior Wobbly president, 5; leadership style of, 119, 139, 179, 188–89, 232, 234; meatball recipe of, 32–33; media coverage of, 62, 65, 117–18, 179–80, 209, 218–21, 232–34, 236–38, 240–41; mob shootings witnessed by, 5; as a mother, 19–20, 32; National Crime Commission testimony by, 57; as NCNW conference speaker, 247; nepotism strategy of, 119, 234, 263; as NFIAO interim president, 64–65, *64*; personality of, xxi–xxii, 5–10, 19–20, 49, 172–74, 179, 236, 239–40, 259, 265; political opponents of, 119, 233–34; "poverty pimps" smear and, 262; pregnancies of, 19–20; Rand School of Social Science attended by, 6–7; "Rebel Girl" sung by, 5, 220; and Red Scare, 19; relationship with Abraham Beame, 260; relationship with Bayard Rustin, 7, 63, 209, 219; relationship with Gladys Harrington, 139–40, 237, 261; relationship with grandmother, 20; relationship with Hubert Humphrey, 65; relationship with John Lindsay, 61–63, 77, 118, 179, 210, 260; relationship with Joseph Gallo, xxii, 177; relationship with mother, 5, 8, 16, 18, 20; relationship with Nancy Seifer, 188–89, 209, 240; relationship with Nicholas Pileggi, 60–61, 141, 167, 173, 177, 235; relationship with Ralph Salerno, 57, 60, 117, 141, 172–73; sexism and, 6, 16–17, 64–65, 119, 263; as social worker, 7–9, 16, 19; as sweatshop worker, 6; Textile High School attended by, 5–6; as UN translator, 17; as a legend, 240; views on AIADL, 64; views on AID, 65; views on CIAO, 179; views on Edward Koch, 264; views on John

Lindsay, 78, 140, 233; views on Joseph Colombo, Sr., 142; views on IACRL, xxii, 117, 119, 235, 240; views on IACU and IAC, 235; views on Liuni adoption case, 51; views on machine politicians, 16, 140, 179, 259; views on Mafia, xxi, 57, 117, 140; views on Mafia stereotype, 57; views on marriage, xxi, 16, 19–20; views on race relations, 7, 62, 118, 140, 166, 180, 209, 220–21, 232, 238; views on Sacco and Vanzetti, 256; wedding of, 18. *See also* CIAO; "Daily Closeup"; Ethni-city and the American Dream; Nobody Speaks for Me!

Sansone, Ralph (son of MS), 20, 234

Sansone, Zachary (husband of MS), 17–19, 141, 221; background of, 17; CIAO founded by, 49–50; as CIAO Mott Street senior center director, 235, 261; as ILA member, 20; as longshoreman, xxi, 20, 220, 235; WWII conscription of, 17

Santangelo, Alfred: as AID president, 176, 197; feud with IACRL, 102, 196, 214; 214; and ILA boycott, 31; relationship with Joseph Gallo, 214

Savitz, Reuven, 264

Scalabrinian Missionaries, 173

Scarfone, Rocco, 109

Scarpa, Gregory "the Grim Reaper," Sr., *23*, 38, 206–207, *212*; acquittal of, 202; as FBI informant on Colombo Crime family, 40, 89–90, 115, 127; as FBI informant on Joseph Colombo, Jr., 87; as FBI informant on Joseph Colombo, Sr., 37–38, 40, 90, 95–97, 100–103, 106, 115, 124, 143, 195, 199, 202, 206–207; FBI informant information on Joseph Gallo, 213; as FBI recruit on solving murders of Chaney, Goodman, and Schwerner, 44; US Senate committee on organized crime testimony of, 211–13; views on IACRL, 213. *See also* Colombo, Sr., Joseph; FBI racketeering files; Top Echelon Criminal Informant program; Villano, Anthony

school reform. *See* education reform

Schwarzenegger, Arnold, 249–50

Scialo, Dominick "Mimi," 103

SCLC. *See* Southern Christian Leadership Conference

Scotto, Anthony, *36*; AIADL supported by, 55; background of, 34; as CIAO conference speaker, 218; as Gambino crime family capo, 81, 158, 195; IACRL supported by, 101, 195; as IACRL Unity Day speaker, 109; John Lindsay mayoral campaign supported by, 79–82; membership in CORE, 34; organizes ILA boycott against apartheid South Africa, 34–35, 140

Scotto, Salvatore "Buddy," 50, 263

Scribner, Harvey, 222–23, 225, 228

Seedman, Albert, 72; views on Joseph Colombo, Sr., 72–73

See It Now (television), 14

segregation. *See* racial segregation

Seifer, Nancy, *237*; background of, 188–89; as CIAO conference speaker, 218; Mary Sansone supported by, 189, 209, 237, 240; as NCNW conference speaker, 247; views on CIAO, 188–89, 209, 237; views on Mary Sansone, 188–89

senior care, senior citizen centers, 17, 166, 179, 189, 209–10, 233–36, 256, 263

Shaughnessy, Donald. 80

Sheepshead Bay (Brooklyn), 249

Index | 335

Sicily: immigrants from, 66, 77, 105, 148, 215, 286n10
"Silk Stocking" District (Manhattan), 257
Sinatra, Frank, 54, *56*, 70, 164; as AIADL national chairman, 53–56, 65–66, 253; civil rights movement supported by, 55; Hubert Humphrey presidential campaign supported by, 66; IACRL supported by, xvii, 142–43, 162–63, 184; John Lindsay mayoral campaign supported by, 81; publicized Mafia ties of, 54, 66; relationship with Joseph Colombo, Sr., 53–54, 192; views on Robert Kennedy, 66
Slater-Hilton Hotel (Manhattan), 218
Slotnick, Barry, 113, *116*, 125–26, 157, 163; and IACRL, 96, 98, 123, 137, 144–45, 156, 200; as lawyer for Joseph Colombo, Sr., 71, 96; as lawyer for Meir Kahane, 180–81; views on Joseph Colombo, Sr., 71
Small, Tolbert Jones, 146–47
socialism, socialists, 7, 16, 19
Son of Sam, 257
Sons of Italy, 27, 102, 196, 236, 238; Vince Lombardi Lodge 2091 (Bronx), 197
Sotomayor, Sonia, 93
South Africa, 34–35, 140
South Brooklyn, xxii, 3, 8, 17, 25, 33, 41, 50, 62–63, 77, 81, 94, 105, 163, 166–67, 173, 194, 203, 209, 233–34, 258. *See also specific places*
South Bronx, 93
Southern Christian Leadership Conference (SCLC), 55
Soviet Union, 181, 244
Staten Island. *See specific places*
Staten Island Advance, 158
St. Bernadette's Church (Bensonhurst), 252

Steinem, Gloria, 148–49, 237; as NCNW conference speaker, 247
stereotypes. *See* Italian Americans; *specific group names*
Stevens, Paul, 74–76, 121
St. Francis Preparatory School (Williamsburg), 21
St. John's University, 92, 119
Stonewall riot, 69, 71. *See also* homosexuality
Straci, Joseph, 151
St. Sabino Church (Williamsburg), 241
Sugarman, Jule, 139, 189
Sullivan, William, 152
Supreme Court (NY), 51, 130, 163
Supreme Court (US), 68, 93, 163
sweatshops, 6

Talbot, Verna, 244
Talese, Gay, 46, 54, 75, 77. *See also* "Frank Sinatra Has a Cold"; *Honor Thy Father*
Tambellini, Aldo, 117, 191, 206; background of, 169–70; views on Joseph Colombo, Sr., 170–71, 206; views on IACRL, 168
Tammany Hall, 25, 54
Teamsters, 200
television, 11–13, *12*, 14, 26–31, 38, 41, 49, 81, 111, 116–18, 147–49, 157, 161, 165–66, 168, *169*, 170, 179, 205, 214–17, 224–25, 238, 245, 257. *See also specific names*
Textile High School (Manhattan), 5–6
Thirteen Most Wanted Men (Warhol), 41, *42*, 43–44
Thomas, Norman, 7
Tilden Houses. *See* Samuel J. Tilden Houses
Time (magazine), 68, 163, 205
Times Square, 122, 244
tipping theory, 223, 229. *See also* Canarsie busing crisis

Today (television), 121
Tolson, Clyde, 120–21
Tomasi, Rev. Silvano, 173, 178–79, *180*, 266
Top Echelon Criminal Informant program, *23*, 37, 40, 44, 87, 206–207, 211. *See also* FBI; Scarpa, Gregory
Tri-Boro Post (NYC), 127, 132, 153, 167–68, 188; IACRL advertises in, 124
Triborough Bridge, 246
Truman, Harry, 182
Tucson, 74–77, 121
Tucson Daily Citizen, 75

Ulster County Welfare Commission v. Michael and Mary Liuni. *See* Liuni adoption case
unemployment. *See* economy
UNICO, 26, 102, 238
unions. *See* labor unions
Union Square (Manhattan), 5
United Canarsie Council, 228
United Nations (UN), 9, 17, 20
Unity Day rally 1970 (IACRL), 97–114, *110, 112*, 117; advertisement for, *102*; estimated attendance at, 106; labor union support for, 100–101
Unity Day rally 1971 (IACRL), 184–85, 193–194, 199–202, *201*, 206, 227; labor unions withdraw support for, 195. *See also* Colombo, Joseph, Sr.: shooting
Unity News, 167–68
Untouchables, The (television), 26–27; ILA boycott against, 28–31, 38, 49, 77
Urban Action Task Force (NYC), 60
Urban Coalition (Washington, DC). *See* New York Urban Coalition
"urban renewal," 169

Valachi, Joseph, 39; McClellan Hearings testimony of, 38, 41; *omertà* broken by, 38
Vale, Peter, 236, 264; views on Mary Sansone, 261–63; relationship with Eugene Cutolo, 236, 261
Valletutti, Joseph, 196; as AID member, 119; background of, 118–19; as *The Challenge* editor, 119; as CIAO president, 118–19, 262; as IACUA executive director, 238, 240
Valli, Frankie. *See* Four Seasons
Verrazano Bridge, 235
Vietnam War, 80, 95–96, 130, 192–93. *See also* antiwar movement
Village Voice, 129, 227, 259, 264
Villano, Anthony: as FBI handler for Gregory Scarpa, 44, 91
violence, xviii, 3–5, 60, 73, 75–76, 108, 116, 157, 165, 171, 174, 192, 2012, 205, 208, 213, 224, 257; racial, 44–45, 146, 208, 216. *See also* nonviolent civil disobedience
Vitale, Caesar, 126, 181, 200; as IACRL secretary-treasurer, 96
Vitello, Philip, 92–93
voter registration, 35, 44, 81. *See also* election

Wagner Administration, 45
Waldorf-Astoria (Manhattan), 63
Wallace, George, 67, 78, 227
Wall Street Journal, 66, 130
Warhol, Andy, 41–43. *See also* Thirteen Most Wanted Men
War on Poverty, 197, 243, 246; maximum feasible participation mandate of, 139, 233–34, 239
Washington, DC, 55, 57, 64–65, 117, 145
Washington Post, 4, 41, 52, 67, 69, 121, 125–26, 238

Index | 337

WASPs (white Anglo Saxon Protestants), 140
waterfront, 101; in Brooklyn, 3, 18, 20, 31, 33–35, 41, 61, 80–81
Waterfront Commission (NYC), 18
Watts (Los Angeles), 59, 80, 190
Weathermen, 146
welfare services, 50, 81, 118, 166, 174, 233, 260. *See also* Great Society; Human Resources Administration
West Indians, 243, 245. *See also* Puerto Ricans
white Anglo Saxon Protestants. *See* WASPs
white ethnics, xvii, 52, 59–60, 62, 65, 78–79, 82, 98, 107, 140, 179, 209, 218, 254; neighborhood movement focuses on, 258, 301n7; as voting bloc, 67, 127–28, 179, 300n7; and white ethnic movement, 218–19, 294n3; and women, xviii
"white flight," 59, 78, 222
White House, 9, 63, 65, 68–69, 80, 96, 253–55
whites, 26, 228; backlash of, xvii, 44–45, 67, 78, 82, 208, 223, 225, 257; working class, 188
Williamsburg (Brooklyn), xviii, 21, 173, 241–50, 255, 298n1; description of, 241

Williamsburg Bridge, 245–46
Willis, Darlene "Corky," 145–49
Wilson Administration, 196
Winchell, Walter, 15, 27
Wobblies. *See* Industrial Workers of the World
Wolfe, Tom. *See* "Radical Chic"
Woman's Day (magazine), 246
women, 7, 9, 17, 46, 51, 172, 189, 223, 227, 230, 234, 240–41, 244, 249; working-class, xviii, 5–6, 145–48, 240, 243, 247, 250
women's movement, xvii–xviii, 144–50, 244, 247, 249, 255
World War II, 7–8, 17–18, 55, 169; post-World War II, xviii, 17, 55, 169; pre-World War II, 46

youth, *1*, 5, 9, 20–21, 32, 44–45, 62, *63*, 107, 111, 118, 130, 133, 136, 151, 166, 172–73, 179, 183–84, 189, 192–93, *203*, 212–13, 216, 222, 233, 236, 238, 242, 245, 248–50, 263, 265
Youth Services Agency (NYC), 62, *63*, 117, 222, 266. *See also* CIAO

Zuccotti, John, 255